100 ALBUMS THAT CHANGED POPULAR MUSIC

100 ALBUMS THAT CHANGED POPULAR MUSIC

A Reference Guide

CHRIS SMITH

GREENWOOD PRESS
WESTPORT, CONNECTICUT • LONDON

Library of Congress Cataloging-in-Publication Data

Smith, Chris, 1968–
    100 albums that changed popular music : a reference guide / Chris Smith.
        p. cm.
    Includes bibliographical references (p.) and index.
    ISBN 0–313–33825–6 (alk. paper)
        1. Popular music—Discography.   2. Popular music—History and criticism.
I. Title.   II. Title: One hundred albums that changed popular music.
    ML156.4.P6S63   2007
    781.64'0266—dc22   2006028662

British Library Cataloguing in Publication Data is available.

Library of Congress Catalog Card Number: 2006028662
ISBN: 0–313–33825–6

First published in 2007

Greenwood Press, 88 Post Road West, Westport, CT 06881
An imprint of Greenwood Publishing Group, Inc.
www.greenwood.com

Printed in the United States of America

∞

The paper used in this book complies with the
Permanent Paper Standard issued by the National
Information Standards Organization (Z39.48–1984).

10 9 8 7 6 5 4 3 2 1

For David, Sean, Carrie,
Casey, and Kim,
who always had music to spare.

CONTENTS

PREFACE

I can hear the jaws dropping already. The first was probably a Dylan fan, who skipped the introduction and went straight to the "D"s in the index, sliding her pinky down to the last entry, blinking a few times, looking at the cover again to make sure she had the right book, then reading once more, utterly bewildered, that although two of Bob's albums made the list, neither *Blonde on Blonde* or *Blood on the Tracks* were among them. The second was a Zeppelin fanatic, a guy so devoted he even listens to *Coda* on occasion. "Are you kidding me?!" he screams upon noticing Led Zeppelin's untitled fourth album and *Physical Graffiti* curiously absent. The inclusion of Zep's debut effort does little to assuage his anger. His roommates try to comfort him. A fresh plate of macaroni and cheese goes uneaten.

If you are reading these words, you are probably one of these people, or, if not a complete vinyl vulture, at least have taken the time to create mental lists of "Favorite Albums," "Least Favorite Albums," and "Albums I Pretend to Like but Really Can't Stand." If, however, you have never really considered an album as anything more than a collection of its songs, then this book is not for you (or, I suppose, it is more for you than for anybody). My point is that no one is going to be entirely pleased with these selections. We all have music we feel passionate about, music that takes us back to a memorable teenage summer, or forward to undiscovered sonic futures, or grounds us in the present, sowing the seeds of nostalgia for subsequent mental lists down the road.

But this book is not about favorites—there are, frankly, albums here that I cannot bear to listen to. However, all attempts have been made to push aesthetics aside and measure to the greatest extent possible the impact these albums have made on American culture. Dozens of music journalists, historians, academics, and industry insiders have provided suggestions and analysis about these selections (fully one-third of the time spent writing this book was exhausted just narrowing down the list). For every album included herein, dozens of others have been considered, dismissed, reconsidered, put on the alternate list, abandoned, then dug out of the trash and placed in the "mystery pile." Outsiders have directly contributed to the content as well, as I attempted to cite critical reception to the albums represented here, either by the journalists of the period, or by later writers and academics who provided insightful commentary on an album's subsequent impact, or by other musicians who were especially influenced by a particular release (many thanks to these colleagues, whom I regard as co-authors rather than cited sources). In doing this I hope to provide a deeper understanding of the influence an album had at the time of its release, to make the reader feel the hairs rising on the neck upon hearing a *Born to Run* or *Birth of the Cool* when the living room speakers first gave them life.

So what makes an album "important"? Sales figures? Chart placement? Longevity? These and many other factors were considered, but in a nutshell, these albums were selected for the impact they made on American music specifically and American culture in general, either directly (such as the hordes of preteen boy toys hatched after Madonna's 1984 *Like a Virgin* and the soundtrack to the summer of love provided by Jefferson Airplane's 1967 *Surrealistic Pillow*) or indirectly (such as the instant revitalization of blues-based rock in the 1960s by Robert Johnson's *King of the Delta Blues Singers* and again in the 1980s by Stevie Ray Vaughan's *Texas Flood*). I would be shocked beyond belief if a single reader agreed with every selection, and there are certainly other ways of weighting the criteria to come up with an entirely different list. But I ask you to set aside for a moment your likes and dislikes, your boredom with overplayed classics and your trepidation of listening to something new (or decades old, but new to you). I ask, when you read these entries, that you suspend judgment on the aesthetic appeal of these selections, and simply try to see how each album, in the context of its own place in time, somehow made a difference.

In technical terms, we are talking about 12" long-player records, or LPs, which came into vogue in the late 1940s (see the Timeline for a more complete dissection of record technology). In 1948, Columbia Records introduced the 12" microgroove LP, the first commercially successful LP record. This was the beginning of the "record album" as we understand it. Up to this point, an "album" was basically a photo album that held several 78-revolution per minute (rpm) singles, but once the LP became popular in the early 1950s, multiple singles were contained on one record (approximately thirty minutes on each side). Suddenly songs were more than individual efforts; they were part of a collection, set within a context of other songs on the same record. As the 12" LP did not become popular until the turn of the decade, the earliest important release that meets our criteria was the 1952 collection *Anthology of American Folk Music*.

Since we are limiting ourselves to post-1948 LPs, some of the most important artists of the century—Chuck Berry, Hank Williams, the Carter Family, Bill Haley, and an entire generation of blues greats—are missing from these pages because their music was recorded on 78s (singles) before the LP was invented, or their influence came from their live performances and radio play, or simply because they lacked a definitive, influential album. Also missing are a number of important compilation albums and collections of old material, as we are focusing here on albums as albums rather than as assemblages of previously released songs. Elvis Presley's 1976 *The Sun Sessions*, for instance, or Mississippi John Hurt's 1963 *Avalon Blues*, or Chuck Berry's 1982 *The Great 28* are no doubt important documents, but the songs had their impact long before the albums were released, thus the albums themselves were not tremendously influential. [It should also be assumed here that from the late-1980s on, when many "albums" were only released as CDs, that the standard CD format is an acceptable replacement (in terms of our criteria) for the 12″ LPs on which they were modeled.] The album-centric focus of this book also precludes inclusion of LPs that contained important singles but had little impact as albums, such as the 1980 self-titled Sugarhill Gang debut and Blondie's *Autoamerican* LP the same year. Though these albums produced the first two rap songs to hit the mainstream—The Sugarhill Gang's "Rapper's Delight" and Blondie's "Rapture"—neither made a significant impact as an album.

Otherwise, the information provided here is straightforward, with each chapter representing a time period of significant change in American albums, an introduction to that period, and a critical overview of the albums that most fed this change (with the featured albums in bold). A timeline at the beginning traces the history of recorded music from the late 1800s to the end of the 20th century, and appendices at the end profile ten significant record producers and ten albums that, for reasons given, barely missed finding homes within these pages.

Finally, a small note on objectivity: It does not exist. Since music history is written by the critics, and each critic writes a different story, then even seemingly provable details such as an album's release date can be a matter of interpretation. Thus every attempt has been made to verify details herein through as many sources as possible, and in the cases where a detail is generally believed to be true but near-certain verification is not possible, I include escape-hatch phrases like "reportedly," "the story goes," and "legend has it." The closest thing to verifiable quantification available in my research has been the chart listings, for which I used the books credited in the bibliography to Joel Whitburn, widely considered the authoritative records of the *Billboard* charts. Everything else is up for speculation.

So disagree with the selections, if you will, argue among your friends, make your own list, and send me an irate email detailing why I do not know I am talking about. But if you have the opportunity, find these albums and give them a good listen, read the reviews and quoted commentary I have included in every entry, and try to put yourself in that place and time and discover the magic each of these selections has brought into the world. And lest you think I am just trying to be charming to shield myself from criticism, here is some fodder for you: I think Miles Davis is the most revolutionary artist represented here, the *Anthology of American Folk Music* is the most important album, and after hearing *The Dark Side of the Moon* at least 100 times over the course of my life, Clare Torry's vocals on "The Great Gig in the Sky" still bring tears to my eyes. God help me if I had actually tried to rank these things.

INTRODUCTION

Scholars have long contended that in matters of war, history is written by the winners. In matters of music, however, history is written by the critics of the winners, famously zinged by antihero Frank Zappa as "people who can't write, interviewing people who can't talk, for people who can't read." Be that as it may, critics and their ilk (academics, historians, journalists, and so on) have been engaging the arts for as long as there has been art to engage. For every caveman that pounded a whittled birch branch against a rock, there was a guy in the back of the room making a mental note that oak would have probably resonated better.

And therein lies the problem with cultural criticism—everyone has an opinion, and in matters of simple aesthetic appreciation, they are all equally valid. The plethora of "best album" lists—from *Rolling Stone's* 500 Greatest Albums of All Time to Johnny Teenager's Top 10 Heavy Metal Records of 1983—lends itself to a wide range of interpretation, and who is to say that one fan's criteria is more legitimate than another's? However, we find that something of a consensus answer can be reached when we tweak the question, asking instead of what are the greatest albums ever made, what are the most important? Within the confines of parameters specified in the preface—12" LPs (and their CD equivalents) released in the 20th century—which ones have had the greatest overall impact on American music specifically and American culture in general?

By rephrasing the question, aesthetic interpretation is put on the back burner and a certain amount of impartial measurement—both quantitative (sales, chart placement, longevity) and qualitative (influence on listeners, imitation by other acts)—takes hold of the decision-making process. Sometimes an album passes all tests to the point of being obvious. The Beatles' 1967 *Sgt. Pepper's Lonely Hearts Club Band*, for instance, was the highest charting album from one of the century's most popular acts. Its sales and airplay have remained impressive decades after its release, it has been imitated or parodied by dozens of other artists, and it is still hailed by many critics (subjective though their opinions may be) as a defining moment in the history of music.

Other selections are less obvious. The Weavers' live performance in 1955 captured on 1957's *The Weavers at Carnegie Hall* is a long-forgotten gem that lacks *Sgt. Pepper's* ubiquitous presence in the country's institutional memory, yet it was an essential document that kickstarted the folk revival at the end of the decade, directly and indirectly influencing other important artists like the Byrds, the Beatles, and Bob Dylan. It is even possible to hypothesize that without *The Weavers at Carnegie Hall*, folk music would have stagnated in the late 1950s, Woody Guthrie would have been less influential at the turn of the decade, Bob Dylan would have remained in Minnesota instead of moving to New York on a pilgrimage to see Guthrie, the Beatles would have remained a pop act without Dylan's lyrical and hallucinogenic influence, the entire California psychedelic scene would have been missing the Beatles' strong presence, and *Sgt. Pepper's*—our obvious choice—would have been a footnote in the history books, or more likely would have never come to be. While it is not possible to imagine every possible scenario of this nature, we are fortunate in this country to have accumulated a wealth of testimony from critics and musicians over the years that allow us to trace "family trees" of influence and determine how and to what degree each artist and album made an impact on the wider culture.

Most of the albums featured here made their impact at either the macro- or the microlevel. To illustrate, let us quickly compare Michael Jackson's 1982 pop smash *Thriller* and the seminal 1973 proto-punk document *Raw Power* by Iggy and the Stooges. *Thriller* represents the macroend of the equation, a phenomenal success that spent nine months in the No. 1 spot, ultimately becoming the bestselling album in the world. The LP put seven singles in the Top 10, with the videos in constant rotation on MTV. For even the most casual media consumer, it was nearly impossible to not hear the music, see the videos, or experience the album's aftershocks, from the sudden rise in Jackson-like fashions to the ubiquitous breakdancing that every teen with a driveway and a large piece of cardboard imitated. *Raw Power*, in contrast, barely cracked the charts, produced no videos, and started no trends in fashion, dancing, or otherwise. Yet, as has been retroactively observed by several critics, even though only a few thousand people heard the album, they all went out and started bands. Over time *Raw Power* became recognized as one of the most influential releases on seventies punk, eighties alternative, and nineties grunge, inspiring a host of acts that appear in these pages with albums of their own, from Sonic Youth to Nirvana, whose frontman Kurt Cobain often hailed *Raw Power* as his all-time favorite album.

Another striking thing about these selections is the degree to which music can evolve in a single year. Sometimes one year will bring extensive transformation to a dominating genre, such as 1967, whose five entries—*The Doors, Surrealistic Pillow, The Velvet Underground and Nico, Sgt. Pepper's Lonely Hearts Club Band,* and *Are You Experienced*— represent the change in psychedelic music coming out of four different cities. In other instances, a single year will reveal significant breakthroughs in multiple genres, as in the case of the six entries from 1975, when *Toys in the Attic* and *Alive!* advanced hard blues in America, *Born to Run* popularized blue-collar rock, *Horses* launched punk and new wave toward the mainstream, *A Night at the Opera* achieved the pinnacle of classical bombast, and *Discreet Music* furthered the aesthetics of electronica. The advances of disparate styles in 1983 were even more dramatic, covering blues (*Texas Flood*), jazz (*Future Shock*), glam metal (*Pyromania*), speed metal (*Kill 'em All*), subtle college alternative (*Murmur*), and anthemic stadium rock (*War*).

Although the book's selection criteria (what makes an album "important"?) is further covered in the preface, it is interesting to take note of how important albums came to be—that is, was there a single ingredient that stood out above all others that led to an album becoming influential in the first place? Overwhelmingly, it seems that an artist simply having an open mind often led to cornerstone releases. This willingness to look beyond the strict confines of one's narrow tastes and experiences manifested itself in a number of ways: experimentation with technology (Jimi Hendrix's *Are You Experienced*, Kraftwerk's *Autobahn*, Herbie Hancock's *Future Shock*), crossing genres lines (the Moody Blues' *Days of Future Passed*, Ray Charles' *Modern Sounds in Country and Western Music*, the Byrds' *Sweetheart of the Rodeo*), rediscovering forgotten pasts (Uncle Tupelo's *No Depression*, the Band's *Music from Big Pink*, Harry Smith's *Anthology of American Folk Music*), discovering alternate presents (Paul Simon's *Graceland*, Run-D.M.C.'s *Raising Hell*, the Dave Brubeck Quartet's *Time Out*), simulating possible futures (David Bowie's *The Rise and Fall of Ziggy Stardust and the Spiders from Mars*, Pink Floyd's *The Dark Side of the Moon*, Parliament's *Mothership Connection*), and even music used as commentary on music (Frank Zappa's *Freak Out!*, Captain Beefheart's *Trout Mask Replica*, the Ramones' *Ramones*).

Of course, we rarely think about these things when we fire up the ipod, CD player, tape deck, or, for the true fans, the good ol' record player. But every release that contains some element of this open-minded vision extends music far beyond the moment it is played. Albums are connected in these webs of influences, feeding off each others' advances and slipping ever forward in a constant march toward some unknown end, which will probably sound much like the beginning, and there will inevitably be some guy in the back of the room making a mental note that silicon probably would have resonated better.

A TIMELINE OF RECORDED SOUND

1878   Thomas Edison invents the earliest form of the phonograph, a tinfoil-wrapped metal cylinder with grooves on its outer surface that plays back recorded sound when mounted onto a phonograph. The phonograph cylinder is the first method of recording and playing back sound and the predecessor to the disc record.

1887   Emile Berliner, a German immigrant to the United States, invents the gramophone and the disc record, adapting Edison's technology to flat wax/rubber discs played on a phonograph.

1894   Emile Berliner founds Berliner Gramophone, the world's first record label. Berliner's first disc records are marketed as toys because of their low audio quality, but the disc record soon begins to compete with the phonograph cylinder.

1901   Emile Berliner and engineer Eldridge Johnson found the Victor Talking Machine Company, which manufactures both phonographs and records. Victor would become the largest record company in the United States, and would invent the concept of signing artists to exclusive recording deals, most notably with opera star Enrico Caruso.

1925   78.26 rpm becomes the standard speed for recording and playing records. The "78," as it eventually comes to be known, is used to record a single song on each side. The 78—also known as a "record," a "standard record," and a "disc record" to distinguish it from a cylinder—remains the dominant format until the mid-1950s.

1930   RCA Victor introduces the first commercial LP record, which not only holds more material than the popular 78-rpm records, but is made of a vinyl plastic that is less prone to breaking and offers a clearer sound than the shellac-based 78s. Due to the Great Depression and the lack of phonographs that could play at the required $33\frac{1}{3}$ speed, the invention is a commercial flop, and the LP does not become a popular medium for another twenty years.

1948   Columbia Records introduces the 12″ microgroove LP, a larger record that plays at a slower speed ($33\frac{1}{3}$ rpm) using thinner grooves, thus capable of holding up to a half hour of material. Though originally a record "album" was a photo album that held multiple 78s, the 12″ LP would become what we understand today as a record album.

1949   In an attempt to compete with Columbia's 12″ LP, RCA Victor introduces the 7″ 45 rpm—known as a "45" or an "EP" (for "extended play"). The LP would eventually win out over the 45 as the dominant medium because of its capacity for holding more songs, but because the 45 was made of a plastic vinyl (less fragile that shellac) and could hold a few more minutes of material, it would quickly replace the 78 as the medium for singles.

1952   The Recording Industry Association of America (RIAA) is founded to promote technical standards for audio recording. Eventually the RIAA would also involve themselves with license and royalty administration, and would create the gold, platinum, and diamond album awards to mark certain levels of an album's sales.

1952   Moses Asch releases *Anthology of American Folk Music* on his Folkways label. The six-record compilation of eighty-four folk songs launched the 1950s folk revival in the United States, and remains perhaps the most important album release in American music history.

1955   Frank Sinatra releases *In the Wee Small Hours*, his first 12″ LP and one of the earliest concept albums. The ballads that Sinatra covers are centered around a late and lonely night for a heartbroken man. Though some earlier albums since the 1920s featured songs tied together by a loose theme, *In the Wee Small Hours* is arguably the first concept album whose songs form a cohesive topic.

1956   RCA releases *Elvis Presley*, the first major album to define rock and roll as a discrete genre.

1958   Two-channel stereo records are introduced by Audio Fidelity in the United States and Pye in the United Kingdom. Though stereo technology was invented in 1931, it was not utilized commercially for twenty-seven years.

1963   The Beach Boys release the car-themed *Little Deuce Coupe* in October, introducing rock and roll to the concept album. Though albums such as Frank Sinatra's 1955 *In the Wee Small Hours* and Marty Robbins' 1959 *Gunfighter Ballads and Trail Songs* had already introduced concept albums, *Little Deuce Coupe* was the first to comprise almost all original material rather than standard covers.

1963   The Dave Brubeck Quartet release the second double album (the first in more than a decade) with their live performance captured on *At Carnegie Hall*. Double albums would soon prove a popular format for releasing live performances because of the wealth of available material.

1963   Phillips introduces the Compact Cassette (now widely referred to as the "cassette tape" or simple "tape"), essentially a smaller version of the reel-to-reel system. The cassette would become a dominant music medium in the 1970s and 1980s, and though largely replaced in the United States by the compact disc, remains a widely used format around the world.

1963   The Beatles and Bob Dylan release their breakthrough albums, *Please Please Me* and *The Freewheelin' Bob Dylan*, beginning a give-and-take process between the two acts that would significantly change the course of popular music.

1964   The eight-track tape is created by Bill Lear, an inventor who helped devise the first car radio and founded the Lear Jet company. The eight-track would become a somewhat popular medium after players were made available in cars in 1965 and home systems were introduced in 1967. The eight-track was only one of several magnetic tape devices available, and would lose out to the popularity of the smaller and higher-fidelity cassette tapes in the 1970s.

1966   Bob Dylan's *Blonde on Blonde* and Frank Zappa and the Mothers of Invention's debut *Freak Out!* premiere as the first studio double albums.

1967   The Beatles release their opus *Sgt. Pepper's Lonely Hearts Club Band* in June, called by many the greatest album of all time. In addition to pioneering studio techniques, *Sgt. Pepper's* is among the first pop albums to include a gatefold sleeve, printed lyrics, and paper cutouts. Though only loosely described as a "concept album" (many of the songs blend into each other but do not share any lyrical connections), the release immediately popularizes theme albums in rock.

1969   The Who release *Tommy*, widely regarded as the first "rock opera." Though the Beach Boys are credited with bringing the concept album to rock with their 1963 *Little Deuce Coupe* and 1966 *Pet Sounds*, the Who's *Tommy* is the first rock album that tells a complete linear narrative through its progression of songs. (Some argue that the Pretty Things' 1968 release *S.F. Sorrow* was a rock opera that predated *Tommy* by a year, but the album was virtually unheard in the United States and was not nearly as appreciated or as influential as *Tommy*.)

1970   George Harrison releases the first triple album with *All Things Must Pass*. Despite its enormous critical and commercial success, triple albums remained very rare because of the abundance of material required to fill them, but after nearly a decade of living in the shadows of fellow Beatles Lennon and McCartney, Harrison had amassed a wealth of quality songs that make *All Things* among the finest post-Beatles releases.

1973   Pink Floyd release *The Dark Side of the Moon* in March, beginning the longest run on the *Billboard* charts ever, spending 741 weeks in the Top 200, the first 591 of them consecutive.

1976   Waylon Jennings, Willie Nelson, Jessi Colter, and Tompall Glaser release *Wanted! The Outlaws*, the first country album to go platinum, jump starting the ascent of country music from a small niche market to the most popular genre in the United States by the 1990s.

1979   Sony introduces the Walkman portable cassette player, originally named "the Soundabout."

1982   Sony and Philips join forces to create the compact disc (CD), introducing it commercially in Asia in 1982 and in other countries the following year. The invention of the CD is seen as a milestone in the digital revolution, and by the mid-1990s largely replaces cassette tapes as the dominant musical medium in the United States.

1982   Michael Jackson releases *Thriller*, the most popular album of all time. *Thriller* spends thirty-seven weeks at the top of the charts and nearly a year and a half in the Top 10, with worldwide sales at more than fifty million copies by the end of the century, reaching platinum status in at least fourteen countries.

1986   Run-D.M.C. release *Raising Hell*, the first rap album to reach a mainstream audience, opening the door for the hip-hop that would dominate the 1990s.

1999   Shawn Fanning creates Napster, the internet's first major peer-to-peer file sharing network for distributing music files. Napster paves the way for song exchanges over the internet, to some degree returning music purchasing to a focus on singles rather than complete albums.

1

THE BIRTH OF THE LONG PLAYER, 1952–1962

It was 1948, and suddenly the music industry was at war. Following the wave of prosperity America enjoyed after emerging victorious from its own international conflict, record companies were battling for supremacy in the growing field of album technology, resulting in a two-year battle known as "the war of the speeds." Columbia Records struck first, introducing the 10" and 12" microgroove long-player album formats, or LP, an improvement over the commercially unsuccessful Vitrolac albums that were attempted by RCA nearly twenty years earlier. The LP album spun at just over 33 revolutions per minute (rpm), and could hold twenty-five minutes of music per side, much more than the 78-rpm discs that could only hold four minutes. In response, Columbia's competitor RCA Victor introduced the 7", 45 rpm EP (for "extended play"), beginning a confrontation whose outcome would determine how Americans would listen to music. Although the EP continued for decades as a format for singles and short collections, Columbia won the skirmish with its longer format that moved the listener to hear songs contextually in relationship to one another. From around 1950 onward, popular music was understood in terms of either individual songs or 12" LPs—the "album" as we know it today—thus beginning the age of the "album" as more than just a collection of songs.

With a dearth of available machines capable of spinning the larger albums, very few LPs were issued in the first few years, but notable among them was the first pop album to be released at 33⅓ speed, Frank Sinatra's 1948 *The Voice of Frank Sinatra* (actually a collection of songs that had already been released as 78s, but repackaged by Columbia to show off their new technology). Sinatra would lead the way for popular music to be recorded on LPs, showcasing his talents on *Christmas Songs by Sinatra* (1948), *Frankly Sentimental* (1949), and *Songs by Sinatra* and *Sing and Dance with Frank Sinatra* (1950). (It should be noted, however, that all of Sinatra's recordings until the 1955 *In the Wee Small Hours* were released as

10″ records rather than 12″, and thus do not fit the constricted definition of "album" used to select this book's entries.) Soon, other record companies began issuing 33⅓ LPs, such as Decca's 1950 Ella Fitzgerald recording *Pure Ella* and RCA Victor's soundtrack for *Porgy and Bess* the same year.

The standardization of the album format was well timed to mark the beginning of rock and roll as a distinct genre—a fact made evident by the overwhelming number of rock and rock-related albums in this book. But in the LP's infant years covered in this chapter, it was folk, jazz, blues, and Ray Charles that ruled the day (Charles may be the only artist in history who deserves his own personal genre). Despite the fact that a multitude of pop crooners kicked off the popularization of the LP in the early 1950s—Bing Crosby, Frank Sinatra, Doris Day, the Ames Brothers, Frankie Laine—it was folk music that first felt the impact of the LP album with the monumental **Anthology of American Folk Music (1952)**, a six-album compilation of forgotten songs from America's traditional canon. The anthology sparked the 1950s folk revival among musicians, one of the most important movements in American music that would directly or indirectly affect many pop genres to follow. Five years later, **The Weavers at Carnegie Hall (1957)** would popularize the traditional music that the *Anthology* had turned so many musicians on to.

In the middle of the folk boom, the first major rock and roll album appeared, **Elvis Presley (1956)**, launching Presley's national career that would make him a legend. The album was buoyed by Presley's appearances on *The Dorsey Brothers Stage Show*, *The Ed Sullivan Show*, *The Steve Allen Show*, and several performances on *The Milton Berle Show*, moving rock and roll forward from fad to phenomenon in an amazingly short span of time. Within a year, major rock releases followed in Presley's footsteps, including Buddy Holly and the Crickets' *The "Chirping" Crickets* and Little Richard's *Here's Little Richard*.

While rock and roll was just learning how to crawl, jazz was leaping and bounding over its own traditions with innovation after innovation, largely fueled by the incomparable Miles Davis, who released a string of landmark albums through the 1950s that included *Bags' Groove, Miles Davis and the Modern Jazz Giants*, **Birth of the Cool (1957)**, *'Round About Midnight, Miles Ahead, Milestones, Porgy and Bess*, and **Kind of Blue (1959)**. Few artists in jazz—in all of American music, in fact—have come anywhere near Davis' prolific and constantly groundbreaking output. In the 1950s, only Ornette Coleman's *The Shape of Jazz to Come* and the Dave Brubeck Quartet's **Time Out (1959)** challenged Davis' rule, the first a shockingly free-flowing avant-garde record, the latter an experiment in unusual time signatures that sounds as fresh now as it did the day it was released. (All respect here to the great Charles Mingus, who released many excellent albums during this period as well.)

But where would popular music be without the blues (and its kid sister, rock and roll)? The turn of the decade marked a number of important milestones in blues, rock, and soul, some tragic—like the 1959 plane crash that killed Buddy Holly, Richie Valens, and the Big Bopper—some promising a bright future, such as Jimi Hendrix buying his first electric guitar, Berry Gordy Jr. founding Tamla Records (later renamed Motown), the Beatles debuting in Hamburg, Germany, and the introduction of stereo albums. In the early 1960s, blues-based rock exploded in the United Kingdom (and subsequently in the United States) with the influence of American recordings such as Albert King's *The Big Blues*, Muddy Waters' **Muddy Waters at Newport (1960)**, Booker T. and the MGs' *Green Onions*, Howlin' Wolf's *Howlin' Wolf*, Bo Diddley's *Bo Diddley*, Robert Johnson's **King of the Delta Blues Singers (1961)**, and a host of singles and album releases by Chicago's Chess Records.

And then there is Ray Charles: 1957's *Ray Charles*, 1958's *Ray Charles at Newport*, 1959's *The Genius of Ray Charles*, 1960's *Genius + Soul = Jazz*, 1961's *The Genius Sings the Blues*, and his international crossover smash, **Modern Sounds in Country and Western Music (1962)**. What more can be said?—Ray's music, frankly, speaks for itself.

Album Title: *Anthology of American Folk Music*
Artist: Various Artists
Recorded: 1926–1934
U.S. release: 1952 (Folkways)
Producer: Harry Smith (editor)

It is appropriate that we begin our journey through this selection of 100 albums with *Anthology of American Folk Music*, as there are only a handful of albums between these pages that were not affected by this extraordinary collection of traditional songs. Considering the enormous footprint this six-record release made on popular music over the five decades following its debut, I would even venture to call it the most important recording of the 20th century, and I would not be alone in doing so.

In 1952, a young bohemian artist named Harry Smith combed through his collection of thousands of 78-rpm records, selecting his favorite 84 tracks as a representation of forgotten American traditional music. All of the tracks had been recorded between 1926 and 1934, bookends of the peak years after the 78-rpm record was standardized and before the Great Depression killed the folk-music market. Many of the great American roots artists were featured in the set, including Mississippi John Hurt, the Carter Family, Blind Willie Johnson, Blind Lemon Jefferson, and Uncle Dave Macon.

Moses Asch, who had worked with seminal folk artists Leadbelly and Woody Guthrie, released *Anthology of American Folk Music* on his Folkways label, using Smith's extensive (and now legendary) liner notes. Smith wrote a short piece about each and every song on the album, and gave each listing a title in a newspaper-headline style. The entry for the Coley Jones song "Drunkard's Special," for instance, was labeled "Wife's Logic Fails to Explain Strange Bedfellow to Drunkard." For Frank Hutchison's

"Stackalee," "Theft of Stetson Hat Causes Deadly Dispute. Victim Iden-tifies Self as Family Man." For the Chubby Parker and His Old Time Banjo tune "King Kong Kitchie Kitchie Ki-Me-O," "Zoologic Miscegeny Achieved in Mouse Frog Nuptuals, Relatives Approve." And so on.

The anthology was released in three volumes, each containing two records—Volume 1: Ballads, Volume 2: Social Music, and Volume 3: Songs. It would almost single-handedly launch the most important movement in 20th-century American music, the folk revival of the 1950s. "Nothing like it ever existed, before or since," claimed Robert Hunter, an early member of the Grateful Dead who wrote many of their most famous songs. "There's no way to estimate how important that Folkways collection was to our mu-sical sensibilities. It radically informed and purified our tastes, as well as the tastes of a whole generation of folk performers, by presenting us with selections from the full spectrum of what had been accomplished in re-corded indigenous American folk music: a lost music after WWII. Sure, the material existed in archives but it might as well have been on the moon for all the good it did us until Harry Smith collected, selected, packaged, and presented his eighty four song sampling of the old disks to the public. To hear them was an initiation. Presto! Instant roots!"[1]

Besides the Grateful Dead, *Anthology of American Folk Music* directly influenced many of the most important folk, country, and rock acts of the 1950s and 1960s, including Bob Dylan, Joan Baez, Dave Van Ronk, Johnny Cash, Eric Clapton, Ry Cooder, the Rolling Stones, the Beatles, John Ham-mond Jr., Mike Bloomfield, Pete Seeger, John Sebastian, Buffy Sainte-Marie, the Seekers, Harry Belafonte, Woody Guthrie, the Byrds, Jerry Lee Lewis, Neil Sedaka, Ike and Tina Turner, and Peter, Paul and Mary. The release had a particularly strong effect on a young Bob Dylan, who performed and re-corded songs from the anthology early in his career—including Clarence Ashley's "The House Carpenter," Frank Hutchison's "Stackalee," the Carter Family's "Little Moses," and Chubby Parker's "King Kong Kitchie Kitchie Ki-Me-O" (recorded as "Froggie Went a Courtin'")—and included Blind Lemon Jefferson's "See that My Grave Is Kept Clean" on his debut album, 1962's *Bob Dylan.*

"Smith's set found its way into beatnik enclaves, collegiate bohemias and the nascent folk scenes in Greenwich Village, Chicago, Philadelphia, Berkeley and Detroit," wrote notable music critic Greil Marcus. "By the early 1960s the Anthology had become a kind of lingua franca, or a password . . . it was the secret text of a secret country. In 1960, John Pankake and others . . . initiated a nineteen-year-old Bob Dylan into what Pankake would later call 'the brotherhood of the Anthology'; the presence of Smith's music in Dylan's has been a template for the presence of that music in the country, and the world, at large. From then to now verses, melodies, images and choruses from the Anthology . . . have been one step behind Dylan's own music, and one step ahead."[2]

Anthology of American Folk Music propelled a wave of forgotten voices back into popularity, bringing new energy and diversity into what had become a glut of predictable, homogenous, prepackaged musical markets. The voices rediscovered on these tracks were treated as if they were from another dimension, establishing a whole new canon of American classics and inspiring a folk-music revolution that would have profound political, economic, social, and artistic effects on American culture. Some artists and academics were so taken with the songs that they ventured to various points around the country in search of the surviving artists, even bringing some of them back with them to perform, which reignited several long-forgotten musical careers. According to Jeff Place, an archivist at the Smithsonian Institution (which was gifted the copyrights to the anthology after Smith's death), artists whose careers were revived after the anthology's release were treated like guests from a forgotten time. When Mississippi John Hurt and Dock Boggs were brought to the Newport Folk Festival, "the audiences thought, 'These are people from the *Anthology*. My gosh they're still alive!'"[3]

In 1997, the six albums were digitally remastered and released as a box set (including a goldmine of historical context in the form of photos, interviews, and extensive commentary, as well as a guidebook to Harry Smith's vision written by Greil Marcus), earning long-overdue public recognition with Grammy Awards for the album and the liner notes. Though *Anthology of American Folk Music* is the earliest album among these selections, its songs are timeless, with themes that have run through every vein of popular music since. As singer-songwriter Elvis Costello eloquently put it, "First hearing the Harry Smith Anthology is like discovering the secret script of so many familiar musical dramas."[4]

Album Title: *Elvis Presley*
Artist: Elvis Presley
Recorded: January 5, 1954–January 30, 1956, in Memphis,
Tennessee, and New York City
U.S. release: May 1956 (RCA)
Producer: Sam Phillips

There were all kinds of reasons *Elvis Presley* should have failed: The 12" album was still a relatively new form of recording, and the kids who would become Presley's core audience mostly bought 45-rpm singles; the album lacked enough new material, filling up space with five songs that were recorded several years earlier at Sun Records; Presley's current single "Heartbreak Hotel"—his first, and at the time only hit—was not even on the album; and Presley's sound, heavily influenced by gospel and blues, was derided as "jungle music" and "negro music" by many inside and outside the record industry, leaving Presley, a white man playing black music, without an established market to break in to. "We were up a gum stump, so to speak," recalled producer Sam Phillips of Presley's earliest recordings. "The white disc jockeys wouldn't touch what they regarded as a Negro's music and the Negro deejays didn't want anything to do with a record made

Elvis Presley's self-titled debut album, which was the first record in history to simultaneously top the country & western, rhythm & blues, and pop charts. *Courtesy of AP/Wide World Photos.*

by a white man. It wasn't a western, and it wasn't a pop tune. There wasn't any ready-made place for it."[5]

However, there were also many reasons for the album, and Elvis, to succeed. Among his allies, Presley counted Sun Records producer Sam Phillips, who recorded one of the first rock and roll records, "Delta 88" by Jackie Brenston and his Delta Cats, and helped launch the careers of Carl Perkins, B. B. King, Ike Turner, Johnny Cash, Roy Orbison, and Jerry Lee Lewis. Also in Presley's corner was his manager, Colonel Tom Parker, a born salesman who was determined to make Elvis a household name; Parker's vision was aided by the timely introduction of Top 40 radio, which gave significant airplay to No. 1 hits. Last, but by no means least, was the quickly spreading phenomenon of television, which beamed Presley's boyish charms and unseemly hip thrusts around the country, much to the chagrin of many a teen's parents, and much to the delight of many a teen.

There were many albums and singles in the 1950s that brought about the rock and roll revolution—Bill Haley and the Comets' 1954 "Rock around the Clock," Chuck Berry's 1955 "Maybellene," Little Richard's 1957 *Here's Little Richard*, and Buddy Holly and the Crickets' 1957 "That'll Be the Day" to name a few. But when Elvis Presley recorded twenty songs for the little-known Sun Records in 1954 and 1955, he was planting a seed that would change the face of music. In 1955, strapped for cash, Sam Phillips sold Presley's contract and the rights to the Sun recordings to RCA for $35,000 (plus a $5,000 bonus to Elvis), an extraordinary sum at the time. Fourteen of the nineteen Sun recordings that survived (twenty songs were recorded) would later be released in 1976 as *The Sun Sessions*. But before going to RCA in 1955, Presley was still mostly a local phenomenon, so RCA released five of the Sun recordings as part of his debut album: "I Love You Because," "Just Because," "Trying to Get to You," "I'll Never Let You Go (Little Darlin')," and "Blue Moon." These songs augmented Presley's first RCA recordings on the album, including the hit Carl Perkins song "Blue Suede Shoes." At the time *Elvis Presley* was released, his first RCA cut "Heartbreak Hotel" was gradually climbing the charts, and even though the song did not appear on the album and few people even bought 12" LPs at the time, the exposure Presley gained from television saturation helped push the single to No. 1 for eight weeks and the album for ten weeks—the first rock album to top the charts.

The enormous success of *Elvis Presley* did much more than put the future king of rock and roll on the path to the throne. It gave Tom Parker the opportunity to market Presley to his fans in unprecedented ways, making Elvis into a larger-than-life character by creating an overly hyped monster. "If a loyal fan so desired, she could put on some Elvis Presley bobby socks, Elvis Presley shoes, skirt, blouse, and sweater, hang an Elvis Presley charm bracelet on one wrist, and with the other hand smear on some Elvis Presley lipstick— either Hound Dog Orange, Heartbreak Hotel Pink, or Tutti Fruity Red. She might put an Elvis Presley handkerchief in her Elvis Presley purse and head for school. Once in the classroom, she could write with her green Elvis Presley pencil, inscribed "Sincerely Yours," and sip an Elvis Presley soft drink between class periods. After school she could change into Elvis Presley bermuda shorts, blue jeans, or toreador pants, write to an Elvis Presley pen pal, or play an Elvis Presley game, and fall asleep in her Elvis Presley pajamas on her Elvis Presley pillow . . . All told, the fan could buy 78 different Elvis Presley products that grossed about $55 million by December 1957."[6]

Within eight months of releasing his debut album, Presley had twelve Top 40 hits, placing five of them at No. 1 for a total of twenty-five weeks, which meant Presley held the top spot on the charts for half of 1956—with a four-month late start. His status as a rock and roll legend from that point on needs no further elucidation—Presley would dominate the charts for several more years, bringing a mix of gospel, blues, rockabilly, rhythm & blues, and country to eager young ears that no longer desired the safety of Frank Sinatra and Burl Ives. His influence would be felt around the world, from starry-eyed young Buddy Hollys and Jerry Lee Lewis's in his own back yard to Beatles and Stones across the ocean, to ultimately become the single most popular act in American music history. His debut recordings for Sun and RCA would be a touchstone for all that rock's future held. As the *Rolling Stone Record Guide* claimed, "Suffice to say that these records, more than any others, contain the seeds of everything rock & roll was, has been and most likely what it may foreseeably become."[7]

Album Title: *Birth of the Cool*
Artist: **Miles Davis**

Recorded: January 21, 1949–March 9, 1950, at WOR Studios in New York City
U.S. release: February 1957 (Blue Note/Capitol)
Producer: Pete Rugulo

"To examine [Miles Davis'] career is to examine the history of jazz from the mid-'40s to the early '90s, since he was in the thick of almost every important innovation and stylistic development in the music during that period, and he often led the way in those changes, both with his own performances and recordings and by choosing sidemen and collaborators who forged new directions. It can even be argued that jazz stopped evolving when Davis wasn't there to push it forward."[8]

The fact that Miles Davis occupies three places in our Top 100 albums list is testament to the monumental footprint he left on American music. Only the Beatles occupy as many spots, and when you stop to consider that every original Beatles LP reached at least No. 2 on the charts, while Davis only had one album ever breach the Top 40, Davis' achievement is only amplified.

Raised in East St. Louis in the 1930s, Davis enjoyed a comfortable childhood few black Americans experienced at the time, particularly during the Great Depression. His father worked as a dental surgeon while his mother hid her talents as a blues pianist, an inappropriate hobby in an upper-middle class home. Miles was given a trumpet at nine, but did not take it up seriously until he was thirteen, when his father bought him lessons. Davis' first instructor did not use vibrato like many trumpet players did, a preference passed on to Davis, who was known for this clear playing throughout his career.

When he was eighteen, Davis managed to get a gig alongside two of the greatest jazz artists of all time, Charlie Parker and Dizzy Gillespie, when their group the Billy Eckstine Band passed through St. Louis (Davis would later famously claim that jazz could be "sweated down" to four words: Louis Armstrong and Charlie Parker). The band's third trumpeter had taken ill, and Davis filled in for two weeks while they played gigs in the area. Davis moved to New York City later that year to study at Julliard, but immediately tracked down Charlie Parker and attached himself to Parker's quintet. Over the next five years Davis would play with several of the great jazz legends—including Charlie Parker, Dizzy Gillespie, Coleman Hawkins, and Benny Carter. It was during this period that he developed his ability to surround himself with talent and bring out their finest work, which would bring about later collaborations with giants like John Coltrane, Charles Mingus, Bill Evans, Herbie Hancock, Chick Corea, and John McLaughlin.

In 1948 Davis moved on from sideman to frontman, forming the Miles Davis Band, performing briefly at the Royal Roost Club in New York City in August and September of that year. The venture was a financial bust, and the group soon disbanded, but after landing a contract with Capitol Records to record twelve sides for 78-rpm releases, Davis reassembled the crew and set to work. Over the course of three sessions in January 1949, April 1949, and March 1950, Davis and company—an expanded roster that included Davis on trumpet; Kai Winding and J. J. Johnson on trombone; Junior Collins, Gunther Schuller, and Sandy Siegelstein on French horn; Al Haig and John Lewis on piano; Al McKibbon, Nelson Boyd, and Joe Shulman on bass; Max Roach and Kenny Clarke on drums; Gerry Mulligan and Lee Konitz on saxophone; Bill Barber on tuba; and Kenny Hagood on vocals—recorded some of the earliest and most significant "cool jazz." Another jazz legend, big band innovator Gil Evans, helped Davis assemble the group and arranged some of the material. (Evans and Davis would again collaborate on some of Davis' celebrated recordings from the late 1950s and early 1960s).

In 1953, Capitol released some of the tracks on a 10″ album, then gathered eleven of the twelve tracks in 1957 for the landmark *Birth of the Cool* (the twelfth track would finally be included on a 1971 re-release of the album). The music on *Birth of the Cool* is generally regarded as a reaction to bebop, an uptempo jazz style from the early 1940s on which jazz artists would explore and improvise over rich harmonies, itself a frenetic, busy reaction to the organized dance numbers of the swing era. On *Birth of the Cool*, Davis moves jazz into a more subdued arena, bringing a fluid, breezy understatement to otherwise complicated melodies. Where bebop constantly pushed against or overtook the beat, cool jazz lagged behind it, replacing dotted eighth- and sixteenth-note sections with legato passages of eighth notes.

Davis was not the first to experiment with cool jazz—tenor saxophonist Lester Young and pianist Leonard Joseph Tristano were extending harmonic boundaries in the cool direction as early as the mid-1930s. But as he would often do, Davis took the form ahead a generation, inspiring an entire school of jazz artists to move the music forward (California was a hotbed for this kind of experimentation, so "cool jazz" is often referred to as "West Coast jazz"). An unusual footnote to cool jazz is that, even though it was largely a reaction to the pent-up energy of bebop, many of Davis' sidemen and colleagues were themselves bebop artists, and would continue playing bebop for years. Even Charlie Parker, who is considered one of bebop's founding fathers, participated in group discussions hosted by Gil Evans, discussions that would lead to the formation of Miles Davis' band.

Davis would take this idea of "musical discussions" to a whole new level, building a reputation not only as a brilliant jazz innovator, but also as a collector of similarly brilliant musicians who would bring about radical changes in musical direction through their work with him. Many of them would move on after playing with Davis to build on the musical advances he brought about. More than a creative figure, Davis was a major hub in the jazz network, constantly redefining music and inspiring others to build on his work. "You've got your late-'50s Elvis, your Rat Pack-era Frank Sinatra and a whole raft of Gucci-toting DJs," noted one adoring scribe on what would have been Miles Davis' seventy-fifth birthday in 2001. "But across the pantheon of 20th-century popular music, no one—but no one—was as cool as Miles Davis."[9]

Album Title: *The Weavers at Carnegie Hall*
Artist: The Weavers
Recorded: December 24, 1955, at Carnegie Hall in New York City
U.S. release: April 1957 (Vanguard)
Producer: Harold Leventhal

With the advances in jazz and rock and roll through the 1950s—brought about by the likes of Miles Davis, Ornette Coleman, Elvis Presley, Little Richard, and Buddy Holly—popular music seemed to be on an upswing, moving the arts into the future with forward-thinking innovation. At the same time, traditional music began to enjoy a resurgence in popularity, not by reinventing folk (that would come a decade later under Bob Dylan's watch), but by rediscovering the roots of American music and celebrating the common man's important place in the American cultural sphere. Unfortunately, to the ears of the powerful House Committee on Un-American Activities (HUAC), any talk of the centrality of the common man smacked of communism, and a number of folk artists got caught up in the sweeping paranoia of McCarthyism. For the Weavers, the intense scrutiny of the federal government led to the group's demise in 1952, and in an odd way, fueled their comeback after the red scare weakened its grip in 1954.

Founded in 1947 in New York's Greenwich Village, the Weavers were a very popular folk group consisting of Ronnie Gilbert (singing alto), Lee Hays (singing bass and baritone), Fred Hellerman (singing baritone and playing guitar), and Pete Seeger (singing tenor and playing banjo). Seeger—a man dubbed "America's tuning fork" by the poet Carl Sandburg—was the central figure in the group and one of America's folk icons, having played with Leadbelly and Woody Guthrie in the 1940s, and, along with Guthrie, founding the popular 1940s folk group, the Almanac Singers.

At first, the Weavers could only find work at the Village Vanguard in New York City, but after signing with Decca Records the group had a hit with Leadbelly's "Goodnight Irene." Their penchant for protest songs and tunes that seemed to support labor unions—not to mention the generally left-wing politics of the group's members—attracted the attention of government watchdogs, who began monitoring the band. Despite the Weavers' attempts to tone down their rhetoric and focus on their less controversial material (a decision unappreciated by the left-wing media, who thought they had sold out), the government succeeded in blacklisting the group, and unable to find work, the Weavers disbanded in 1952.

Two years later, Pete Seeger, still under FBI surveillance, was called to testify before HUAC, where he refused to identify friends who had communist leanings. This might have been the end of Seeger's career had McCarthy himself not been discredited in 1954, leading to a decline in anticommunist propaganda and a rise in folk music's popularity. On Christmas Eve 1955, the Weavers reunited for a sold-out performance at New York's Carnegie Hall, a concert that signaled their reemergence as a popular act. Their new label, Vanguard Records, released the live recording as *The Weavers at Carnegie Hall*, an album that sparked the folk boom of the late 1950s and early 1960s. Where *Anthology of American Folk Music* inspired performers, *The Weavers at Carnegie Hall* inspired the audiences, making them receptive to the coming strains of emerging folk giants like the Kingston Trio, Joan Baez, Bob Dylan, and Peter, Paul and Mary. Though folk was often regarded by its practitioners as decidedly anticommercial, the popular attention *The Weavers at Carnegie Hall* received took the genre to new heights. "Commercialization has actually helped folk music," said Seeger. "It revived interest in it in the cities where it had almost died. Country interest never really stopped. Now, there are kids all over the nation plinking their banjos, and folk music is a living, vibrant thing again."[10]

More than just a great concert, *The Weavers at Carnegie Hall* expanded the listener's perception of what kind of music was out there. The band included a wide variety of songs in their set—from their first hit, Leadbelly's "Goodnight Irene," to the unknown "Wimoweh," which would become a No. 1 hit for the Tokens in 1961 as "The Lion Sleeps Tonight"; from "Sixteen Tons," which was at the top of the charts (sung by Tennessee Ernie Ford) the night of the concert, to "Kisses Sweeter than Wine" and "Rock Island Line," both of which would be Top 10 hits for other artists over the next few years; from black American spirituals to international folk tunes (sung in their original languages) to the gospel number "Three Hymns, a Lullaby and Goodnight." *The Weavers at Carnegie Hall* thus opened the door to a universe of potential influences, priming the audience for the unprecedented variation the popular music world would produce over the next decade.

Central to the import of *The Weavers at Carnegie Hall* is the role it played in reviving Pete Seeger's career. Seeger would continue playing on and off with the Weavers while working as a notable solo artist, penning landmark folk songs such as "Where Have All the Flowers Gone," "If I Had a Hammer," "We Shall Overcome," and "Turn! Turn! Turn!" "No music-maker of any genre occupies quite the position that Seeger does," claimed a later folk chronicler. "The bearded stringbean in the old work shirt and denims, bent over his long-necked five-string banjo has, in thirty years of performing, done as much as anyone to shape popular taste in folk, topical and protest music. Seeger is the eternal teacher, but is rarely the pedant. He has always believed that there is a power in music to inform, to stir, to rally, to direct and to cause social and personal interaction. His career has been a study in reverence for the creative spark that courses through the world's peoples. He hears melodies everywhere, and he relates them to the causes he most venerates: peace, equality, decency in a troubled world."[11]

Seeger's proficient songwriting and common touch, not to mention his strength and courage in facing down the communist witch-hunters, made him an enduring idol of the folk movement, and *The Weavers at Carnegie Hall* became not only a valuable document of one of folk's most important groups, but a testament to the power of folk music to brave the dark shadows of xenophobia and ultimately inspire social progress through the arts. In 1982, a documentary was released about the recording of *The Weavers at Carnegie Hall* entitled *The Weavers: Wasn't That a Time*. The film would inspire a mockumentary in 2003, *A Mighty Wind*.

Album Title: *Kind of Blue*
Artist: Miles Davis
Recorded: March 2–April 22, 1959, at Columbia Studios in New York City
U.S. release: August 1959 (Columbia)
Producer: Irving Townsend

Often hailed as the best-selling jazz record of all time, Miles Davis' *Kind of Blue* is no less than a foundation album for jazz fans, the cornerstone of any jazz collection. Nearly fifty years after its initial release, *Kind of Blue* still sells approximately 5,000 copies a week, giving it a shelf life that would be the envy of any forgotten rock god who once sold millions.

As became Davis' style, he gave only partial direction to his bandmates before laying down tracks for the album. Much of Davis' import was from drawing together the best jazz musicians and giving them the freedom to show off what they could do without overshadowing their colleagues. The result, on *Kind of Blue*, is breathtaking, occasionally described as an album where not a single note is wasted. This is all the more remarkable in that the notes were not written beforehand. Davis gave each band member instructions to shape their playing around a particular melody or scale and then allowed them to improvise at will during the recording with only minor direction by Davis.

For this particular outing, Davis brought together one of the finest assemblies of artists in jazz, featuring Davis on trumpet, Julian "Cannonball" Adderly on alto saxophone, John Coltrane on tenor saxophone, Wynton Kelly and Bill Evans on piano, Paul Chambers on bass, and Jimmy Cobb on drums. Other than Evans, none of the band knew what they were set to record when Davis called them to the studio. Davis liked to capture the raw, spontaneous energy that came with a musician trying a piece for the first time. Recalls Bill Evans of the sessions, "The first time we played each thing through, that was the take that's on the record, so there are no complete outtakes. I think maybe that accounts for some of the real freshness, because first-take feelings are generally your best. If you don't take that one, generally you take a dip emotionally, you go down, and then you have to start working your way up. And that may account for some of the success of this album. All of those takes are first takes."[12]

Evans was particularly important to the album, as he had recently introduced Davis to the work of classical composers Béla Bartók and Maurice Ravel, whose music often focused on modal progressions. Up to this point, jazz was largely based on chord progressions, limiting soloists in their efforts to improvise original passages. When modal music was rediscovered by early-20th-century composers such as Claude Debussy and George Russell, it allowed soloists a greater degree of innovation in their playing, as they could now wander freely through the scales rather than being compelled to revisit important notes in a chord.

Between them, Evans and Davis worked for more than a year creating basic compositional sketches of what they might like to hear in their collaboration. At one point, Davis simply gave Evans a piece of paper containing the musical notation for G Minor and A Augmented, telling him "See what you can do with this."[13] Evans used the guidance to create a chord cycle that provided the scaffolding for the solos on "Blue in Green." Many of the songs on the album, including "Blue in Green," were shaped around Evans' piano playing, generally subtle and inviting modal progressions that provide a flavorful backing for the other musicians' unassuming yet uniquely compelling solos. The opening track, "So What," became the cornerstone of modal jazz, required listening (and learning) for any jazz artist from that point on.

The magic of the compositions lie in their simplicity, or, more specifically, Davis and Evans' ability to create worlds of sound out of relatively simple orchestrations. It is generally held that the undemanding nature of the tunes is what accounts for the album's enduring status, as listenable and inviting forty-five years later as it was the day it was released. "An examination of Miles's work reveals a musical visionary balancing personal limitations with an expansive, intrepid spirit," wrote *Kind of Blue* drummer Jimmy Cobb in the introduction to *Kind of Blue: The Making of the Miles Davis Masterpiece.* "Miles could not launch into the virtuosic, high-register fury of a Dizzy Gillespie, but he could plumb the emotional depths of a melody with economy and intensity.... He lacked the compositional talent of Duke Ellington, but he knew how to assemble a great band, how to play one outstanding sideman off another. While others opted for the security and comfort of playing the same old same old Davis plowed ahead, cock sure that inspiration, value and musical discovery lay somewhere ahead."[14]

It should be noted that Ornette Coleman's groundbreaking album, the appropriately titled *The Shape of Jazz to Come,* was recorded just a month after Davis' *Kind of Blue,* helping to found the avant-garde and free-jazz movements, which were similar in style to modal jazz in their emphasis on improvisation, though without the modal underpinning. It is only with great reluctance that *The Shape of Jazz to Come* is not listed among these 100 albums, but to do so would have probably meant the exclusion of *Kind of Blue,* which would have been an unthinkable omission.

With the 1957 release of *Birth of the Cool,* Davis had already redefined jazz, as he would again do in 1970 when *Bitches Brew* set the rock and jazz worlds on their ears with the introduction of fusion (see p. 78). Davis' influence on American music was so vast that he was inducted into the rock and roll hall of fame in 2006 despite never having considered himself a rock musician, giving credence to his reputation as one of the most important American artists for "the planet-shifting effect the man had on mid-20th century music."[15]

Album Title: *Time Out*
Artist: The Dave Brubeck Quartet
Recorded: June 25–August 18, 1959, at Columbia Studios in New York City
U.S. release: 1959 (Columbia)
Producer: Teo Macero

Stylistically, Dave Brubeck was one of the more provocative figures in jazz, often praised and derided in the same breath, his music described by one reviewer as "the sounds of the conservatory and the cathouse."[16] Enormously popular with jazz fans throughout the 1950s and 1960s, Brubeck headlined major jazz festivals all over the world, often winning popularity polls in magazines ranging from *Down Beat, Melody Maker,* and *Cash Box* to *Billboard* and *Playboy.* His name is spoken with the same reverence as Miles Davis and John Coltrane, and between the three of them they all but defined jazz in the middle of the century.

Performing in the 1940s with various twelve-, eight-, and three-piece jazz combos, Brubeck became the darling of the college circuit, one of the hippest of the intelligentsia. In 1951 he formed the first incarnation of the Dave Brubeck Quartet, featuring a partnership with alto saxophonist Paul Desmond that would elevate Brubeck's music and his status and help create a jazz renaissance in San Francisco, where they regularly performed. Among white jazz audiences, Brubeck was appreciated for his thick chord structures, complex improvisations, and his ability to dip a toe into dischord and atonality without drenching himself in chaos. The year *Time Out* was released, a *Time* magazine cover story praised Brubeck's ability to excite the listener by grabbing a "huge fistful of notes," building them into "a sonata-size movement that ignores the stock thirty-two chorus. The notes grow progressively dissonant.... His fingers seem to take on a life of their own. At this point, both musicians and laymen in the audience are apt to wonder whether Brubeck will ever be able to make it back to home base. He creates an illusion of danger.... Suddenly the rhythm seems to shift gears. Bits of familiar harmonies reappear. In a few moments it is all over and the music relaxes."[17]

Though Brubeck's music was criticized by some reviewers for lacking the swing of his contemporaries' productions, his imagination and willingness to experiment (not to mention the skills of Paul Desmond) gave his quartet a distinctive voice, made all the more distinguished when *Time Out* was released in late 1959. Featuring the extraordinary talents of Brubeck on piano, Paul Desmond on alto saxophone, Gene Wright on bass, and Joe Morello on drums, the album was a wild experiment in time signatures, inspired by a tour his band had taken of the Middle East and India in the late 1950s where Brubeck was impressed by the wide variety of rhythms they encountered. Jazz had historically been married to American dance rhythms with a 4/4 time signature (an even four-quarter notes per measure), giving it a steady, easily tappable rhythm. Though jazz drummer Max Roach had expanded hard bop into 3/4 time (basically a waltz rhythm) in the mid-1950s, popular jazz was otherwise generally held to 4/4 time. But the modal music Brubeck experienced overseas opened his eyes to the possibilities of odd time signatures such as 5/4, 6/4, and 9/8, which he developed on *Time Out.* Many of the songs even change time signatures as they go, such as the alternating between 9/8 and 4/4 on the memorable opening track "Blue Rondo á la Turk," and the steady back and forth between 3/4 and 4/4 on "Three to Get Ready."

Although Brubeck wrote all but one of the tracks on *Time Out*, it was the Desmond-penned "Take Five" that stole the show (the album was often marketed as *Time Out Featuring Take Five*) and became Brubeck's signature tune. Originally intended as a drum solo for Morello, the song's 5/4 time was "one of the most defiant time-signatures in all music, for the performer and listener alike. Conscious of how easily the listener can lose his way in a quintuple rhythm, Dave plays a constant vamp figure throughout, maintaining it even under Joe Morello's drum solo. It is interesting to notice how Morello gradually releases himself from the rigidity of the 5/4 pulse, creating intricate and often counter-patterns over the piano figure. And contrary to any normal expectation—perhaps even the composer's!—"Take Five" really swings."[18]

Although very complex and cerebral, and despite the unusual time signatures, *Time Out* never loses this ability to swing, making it all the more an extraordinary achievement. Critics were initially hesitant to appreciate Brubeck and Desmond's ingenuity, feeling they had violated the rhythmic underpinning that made jazz what it was. But *Time Out* was a surprisingly popular success, reaching No. 2 on the *Billboard* charts, something wholly unexpected from an avant-garde jazz album. The album remained on the charts for more than three years, buoyed by the hit single "Take Five," and has gone on to become one of the best-selling jazz albums in history. Though its strains have become familiar—particularly "Take Five" and "Blue Rondo á la Turk"—to even the most casual jazz listener, the album is anything but dated, retaining the energy and excitement of Brubeck's and Desmond's formidable composing talents that made them enduring personalities on the world's jazz stage. "Some have come to disdain *Time Out* as it's become increasingly synonymous with upscale coffeehouse ambience," wrote Steve Huey in the *All Music Guide*, "but as someone once said of Shakespeare, it's really very good in spite of the people who like it."[19]

Album Title: *Muddy Waters at Newport*
Artist: Muddy Waters
Recorded: July 3, 1960, at the Newport Jazz Festival in Newport, Rhode Island
U.S. release: November 15, 1960 (Chess)
Producer: Leonard Chess

The story goes that Keith Richards spotted Mick Jagger in a train station in London. They had known each other years earlier in grammar school, but the reason Keith walked over to Mick was to ask about the album under his arm—Chess Records LP-1427, *The Best of Muddy Waters*. They were both blues fans, and the quick chat led to a collaboration that became one of the all-time biggest acts in rock music, the Rolling Stones. In the context of Muddy Waters' enormous contribution to blues and rock in the 1960s and beyond, this chance meeting barely deserves mention. The Stones—and many of their contemporaries—patterned themselves on Muddy Waters' electric blues, even borrowing their name from one of his early tunes, "Rollin' Stone." Rock music, it has been said, can be boiled down to a partnership between Hank Williams' honky tonk and Muddy Waters' blues.

Waters was discovered by accident, when famed ethnomusicologist Alan Lomax descended on the Mississippi delta in search of the legendary blues guitarist Robert Johnson. Disappointed to learn that Johnson had died two years earlier, Lomax was pointed in the direction of the Stovall Plantation near Clarksdale, Mississippi, to check out local harmonica and guitar player McKinley Morganfield, aka Muddy Waters. After Lomax recorded several of Waters' songs for the Library of Congress folk collection, Waters decided he wanted to take a stab at being a professional musician, and moved to Chicago in 1943. With the help of fellow bluesmen Big Bill Broonzy, Memphis Slim, Sunnyland Slim, and John Lee "Sonny Boy" Williamson, Waters broke into the scene, eventually recording a few hits for Leonard and Phil Chess on the Aristocrat label. The country blues had lately been absorbing more of the city's urban influence, a dynamic mingling that led Muddy to amplified performances (soon favoring electric guitar over acoustic simply because it was hard for the audience to hear acoustic blues in crowded, noisy venues). Over the next decade and a half he would become the undisputed heavyweight of Chicago blues, helping the Chess brothers launch Chess Records with his early hits "I Can't Be Satisfied" and "I Feel Like Going Home." Waters' influence would draw many future blues greats to Chicago to record for Chess, sparking an energetic revival in the genre and, largely thanks to Waters, giving birth to the electric blues.

The Best of Muddy Waters, released in 1957, was Waters' first LP, a collection of enormously influential acoustic and electric blues singles recorded by Waters over the course of the 1950s. Chess Records was the home of Chicago blues, and Waters was the landlord, singing and playing guitar with the support of a double bass, harmonica, and rhythm section. Waters' ensemble would be the first electric blues band (essentially the first rock band), all of its members contributing to a raw, energetic sound rather than simply backing up a single star. Throughout the 1950s, Waters defined the Chicago blues style, drawing some of the all-time blues greats to his band over the years, including Willie Dixon, Little Walter, Big Walter Horton, James Cotton, Junior Wells, Leroy Foster, Pinetop Perkins, Otis Spann, Jimmy Rogers, and Buddy Guy.

Muddy's status as the man who moved acoustic blues forward into electric territory was solidified with his July 3, 1960, performance at the venerated Newport Jazz Festival in Newport, Rhode Island. In a sizzling set to close out the show, Waters brought all the weight of his blues influences to bear—Robert Johnson, Son House, Willie Brown—but amplified and electrified, blowing away an enthusiastic crowd, for which he is credited with introducing the richness of Chicago blues to an appreciative jazz audience. With his stellar assemblage of James Cotton, Otis Spann, Pat Hare, Andrew Stephenson, and Francis Clay, Waters burned up the stage with flaming renditions of "Got My Mojo Working," "I've Got My Brand on You," "Hoochie Coochie Man," "Feel So Good," and "Tiger in Your Tank." Some overzealous teenagers had gotten drunk in town the previous evening, leading to the announcement that the festival would be cancelled after Waters' performance, prompting poet Langston Hughes to write "Goodbye Newport Blues," which Waters used to close the show. But even the cancellation did not seem to dour the spirits of the festival-goers, who were captured on film dancing along to Waters, who was shaking and shimmying onstage like a man half his age, and belting out the blues in a manner that put his studio recordings to shame. When Chess released *Muddy Waters at Newport* later in the year, its effects were felt in the blues and rock worlds in both the United States and the United Kingdom. Waters had toured Great Britain in 1958, bringing his electric blues to the other side of the ocean and influencing many of England's future rockers, but *Muddy Waters at Newport* provided a major inroad to white audiences in the United States, many of whom had never heard live blues on record before.

With *The Best of Muddy Waters* and *Muddy Waters at Newport*, rock and roll began a transformation into the harder rock music soon to take over the airwaves and album stands. Waters' powerful recordings of the 1950s made him one of the most influential artists of the 1960s. His songs (as well as those of Willie Dixon, who penned a number of Waters' hits) were recorded by a who's who of future rock greats. Led Zeppelin's biggest hit "Whole Lotta Love" is based on the Dixon/Waters hit "You Need Love." Hard rockers Foghat remade the song "I Just Want to Make Love to You" into a scorching radio favorite in the 1970s. "Mannish Boy" was covered by Jimi Hendrix, and also borrowed by David Bowie to name one of his early bands. When AC/DC covered "Baby, Please Don't Go," singer Bon Scott joined a long list of rock heavyweights to cite Waters as an influence.

Throughout the 1950s and 1960s, Waters did double duty as an innovator of electric blues (which appealed to fans of the harder style) and as a gifted interpreter of the more traditional, rural-tinged acoustic blues, which had its own broad audience of authenticity-seeking patrons. His distinctive style of playing traditional Delta-blues bottleneck guitar with a thick, round flavor earned him notice in the Chicago blues scene, but it was his growly vocal presentation, energetic stage presence, and electrifying (literally and figuratively) performances—particularly on *Muddy Waters at Newport*—that helped give birth to the electric blues and the second incarnation of rock and roll, in the process transforming Muddy Waters into a living legend.

Album Title: *King of the Delta Blues Singers*
Artist: Robert Johnson
Recorded: November 23, 1936–June 20, 1937, in Dallas
and San Antonio, Texas
U.S. release: 1961 (Columbia)
Producer: Don Law

As stated in the introduction, one of the criteria for choosing these albums for inclusion is that the album itself had to be influential, not just the songs on the album, which accounts for the dearth of compilations among these selections. Robert Johnson's *King of the Delta Blues Singers*, however, is truly an exception, a compilation of sixteen 78-rpm releases that were as influential when they were released in a compilation album in 1961 as they were when first released as singles twenty-five years earlier.

There are few artists who exhibit such a wide gulf between the amount of their commercial output and their long-term status in the musical canon. Robert Johnson recorded and released a mere twenty-nine songs in his lifetime, but his style was copied by hordes of bluesmen in the 1940s and 1950s, and when sixteen of those twenty-nine cuts were released as *King of the Delta Blues Singers* in 1961, it sparked a whole new era of blues-based rock, influencing some of the biggest names in music through the 1960s.

Johnson lived a brief, secretive life that made him into one of music's most mythical figures (in the absence of known facts, myth makes a more than adequate substitute for mere truth). His birth is placed somewhere between 1907 and 1912, and his death in 1938 has been attributed to pneumonia, syphilis, stabbing, and even poisoning by a jealous husband (Johnson was known to recklessly enjoy the arms of his female fans). Much of the anecdotal evidence concerning Johnson comes from his mentor Son House, perhaps the only man who can claim to have had more influence on the blues.

In the mid-1930s, Son House and Charley Patton were the undisputed heavyweights of Delta blues, playing clubs and front porches all over Mississippi and beyond. Johnson was a respected jew's harp and harmonica player, but he wanted to be a blues guitarist. When House and Patton would play the local Saturday night ball, a teenaged Johnson would hound them with his mediocre strumming. "He'd sit at our feet and play during the breaks and such another racket you'd never heard,"[20] House later recalled. "I think it was in Robinsonville I met him. I got friendly with his mother and father, and he was blowing jew's harp. Why then he could blow the pants off just about anyone, but he wanted to play guitar. When he grabbed the guitar the people asked why don't he stop; he was driving 'em all crazy with his noise. Then he slipped off to Arkansas somewhere but sure enough he came back and he found us (Son was with Willie Brown at the time). We was asking if he remembered what we'd showed him but then he showed us something and we didn't believe what we saw. I said to old Bill 'that boy's good'."[21]

It was Johnson's sudden—and drastic—improvement as a guitar player that gave birth to one of music's most enduring legends: that Robert Johnson had sold his soul to the devil. The story goes that Johnson wanted to become a guitarist so badly that he met the devil at an out-of-the-way crossroads, offering his soul in exchange for becoming the finest blues guitarist of all time (allegedly the devil tuned Johnson's guitar and handed it back to him, sealing his fate). When he returned to the scene after an absence of several years, his guitar playing was stunning. Johnny Shines, who partnered with Johnson for a short period, claimed that "some of the things that Robert did with the guitar affected the way everybody played. He'd do rundowns and turnbacks. He'd do repeats. None of this was being done. In the early '30s, boogie on the guitar was rare, something to be heard. Because of Robert, people learned to complement theirselves, carrying their own bass as their own lead with this one instrument."[22] The rumor that Johnson had made a deal with the devil was aided by his sudden and mysterious death less than one year after his first recordings. It is generally believed by scholars that Johnson simply applied himself, absorbing as many styles of blues playing as he could when other Delta bluesmen generally stuck to following local heroes. Over the several years Johnson went missing, he could have easily studied hundreds of recorded blues artists and traveled throughout the South, picking up local styles wherever he went.

The twenty-nine singles that Johnson released were influential enough the first time around—despite the fact that blues had started to become urbanized and mixed with jazz, so a single blues artist on a guitar was considered old-fashioned. Fast forward more than two decades, and once again a solo artist on a worn-out six-string would inspire a generation of musicians. The hard rock of the 1960s, particularly the strains bleeding from the United Kingdom, was largely based on the Delta blues. Johnson influenced these sounds indirectly, through his influence on seminal bluesmen like Muddy Waters, Howlin' Wolf, and Elmore James, as well as directly, as his own paltry output was covered by the likes of Bob Dylan, the Rolling Stones, Fleetwood Mac, John Hammond Jr., and Eric Clapton, who has covered at least 75 percent of Johnson's material. "The archetype of the tortured drifter, wrestling both inner demons and the outer material world of the racist, apartheid South with nothing but his music and the prospect of the next woman, the next dollar and the next bottle to keep him going, has proved an enduring one, and the music he left behind backs it up all the way," was how a later critic described Johnson's career. Indeed, Johnson's output was short on volume but long on impact, plumbing the emotional depths of hard living in the Mississippi Delta to create a prototype of the southern bluesman. "Johnson's music is the Delta blues with all hints of meditation or repose stripped away: bare-wire, tendon-taut. His wired, wiry tenor voice and driving, driven guitar provide the scaffolding for epigrammatic lyrics with the enigmatic force of Delta haikus. Listening to songs like 'Me and the Devil' and 'Hellhound on My Trail' renders utterly irrelevant any questions concerning the 'objective truth' of whether Johnson did or did not, in any sense which Western rationalism can comprehend, sell his soul to the devil. The point is that he evidently believed it, and listening to him, we do, too."[23]

Album Title: *Modern Sounds in Country and Western Music*
Artist: Ray Charles
Recorded: 1961–1962, at Capitol Studios in New York City,
United Recording Studios in Hollywood, and
RPM International Studios in Los Angeles
U.S. release: April 1962 (ABC-Paramount)
Producer: Ray Charles

In an adoring profile of Ray Charles written just after his death in 2004, critic Al Aronowitz opens with a well-worn joke. Apparently, Ronald Reagan somehow got into heaven. St. Peter welcomes him with open arms and shows him his posh mansion in an affluent neighborhood, bordered by neighbors Albert Einstein, Madame Curie, and Pope John Paul. When Reagan notices a shimmering palace on the hilltop, he comments that it must be where the Lord lives. "No, that's Ray Charles's place," said Peter. Reagan's smile faltered for a moment. "Ray Charles lives there? How come all the Presidents, scientists and Popes live here, and Ray Charles lives up in that palace? I don't get it." St. Peter chuckled. "Ronnie," he said, "Presidents and Popes are a dime a dozen. But baby, there's only one Ray Charles."[24]

Hailed by no less a legend than Frank Sinatra as "the only true genius in our business," Ray Charles united the disparate sounds of rock, gospel, R&B, country and western, soul, and jazz as much as any figure in American music. By the time he had reached a position in the late 1950s to write, arrange, and perform his material without restrictions, he was an unstoppable force, scoring crossover hits with "Georgia on My Mind," "I Got a Woman," and soul music's all-time greatest call and response, "What'd I Say."

Charles was born to a desperately poor family in Albany, Georgia, in 1930, surviving a tragic childhood that would prepare him for the hardships ahead. When he was four years old, his infant brother drowned in a wash basin in the front yard as Ray could only watch in horror. After going blind from glaucoma at age seven, Charles lost his father at age ten, and his mother at age fifteen, leaving him with music as his constant, and only, permanent companion. He disappeared into his piano, absorbing everything he heard and ignoring where it came from, as long as it served to help him create new music. At a time when artists were criticized for borrowing from other traditions—particularly crossing race lines—he defended the mix of rock and roll and rhythm and blues that was coming out of the Elvis Presley contingent. "I believe in mixed musical marriages," he later claimed, "and there's no way to copyright a feeling or a rhythm or a style of singing. Besides, it meant that White America was getting hipper."[25]

His own influences reached almost without limit across the spectrum of music, the smooth vocals of Charles Brown and Nat King Cole, the technical mastery of Bach, the honey softness of Sibelius and Chopin, the emotive strains of Artie Shaw, the wit of Minnie Pearl, the gentle simplicity of

Roy Acuff and Gene Austin, the virtuosity of Art Tatum—Charles was both a jack, and a master, of all of music's stylistic trades.

His wide-reaching tastes are demonstrated on *Modern Sounds in Country and Western Music* as well as on any of his albums. After a successful decade creating some of soul and R&B's most enduring sounds through the 1950s, Charles signed to ABC-Paramount with a contract that gave him unprecedented creative control of his music. Charles took advantage of the opportunity to break from his gospel-infused soul and record an album of country and western covers—a bizarre move for a blind, black R&B pianist from the Deep South. Charles had called his former producer, Sid Feller, and asked him to bring him the best country and western songs of the past twenty years. Though Feller had no idea what Charles was up to, he collected 150 songs for him, which Ray culled down to twelve tracks for his unusual experiment.

Ray got the idea for a country and western album in 1959 when he recorded the Hank Snow song "I'm Movin' On," which was the B-side to one of his last Atlantic singles, "I Believe to My Soul." But there is a difference between slipping an odd tune onto the B-side of a single and making a whole album outside your established genre, especially when a label just paid a pretty penny for your name. Ray, however, saw little difference between the blues and country and western. "I didn't want to be Charlie Pride, now," he told a later *Rolling Stone* interviewer, "...I just wanted to take country-western songs. When I sing "I Can't Stop Loving You," I'm not singin' it *country-western*. I'm singin' it like *me*. But I think the words to country songs are very earthy like the blues, see, very *down*. They're not as dressed up, and the people are very honest and say, "Look, I miss you, darlin', so I went out and I got drunk in this bar." That's the way you say it. Wherein Tin Pan Alley will say, "Oh, I missed you, darling, so I went to this restaurant and I sat down and I had dinner for one." That's cleaned up now, you see? But country songs and the blues is like it is."[26]

Despite Charles' reputation as a popular act, his new label was troubled by this sudden switch in genre. Even ABC's distributor thought it was some kind of practical joke. Nonetheless, *Modern Sounds in Country and Western Music* was a surprise smash, spending 14 weeks on top of the charts—by far the biggest success of Ray Charles' career—and spawning two hit singles, the Eddy Arnold and Cindy Walker number "You Don't Know Me" and the No. 1 Don Gibson tune, "I Can't Stop Loving You." More than a hit album, Charles performed a crossover miracle, becoming the first black man to be chosen by the Country Music Association as one of the Top 10 country and western artists. "Ray Charles hipped a lot of black people to country and western bands," claimed Gladys Knight. "We was kind of listening before, but he made it even more down-to-earth where you could dig it."[27] The album was popular enough for a sequel six months later, *Modern Sounds in Country and Western Music, Volume II*. Though ABC began a subsidiary label just for Charles, he eventually started his own label called—what else?—Crossover Records.

NOTES

1. Hunter archive, www.bobdylan.com.

2. Greil Marcus, "American Folk," *Granta*, January 9, 2002.

3. National Public Radio, "America's Folk Music Anthology," www.npr.org.

4. Smithsonian Folkways website, www.folkways.si.edu.

5. David Dalton and Lenny Kaye, *Rock 100*. New York: Putnam, 1976.

6. David Szatmary, *A Time to Rock: A Social History of Rock And Roll*. New York: Schirmer, 1996 (1987), 53.

7. Dave Marsh and John Swenson, *The New Rolling Stone Record Guide*. New York: Random House, 1983 (1979), 395.

8. William Ruhlmann, www.allmusic.com.

9. Joel McIver, "The Re-Rebirth of the Cool: Miles Davis at 75," *Record Collector*, Summer 2001.

10. Szatmary, 1996, 97.

11. Dave Laing et al., *The Electric Muse: The Story of Folk into Rock*. London: Methuen, 1975, 14.

12. Jim Luce, "Jazz Profiles from NPR," www.npr.org.

13. Ibid.

14. Ashley Kahn, *Kind of Blue: The Making of the Miles Davis Masterpiece*. New York: De Capo, 2000, introduction.

15. McIver, Summer 2001.

16. David Ewen, *All the Years of American Popular Music*. London: Prentice-Hall, 1977, 549.

17. Ibid., 548–549.

18. Steve Race, *Time Out* liner notes.

19. Steve Huey, www.allmusic.com.

20. Cub Koda, www.allmusic.com.

21. Jerry Gilbert, "Unraveling the Legend of Robert Johnson," *Sounds*, June 19, 1971.

22. Koda, www.allmusic.com.

23. Charles Shaar Murray, "Turning Points: Robert Johnson," *Daily Telegraph*, November 1999.

24. Al Aronowitz, "The Great Ray Charles Needed No Justifying," *The Blacklisted Journalist*, July 1, 2004.

25. Glenn C. Altschuler, *All Shook Up: How Rock 'n' Roll Changed America*. New York: Oxford, 2003, 51.

26. Ben Fong-Torres, *Not Fade Away: A Backstage Pass to 20 Years of Rock & Roll*. San Francisco: Miller Freeman Books, 1999, 126.

27. Ibid., 120.

2

STOP, HEY, WHAT'S THAT SOUND? 1963–1967

If the 1940s and 1950s were the age of jazz, blues, folk, and rock-n-roll, then the mid-1960s was certainly focused around the development of rock as an emerging genre distinct from rock and roll, when heady and hardy songcraft took over catchy pop to create music you could feel and think about instead of just dance to. Just as folk music had maintained a political and social agenda in the 1940 and 1950s (making itself a tasty snack for McCarthyism), folk, folk-rock, and psychedelic music became important vehicles for engaging the surrounding culture in the mid-1960s. Rock music became the people's voice, rallying for community causes that ranged from saving local parks to the Civil Rights movement, and rallying against police brutality and America's ever-extending involvement in the Vietnam conflict. But more than just another developing musical genre and outlet for disillusioned youth, rock catapulted album sales into unexpected territory, surpassing the $1 billion-per-year mark in 1967 (by this time the album format had largely eclipsed the sale of singles, holding 82 percent of the record market).

Advancing technology helped move albums into other audio media as the cassette tape was introduced in 1963 and the eight-track tape in 1964, both eventually becoming standard features in automobiles, which created a new listening space for cassette and eight-track versions of albums. Stereophonic sound (stereo) technology had come to the LP in 1958, giving albums two channels so different elements of the music come from different speakers, making it sound more natural than the one-channel mono recordings. Within a decade, stereo dominated mono albums on the market (many albums were released in both stereo and mono versions, and until 1963 the *Billboard* charts had separate listings for the two categories). Sonic pioneers such as Augustus Owsley Stanley III and Phil Spector revolutionized the way people listened to music, with Stanley and others developing advanced public-address systems that carried sound farther and more clearly than before, paving the way for larger concerts, festivals, and eventually stadium rock.

Spector, meanwhile, became one of rock's legendary producers when he used girl groups to develop his famous "wall of sound" studio technique that used extra musicians and an echo chamber to give music a fuller, more layered feel (however, Spector's distaste for innovations such as stereo and the album format was widely known).

Popular music continued its explorations into a variety of sounds: girl groups like the Chiffons, the Ronettes, and the Shirelles created strings of hit singles off of Phil Spector's magical fingertips; California (and California-at-heart) boys like Dick Dale, the Ventures, the Surfaris, Jan and Dean, and the Beach Boys popularized surf music; Herb Alpert and the Tijuana Brass single-handedly brought Latin music into millions of homes despite the fact that none of Alpert's musicians were Latino, rivaling the Beatles and the Monkees in chart popularity; and Motown defined soul and R&B with 110 Top 10 hits in the 1960s by acts such as the Miracles, the Supremes, the Temptations, the Four Tops, Marvin Gaye, and a twelve-year-old miracle named Little Stevie Wonder. While jazz was largely crowded out of the market by such an influx of disparate styles, some of the genre's most inspiring artists left their mark with magnificent releases like Stan Getz and Joao Gilberto's 1964 bossa nova classic *Getz/Gilberto*, John Coltrane's immortal 1965 suite *A Love Supreme*, and Miles Davis' 1966 masterpiece *Miles Smiles*.

Albums themselves underwent a number of important developments in the mid-1960s as well. "Theme albums"—also known as "concept albums"—had been loosely constructed as collections of songs with similar premises as early as Woody Guthrie's 1940 *Dust Bowl Ballads* (released as a 12" LP in 1964), Frank Sinatra's 1955 *In the Wee Small Hours*, and Marty Robbins' 1959 *Gunfighter Ballads and Trail Songs*. But while early concept albums were trying to portray a certain mood or general theme, the Beach Boys brought a tight focus on car culture with their 1963 hit *Little Deuce Coupe*, topping it three years later with their loss-of-innocence themed **Pet Sounds (1966)**.

The same year, Frank Zappa and the Mothers of Invention stunned listeners with the first theme album that was also a double album, the shocking criticism of American culture **Freak Out! (1966)**. Double albums were a rare phenomenon, starting with Benny Goodman's 1950 *Live at Carnegie Hall* and the Dave Brubeck Quartet's 1963 *At Carnegie Hall*, but very uncommon until being popularized in the 1960s with Zappas' *Freak Out!* and Bob Dylan's *Blonde on Blonde* (the first studio double albums). By the 1970s, double albums would become an inevitable catalog-filler for popular acts, especially live performances that provided plenty of material for four sides of vinyl.

If one had to name a single phenomenon that defined the tone of 1960s' popular music and the future of music in America, it would have to be the ongoing conversation between Bob Dylan and the Beatles. In 1963, the Beatles released their debut **Please Please Me (1963)** in the United Kingdom just two months before Bob Dylan released his breakthrough sophomore effort **The Freewheelin' Bob Dylan (1963)** in the United States. Dylan's album ignited the folk crowds in America while the Beatles' effort united rock fans all over the world, and before long the two acts would inspire each other enormously. Dylan demonstrated that popular music could be literate (and an artist could express his independence) with albums such as *Freewheelin'*, 1964's *Another Side of Bob Dylan*, **Bringing It All Back Home** (1965), 1965's *Highway 61 Revisited*, and 1966's *Blonde on Blonde*. The Beatles, meanwhile, made rock respectable and elevated pop music to a new level of craftsmanship with *Please Please Me*, 1964's *A Hard Day's Night*, **Rubber Soul** (1965), and 1966's *Revolver*.

One of the first and biggest American acts to incorporate both Dylan and the Beatles into their sound was the California folk-rock quintet the Byrds, forever changing the landscape of American pop with their seminal hits **Mr. Tambourine Man** (1965) and *Turn! Turn! Turn!* the same year. Before long all of California rang with the sound of folk-rock, and when hallucinogenic drugs entered the equation, San Francisco became the epicenter of psychedelic rock with bands like the Grateful Dead, Quicksilver Messenger Service, Big Brother and the Holding Company, Moby Grape, the Charlatans, and Jefferson Airplane, whose **Surrealistic Pillow** (1967) provided a soundtrack to the "summer of love." Though psychedelic music thrived in San Francisco for two years before becoming commercially popular, 1967 was its peak as a national and international phenomenon, influencing artists outside of San Francisco to create treasures such as the 13th Floor Elevators' *Easter Everywhere*, Pink Floyd's *The Piper at the Gates of Dawn*, the Doors' **The Doors** (1967), Jimi Hendrix's **Are You Experienced** (1967), and the Velvet Underground's **The Velvet Underground and Nico** (1967). Each of these acts mingled psychedelic music with their own local influences creating numerous rock offshoots in a short period of time (this is especially true of the New York City band the Velvet Underground, whose work was so original that it almost seemed autochthonous). The exclamation point to the psychedelic era appropriately circled back to one of its greatest influences, the Beatles, whose **Sgt. Pepper's Lonely Hearts Club Band** (1967) opened the floodgates for what was possible in a studio album.

Album Title: *The Freewheelin' Bob Dylan*
Artist: Bob Dylan
Recorded: July 9, 1961–April 24, 1963, at Columbia Studios
in New York City
U.S. release: May 27, 1963 (Columbia)
Producer: John Hammond Sr.

"A bright new face in folk music is appearing at Gerde's Folk City," wrote Robert Shelton in the *New York Times* in the fall of 1961. "Although only 20 years old, Bob Dylan is one of the most distinctive stylists to play in Manhattan cabarets in months. Resembling a cross between a choir boy and a beatnik, Mr. Dylan has a cherubic look and a mop of tousled hair he partly covers with a Huck Finn black corduroy cap. His clothes may need a bit of

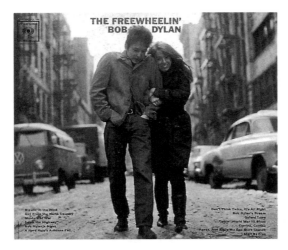

Bob Dylan's 1963 sophomore release *The Freewheelin' Bob Dylan*, the first major folk album to feature mostly original material. *Courtesy of Photofest.*

tailoring, but when he works his guitar, harmonica, or piano and composes new songs faster than he can remember them, there is no doubt that he is bursting at the seams with talent."[1]

One month later, Bob Dylan released his self-titled debut album to a small, but appreciative audience. While *Bob Dylan* certainly announced a talented new busker on the folk-revival scene, it was not monstrously different from other folk albums, largely interpreting traditional material (albeit with Dylan's distinctive nasal singing and a stronger blues influence than his contemporaries) with only a hint of Dylan's songwriting ability—the talkin' blues of "Talkin' New York" and the touching ode "Song to Woody," both tunes inspired by Dylan's hero, Woody Guthrie.

Bob Dylan failed to chart, but earned Dylan street cred in the bustling Greenwich Village folk scene, credibility that would grow a hundred-fold the following year with the release of *The Freewheelin' Bob Dylan* in the spring of 1963. Composed almost entirely of originals (unusual in the pop-music world, and almost unheard of in the tradition-minded folk scene), *The Freewheelin' Bob Dylan* was a landmark album. Dylan's songs were not only important for showing that an artist's self-penned tunes could be as significant (if not more so) as the prepackaged pop coming out of the Brill building or the endlessly reworked traditional material in the folk canon, but also because Dylan's tunes were so far-reaching, impressing pop-music fans with his sophisticated songwriting and hijacking the folk scene with his social and existential insight. "Dylan's songs can serve as metaphors," wrote a *Rolling Stone* critic in 1970, "enriching our lives, giving us random insight into the myths we carry and the present we live in, intensifying what we've known and leading us towards what we never looked for, while at the same time enforcing an emotional strength upon those perceptions by the power of the music that moves with his words."[2] Though only his second album, *The Freewheelin' Bob Dylan* launched Dylan almost overnight from notable new songwriter to voice of his generation.

Several of the songs on the album became landmarks in their own right, particularly Dylan's most famous composition "Blowin' in the Wind," which had been a hit as a cover for Peter, Paul and Mary several months before Dylan released his version, and was to become one of the most covered songs in American popular music. Dylan also ignited the protest movement with his diatribe against war profiteers in "Masters of War" and his vaguely apocalyptic predictions in "A Hard Rain's A-Gonna Fall." At the same time, Dylan showed his ability to pen touching ballads with "Girl from North Country" and "Don't Think Twice, It's All Right," as well as intelligent humor with "Bob Dylan's Dream" and "Bob Dylan's Blues," demonstrating his wide-reaching talents as a troubadour, a critic, and a clown. (Though it should be noted that even some the songs that are credited to Dylan relied heavily on traditional folk—"I Shall Be Free" is a rewrite of Leadbelly's "We Shall Be Free," and "Masters of War" was based on an arrangement of the English riddle song "Nottamun Town.")

Despite the extent to which Dylan is credited with leading a whole generation of protest music, it was not long before he began distancing himself from his message, or at least the message many took from his songs. "I agree with everything that's happening, but I'm not part of no movement," he told writer Nat Hentoff not long after the release of *The Freewheelin' Bob Dylan*. "If I was, I wouldn't be able to do anything else but be in 'the Movement.' I just can't sit around and have people make rules for me.... Those protest records I made, I'll stand behind them but some of that was jumping on the scene to be heard and a lot of it was because I didn't see anybody else doing that kind of thing. Now a lot of people are doing finger-pointing songs... Me, I don't want to write for people anymore. You know—be a spokesman."[3]

Many of Dylan's biggest fans would turn their backs on him when he entered his electric phase with *Bringing It All Back Home* (see p. 30) two years after *The Freewheelin' Bob Dylan*. But Dylan, it seemed, had never agreed with his fans in the first place, telling *Newsweek* in 1965, "I've never written a political song. Songs can't save the world. I've gone through all that. When you don't like something, you gotta learn to just not need that something."[4] Such independent thought was anathema to the folk-protest tradition, and Dylan, for a brief two years the crown prince of the new protest kingdom, had become folk music's Judas Iscariot. But Dylan's songs were mercurial enough to be appreciated without having to appreciate the man who wrote them. Though he lost many fans upon entering his electric phase, no one doubted his talent as a songwriter, and his songs from *The Freewheelin' Bob Dylan*—especially "Blowin' in the Wind," which became an anthem for the Civil Rights movement—retained their cache as intelligent, thought-provoking discourse that would earn a place among the century's most enduring music.

Album Title: *Please Please Me*
Artist: The Beatles
Recorded: September 11, 1962–February 11, 1963, at Abbey Road Studios in London
U.K. release: March 22, 1963 (Parlophone)
U.S. release: July 1963 (as *Introducing... The Beatles*) (Vee-Jay)
Producer: George Martin

The Beatles' debut LP is unique among the albums in this book in that it is the only foreign entry—that is, in terms of influence, the U.K. version *Please Please Me* was more important even in the United States than its later U.S. version, *Introducing... The Beatles*.

In the early 1960s, British bands would only release an LP if it could be supported by at least one hit single. For the Beatles, that song was their second release "Please Please Me," which went to No. 1 in Britain after their first single, "Love Me Do," reached No. 17 in late 1963. Seizing the opportunity, producer George Martin hurried the future Fab Four into the studio for a thirteen-hour session on February 11, 1963 to record the remainder of the album. With extremely clever marketing by manager Brian Epstein and tight pop arrangements by Martin, *Please Please Me* rocketed to No. 1 on the British charts where it remained for more than six months.

The ensuing hysteria over the group was labeled "Beatlemania," a phenomenon which reached beyond mere fandom to be described almost as a medical condition (psychologist F. R. C. Casson tried to explain to readers of the *London Times* that the Beatles' music "has a rhythmic stimulation on the brain. A similar result... is seen in some types of epileptic fit which may be caused by rapidly flickering light."[5]). Besides the eponymous single (penned by Lennon and McCartney), the album included a heavy and varied dose of original material—including the rocker "I Saw Her Standing There," the schmaltzy "P.S. I Love You," and their poppy debut single "Love Me Do"—at a time when most bands debuted with covers of standards or tunes penned by a label's professional songwriters. Among the covers is the most famous single take in rock, John Lennon belting himself hoarse on the classic Medley and Russell hit "Twist and Shout."

Please Please Me was accompanied by a string of hit singles and sold-out shows through 1963 to make the band a monster in Britain, but Capitol Records—the American arm of the Beatles' U.K. label—was wary of introducing the group to American audiences, which had never warmed to a British act. The American independent labels Swan and Vee Jay had released several Beatles singles in the United States in 1963, as well as *Introducing... The Beatles*, but to limited success.

Eventually Martin and Epstein were able to convince Capitol to spend the princely sum of $50,000 for a massive marketing push in America, which put the phrase "The Beatles Are Coming" on the lips of millions (many who didn't know what a Beatle was), generating stories in *Time, Life*, and *Newsweek*, which reported that the Beatles produced "a sound that is one of the most persistent noises heard over England since the air-raid sirens were dismantled."[6]

By the time the Beatles landed in New York City on February 7, 1964, they were already a phenomenon in the United States. The group's second American album, *Meet the Beatles*, had just been released the previous week and would find a home in the top spot for eleven weeks, shadowed for nine weeks at No. 2 by *Introducing... The Beatles*, which had finally found respect in the states almost a year after the U.K. version's release. Most who remember the Beatles' first visit to the United States—which included their legendary appearance on the *Ed Sullivan Show* in February—will associate American Beatlemania with their *Meet the Beatles* album. Indeed, *Meet the Beatles* was a major boon to the foursome's stateside spectacle (as many a screaming fifteen-year-old girl would have told you in 1964), but by the time it was released the furor had already reached a boiling point, and by April the band held the top five positions on the charts with "Can't Buy Me Love," "Twist and Shout," "She Loves You," "I Want to Hold Your Hand," and "Please Please Me"—a monopoly no artist has come close to achieving before or since.

As the band's first album, *Please Please Me* also offered important clues to the Beatles' original influences. Since their early days, the group demonstrated a debt to American musical traditions—particularly to the skiffle and R&B styles—as the quartet's repertoire consisted mostly of covers of tunes by Chuck Berry, Little Richard, Buddy Holly, Ray Charles, the Isley Brothers, and Brill Building and Motown hits. The lads emulated Elvis Presley and wanted to be a rockabilly band—even adopting the name "The Foreverly Brothers" at one point (in homage to the Everly Brothers), and George Harrison calling himself Carl Harrison in honor of his hero Carl Perkins. They eventually decided on the Beatles since it was similar to the Crickets (Buddy Holly's band) but evoked the specter of the Beat poets.

Please Please Me is drenched in these and other American influences. Of the album's six covers tunes, five were written and popularized by American artists, including Arthur Alexander's "Anna," the Goffin/King collaboration "Chains," the Shirelles' "Boys" and "Baby It's You," and the Isley Brothers' No. 2 hit "Twist and Shout." Much of the album's original material can be traced to specific influences as well—the Roy Orbison-inspired title track, the Chuck Berry-drenched guitar and bass on "I Saw Her Standing There," the girl-group themes on "Misery" and "There's a Place," the doo-wop vocals of "Do You Want to Know a Secret"—most molded into a positive, energetic Merseybeat sound that gave the group a distinctive voice and launched them to stardom in the United Kingdom and eventually around the world.

It could be argued that the band's first U.S. release *Introducing . . . The Beatles* or their much more successful sophomore release *Meet the Beatles* were more important to their success in the states. But foreign acts rarely made an impact in North America before the Beatles, and it took the overwhelming success of *Please Please Me* to make the group giants at home and across Europe before their label was willing to risk the American market. The risk that *Please Please Me* inspired changed the very nature of rock music in the United States, opening the door for a wealth of fresh, original acts—including the Kinks, the Who, the Rolling Stones, the Yardbirds, and dozens of imitators—to find a new audience across the ocean.

Album Title: *Bringing It All Back Home*
Artist: Bob Dylan
Recorded: January 13–15, 1965, at Columbia Studios in New York City
U.S. release: March 22, 1965 (Columbia)
Producer: Tom Wilson

Bob Dylan's 1965 *Bringing It All Back Home,* which marked a return to his electric origins and the advent of folk-rock. *Courtesy of Photofest.*

In light of the fact that Dylan was a revered folkie before releasing *Bringing It All Back Home,* and that this is the album where he turns off much of his adoring audience by turning on the amplifiers for the first time, it may seem that the album is poorly named—folk music was Bob Dylan's home, and if anything he was running away from it rather than "bringing us all back" to it.

But the fact is that Dylan had always been an electric musician, with his journey into folk music only a temporary departure from his true home of pompadour haircuts and electric guitars. Counting bluesmen like Muddy Waters and Jimmy Reed and rockers like Elvis Presley and Buddy Holly among his early influences, Dylan formed his own rock band in high school, the Golden Chords, in which he emulated Little Richard's percussive piano playing, as well as the outlaw attitudes of Marlon Brando and James Dean. During one performance at his high school, the vice principal pulled the plug on the band (literally), an eerie foreshadowing of Dylan's reemergence as a rocker at the famous 1965 Newport folk festival (at which he was practically booed off the stage) shortly after *Bringing It All Back Home* was released.

After a short period as a backup pianist for rockabilly star Bobby Vee, Dylan converted to the guitar and began exploring folk territory, heavily influenced by folk legend Woody Guthrie, whose potent celebrations of the common man would lure Dylan away from rock and roll and into New York's acoustic Greenwich Village scene. Over the course of his first four albums he would largely stick to the acoustic folkie formula, making a name for himself as a talented lyricist and an increasingly important part of the folk revival. But he never strayed far from his electric influences, and only the restraining hand of his producer John Hammond Sr. kept Dylan's rock and roll cuts off his early albums, as Hammond knew Dylan was best marketed as an acoustic act. By 1964, however, Dylan's manager Albert Grossman had so alienated Hammond, and Dylan had grown in such confidence over his own material, that a return to rock was inevitable.

Bringing It All Back Home marked a transition in American songcraft as much as it marked a transition in Dylan's own career, forever changing the face of popular music. "Dylan's imagery got really wild here, though it still maintained links—sometimes melodic, sometimes lyric—to the folk tradition and still festered with elliptical protest," wrote critic Dave Marsh in the *Rolling Stone Record Guide*. "More importantly, by fusing the Chuck Berry beat of the Rolling Stones and the Beatles with the leftist, folk tradition of the folk revival, Dylan really had brought it back home, creating a new kind of rock & roll...that made every type of artistic tradition available to rock....Dylan opened up new country for everyone in popular music, because his songs were unrestricted in meter, because his lyrics were so untamed and because his singing voice, once described as sounding like "a cow with its leg caught in a fence," made it clear that there was a difference between the great voice and the great rock & roll voice."[7]

It was for ushering in the age of folk-rock that Dylan is best remembered (and for which he received his most trenchant criticism). His troubled (yet seminal) appearance at Newport should not have come as such a surprise to his fans who had listened to *Bringing It All Back Home*, released several months before the festival. (After revisiting audio and video footage of the event, some have come to believe that the booing during Dylan's set was in response to the poor quality of the P.A. system and the short set, but the year that followed would see Dylan face scorn and ridicule—sometimes bordering on violence—at a number of shows). With one foot firmly rooted in the folk tradition and the other stretching out toward rock's future, *Bringing It All Back Home* introduced classic Dylan material like the painfully shy "She Belongs to Me," the rural rocker "Maggie's Farm," the "ultimate protest song" (according to Dylan's biographer) "It's Alright, Ma (I'm Only Bleeding)," and the stream-of-consciousness monster "Subterranean Homesick Blues," which was Dylan's first single to show off his rock and roll interest.

After *Bringing It All Back Home*, Dylan's career would be scrutinized and picked apart, album after album, like no artist before or since. At one point, Toronto newspaper columnist Scott Young (father of folk-rocker Neil Young) came to Dylan's defense on a Toronto talk show. "I believe there's a freedom to just sit down if you want to...The public doesn't own Dylan; that's why he appealed to you in the first place. There's something sad about it; it's like Hemingway writing one book and the audience reading it over and over again and wanting nothing else."[8] Dylan, of course, would endure the slings and arrows of outrageous proportions and come to be hailed as one of American music's great innovators, heavily influencing the course of folk and rock in the 1960s (in no small part through the enormous effect he had on the Beatles). "The first few months of folk-rock were strange, indeed," wrote a later scribe of Dylan's adventurous foray into undiscovered territory. "Critics were caught off guard. The audiences booed Dylan for part of a year . . . but while some were booing him, the musicians were busy imitating him, and by the late summer of 1965, folk-rock was all about us . . . The singer-songwriters were plugging in."[9]

Album Title: *Mr. Tambourine Man*
Artist: The Byrds
Recorded: January 20–April 22, 1965, at Columbia Studios in Hollywood
U.S. release: June 21, 1965 (Columbia)
Producer: Terry Melcher

"Rock history is striated by the influence of the Byrds," wrote critic Barney Hoskyns decades after this seminal California pop band's influence was first felt. "Theirs is one of the great stylistic lineages, forever shadowing those of the Fabs and the Stones. Without them we would never have had Big Star, Tom Petty & the Heartbreakers, R.E.M., The Stone Roses or Teenage Fanclub—that blissed-out, churningly harmonic, quintessentially white sound which continues to thrive in the age of Britpop. Come to that, we would never have had Dillard and Clark, Crosby, Stills and Nash, The Flying Burrito Brothers and a dozen other folk-country-rock aggregations of the late '60s. 'Influential' is the understatement of the epoch."[10]

Starting with *Mr. Tambourine Man* and continuing through to their 1968 country-rock landmark *Sweetheart of the Rodeo* (see p. 61), the Byrds joined the company of Miles Davis, Bob Dylan, Woody Guthrie, Hank Williams, and Elvis Presley as among the most important American musical acts of the 20th century. The band started out in 1964 as a Los Angeles quintet consisting of vocalist and guitarist Jim McGuinn (who later changed his name to "Roger" for religious reasons), vocalist and guitarist David Crosby, bassist Chris Hillman, drummer Michael Clarke, and vocalist, guitarist, and percussionist Gene Clark. Between them they added a number of traditional folk instruments such as banjo, mandolin, harmonica, and appropriately, tambourine.

The Byrds' 1965 *Mr. Tambourine Man*, an early Dylan/Beatles-infused masterpiece that helped bring folk-rock into the mainstream. *Courtesy of Photofest.*

Most of the band's members had been doing traditional

folk material until hearing the Beatles made them want to form a band and experiment with pop noise. McGuinn even created a signature sound for the band with his twelve-string Rickenbacker guitar, which he bought after seeing George Harrison play one in the film *A Hard Day's Night*, giving many of the Byrds' songs a warm, upbeat tone. "I did feel that the real folk scene was in the Village," McGuinn said of his early folk years. "But the Beatles came out and changed the whole game for me. I saw a definite niche, a place where the two of them blended together. If you took Lennon and Dylan and mixed them together, that was something that hadn't been done."[11]

Much of the creative force in 1960s rock came about through Bob Dylan and the Beatles reacting to each others' musical ideas: Dylan showed the Fab Four that folk could be exciting, while the Beatles showed the Village folkie that rock and roll could be intelligent. Between them they revolutionized the way people thought about rock music, and it was the Byrds that first stood at this crossroad of folk tradition and pop sounds.

Upon the release of their debut album, the Byrds were immediately hailed as America's response to the Beatles. Though many record labels made similar claims about their acts, in this case it was quite true, a claim supported by many fans and imitators since, not the least of which the Beatles' own George Harrison.

Dylan and the Byrds played folk themes to rock rhythms. Between the 1965 release of *Mr. Tambourine Man* and Dylan's landmark album *Bringing It All Back Home* issued just three months earlier, the genre of folk-rock was born. When the Byrds fused the Beatles' pop sensibilities with Dylan's meaningful lyrics, they got the best of both worlds, "holding on to meaning but making things dance."[12] The band applied their warm, jangly pop and sweet California harmonies to a diverse selection of tunes, including uber-folkie Pete Seeger's "The Bells of Rhymney," several of their own compositions (which was unusual for a rock act at the time), and no less than four Bob Dylan songs, including the classic "All I Really Want to Do" and the band's first recording, "Mr. Tambourine Man."

Dylan's "Mr. Tambourine Man" was brought to the Byrds by their manager Jim Dickson, who encouraged the band to rearrange and record the song to generate label interest. "McGuinn all but rewrote the song," a later reviewer wrote about the classic track. "He axed three verses, leaving the most 'contemporary' of the original four in between the choruses. He slowed it down by half, allowing himself a very deliberate and clearly articulated vocal very much in contrast with Dylan's breathless rush. Using the bass guitar as a lead counterpoint to his own jungle jangle electric twelve-string he could play both lead and rhythm phrases, mostly the latter, jet-driven magic carpet textures that rise and fall in perfect cycles. But the voice is quite as important as the guitar, at once puzzled and cynically wise, weary and elevated, punkish and dignified..."[13]

This title track became the Byrds' first No. 1 hit, and as the first widespread folk-rock crossover, one of the most important singles in rock history. Due to limited studio time, only Roger McGuinn plays on the title cut—the amateurish band members were replaced by seasoned pros to turn the work out quickly—but Crosby and Clark do deliver harmonized vocals as McGuinn plays. Six months later the Byrds would score another No. 1 hit with "Turn! Turn! Turn!," a Pete Seeger song based on a biblical passage from the book of Ecclesiastes. Their ability to turn intelligent, folk-based anthems into bouncy radio hits would help them define a new sound for rock in the 1960s—strummed guitar, fluid harmonies, and relevant lyrics copied by scores of imitators—and their later opus *Sweetheart of the Rodeo* would have the same effect in founding the country-rock sound of the 1970s.

Folk-rock would soon incorporate bluegrass, jazz, country, honky-tonk, and other genres into its mix, helping to spur on an unprecedented explosion of musical creativity through the late 1960s, influencing the psychedelic rock coming out of San Francisco, the art-rock bouncing around in London clubs, the Southern rock reaching out from Florida's hinterland, and of course the soft rock of the 1970s, dubbed the "West Coast sound." One can draw a direct musical lineage from the early Byrds hits to the biggest groups of the 1970s, including the Eagles, Fleetwood Mac, and Crosby, Stills, Nash and Young, all of which share the folksy pop of *Mr. Tambourine Man* and the country grooves of *Sweetheart of the Rodeo*. During the spread of time between these albums, the Byrds went through a constantly rotating lineup with McGuinn remaining as the only original member by the end—yet the band somehow managed to retain a solid, defining sound and release high-quality albums throughout. It has been widely asserted that had they been able to maintain a steady roster, they would have out-Beatled the Beatles. Nonetheless, even with the Byrds' constant personnel changes, few bands would have such sweeping impact on musical history.

Album Title: *Rubber Soul*
Artist: The Beatles
Recorded: June 17–November 11, 1965, at Abbey Road Studios in London
U.K. release: December 3, 1965 (Parlophone)
U.S. release: December 6, 1965 (Capitol)
Producer: George Martin

In previous entries I've spoken about the exchange of ideas between the Beatles and Bob Dylan, a series of back-and-forth influences that fueled the rapid expansion of musical genres and demonstrated that rock and roll could be taken seriously. From Dylan, the Beatles learned that folk music could be exciting and energetic without losing its power as social commentary, prompting a change in the group's lyrics to tackle issues more substantial that the old "boy-meets-girl" standby. "I wasn't too keen on the lyrics in those days," Lennon once said. "I didn't think they counted. Dylan used to say 'Listen to the words, man.' And I'd say 'I don't listen to the words.'"[14]

But Lennon—and his bandmates—began to listen to the words and increased their range as both musicians and as lyricists. In the short time between their February 1964 arrival in New York and their December 1965 release of *Rubber Soul*, the Beatles had changed dramatically. Although their upbeat, poppy grooves had made them the most popular act in the western world, they had since discovered marijuana and LSD, had begun to assert more control over their music, and had sought out new ways to incorporate alternative instruments, structures, and technology into their releases. In modern parlance, the band that released *Rubber Soul* might be described as "Beatles 2.0." Though they would really stretch their wings on *Revolver* eight months later and *Sgt. Pepper's Lonely Hearts Club Band* the following year (see p. 46), it was *Rubber Soul* that first gave audiences a hint that the lads from Liverpool could do more than make teenage girls faint. Dylan took early note of the Beatles' potential, claiming "Everybody else thought they were for the teenyboppers, that they were gonna pass right away. But it was obvious to me that they had staying power. I knew they were pointing the direction of where music had to go."[15]

With *Rubber Soul* the group began exploring themes beyond boy/girl relationships that made them stars with songs such as "I Want to Hold Your Hand," "Love Me Do," and "She Loves You." A weightier, more universal awareness came to light through tunes like "The Word" (a semipolitical song calling for brotherly love) and "In My Life" (an homage to past and future friends). The stark, introspective "Nowhere Man," which Lennon claimed he wrote about himself, is known as the first Beatles song that moved entirely beyond the relationship theme, foreshadowing future albums that would sit heavy with philosophical pondering.

The album began to explore more territory sonically as well. The Harrison-penned "Think for Yourself" introduced the fuzz-tone bass and an uncomfortable blending of major and minor modes (which serves as an ingenious complement to the lyrics about deception). The romantic "Michelle" incorporates French lyrics that rhyme with their English counterparts. On the aforementioned "In My Life," the band simulates a harpsichord by taping a piano performance and speeding up the playback, presaging future tape experimentation mastered on 1966's *Revolver* and 1967's *Sgt. Pepper's Lonely Hearts Club Band*. The Beatles' first use of sitar appears on "Norwegian Wood (This Bird Has Flown)," an instrument that would become a recognizable weapon in the Beatles arsenal and would spread to other bands ranging from Donovan to the Rolling Stones (and would ultimately make George Harrison's mentor, Ravi Shankar, something of a rock star).

Such experimentation would presage their monumental follow-up, *Revolver*, released in August 1966. *Revolver* was itself a landmark album, often listed among rock's all-time greatest, introducing orchestral instruments such as French horn on "For No One" and strings on "Eleanor Rigby," twin-guitar harmony on "And Your Bird Can Sing," extraneous noises (coughing) on the lead track "Taxman," and all manner of odd syncopation and tape looping on "Tomorrow Never Knows," which really stretched the band thematically with an interpretation of the Tibetan *Book of the Dead*. Though it is somewhat unfair that such a brilliant and groundbreaking album is not found among this book's entries, its salient features are covered in this listing for its predecessor *Rubber Soul* (which marked the band's evolution into sonic and lyrical experimentation) and *Revolver*'s follow-up *Sgt. Pepper's Lonely Hearts Club Band* (on which the Beatles mastered their experiments).

The U.S. version of *Rubber Soul* was missing several tracks that appeared on the U.K. version, a marketing decision commonly used with the Beatles' pre-*Sgt. Pepper's* releases to make the album appeal specifically to an American audience. Since these decisions were usually made by the label without the consent of the band, often the group decried the changes as altering the album's cohesiveness. In the case of *Rubber Soul*, however, these changes worked to the band's advantage, making the U.S. version even more of a landmark for its inclusion of folk-influenced tunes.

For *Rubber Soul*'s U.S. release, the songs "Drive My Car," "Nowhere Man," "What Goes On," and "If I Needed Someone" are dropped in favor of the country and western-tinged "I've Just Seen a Face" and the acoustic "It's Only Love," removing some of the album's heavier vibes and revealing the Beatles' debt to Bob Dylan, the Byrds, and other acts that were bringing electrified folk to the forefront of the American music scene. The Byrds' guitarist Roger McGuinn was particularly influential to George Harrison (and vice versa), and soon the Beatles would continue their exchange of musical ideas with the advent of the San Francisco psychedelic scene. In the words of rock critic Robert Christgau, "*Rubber Soul* smashed a lot of alienation. Without reneging on the group's masscult appeal, it reached into private lives and made hundreds of thousands of secretly lonely people feel as if someone out there shared their brightest insights and most depressing discoveries.... Psychedelia starts here."[16]

Album Title: *Pet Sounds*
Artist: The Beach Boys
Recorded: July 12, 1965–April 13, 1966, at Gold Star Recording Studios, Columbia Studios, Western Recorders, and Sunset Sound in Hollywood
U.S. release: May 16, 1966 (Capitol)
Producer: Brian Wilson

Rivaling *Rubber Soul* and *Sgt. Pepper's Lonely Hearts Club Band* for the title of rock's greatest album, the Beach Boys' *Pet Sounds* had the unfortunate luck of being buried between the two Beatles masterpieces, released five months after *Rubber Soul* and thirteen months before *Sgt. Pepper's*. While this fact may have dulled the album's commercial popularity—reaching only No. 10 on the charts (below par for the band)—*Pet Sounds* still stands as one of the most innovative recordings in rock and elevated producer Brian Wilson from talented bandleader to studio genius.

Unlike its British counterparts, which were largely collaborations between John Lennon, Paul McCartney, and producer George Martin, *Pet Sounds* was masterminded almost entirely by Brian Wilson, who had led his brothers Carl and Dennis, their cousin Mike Love, and their friend Alan Jardine to become the definitive voice of surf music in the 1960s as the Beach Boys.

In the three years between 1962 and 1965, the Beach Boys were on top of the pop world with eight albums charting in the Top 10, six of them in the Top 5. But for Brian Wilson, who shouldered most of the creative burden for the band, the pressure was too great, and after suffering a breakdown on a flight during a late-1964 tour, Brian stopped touring altogether and began spending more time in the studio. With the rest of the group away fulfilling tour commitments without him, Brian hired studio musicians to complete the half-recorded *The Beach Boys Today!*, whose complex arrangements and more developed themes foreshadowed the lush orchestration and maturity of *Pet Sounds*.

When the band returned to the studio to lay down vocal tracks for *The Beach Boys Today!*, Brian informed them that he could no longer handle the pressures of touring, and an odd new arrangement was reached: the band would continue touring with Glenn Campbell (and later Bruce Johnston) rounding out the group, while Brian would devote himself to composing and producing their albums with studio musicians.

With the sudden freedom Brian gained, his creative energy grew by leaps and bounds with each album, but it took the release of the Beatles' *Rubber Soul* in December 1965 to fuel the fire. "I really wasn't quite ready for the unity," Wilson remarked on first hearing the record. "It felt like it all belonged together. *Rubber Soul* was a collection of songs...that somehow went together like no album ever made before, and I was very impressed. I said, 'That's it. I really am challenged to do a great album.'"[17]

All Brian lacked was a collaborator to help him write the lyrics, which he found in Tony Asher, who wrote jingles for an advertising agency in Los Angeles at the time. Brian had crossed paths with Tony in the studio on several occasions, and asked him to take a leave of absence from his job to help compose some songs for a new album. Over the next month the two worked together writing the lyrics, and Brian spent countless hours in the studio laying down tracks and—heavily influenced by his favorite producer, Phil Spector—experimenting with the songs' sonic possibilities. When the band returned from a successful tour in early February, they found half a dozen tracks awaiting their vocals.

"We came back, and there was *Pet Sounds* sitting there for us to do," recalled Alan Jardine. "There was this masterpiece sitting there, kind of an uncut gem. And we're going, 'Wow, hmm, what's up, Brian?' Really, it was a whole new horizon for us. We were a surfing group when we left the country, and now basically we came back to this new music. And it took some getting used to."[18] The band eventually accepted the project for what it was—essentially a solo album for Brian on which he could put to vinyl what he wanted to hear (hence the name *Pet Sounds*, as this was Brian's pet project).

Though the Beach Boys had made their name with songs about surfing, cars, and high-school sweethearts, *Pet Sounds* was a radical departure encompassing themes of isolation, transition to adulthood, hope, and loss of innocence. The lyrics are complemented—at times overshadowed—by melodies that are at their heart fairly simple but are layered by Brian in extraordinarily complex ways. Several dozen musicians ultimately had a hand in the album—some playing instruments that were alien to rock, including the glockenspiel, ukulele, accordion, theremin, bongos, harpsichord, violin, viola, cello, trombone, and a drummer pounding on two empty Coke cans—all arranged to the last detail by Brian. Just as *Sgt. Pepper's* would do a year later, odd sounds like barking dogs, trains, and bicycle bells were incorporated into the songs. More than a month was spent just laying down the vocal tracks, which Brian had arranged in precise pitches and tight harmonies, recorded again and again to absolute perfection.

Among the songs are the memorable opening track "Wouldn't It Be Nice," the instrumental "Let's Go Away for a While," which Brian called "the most satisfying piece of music I have ever made,"[19] and a remake of the Kingston Trio's Caribbean folk classic "Sloop John B.," which landed at No. 3 on the U.S. singles charts and No. 2 in Britain. Oddly, the song that Brian eventually cut from the album, the brilliant "Good Vibrations," was released months later as a single and has been hailed by many critics as one of the greatest songs ever composed (mostly for its intricate production value). Had it been included in *Pet Sounds*, however, it might have been a very different song—Brian wanted to finish the album so he could devote time to "Good Vibrations," and in the end he spent more time on that one song than on the entirety of *Pet Sounds*.

From the day it was released, *Pet Sounds* was hailed as a masterpiece and became enormously influential. But much to Brian's disappointment (nearly crushing his notoriously fragile ego), its sales were weaker than the band had come to expect from their albums, largely due to an apathetic marketing campaign by the record label. Nonetheless, with *Pet Sounds* Brian Wilson returned the favor to the Beatles for their influential *Rubber Soul*—the Fab Four praised the album as a major influence on *Sgt. Pepper's Lonely Hearts Club Band*, with Paul McCartney calling it his favorite album. But for Brian, *Pet Sounds* was a prelude to his opus *Smile*, which he worked on for the remainder of the year and might have been an album of "Good Vibrations" quality, had pressure from his band and label not led him to abandon the project, making *Smile* possibly the greatest album that never was.

Album Title: *Freak Out!*
Artist: Frank Zappa and the Mothers of Invention
Recorded: March 9–12, 1966, at Sunset-Highland Studios in Los Angeles
U.S. release: July 1966 (Verve)
Producer: Tom Wilson

There are many ways that a band or an artist can use their albums as a way of critiquing the popular music exploding around them. Progressive groups like the Moody Blues borrowed symphonic elements to challenge the guitar-centered assumption of the classic rock band. Glam artists such as David Bowie borrowed from the theatre and androgynous culture to make a statement about the testosterone-heavy rock idols. Avant-garde bands like Captain Beefheart defied conventional pop themes with surreal lyrics and unusual arrangements. And later punk/new wave acts such as Elvis Costello attacked the record industry's hypocrisy with direct, scathing lyrics.

Frank Zappa and his band, the Mothers of Invention, did all these things, and in most cases they did them long before anyone else. Zappa was the original hippie freak, always railing at the establishment, using his considerable musical talents to lampoon the record business, his musical contemporaries, even himself. "More accessible than the New York Dolls yet more underground than the Moody Blues, Zappa was an unstoppable champion of authenticity and ruthless adversary of conformity. His bizarre music and over-the-top performances were simultaneously derided as the work of a madman and celebrated as brilliant modern extensions of classical, jazz, blues, and rock genres. Denigrated as a hippie, lauded as a genius, castigated as a troublemaker, honored as a patriot, Zappa had as many sides as there were people to hear his music. Whether one liked him or hated him, his pointed wit and tremendous musical talent made it simply impossible to ignore him."[20]

Zappa burst onto the scene in the summer of 1966 with *Freak Out!*, one of the most mind-bending debuts in the history of rock, as well as one of the first studio double albums (predated just two months by Bob Dylan's *Blonde on Blonde*). Exhibiting a dazzling combination of jazz, pop, doo-wop, bubble-gum, protest, punk, close-harmony group vocals, spoken word, musique concrète, and satire, the album disintegrated rather than stretched the boundaries of what was possible in a rock album. With songs ranging from "Help, I'm a Rock" to "Who Are the Brain Police," to "The Return of the Son of Monster Magnet," *Freak Out!* demonstrated a mastery of the unpredictable and unorthodox while somehow maintaining ties to the pop craftsmanship the album ridicules. Where Zappa's friend and colleague Captain Beefheart completely escaped the pop mentality with his avant-garde gem *Trout Mask Replica* (see p. 73), Zappa worked within pop frameworks to lampoon his own profession. From the straight-up rocker "Trouble Every Day," a song about the Watts riots that received the most mainstream acceptance of all the tracks, to the kazoos, vibraphone, and off-key singing in the opening track "Hungry Freaks, Daddy," *Freak Out!* brought to the public eye an unusual, creative, and outspoken force in Frank Zappa.

"I think of the art of composition as time-painting you know," Zappa told one critic in 1969. "You're being employed by your audience to decorate a piece of time for them. In the same way a painter uses a piece of canvas and he's got to slap it on that, I have the opportunity of taking a piece of time and sticking little things on it. In a live performance I get to do it with visual and audio material, on a record I can do it with pieces of time from all over. In some albums I've condensed as much as ten years into one little piece of plastic."[21]

The bizarre experimentation on *Freak Out!* would not only herald the beginning of Zappa's extraordinarily prolific recording output (releasing eleven albums in the Mothers' first four years, and almost sixty albums in Zappa's thirty-year career), but would also influence the Beatles to such an extent that they credited it with inspiring their 1967 landmark *Sgt. Pepper's Lonely Hearts Club Band* (see p. 46) (an album that Zappa lampooned, ironically, with his 1968 attack on hippie culture *We're Only in It for the Money*, which featured a parody of *Sgt. Pepper's'* famous album cover). Far from participating in the peace-and-love ideology of their Californian contemporaries, Zappa and the Mothers sought to tell it like it is rather than like it should be, lambasting the hypocrisy of both the status quo and the counterculture, even taking pot-shots at themselves in the process. "If it were possible to get whiplash just listening to music," wrote one reviewer, "Frank Zappa would be the one to give it to us."[22]

Album Title: *The Doors*
Artist: The Doors
Recorded: August–September 1966, at Columbia Studios in Hollywood
U.S. release: January 1967 (Elektra)
Producer: Paul Rothchild

"If the doors of perception were cleansed, everything would appear to man as it is, infinite."[23] This William Blake quote, borrowed by novelist Aldous Huxley for his 1963 masterpiece *The Doors of Perception*, not only gave the Doors their name, but well-encapsulated their attitude and what they sought from their music: a clear, un-coerced view into the nature of reality. Such existential straw-clutching has earned the group—lead singer Jim Morrison in particular—both wide appreciation as a truly deep and original act and wide derision as a band not talented enough to pull it off. Sometimes the praise and condescension would appear on the same page, such as in the *Rolling Stone Record Guide*, which hails Morrison as "a genuinely dangerous teen idol. In this way, the Doors take their place in pop history as the progenitors of a whole wave of teenybopper anti-icons, the genuine precursors of Alice Cooper and Kiss." But in the end, the writer posits the question, "Is this the most overrated group in rock history? Only a truly terminal case of arrested adolescence can hold out against such a judgment for very long."[24]

It was this arrested adolescence in their fans that fueled the Doors' success as Los Angeles' hottest rock act in the late 1960s, distilling a potent brew of psychedelic tonic much darker than the pleasant hippie vibes coming from the Haight-Ashbury scene to the north. Though the psychedelic bands of Los Angeles and San Francisco had much in common—open sexuality, freedom of individual expression, and rebellion against corporate authority—the Doors took themselves more seriously, and Morrison in particular was fascinated by death (not only corporeal, but spiritual and artistic transformations as well). Morrison considered himself a poet much more than his contemporaries, and his heavy lyrics, complemented by the sometimes brooding, sometimes frenzied guitar work of Robby Krieger, organ of Ray Manzarek, and drums of John Densmore, played to "the darker dreams lurking in the subconscious of the young."[25]

Morrison and Manzarek had met at UCLA film school in the early 1960s, and a year after graduation, had a chance encounter on Venice Beach, where Morrison recited one of his poems to Manzarek and the two decided to put together a band. Manzarek recruited Krieger and Densmore from a Maharishi meditation class the three attended, and in 1965 the Doors were born. After a stint at the Whisky-A-Go-Go in Los Angeles, the group were signed to Elektra Records by Elektra founder Jac Holzman, who caught one of their shows at the Whisky. Three days after being signed, the band was fired from the Whisky for an obscenity-laced set by an overmedicated Morrison, establishing a pattern of drug abuse and lewd behavior that would haunt the singer for the remainder of his short life.

The Doors were "about revolt, disorder, chaos," Jim Morrison told the *New York Times*. "It seemed to me to be the road toward freedom—external revolt is a way to bring about internal freedom.... When I sing my songs in public that's a dramatic act, but not just acting as in theater, but a *social* act, real action."[26] With the release of *The Doors* in January 1967, Morrison got to see his social action writ large. Produced by Paul Rothchild, who claimed he wanted to create an "aural documentary" of the band's live shows (and who would continue to produce most of the Doors' albums), *The Doors* was a stunning debut—thoughtful, moody, dark, and dripping with an introspective charm, unusual for the community-focused psychedelic music that had become the radio staple and that would define the summer of 1967.

The Doors slowly rose to No. 2 on the charts, propelled by the No. 1 single "Light My Fire," which would be their biggest hit. Though the band was largely defined in the public eye by Morrison's good looks, ego, and desire to make scandalous headlines, he had little to do with the hit—Manzarek developed the melody, Krieger wrote most of the lyrics, Densmore created the beat, and Rothchild edited the lengthy song down to a catchy radio version. Other songs from the album, including "Twentieth Century Fox" and "Break on Through (to the Other Side)," became staples of classic rock radio. The album's final track, appropriately titled "The End," became a signature song for Morrison's tortured-poet persona, a disturbing, schizophrenic acid trip of murder and incest that got the band in trouble at more than one gig (it was this song that had gotten them fired from the Whisky). If "The End" had a film equivalent, it would be the 1979

Coppola masterpiece *Apocalypse Now*, which uses the song to provide a soul-shattering exclamation point to the film's final scenes.

"Each generation wants new symbols, new people, new names," Morrison told *Rolling Stone*, "they want to divorce themselves from the preceding generation; they won't call it rock. . . . Don't you see a cyclical thing every five or ten years, when everybody comes together and swarms and breaks apart?"[27] The mid-1960s was just such a swarm in popular music as all of rockdom bowed to the Beatles and Dylan, and the Doors helped fuel the breaking apart later in the decade with their compellingly personal music, foreshadowing the 1970s when rock ceased being about the "us" and focused on the "me."

Album Title: *Surrealistic Pillow*
Artist: Jefferson Airplane
Recorded: November 1966, at RCA Victor's Music Center of the World in Hollywood
U.S. release: February 1967 (RCA)
Producer: Rick Jarrard

Jefferson Airplane's 1967 *Surrealistic Pillow*, the soundtrack for San Francisco's 1967 Summer of Love. *Courtesy of RCA Music Group.*

Though the psychedelic scene in San Francisco was on fire in 1965 and 1966, it was largely a local phenomenon, with artists from the Charlatans, the Great Society, Moby Grape, Quicksilver Messenger Service, Jefferson Airplane, the Warlocks, and Big Brother and the Holding Company jamming in each others' basements and the local music halls. By late 1966, the secret hippie enclave had been breached, and wanna-beatniks from around the country flocked to Haight-Ashbury to take the revolution up on its promise of free sex, cheap drugs, and mind-bending rock and roll.

One of the chief exporters of the bay area's psychedelic music was Jefferson Airplane, the first underground act to reach out to a national audience with their 1966 debut *Jefferson Airplane Takes Off*, called by *Crawdaddy!* "Perhaps the best rock album ever produced,"[28] though with the explosion of incredible rock landmarks that followed over the next two years, the album quickly became a footnote in the grander music scheme. Though *Jefferson Airplane Takes Off* introduced the band (and the San Francisco scene) to a wider audience, it was not until their sophomore release the following year, *Surrealistic Pillow*, that the group really cemented themselves in the wider pop arena, reaching the No. 3 spot and scoring Top 10 hits with "White Rabbit" and "Somebody to Love."

Jefferson Airplane Takes Off was dominated by the composing skills of frontman and singer Marty Balin, who penned most of the tunes and managed a tight ensemble that included blues guitarist Jorma Kaukonen, folk guitarist Paul Kantner, folk- and jazz-influenced backing singer Signe Anderson, drummer Skip Spence, and jazz bassist Jack Cassady. The pastiche of genres gave the band a sophisticated and original sound, earning it gigs at such diverse venues as the Monterey Jazz Festival, the Monterey Pop Festival, the Berkeley Folk Festival, and performances alongside the San Francisco Symphony. Like nearly every American pop act at the time, the band found their influences in the Beatles, Bob Dylan, and the Byrds—the holy trinity of mid-1960s folk-rock. But after their debut, Jefferson Airplane adopted vocalist Grace Slick from the Great Society, giving the group a powerful female lead singer, as well as fresh material that Slick brought with her from her old band. When *Surrealistic Pillow* was released in February 1967, it was like San Francisco's entire underground scene shouting at the world through a megaphone.

The release of *Surrealistic Pillow* was the first major event of the Summer of Love, San Francisco's overhyped but still magical year that started with the Gathering of the Tribes festival in January, and led up to the Monterey Pop Festival in June, arguably the most important concert in the history of rock music. Throughout the spring and summer, when all eyes were on San Francisco's psychedelic scene, *Surrealistic Pillow* provided the soundtrack to the season. "For the past year and a half the combo with the singular name has fashioned a freewheeling style of music that has made it the hottest new rock group in the country," wrote *Time* magazine soon after the album's release. "The Airplane is the anointed purveyor of the San Francisco Sound, a heady mixture of blues, folk and jazz that began as the private expression of the hippie underground and only recently bubbled to the surface. Now, in such cavernous San Francisco halls as the Fillmore and the Avalon Ballroom, as well as in rollerskating rinks, movie theaters, veterans' halls, park bandstands, college gyms and roped-off streets from Pacific Heights to Butchertown, about 300 bands are inviting the faithful to 'blow your mind' with the new sound."[29]

At the center of this sound were the two hits from *Surrealistic Pillow* that Slick had brought with her from the Great Society: "Somebody to Love," written by Slick's brother-in-law Darby, and "White Rabbit," the Slick-penned tune that became Jefferson Airplane's signature song. With a melodic pattern borrowed from Ravel's "Bolero," a lyrical construction inspired by Lewis Carroll's *Alice in Wonderland*, and a strict "think for yourself" message, "White Rabbit" functioned as both an invitation to expand one's consciousness with LSD and a call to arm oneself with awareness of social inequality, both encapsulated in the closing line that could have been (and in many ways, was) the subtitle for the Summer of Love: feed your head.

With the enormous success of *Surrealistic Pillow*, Jefferson Airplane opened up San Francisco's psychedelic scene for national gawking, helping further the careers of bay-area-based acts like the Grateful Dead (formerly the Warlocks), the Steve Miller Band, Quicksilver Messenger Service, Big Brother and the Holding Company (now featuring singer Janis Joplin), and Country Joe and the Fish. Beyond the musical influence, the Airplane became the ambassadors for hippiedom, not just preaching communal values, but living them through their music. "The stage is our bed," Marty Balin told a reporter on the eve of the magic summer, "and the audience is our broad. We're not entertaining, we're making love."[30]

Album Title: *The Velvet Underground and Nico*
Artist: The Velvet Underground
Recorded: April–November 1966, at Scepter Studios and Mayfair Studios in New York City and T.T.G. Studios in Hollywood
U.S. release: March 1967 (Verve)
Producer: Tom Wilson, Andy Warhol

The Velvet Underground's 1967 debut *The Velvet Underground and Nico*, an important early influence on American punk and new wave. *Courtesy of Universal Music Enterprises.*

Common wisdom dictates that the more albums a band sells, the more influence that album should have on the music scene and the wider public. The Velvet Underground's 1967 debut *The Velvet Underground and Nico* is an exception to this rule, peaking at No. 173 on the pop charts and spending only twelve weeks in the Top 200 despite heavy anticipation brought about by the band's benefactor and spiritual guru, Andy Warhol. Although only a few thousand people purchased the album in the first year of its release, it was an extraordinarily influential document, as famously pointed out by 1970s avant-garde king Brian Eno, because almost everyone who bought it went out and started a band.

The Velvet Underground are the undeniable primogenitors of much that was good and holy in the punk, new wave, and avant-garde scenes of the

1970s, "playing experimental rock in 1965 when the Beatles just wanted to hold your hand and San Francisco was still the place where Tony Bennett left his heart," said the *New York Times* in 1970, attributing to the band "a hard rock that is powerful and tight as a raised fist; so unified and together that it just rolls itself into a knot and throbs...they make 80 percent of today's popular rock groups seem pointless and amateurish."[31]

Just as it took years for the band to earn a wider appreciation—reportedly a decade went by before their debut album passed the 100,000 mark—it took a long time for the Velvet Underground to become noticed by the underground in the first place. The members largely responsible for the band's distinctive style and uncommon originality were guitarist, singer, and songwriter Lou Reed, and bassist, violist, and organist John Cale. The two met while Reed was working as a staff writer for Pickwick Records ("a poor man's Carole King" is how Reed later described himself). Cale, a classically trained musician from Wales, had moved to the United States to continue his studies of "serious" music, but found himself increasingly drawn to rock and roll. The two found in each other kindred spirits, Cale looking for a songwriter to complement his unusual arrangements, Reed looking for a composer to bring distinct melodies to his songwriting, and both interested in fusing rock and roll with avant-garde sensibilities.

After a number of incarnations in 1964 and 1965—performing as the Primitives, the Warlocks, and the Falling Spikes—the group settled into a quartet with Reed's friends Sterling Morrison on bass and guitar and Maureen Tucker playing drums, drawing their new name from *The Velvet Underground*, a book about sadomasochism written by Michael Leigh. The band made it a point to be unusual. Dowd would play her drums with mallets rather than drumsticks, and would sometimes lay the bass drum on its side, pounding out the beat from a standing position. Cale was fascinated with the antirock notion of drones, and would create low, moody antimelodies with his viola to complement Reed's speak-sing vocals and gritty lyrics about sex, drugs, and transvestism in New York City's gritty underbelly.

To call the band uncommercial is an understatement—for a country fawning over the inoffensive jangle of Herb Alpert and the Tijuana Brass, the slick pop of pre-*Rubber Soul* Beatles, and heading into a love affair with San Francisco's positive hippie vibes, the heady experimentalism of the Velvets never had a chance. Enter Andy Warhol, undisputed guru of the 1960s' bizarre bazaar, who took the group under his wing. Warhol was seeking a band for his multimedia circus called The Exploding Plastic Inevitable, an experiential collage of music, film, dance, art, and theatre that was well suited to the Velvet Underground's atypical sound.

Warhol introduced the band to Nico, a European chanteuse who teamed up with the Velvets for their debut release, the groundbreaking *The Velvet Underground and Nico*. Simultaneously prepunk and postmodern, the album is thematically driven by Reed's lyrical journeys through the unseemly streets of counterculture New York. By the time the album was released (a year after it was recorded), the drugs and sex coming out of San Francisco's flower-powered amplifiers were finding mainstream acceptance, even on the national stage. But where bay-area bands sang of chemical and sexual liberation, Reed explored the more depraved—and occasionally destructive—side of the equation, with themes of addiction and sexual perversion in songs like "Heroin," "Waiting for the Man," and "Venus in Furs." Musically, the album is surprisingly eclectic, with Cale and Reed combining crunchy rock, rhythm and blues, free jazz, and avant-garde experimentation in a brew that would influence punk, glam, new wave, heavy metal, and grunge over the next three decades.

"The Velvet Underground marked a turning point in rock history," claimed one retrospective. "After the release of *The Velvet Underground & Nico*, knowing the power of which it was capable, the music could never be as innocent, as unselfconscious as before.... In perverse subject matter ("Heroin," "Venus in Furs"), deceptively simple musical forms and anarchic jamming, the Velvets displayed the rebellious traits new wave bands would pick up on ten years later."[32]

Though Reed and Cale deserve the musical credit, Warhol is permanently associated with the album for his financial support of the band, his willingness to let Reed retain creative control of the work (despite Warhol's insistence that Nico participate), and most notably for his design of the album cover: a peel-off banana sticker that revealed a phallic symbol when removed. It is doubtful that the band would have been nearly as influential (or for that matter, ever heard) without Warhol's support, and the combination of his mentoring and the band's vision created one of the most extraordinary releases in American music. "Few rock albums are as important as *The Velvet Underground and Nico*," it was later claimed, "and fewer still have lost so little of their power to surprise and intrigue more than 30 years after first hitting the racks."[33]

Album Title: *Sgt. Pepper's Lonely Hearts Club Band*
Artist: The Beatles
Recorded: December 6, 1966–April 1, 1967, at Abbey Road Studios
in London
U.S. release: June 2, 1967 (Capitol)
Producer: George Martin

When *London Times* critic Kenneth Tynan famously gushed that *Sgt. Pepper's Lonely Hearts Club Band* was a "decisive moment in the history of Western civilization,"[34] it was only one hyperbole in a long line of hyperboles heaped upon the album in the four decades since. The LP has appeared near the top or at the top of almost every major album "best of" list, and continues to dominate the consciousness of 1960s psychedelic rock the way the 1977 film soundtrack *Saturday Night Fever* embodies disco (see p. 141) and Nirvana's 1991 release *Nevermind* personifies grunge (see p. 214). Though its popularity has waned a bit over time—forty years of

The Beatles' 1967 *Sgt. Pepper's Lonely Hearts Club Band*, the group's highest charting release and one of the most influential albums of the 1960s. *Courtesy of Photofest.*

praise is bound to create some kind of backlash—few would argue that it was an extraordinary feat that catapulted music several years into the future. Critics' opinions aside, the numbers speak for themselves: spending fifteen weeks at No. 1 and nearly four-and-a-half years in the Top 200, *Sgt. Pepper's* was by far the highest and longest charting Beatles album in America, and by the end of the century was among the twenty best-selling albums of all time worldwide.[35]

In a sense, *Sgt. Pepper's* was inevitable—a climactic exclamation point to the wild and experimental rock of the mid-1960s. With the release of *Rubber Soul* in December 1965 (see p. 34), the Beatles demonstrated an ability to reach beyond the confines of acceptable rock and roll techniques and bring to the studio truly innovative ideas such as layering bass and fuzz-bass guitars, creating rhymes in different languages, mixing modes on a single song, utilizing tape manipulation to give instruments entirely new sounds, and introducing the sitar—a most unusual instrument for a rock band. When they recorded *Revolver* the following spring (an album described by critic Stephen Thomas Erlewine as "the Great Leap Forward"[36]), the group really took it up a notch, employing orchestral instruments such as the French horn and strings, offering more insightful and worldly lyrics, introducing the use of "chance" noise, and experimenting with tape-looping techniques.

Meanwhile, nearly 6,000 miles away from their Abbey Road studio in London, San Francisco's psychedelic scene was in full swing. Bands including the Grateful Dead (at the time called the Warlocks), Jefferson Airplane, the Charlatans, and Big Brother and the Holding Company were producing sophisticated, LSD-inspired grooves that were changing the nature of live performance as much as the Beatles were changing the nature of the studio. Largely inspired by the Beatles and the new electric Dylan, California music was pointing the way toward the unchecked experimentalism in rock's near future. A visit by Paul McCartney to the bay area in 1966 is largely credited with the extensive psychedelia that fuels *Sgt. Pepper's* (as is the work of another Californian, the avant-garde composer Frank Zappa, who released his debut *Freak Out!* in July 1966 [see p. 38]).

On December 6, 1966, the Beatles settled into the Abbey Road studio for what might have been the longest recording session in history. Over the following four months the band would spend 700 hours and $100,000 (an extraordinary sum at the time) to produce the thirteen tracks that make up *Sgt. Pepper's*. It was a monumental effort that resulted in an actual musical monument, and when compared to their 1963 debut *Please Please Me*—which was recorded in a single day—demonstrated the extensive personal investment the group had begun to make in their music.

From the eponymous opening track to the "A Day in the Life" finale, *Sgt. Pepper's* is an alternate, fanciful version of the Beatles. The group had played their last official concert on August 29, 1966 at San Francisco's Candlestick Park, and without the burden of future tours hanging over their heads, the lads were free to create sounds in the studio that they wouldn't have to recreate in live performances. The fictional Sgt. Pepper's band was a way for the Beatles to simulate a tour on vinyl, complete with crowd noise on the opening track and several songs that lead into each other without a break (as live medleys do). The revolutionary jacket design also participated in the illusion, offering cardboard cutout props for the listener (as if they were souvenirs from an actual tour), a gatefold album sleeve (the first) with a photo of the band for the "concertgoer" to look at, and lyrics printed on the back (another first) so the audience could sing along. The album cover—matching the album itself in terms of historical status—featured the foursome dressed in character surrounded by dozens of life-sized cardboard images of miscellaneous cultural icons, ranging from the musical (Bob Dylan, Elvis Presley, and Karlheinz Stockhausen) to the cerebral (Albert Einstein, Carl Jung, and Karl Marx) to the comical (Mae West, W. C. Fields, and Lenny Bruce) to the literary (Dylan Thomas, George Bernard Shaw, and Aldous Huxley) to the downright odd (occultist Aleister Crowley, architect Simon Rodia, and 19th-century British Prime Minister Sir Robert Peel). With the lads in full costume and holding instruments, the entire group represents an entourage of sorts, like a backstage photograph of musicians surrounded by their stagehands from a very, very strange tour.

But the real impact of the album was of course the music, brilliantly crafted by Lennon and McCartney (except George Harrison's haunting solo effort "Within You Without You") and brought together by uber-producer George Martin in a pastiche of ideas as wide-ranging and complicated as the cover. The album's cohesive whole was underlined by the fact that none of the songs were released as singles, though many—including "With a Little Help from My Friends," "When I'm Sixty-Four," and the psychedelic cornerstone "Lucy in the Sky with Diamonds"—survive to this day as radio standards. One song that was cut from the album and released on its own (with "Penny Lane" on the B-side) was "Strawberry Fields Forever," which Lennon played two versions of in different keys and tempos and had Martin meld into one song, to startling effect.

Oddities abound throughout the record, including a French horn quartet on "Sgt. Pepper's Lonely Hearts Club Band," circus instruments that were played backwards and spliced together on "Being for the Benefit of Mr. Kite!," clucking chickens on "Good Morning Good Morning" (which Lennon based on a Corn Flakes commercial), and various other "instruments" and techniques including farm animals, a steam organ, variable-speed tape recorders, oscillators, vocal echo, forty-two classical musicians, and a pack of foxhounds. In the extraordinary closing song "A Day in the Life," the final lyrics "I'd love to turn you on" (a fitting epitaph for the album) are followed by a gradually escalating collision of noises that Lennon described as "a sound building up from nothing to the end of the world,"[37] followed by a piano chord that fades into a drone at 15 kilocycles (well beyond the range of human hearing), which itself is followed (on the U.K. release) by the final record groove cut back into itself so the album would play, theoretically, for infinity.

If *Rubber Soul*—with its significant evolution of the Beatles sound— was the end of the beginning, then *Sgt. Pepper's* was the beginning of the end. The Beatles had long since decided to stop touring, and subsequent albums—though many excellent in quality—were largely collages of individual efforts rather than true examples of teamwork, and with the death of longtime manager Brian Epstein that August, the Beatles knew their own end was near. When released in June 1967, *Sgt. Pepper's* stunned the music community, reaching the top of the charts around the world and rivaling Jefferson Airplane's *Surrealistic Pillow* (see p. 42) as the soundtrack to the Summer of Love. The influence of *Sgt. Pepper's* was quickly demonstrated on albums such as the Rolling Stones' November 1967 release *Their Satanic Majesties Request*, Jefferson Airplane's December release *After Bathing At Baxter's*, and Frank Zappa's brilliant *Sgt. Pepper's* parody that January, *We're Only in It for the Money*. With *Sgt. Pepper's*, the Beatles were the first band to fully utilize the studio as an instrument in itself, opening the door for other acts to do the same and influencing countless artists since.

Album Title: *Are You Experienced*
Artist: The Jimi Hendrix Experience
Recorded: October 26, 1966–April 3, 1967, at Olympic
Studios in London
U.S. release: August 23, 1967 (Reprise)
Producer: Chas Chandler

When talking about American music, there are few claims one could make that would elicit the subtle gasp, the jealous smile, the quiet, resigned "wow" from your listener than to reveal you once saw Jimi Hendrix live. Few could burn up the stage or ignite an audience with such heat—the Who, perhaps, in their heyday, maybe pre-*Presence* Zeppelin, James Brown on an average night, or the King of rock and roll when he was still a prince— but Hendrix was short on time, and far fewer people got to stand next to his fire. From the moment he dropped the match on his guitar at the 1967

Monterey Pop Festival to the day his own flame went dark only three years later, he was the brightest star in rock. His candle burned at both ends, to quote Edna St. Vincent Millay, but oh, he gave a lovely light.

"The Jimi Hendrix Experience are a musical labyrinth," wrote an early reviewer, "you either find your way into the solid wall of incredible sound, or you sit back and gasp at Hendrix' guitar antics and showmanship, wondering what it's all about. The sounds are something new—you either dig it or you do not."[38] Fortunately for the rest of us, Chas Chandler dug it. After a stint playing bass for the popular English blues band the Animals in the mid-1960s, Chandler settled in New York, searching for other projects. A friend of Chandler pointed him in the direction of Hendrix, who was playing gigs at Greenwich Village's Café Wha? in 1965. Chandler was amazed at what he found. When Hendrix played his laid-back, electric version of the folk song "Hey Joe," Chandler reportedly spilled his drink on himself.

Hendrix accompanied Chandler to England, where Chandler found him gigs to display his unusual guitar skills and helped organize a backing band that became the Jimi Hendrix Experience. The buzz soon spread, and before long notables such as Eric Clapton, Jeff Beck, Pete Townshend, John Mayall, and Paul McCartney were dropping their jaws at Hendrix's gigs. Ironically, this was how the unknown guitar slinger from Seattle was discovered, not for his supporting work with the Isley Brothers, Little Richard, and Ike and Tina Turner in the early 1960s, but on the other side of the ocean, where many of rock's greatest musicians departed for American shores to earn wider fame.

Hendrix settled in London where he signed with the Who's label, Track Records, and released a string of Top 10 singles, including "Hey Joe," "Purple Haze," and "The Wind Cries Mary." Meanwhile his live performances shook the foundations of British rock, leading to his eagerly anticipated debut album *Are You Experienced*, released in May 1967. Although the album did not contain any of his hit singles, it soared to the Top 5 on the British charts on the strength of cuts like "Are You Experienced," "Foxey Lady," "I Don't Live Today," and "Manic Depression," kept out of the No. 1 spot only by the timing of the Beatles' magnum opus, *Sgt. Pepper's Lonely Hearts Club Band*, released several weeks later (see p. 46).

However, Hendrix was still completely unknown in the United States. In June, only five weeks after *Are You Experienced* hit the London streets, Hendrix was introduced to American audiences at the Monterey International Pop Festival in northern California, playing at the request of Paul McCartney who was serving on the festival's board of directors. Jimi's appearance became the stuff of rock lore. The Who were also making their first American appearance at the festival, and a battle ensued between Hendrix and the Who to determine who would go on first—they were the two most energetic acts in Britain, and neither wanted to follow the other.

A coin toss favored the Who, prompting Hendrix to stand on a chair and tell the crowd assembled backstage that if he had to follow the Who, he would pull out all the stops.

Hendrix was true to his word, blazing through a set that had him playing his guitar behind his back, between his legs, and with his tongue. Already having whipped the crowd into a frenzy, Hendrix ended his show by dousing his guitar in lighter fluid, setting it on fire, and throwing the pieces into the crowd. In the course of one short evening, Jimi had graduated, according to *Los Angeles Times* coverage of the event, "from rumor to legend."[39]

Not everyone appreciated Hendrix's wild stage act. Some blacks decried his eccentric performances and flashy dress as selling out to a white audience—Hendrix became the first black rock artist to entertain mostly white crowds—and feeding stereotypes of black sexuality and exoticism (despite the fact that he learned his moves by watching James Brown and Little Richard). But Hendrix had little patience for outsiders telling him how to perform. "Man, it's the music, that's what comes first," he told a *New York Times* reporter in 1968. "People who put down our performance, they're people who can't use their eyes and ears at the same time. They've got a button on their shoulder blades that keeps only one working at a time. Look, man, we might play sometimes just standing there; sometimes we do the whole diabolical bit when we're in the studio and there's nobody to watch. It's how we feel. How we feel and getting the music out, that's all. As soon as people understand that, the better."[40]

One week after his performance at Monterey, the U.S. version of *Are You Experienced* was released in the States. As word of his incredible skill circulated—with proper credit going to drummer Mitch Mitchell and bassist Noel Redding, both of whom gave Hendrix's songs a solid blues and jazz grounding—the album slowly climbed the charts, eventually reaching the No. 5 spot the year after it debuted. For the American version of the album, the songs "Can You See Me," "Remember," and "Red House" were all removed (the latter against Jimi's wishes), and replaced by his three U.K. hits. Though rock purists will insist that originals are always the better version, it is hard to argue that the addition of "Hey Joe," "Purple Haze," and "The Wind Cries Mary" somehow made it a lesser album. More than just one of the greatest debuts in the history of American music, *Are You Experienced* was a landmark in a summer of landmark albums (five releases from 1967 appear on our list here). The wide breadth of material on the album (all but one penned by Hendrix) demonstrated his uncanny ability to tackle psychedelic jams ("Purple Haze" and "Are You Experienced") smooth ballads ("The Wind Cries Mary" and "Hey Joe"), and blistering R&B ("Stone Free" and "Highway Chile") with equal wizardry. Hendrix was a true innovator of guitar technique, eliciting sounds from his instrument no one had ever heard, forever changing the boundaries of what was possible in rock music.

NOTES

1. Robert Shelton, *New York Times*, September 29, 1961.

2. Paul Friedlander, *Rock And Roll: A Social History*. Boulder, CO: Westview, 1996, 134.

3. David Szatmary, *A Time to Rock: A Social History of Rock And Roll*. New York: Schirmer, 1996 (1987), 107.

4. Ibid., 107–108.

5. Ibid., 123.

6. David Ewen, *All the Years of American Popular Music*. London: Prentice-Hall, 1977, 614.

7. Dave Marsh and John Swenson, *The New Rolling Stone Record Guide*. New York: Random House, 1983 (1979), 154.

8. Ben Fong-Torres, *Not Fade Away: A Backstage Pass to 20 Years of Rock & Roll*. San Francisco: Miller Freeman Books, 1999, 160.

9. Dave Laing et al., *The Electric Muse: The Story of Folk into Rock*. London: Methuen, 1975, 42.

10. Barney Hoskyns, "The Byrds: *Mr. Tambourine Man, Turn! Turn! Turn!, Fifth Dimension, Younger Than Yesterday*," *Mojo*, June 1996.

11. Szatmary, 1996, 110.

12. Laing, 1975, 42.

13. Andrew Weiner, "Dylan, the Byrds, and the First Hippy Hymn," *Creem*, April 1972, 43.

14. Friedlander, 1996, 89.

15. Glenn C. Altschuler, *All Shook Up: How Rock 'n' Roll Changed America*. New York: Oxford, 2003, 183.

16. Robert Christgau, *Grown Up All Wrong: 75 Great Rock and Pop Artists from Vaudeville to Techno*. Cambridge: Harvard, 1998, 115.

17. www.beachboysfanclub.com.

18. Ibid.

19. Ibid.

20. Chris Smith, *The Greenwood Encyclopedia of Rock History: The Rise of Album Rock, 1967–1973*. Westport, CT: Greenwood, 2005a, 127.

21. Miles, *International Times*, August 29, 1969.

22. Michael Campbell and James Brody, *Rock and Roll: An Introduction*. New York: Schirmer, 1999, 195.

23. Aldous Huxley, *The Doors of Perception*. New York: Harper and Row, 1963, introduction.

24. Marsh and Swenson, 1983, 149.

25. Ewen, 1977, 634.

26. Szatmary, 1996, 173.

27. Fong-Torres, 1999, 46.

28. Gene Sculatti, "San Francisco Bay Rock," *Crawdaddy!*, 1966.

29. Uncredited, "Jefferson Airplane: Open Up, Tune In, Turn On," *Time*, May 23, 1967.

30. Ibid.

31. Mike Jahn, "Velvet Rock Group Opens Stand Here," *New York Times*, July 4, 1970.

32. Scott Isler and Ira Robbins, "Velvet Underground," *Trouser Press*, www.trouserpress.com.

33. Mark Deming, www.allmusic.com.

34. Friedlander, 1996, 91.

35. www.riaa.com.

36. www.allmusic.com.

37. Colin Larkin, ed., *The Virgin Encyclopedia of Popular Music*. London: Muse UK, 1997, 107.

38. Keith Altham, "The Jimi Hendrix Experience: Finsbury Park Astoria," *New Musical Express*, April 8, 1967.

39. Jerry Hopkins, *Hit and Run: The Jimi Hendrix Story*. New York: Perigee, 1983, 118.

40. Michael Lydon, "Jimi Hendrix 1968," *New York Times*, March 1968.

3

A BRIDGE OVER TROUBLED WATER, 1968–1971

Music in 1960s' America will forever be linked with the hippie phenomenon that spilled out of San Francisco and onto the world stage between 1965 and 1970—even the term "the sixties" reflects less the actual calendar decade and more the peace-and-love movement it is known for. The Human Be-In and the Monterey Pop Festival of 1967 brought about a rash of concert festivals through the remainder of the decade, as amplification technology allowed large crowds to gather for performances, creating a communal atmosphere most famously exemplified by the Woodstock Music and Art Fair in upstate New York in 1969.

Music as a communal experience was devastated, however, by the late 1969 tragedy at Altamont Speedway in California, where nineteen-year-old Meredith Hunter was beaten to death right in front of the stage as the Rolling Stones performed, murdered in plain sight (and on camera) by a gang of drugged-up Hell's Angels hired as security for the event. A quick succession of tragedies over the next two years—the elevating body count in Vietnam, the Kent State and Jackson State shootings, the American invasion of Cambodia, the deaths of Jimi Hendrix, Janis Joplin, and Jim Morrison—would squelch the community-focused vibes of the bay area in favor of a more introspective and egocentric (and eventually hedonistic) society.

American music would follow and reinforce these trends as it became an increasingly powerful social force. Between 1967 and 1973, album sales in the United States doubled from $1 billion to 2 billion per year, overtaking the amount of money spent on movies and sporting events as forms of entertainment. The post-World War II baby boom generated a steady growth in the number of young teens, and as pop music splintered into endless subgenres, greater musical variety brought in a greater number of listeners who found audio equipment and albums increasingly affordable (coupled with the expanding number of festivals nationwide, which were often either free or easy to sneak in to). All of these factors contributed to an exponential rise in the purchase of albums—particularly rock albums, which accounted for approximately 80 percent of all album sales by the turn of the decade.

In the mid-1960s, the Beatles made an indelible stamp on American music by becoming the first British act to receive widespread acceptance in the United States, opening the floodgates for dozens of blues-based musicians to land on U.S. soil. After the initial blues-rock invasion, the Brits kept coming, bringing with them even more radical musical ideas. European music edged out blues influences in U.K. progressive rock albums, such as the Moody Blues' *Days of Future Passed* (1968), King Crimson's *In the Court of the Crimson King* (1969), and Yes' 1971 *The Yes Album*, influencing a decade of progressive rock to come with bands like Jethro Tull, Procol Harum, the Electric Light Orchestra, and Emerson, Lake and Palmer. The Who and the Pretty Things capitalized on the uniquely European musical theater to create the first rock operas, with the Pretty Things' little-heard 1968 release *S.F. Sorrow* and the Who's monumental *Tommy* (1969).

In 1968, a harder psychedelic music made up of lingering hippie vibes created heavy metal, which first emerged in the United States with Blue Cheer's *Vincebus Eruptum* and Iron Butterfly's roof-shaking trio *Heavy, In-A-Gadda-Da-Vida*, and 1969's *Ball*. Close behind were the footsteps of proto-punk, found in the Stooges' self-titled debut in 1969 and *Kick Out the Jams* (1969) by the Detroit-based MC5. Simultaneously in the United Kingdom, Led Zeppelin's debut *Led Zeppelin* (1969) and its quick follow-up *Led Zeppelin II* paved the way for the worldwide popularity of heavy metal, soon realized through releases such as Deep Purple's 1970 *Deep Purple in Rock*, Alice Cooper's 1971 *Love It to Death*, and Black Sabbath's *Paranoid* (1971) and *Master of Reality* the same year.

Heavy metal and progressive rock were just two new subgenres born at the turn of the decade. Lineup changes in the Byrds—who had already changed the face of American music with the 1965 classics *Mr. Tambourine Man* and *Turn! Turn! Turn!*—moved the band in a more country direction with the country-rock crossover *Sweetheart of the Rodeo* (1968), an album that was followed by Bob Dylan's 1969 *Nashville Skyline* and the Flying Burrito Brothers' 1969 *The Gilded Palace of Sin*, to bring about a new interest in Americana. More rock-oriented country-rock hybrids were found in the music of Bob Dylan's backing group, the Band, and their debut album *Music from Big Pink* (1968), whose style took on a distinctive gospel and southern blues flavor in releases by the early southern rock outfit, the Allman Brothers Band, crafting 1968's *The Allman Brothers Band* and 1971's *At Fillmore East*. Miles Davis, meanwhile, continued his reign as the focal point of the jazz world with some of his finest work, including 1969's *In a Silent Way*, 1970's *A Tribute to Jack Johnson*, and *Bitches Brew* (1970), which ignited a fury of jazz-rock from bandmates such as John McLaughlin, who formed the Mahavishnu Orchestra for the seminal fusion album *The Inner Mounting Flame* (1971).

In one sense, social and political challenges moved popular music in opposite directions for white and black artists. Early solo efforts, including Simon and Garfunkel's 1968 *Bookends* and soundtrack to *The Graduate*, James Taylor's 1968 *James Taylor*, and Joni Mitchell's 1968 debut *Song to a Seagull*, opened the door for the singer-songwriter set that had largely been blockaded when Dylan turned electric in 1965. At the beginning of the 1970s, middle-class whites focused less on their community and more on their own needs, as communal living became outmoded, and primal scream therapy, the women's independence movement, and eastern meditation recentered attention on the self (leading to a doubling of the divorce rate by the end of the decade). Suddenly, the singer-songwriter was the new vogue for self-aware survivors of hippie counterculture, and landmarks like James Taylor's **Sweet Baby James** (1970), Neil Young's 1970 *After the Gold Rush*, Don McLean's 1971 *American Pie*, Joni Mitchell's 1971 *Blue*, and Carole King's **Tapestry** (1971) took listeners on an unpaved journey to the center of themselves.

Soul and R&B artists, however, began to move past the feel-good pop ditties of the Motown and Brill Building assembly lines and into more literate and focused territory. The growing Civil Rights movement brought about an interest in black consciousness and empowerment of the black community. Albums from some of the top R&B artists reflected these trends, ranging from the positive vibes of Sly and the Family Stone's 1969 *Stand!* to the self-assertion of Isaac Hayes' 1969 *Hot Buttered Soul* and Aretha Franklin's 1971 *Young, Gifted and Black* to the personal and political sentiments on Marvin Gaye's **What's Going On** (1971) and Sly and the Family Stone's **There's a Riot Goin' On** (1971). And with the debut trio of albums by his new band Funkadelic—1970's *Funkadelic*, 1970's *Free Your Mind...and Your Ass Will Follow*, and 1971's *Maggot Brain*—funk mastermind George Clinton began to pull off bizarrities at least as revolutionary as Captain Beefheart's **Trout Mask Replica** (1969), which simply defies a one-sentence description.

Album Title: *Days of Future Passed*
Artist: The Moody Blues
Recorded: May–June 1967
U.S. release: April 1968 (Deram)
Producer: Tony Clarke

"The five rather dapper looking musicians on the Fillmore East stage began a song, and some members of the audience craned their heads to look for the orchestra that evidently backed the group."[1] This performance review clip, written in 1970, captures the legacy the Moody Blues left behind after a string of successful albums in the late 1960s and early 1970s (in a career that would continue for several decades with a dwindling, but still respectable, level of success). The Moodies, as fans called them, were known as a sophisticated orchestral rock band, combining lush symphonic instrumentation (using mellotron and synthesizers during live shows, as in the performance reviewed here), with heady lyrics and a whisper of their blues background to create an overwhelming—though placid—psychedelic experience for the listener.

Like nearly all of their struggling contemporaries in early 1960s British rock, the Moody Blues found a home in the American R&B tradition. With Ray Thomas on harmonica and vocals, Mike Pinder on keyboards and vocals, Denny Laine on guitar and vocals, Clint Warwick on bass and vocals, and Graeme Edge on drums, the group were signed for a recording contract with Decca Records within six months of their formation in 1964, and scored a hit with their second single, "Go Now," that November. "Go Now," a cover of an R&B classic recorded by Bessie Banks, reached No. 1 in the United Kingdom and No. 10 in the United States, earning the group an opening spot for the Beatles and a generous amount of press.

On the strength of their hit, the band released a well-received debut album in the United Kingdom entitled *The Magnificent Moodies* (its American version was simply called *Go Now*). However, the band could only sail for so long on the winds that "Go Now" generated, and unable to muster a follow-up hit, the group soon returned to bar-band status, in debt to their label and bound, seemingly, for one-hit-wonderdom. By August of 1966, Laine and Warwick had left the group, replaced by John Lodge on bass and Justin Hayward on guitar. Hayward and Pinder began collaborating on new, less rock-oriented material, but for a while the group continued touring small venues in Europe as recent has-beens. "Things just got worse and worse," Edge told a later biographer, "until one week, when we were in cabaret in Newcastle, we were so broke and it was such a misery that we said, 'fuck it, we're miserable and unhappy and broke playing music we don't like, so let's be miserable, unhappy and broke playing music we do like' . . . we stopped trying to do things that others were doing and just did it as we felt. There was no point in trying to make Justin (Hayward) leap about on stage because Townshend could do it better and it was not in his nature. When Justin gets worked up he taps his foot."[2]

The group moved into more sophisticated territory, replacing blues standards with psychedelia, world music, and heavily textured folk-rock. Their timing could not have been better. Decca was introducing a new sound system known as "Deramic Stereo"—though stereo had swept the United States by the early 1960s, in 1966 Britain it was still something of a novelty—and wanted to release a rock version of Dvořák's "New World Symphony" to showcase the technology. The label slated the Moody Blues, with their increasingly erudite sound, to record the piece. The band, however, convinced the producer Tony Clarke to instead record a symphonic song cycle they had been working on. Clarke liked the Moodies' new material and championed the idea. With background arrangements from the London Festival Orchestra (actually a hastily cobbled assortment of studio musicians), Clarke and the band produced one of the gems of late 1960s progressive music: *Days of Future Passed*.

An unusual mix of rock and classical, the label did not know what to do with the album, fearing rock fans would not buy it, and classical fans would be incensed by this aberration. But strong songwriting by the band, inventive arrangements by conductor Peter Knight, and seamless production by Clarke propelled the album up the charts in the United Kingdom and eventually to the No. 3 spot in America, adding the singles "Tuesday Afternoon" and "Nights in White Satin" to the American classic rock canon. *Days of Future Passed* seemed to satisfy the appetites whetted by the Beatles' *Sgt. Pepper's Lonely Hearts Club Band* (see p. 46) the previous summer, a thickly textured departure from amplified, blues-based rock. The Moodies felt they had passed through their "fascination with American blues" phase, and sought to emphasize rock's European roots that had been forgotten by English bands who bowed down to Muddy Waters and Robert Johnson. "When Graeme and Mike were asked what they thought of the Stones and the other English bands that have continued to play music with American black roots, Graeme smiled and said, 'It's like Sonny Boy Williamson singing about King Arthur.'"[3]

Days of Future Passed was also one of the earlier theme albums, a loose story told of a man's journey over the course of a day (as a metaphor for the course of a life). From track one, "The Day Begins," to the final cut, "Nights in White Satin," the album flutters back and forth between English psychedelia, buttery smooth vocal harmonies, and symphonic arrangements to propel rock into a whole new territory. "The Moodies have become the first breed of artist who see the recording studio as their platform," read one review of the album. "Their intricate work is the result of hours of work laid down in the studio. Producer Tony Clarke is considered a sixth member of the group. [If] they had mixing equipment onstage, Tony would be up there playing it."[4]

The album paved the way for a host of English progressive bands to experiment with sophisticated studio technology and elaborate stage productions, popularizing progressive rock to become one of the hottest genres of the 1970s in the United States, bringing stardom to bands like Yes, Procol Harum, Jethro Tull, the Electric Light Orchestra, and Emerson, Lake and Palmer. The Moody Blues would continue along a path of success themselves, replacing the orchestra with the mellotron and synthesizers on subsequent albums, and continuing to pioneer a thick, mature blend of rock and symphonic sounds to push the ever-expanding envelope of popular music.

Album Title: *Music from Big Pink*
Artist: The Band
Recorded: 1968, at Big Pink in West Saugerties, New York
U.S. release: July 1, 1968 (Capitol)
Producer: John Simon

One of America's most successful and influential rock acts during the transition between the late 1960s and the early 1970s, the Band sounded like none of their contemporaries. With Robbie Robertson on guitar, Levon Helm on drums, Rick Danko on bass, and Richard Manuel and Garth Hudson on keyboards, the group formed the cornerstone of the country-rock movement that swept American music at the turn of the decade, beginning with their 1968 debut, *Music from Big Pink*.

Throughout most of the 1960s, the Band were known as the Hawks, once the backing group for singer Ronnie Hawkins. But the Band became famous—or, as some believe, infamous—several years before their first album was released for supporting Bob Dylan in his electric phase beginning in 1965. As the Hawks, the Band had become talented and precise musicians, heavily influenced by the sounds coming out of Chicago on Chess Records and Memphis on Sun Records. They played rockabilly and straight-up rock and roll, and they expected their audiences to dance to it. But once the group began backing Dylan, they had to adjust to Dylan's improvisational style, often changing a song as he played it. Their collaborations with the folk king made the Hawks more adaptable during their live sets and gave them something of a jam-band feel.

After several years backing Dylan, the Hawks joined him in early 1968 at his retreat near Woodstock, New York, where Dylan was convalescing after a motorcycle accident that kept him out of the public eye for a year and a half. Dylan's manager, Albert Grossman, had taken the Hawks under his wing and saw an opportunity for the group to work with Dylan in seclusion after two years of heavily scrutinized collaboration on stage. The recordings made during this period are the stuff of rock legend, and were not released until 1975 as *The Basement Tapes*, by which time the Band were one of the biggest groups in music. Following their stay at Dylan's house—dubbed "Big Pink" for its colorful exterior—the Hawks renamed themselves and released their debut, an unexpectedly powerful album that would launch them to stardom.

Along with the Byrds' *Sweetheart of the Rodeo* (1968) (see p. 61), Bob Dylan's *Nashville Skyline* (1969), and the Flying Burrito Brothers' *The Gilded Palace of Sin* (1969), *Music from Big Pink* was a foundation album for a blend of country and rock that seemed to come out of nowhere, as at this point the United States was being swept away by San Francisco's psychedelic rock and the British Invasion. Under the influence of Dylan (who penned or copenned three songs on *Music from Big Pink* and painted the cover art), the Band had acquired a folksy feel and an appreciation for the history of the American common man. Notable critic Greil Marcus would later posit that the Band (along with fellow early 1970s' rockers Grand Funk Railroad) were the rock alternative to the "neutralization" of music by the singer-songwriter set of James Taylor and company. "The importance of their work lay in the chance that they might reunify the new cultural forces of the sixties because of their concern with America, its history and mythologies."[5] This was an incredible feat considering four of the five members were actually Canadian (Levon Helm was from Arkansas, but he neglected to join the band on their Dylan tours and at Dylan's house in

Woodstock)—though it is also believed that as outsiders, the group's members were in a unique position to appreciate American folklore and mythology. Nonetheless, with their debut album and its follow up the next year, *The Band*, the Band helped found the genre of Americana, which would make its influence felt in decades to come.

With their passionate, free-flowing delivery and vocal harmonies that were as powerful and ragged as Crosby, Stills and Nash's were powerful and smooth, the Band redefined how a rock group worked together—neither as a single, melodious unit nor as a backup band supporting a single frontman, but as five talented individuals bouncing musical ideas off each other like a heavily amplified porch quintet. Robbie Robertson was recognized as one of the most soulful guitarists of his day, Rick Danko became accomplished at sliding notes around on his fretless bass, the dueling organ and piano strains of Manuel and Hudson lent the band a sweeping feeling that was copied by a number of acts, and the folksy drawl of Helm, Manuel, and Danko complemented the lyrics that often seemed right out of an American Civil War songbook.

The Band's first two albums were, as has been pointed out in retrospect, an attempt to create a "national" form of rock at a time when the unifying strains of hippie rock were gasping their last breaths in the face of political and social defeats (Altamont, Kent State, Vietnam, and so on). Songs such as "Tears of Rage," "Chest Fever," the Dylan-penned "I Shall be Released," and the Band's best-known tune "The Weight" were powerful statements on rural themes of faith and community that lay the groundwork for an entire genre of roots-rock, leading one critic to call the Band's early releases "as close to a perfect statement of purpose as any rock group has ever come."[6]

As important as *Music from Big Pink* was to later generations, its immediate commercial reception was lukewarm, rising only to No. 30 on the charts and slipping out of the Top 200 after forty weeks. The fact that it found a commercial audience at all was largely to the credit of veteran rocker and *Rolling Stone* critic Al Kooper, who exclaimed, "Every year since 1962 we have all singled out one album to sum up what happened that year. It was usually the Beatles with their double barrels of rubber souls, revolvers and peppers. Dylan has sometimes contended with his frontrunning electric albums. Six months are left in this proselytizing year of music; we can expect a new Beatles, Stones, Hendrix, perhaps even a mate for JW Harding; but I have chosen my album for 1968. *Music from Big Pink* is an event and should be treated as one. . . . This album was recorded in approximately two weeks. There are people who will work their lives away in vain and not touch it."[7]

Album Title: *Sweetheart of the Rodeo*
Artist: The Byrds
Recorded: March 9–May 27, 1968, in Nashville and Hollywood
U.S. release: July 22, 1968 (Columbia)
Producer: Gary Usher

The Byrds' 1968 *Sweetheart of the Rodeo*, one of the earliest albums to popularize the hybrid of country-rock. *Courtesy of Photofest.*

By 1968, the Byrds had already established themselves as among the more intrepid explorers at the forefront of rock music. Their 1965 masterpiece *Mr. Tambourine Man* (see p. 32) was one of the most important debut albums in history, using Roger McGuinn's signature Rickenbacker twelve-string guitar to blend the folk balladry of Bob Dylan with the pop jangle of the Beatles, creating literate but catchy songs that would immediately popularize the genre of folk-rock while it was still in its infancy. The Byrds also joined the Beatles in bringing about a raga sound to rock music, using sitar on tracks such as their 1966 hit "Eight Miles High" from their album *Fifth Dimension*. Despite diverse experimentation with what might fit into a pop mold, and a constantly changing lineup (which many assert kept the band from becoming bigger than the Beatles themselves), the Byrds managed to maintain a high standard of quality throughout the decade, releasing landmark songs including the folk-rock lodestone "Mr. Tambourine Man," the early hippy anthem "Turn! Turn! Turn!," the prepsychedelic acoustic gem "Eight Miles High," and the sardonic attack on the music industry "So You Want to Be a Rock and Roll Star."

However, the Byrds that made *Sweetheart of the Rodeo* were a very different band than the Byrds who popularized folk-rock with *Mr. Tambourine Man*. What started as a quintet dwindled to a duo after guitarist David Crosby, drummer Michael Clarke, and guitarist and percussionist Gene Clark split the band by 1968. Bassist Chris Hillman and frontman and guitarist Roger McGuinn recorded with studio musicians for their excellent 1968 album *The Notorious Byrd Brothers*, a sophisticated mix of folk, rock, protest music, country, and early electronica that merely hinted at what was lurking around the corner. With the addition of guitarist and keyboardist Gram Parsons and drummer Kevin Kelley (Hillman's cousin), the group took a definite turn toward roots music as Parsons imported his country influences into the band. Parsons had hinted at the possibility of country-rock with his previous group, the International Submarine Band, and their 1968 debut album *Safe at Home*. But *Safe at Home* was more country than rock, and the International Submarine Band was barely known, so it was not until *Sweetheart of the Rodeo* that rock and country were fully united in one landmark release.

Thanks to the unexpected leadership role that Parsons took on in the band, *Sweetheart of the Rodeo* became the first album widely recognized as country-rock. The Byrds' previous albums *The Notorious Byrd Brothers* and *Younger than Yesterday* had dabbled in country as much as Parsons' *Safe at Home* had dabbled in rock, but with *Sweetheart of the Rodeo*, a fully integrated vision was finally realized. Utilizing the talents of country musicians such as John Hartford and Clarence White (who would continue playing in the Byrds for another five years), and incorporating traditional country instruments such as pedal steel guitar, fiddle, banjo, and mandolin, *Sweetheart of the Rodeo* recalled the timeless twang of Hank Williams without abandoning the strides the Byrds had made toward giving folk music a steady beat and an electric kick.

Although the Byrds were one of the first American rock groups to write their own songs—a practice soon followed by many of the 1960s' rockers—with *Sweetheart of the Rodeo* they reverted to traditional tunes penned by Woody Guthrie, Merle Haggard, and the Louvin Brothers, with two more Bob Dylan songs thrown in to boot. The two original songs included—the Gram Parsons and Bob Buchanan tune "Hickory Wind" and the Parsons-penned "One Hundred Years from Now"—melded the Byrds' two distinct phases, with "Hickory Wind" decidedly twangy and rootsy like their new material, and "One Hundred Years from Now" recalling their early vocal harmonies. With country covers, of course, come country themes of God, lost love, and alcohol, which gives *Sweetheart of the Rodeo* a retro-western theme through its lyrics as well (with the exception of "One Hundred Years from Now," which, again, echoes the early Byrds songs that ached of traditional folk, but were simultaneously modern and forward-looking).

Though Parsons was only with the Byrds for about six months, his sound is indelibly stamped on country-rock through this enduring release. In keeping with the Byrds' practice of constant lineup changes, Parsons and Hillman soon left the band to form the Flying Burrito Brothers, whose 1969 debut *The Gilded Palace of Sin* would become another foundation album for country-rock. Between the Band's 1968 debut *Music from Big Pink* (see p. 59), Bob Dylan's 1969 *Nashville Skyline*, and *The Gilded Palace of Sin*, the Byrds' *Sweetheart of the Rodeo* served as a blueprint for country-rock that would be copied for decades. This country-rock sound would be enormously important in establishing the popularity of some of the 1970s' biggest acts, including the Eagles, Linda Ronstadt, and Crosby, Stills, Nash and Young.

Roger McGuinn filled in the spots left by Parsons and Hillman and continued with the Byrds for three more years before dissolving the band in 1972. Though several of the members had notable careers after their respective stints in the band—David Crosby formed the supergroup Crosby, Stills and Nash (and later Young), and Parsons and Hillman moved on to the Flying Burrito Brothers—in terms of influence, none of them were able to top (if it were possible to do so) the enormous contribution to popular music brought about by the Byrds' early albums and the specific contribution to country-rock made by *Sweetheart of the Rodeo*. As Steve Turner eloquently put it shortly before the band called it quits, "They came up in '64 with what was to be the beginning of everything we'd like to preserve in our rock-art galleries if we had them. It was the fusion of poetry and electricity, of literature and rock. The group however didn't wait around to get old and mellow—that process was left up to the imitators and the musical xerox machines. Not content to remain simple folk-rockers they went on to space rock and then a little acid rock. Then, when everyone else was coming into their interstellar rock period, the Byrds were off playing country rock. Soon after, Dylan joined up with Johnny Cash, the Burritos took to country style and just about everyone hired their local steel guitar player for the next session. Meanwhile the Byrds were into something else."[8]

Album Title: *Led Zeppelin*
Artist: Led Zeppelin
Recorded: October 1968, at Olympic Studios in London
U.S. release: January 12, 1969 (Atlantic)
Producer: Jimmy Page

Over the years, several acts have attempted to lay claim (or have had the claim laid upon them) to the title "the definitive heavy-metal band"—including AC/DC, Black Sabbath, Metallica, and Van Halen, each of whom occupy their own corner of these pages. But in terms of pedigree, talent, sales, influence, showmanship, and let's face it, just plain volume, Led Zeppelin arguably dwarfs them all.

An accidental byproduct of the Yardbirds' breakup in 1968, Led Zeppelin was formed as the New Yardbirds when guitarist Jimmy Page attempted to complete the Yardbirds' remaining tour commitments. The Yardbirds had been one of the prime movers of Britain's hard-rock scene in the mid-1960s, with three of rock's most extraordinary guitar talents—Eric Clapton, Jeff Beck, and Jimmy Page—members of the group during its short history. When the band folded in the summer of 1968, Page gathered well-known bassist/keyboardist John Paul Jones and—unable to recruit the musicians they wanted—settled for unknown vocalist Robert Plant (singer for the struggling group Hobbstweedle) and Plant's friend, drummer John Bonham.

The quartet found themselves to be kindred spirits, and upon fulfilling the New Yardbirds' tour commitments in Scandinavia, renamed themselves Led Zeppelin (reportedly after a quip by Who drummer Keith Moon that their band would go over like a lead zeppelin) and set to work recording their first album in October 1968. The self-titled result, released the following January, was a watershed moment in the evolution of hard blues and the nascent heavy metal.

"I've never been so turned on in my life," said Plant of the thirty-hour session that produced the album. "Although we were all steeped in blues and R&B, we found out in the first hour and a half that we had our own identity."[9] That identity, a combination of their American blues and rock influences (Chuck Berry, Willie Dixon, B. B. King, Scotty Moore) and the heavier sounds coming out of their native London (the Yardbirds, the Who, Cream), would fuel *Led Zeppelin* with a raw energy and explosiveness that was initially derided by the more influential critics, but propelled the band to the top of the rock world.

Among the tracks from their debut are two heavily amplified Willie Dixon covers—"You Shook Me" and "I Can't Quit You Baby"—and a re-write of Howlin' Wolf's "How Many More Years" (renamed "How Many More Times"), demonstrating the band's debt to the American blues tradition. But while Zeppelin largely had predecessors like the Who and the Rolling Stones to thank for their initial reception in the United States (millions of post-hippie-era teens hungry for less peace and more volume), the group brought a subtlety and variation to hard blues and heavy metal that has never been matched. From the aforementioned bluesy rockers to the folksy strains on "Babe I'm Gonna Leave You," "Black Mountain Side," and "Dazed and Confused" (originally a folk ballad by Jake Holmes) to the punk strains of "Communication Breakdown" to the psychedelic wanderings that appear throughout the album, *Led Zeppelin* was but a taste of what the band could do, and provided the momentum to allow them to do it with their follow-up albums, and more importantly, with their live performances.

"The statement of our first two weeks together is our first album," Page told the English magazine *ZigZag*. "We recorded them almost exactly as we'd been doing them live."[10] Before Zeppelin, a thick line separated studio tracks from live tracks on albums (although at this point even live albums were rare, and live-sounding tracks on studio albums almost unheard of). But for Page and the gang, live was the only way to go (the band embarked on six tours in their first year and a half together), and none of the group's members toned down their sound whether they were facing a studio engineer or a crowd of 50,000. Though the band would later record an actual live album, 1976's *The Song Remains the Same*, the drive and forcefulness of each virtuoso's performance—Robert Plant's banshee screams, Page's imaginative fretwork, John Paul Jones' thundering bass, and John Bonham's relentless drumming—was captured on every album, and with their debut, Page made it clear that he was not only one of rock's top guitarists, but an extremely competent producer.

Not everyone was thrilled with this new powerhouse of a band. With rock journalism still in its infancy, the San Francisco magazine *Rolling Stone* was considered the authoritative voice of rock's horizon, and they did not like *Led Zeppelin* one bit. The album was decried as "self-indulgent" and "restricted," and Page lambasted as "a very limited producer and a writer of weak, unimaginative songs."[11] Even in later editions of the famous *Rolling Stone Record Guide*—long after the band had established themselves as the world's top act—the authors dismiss *Led Zeppelin* as the product of "a band that, when not totally demolishing classic blues songs, was making a kind of music apparently designed to be enjoyable only when the listener was drugged to the point of senselessness."[12] It took time for the new sound of heavy metal to be accepted by the rock intelligentsia—especially the bitter scribes who fawned over the nascent mid-1960s San Francisco scene, only to watch it commercialized and disposed of within a few years. Though today many wizened critics claim they liked *Led Zeppelin* from the beginning, there was initially a disparity between critical reception of the album (and the band) and its (their) popularity. It was not until the band's successive albums—*Led Zeppelin II*, *Led Zeppelin III*, and their untitled fourth album containing their biggest hit "Stairway to Heaven"—that the group found critical acceptance, often in hyperbolic terms that reeked of making up for lost time: "Like their namesake, they defy gravity to ride a core of flaming vapor, the acknowledged heavyweight band champions of the world."[13]

Led Zeppelin would touch their audiences in the same way Elvis and the Beatles stirred the spirits of their adolescent female fan base. The band would become emblematic of the rock-god excess of the 1970s' super-groups, trashing hotel rooms, selling out stadiums, and oozing such potent sexual power on the stage that much of their teen male audience would be transported from adoring fan to rabid devotee. In 1975, a Led Zeppelin concert in Boston was cancelled after 3,000 fans inflicted $30,000 worth of damage to a performance venue *just in the process of buying tickets*—weeks before the actual show.[14] Though *Led Zeppelin*'s commercial success paled in comparison with the band's later releases—reaching only the No. 10 spot, with all of their other albums reaching No. 1 or 2—the album announced to the world that there was a new sound in rock and roll, and the group's masterful recordings, their renowned live performances, and their loyal fans elevated the band to become the third most successful act in rock after Elvis Presley and the Beatles.

Album Title: *Kick Out the Jams*
Artist: MC5
Recorded: October 30, 1968–October 31, 1968, at the Grande Ballroom in Detroit
U.S. release: February 1969 (Elektra)
Producer: Jac Holzman and Bruce Botnick

There was punk before punk, but nobody knew what to call it. Until *Creem* magazine critic Dave Marsh gave this loud, fast, disobedient noise a name in 1971, music from amateurish bands like the Standells, the Seeds, and ? and the Mysterians was called "garage rock." But there were a very few acts that were so far ahead of the curve that they simply defied definition. Two of the greatest were Iggy and the Stooges (see *Raw Power*, p. 100) and the Detroit proto-punk band Motor City Five, nicknamed "The Five" by fans, but commonly known as MC5.

Kick Out the Jams was the first of three albums released by the band over its short lifespan, and the only one to peek into the Top 40, a notable feat considering the group did not have much of a national audience and suffered a poor relationship with their label and record retailers. MC5 were not just an early punk act, they were the first overtly political punk act, and if their heavily distorted power chords were not enough to frighten off their corporate partners, then their vulgar language and outspoken politics were. A decade before the Sex Pistols offended their native England with words like "bollocks" and the Clash frightened timid listeners with political diatribes, MC5 were making waves in the uncharted musical seas of the hinterland.

Initially founded in 1964 as a midwest version of a San Francisco psychedelic band, MC5 found a leader in their manager John Sinclair, an outspoken activist and popular beat figure in Detroit. By the time *Kick Out the Jams* was recorded in the fall of 1968, the group had transformed into a politically oriented hard-blues act, playing for the protesters at the heated 1968 Democratic National Convention and engaging in all sorts of community-focused activities, including founding the White Panther party in 1968.

Although such activities made MC5 the most popular underground act in Detroit—Led Zeppelin opened for the band on Zep's first American tour—they led to considerable friction with the group's Elektra label. When *Kick Out the Jams* was released in February 1969, the label was dismayed with the rallying cry preceding the title track, in which singer Rob Tyner exhorts the crowd to "KICK OUT THE JAMS, MOTHERFUCKER!" Michigan's largest department store chain, Hudson's, refused to carry the album, leading the band to purchase a full-page advertisement in *The Fifth Estate*—Detroit's leading underground paper—encouraging their fans not to shop there (though stated in much less polite terms). When Hudson's ceased to carry all Elektra titles in protest, MC5 were dropped from the label and would record their last two albums with Atlantic.

As much as the band's attitude, it was the fuzzy guitar riffs of Fred "Sonic" Smith—adopting a lineage that reached back to Pete Townshend, the Kinks' Dave Davies, and Link Wray—that gave the band an edgy feel and established them as progenitors of the late 1970s' punk sound. When Norman Mailer wrote about MC5 playing in Chicago just before *Kick Out the Jams* was recorded—in an article titled "Had the Horns of the Huns Ever Had Noise to Compare?"—he described the sound as "an electric caterwauling of power corne out of the wall . . . and the singer not bending it, but whirling it, burning it, flashing it down some arc of consciousness, the sound screaming up to a climax of vibrations like one rocket blasting out of itself, the force of the noise a vertigo in the cauldrons of inner space—it was the roar of the beast in all nihilism, electric bass and drum driving behind out of their own non-stop to the end of mind."[15]

It was this loud, raucous sound that MC5 wanted to capture in their first album, and a live set was the only way to get it, to set to vinyl what one

Creem reviewer called "an indescribable and frenzied mood. The voice of the Five resounds all that is the youth of today. An aura of all our sought-after goals; love, peace, freedom, and f–king in the streets—they are . . . an incarnation of our will. We receive them with appropriate joy and rapture."[16]

Despite critical acclaim from some corners, including the January 4, 1969 cover of *Rolling Stone* (an unusual feat for a local Detroit band that had little national exposure and had yet to release their first album), MC5 ultimately failed to capture the national imagination. *Kick Out the Jams* quickly dropped off the charts after peaking at No. 30, and their two follow-ups, 1970's *Back in the USA* and 1971's *High Time,* barely made a dent. The group wisely broke up in 1972 while they were still heroes of the underground, and it would be several more years before the strains of MC5 and the Stooges would inspire musical revolution on the tiny stage of CBGB in New York City, where punk legends like the Ramones and Television would build on this foundation and export it to England and the west coast.

Serving as an important conduit between the hard blues of the 1960s (the Yardbirds, Cream, the Who) and the in-your-face politics of later punk (the Clash especially), *Kick Out the Jams* demonstrated all the power and sophistication of the period's other classic live albums (the Who's 1970 *Live at Leeds* and the Allman Brothers' 1971 *At Fillmore East*) with more than a dash of the street-preacher politics the group were renowned for. "I want to hear some revolution out there, brothers," exhorts Brother J. C. Crawford as he introduces MC5 on the album. "The time has come for each and every one of you to decide whether you are going to be the problem or you are going to be the solution. . . . are you ready to testify? Are you ready!? I give you a testimonial—the MC5!"

Album Title: *Tommy*
Artist: The Who
Recorded: September 19, 1968–March 7, 1969, at IBC Studios in London
U.S. release: May 23, 1969 (MCA)
Producer: Kit Lambert

Following the Beatles and the Rolling Stones as the third wave of the British Invasion, the Who made their first significant splash in the United States with their landmark 1969 release *Tommy*, one of the seminal texts in the hard-rock canon. Hailed by many as the first "rock opera"—so named for its libretto-like narrative that tells a complicated story through a progression of songs—the album was a major leap forward in the artistic capacity of the rock world, which was still reeling from the complex narratives of the Beach Boys' 1966 *Pet Sounds* and the Beatles' 1967 *Sgt. Pepper's Lonely Hearts Club Band* (see pp. 36 and 46, respectively).

The irony of *Tommy* is that it came from a band generally known for turning the volume up too high and smashing their instruments on stage, barbaric behavior even for a rock band at the time. Though the Who were

The Who's 1969 *Tommy*, which moved the concept album into the realm of rock opera. *Courtesy of Universal Music Enterprises.*

somewhat respected in their home country and created a stir in the United States after an electrifying set at the 1967 Monterey Pop Festival in California, their material before *Tommy* was generally regarded as more attitude than substance, and with metal still in its infancy and punk years away, the Who were just another loud British band riding the coattails of their predecessors.

But Pete Townshend's lyrical and compositional gifts would not be denied, and the swirling cacophony of sound the band produced— with Townshend's solid guitar skills providing a foundation for Keith Moon's chaotic drumming, John Entwistle's adventurous bass, and Roger Daltrey's vocal acrobatics—would find grounding and maturity in *Tommy*, elevating rock to the world of high art. "The thing is, we wanted it to work on lots of levels," said Townshend of the project. "We want to turn on the spiritually hip, we want to turn on the fuckers and the street fighters ... we want to turn on the opera lovers and we succeeded in turning on a lot of people that weren't reached before."[17]

The album tells the story of Tommy Walker, a boy struck deaf, dumb, and blind by the shock of witnessing his stepfather's murder at the hands of his real father, who unexpectedly turns up years after he went missing in action in World War I. Although Tommy shuts himself off from the real world, he finds a spiritual connection with a pinball machine and becomes such a skilled player that he inspires a cult following, eventually becoming a messiah figure to his fans. After Tommy's family takes advantage of his legion of worshippers, his followers revolt against him even as Tommy continues to bring them spiritual enlightenment.

Originally titled *Amazing Journey* and then *Brain Opera, Tommy* unfolds over four sides of a double album, not only opening the rock world up to complex narrative structures, but demonstrating the possibilities of combining astute lyricism with crunchy guitars and piercing vocal shrieks, demonstrating that the nascent heavy-metal genre could be more than just noise. Townshend later characterized this period in popular music as having a "strong connection with the roots of spiritual theosophy and the language that rang with it—the idea that pop music was about spiritual uplift, human potential, solidarity, and unification."[18]

It was not easy for American pop-music critics and their high-art counterparts to accept the marriage of distortion and erudition. As *Tommy* was lining the record store shelves, a heated discussion was already underway about the artistic merits of rock as the bands King Crimson, Procol Harum, the Moody Blues, and Frank Zappa and the Mothers of Invention were incorporating classical structures and instruments into their music. But the literary sophistication of *Tommy* scored it critical acceptance in the United Kingdom, where the dominant musical publication *Melody Maker* named it album of the year. There was even some praise by forward-thinking critics in the United States, with *New York Times* critic Albert Goldman calling the album a "work of innovative power and philosophical profundity."[19]

The Who had scored several hit singles in the United States before *Tommy*, but this was their first album to break the American Top Ten (reaching the No. 4 spot a year after its release). Over the following two years, they would set fire to the American market with less literary but still powerful albums such as *Live at Leeds* and *Who's next*. Songs from *Tommy* would appear on future albums in various forms, and tracks, such as "Pinball Wizard," "I'm Free," and "We're Not Gonna Take It" would become staples in the classic-rock archive, with the immortal refrain "see me, hear me, touch me, feel me" taking on iconic proportions as American popular music slipped out of the community-driven 1960s and into a more egocentric and relationship-oriented 1970s.

After forty-seven weeks in the American Top 40, the growing critical appreciation for *Tommy* was demonstrated by its acceptance in other media and performance outlets not generally receptive to rock bands. The Who took the album on a tour of European opera houses, and even booked two nights in Manhattan's Lincoln Center. Eventually a symphonic rendition of *Tommy* by the London Symphony Orchestra reached No. 5 on the American charts, and a ballet and a Broadway version found homes on the New York stage. In 1975, the noted British producer Robert Stigwood backed a film based on the album starring such musical greats and Hollywood luminaries as Jack Nicholson, Elton John, Ann-Margret, Eric Clapton, Tina Turner, and the members of the Who themselves. The film's soundtrack reached No. 2 on the American charts and Elton John scored a hit with his rendition of "Pinball Wizard."

Townshend has received criticism over the years for the similarities between *Tommy* and a 1968 album by the London band the Pretty Things entitled *S.F. Sorrow*. Many rock aficionados regard *S.F. Sorrow* as the first true rock opera, and Townshend admits that he was greatly influenced by the album when he was penning *Tommy*. But many of *Tommy*'s structural elements can be seen in Townshend's earlier works, and with so many groundbreaking albums being released in such a short period, none of them could help being influenced by the staggering advances of the others. *Tommy* would remain one of the most important recordings of this transition period, and would go on to influence bands like Jethro Tull and Pink

Floyd to create story albums of their own, ultimately inspiring rock musicals such as *Godspell*, *Grease*, and *Jesus Christ Superstar*.

Album Title: *In the Court of the Crimson King*
Artist: King Crimson
Recorded: August–September 1969, at Wessex Sound Studios in London
U.S. release: October 10, 1969 (Atlantic)
Producer: King Crimson

King Crimson's 1969 *In the Court of the Crimson King*, the first album to mark progressive rock as a distinct genre. *Courtesy of Photofest.*

The late 1960s was a period of explosive change for music in both the United Kingdom and the United States. Artists were breaking down musical barriers and creating new genres more or less after every meal. Many new types of music were brought about by combining elements of different genres to create new sounds, such as the Byrds' *Sweetheart of the Rodeo* and the Band's *Music from Big Pink* (both featured in this chapter) toning down rock with elements of country and folk to create the hybrids of country-rock and Americana. Aiming in the opposite direction, bands such as the Moody Blues, Procol Harum, and King Crimson brought elements of classical music into the rock arena to create heavy, bombastic rock symphonies that were dubbed "progressive rock," a genre that brought about massive LP sales and sold-out arena tours through the early and mid-1970s.

Although the Moody Blues, Procol Harum, and Jethro Tull predated King Crimson in the use of classical instruments in a rock setting, King Crimson—largely through the efforts of frontman/guitarist Robert Fripp—went beyond the use of classical instruments to generate rock with sophisticated classical ideas. Using a wide range of effects, styles, meters, and volume to create complex, multimovement works, Fripp orchestrated lush compositions that advanced a moody, postpsychedelic agenda that was called by one critic "a thinking man's Pink Floyd."[20] With Fripp on guitar, Ian McDonald playing a wide variety of instruments not traditionally found in a rock band (including mellotron, vibes, woodwinds, reeds, and keyboards), Greg Lake on bass, and Michael Giles on drums, the band's debut album was a significant influence on the heavy metal and progressive rock to come, later described by Fripp as "the sound of 170 guitarists almost hitting the same chord at the same time."[21]

After the Beatles, the San Francisco psychedelic scene, and the London art-rock scene brought about the death of the three-minute pop song in the late 1960s, progressive bands took it a step further by creating entire song cycles with the pastoral themes found in classical music's romantic period. With fantasy-laden, nearly indecipherable lyrics drawn from authors such as J. R. R. Tolkien and musical ideas from composers like Edgard Varése, Johann Sebastian Bach, and Karlheinz Stockhausen, prog-rockers attempted to elevate rock music to high-art status by removing its blues-based tradition (imported to the United Kingdom by American blues and rock acts) and replacing it with a European symphonic foundation. King Crimson found influence in the early 20th-century English composer Gustavus Theodore von Holst and the Hungarian pianist Béla Bartók.

With *In the Court of the Crimson King*, King Crimson married rock's driving energy and baroque music's sophisticated use of counterpoint to produce the first fully progressive rock album, believed by many to be the point where progressive rock begins as a distinct genre. Fueled by producer Peter Sinfield's opaque lyrics, the mellotron-rich release was an echo of the Moody Blues' 1968 album *Days of Future Passed*, which assembled the London Festival Orchestra to create a classical arrangement of blues-based rock (see p. 57). In their attempt to remove the blues altogether, King Crimson constructed a stunning debut that functioned as a cohesive unit rather than a mere collection of songs. Although the title track has survived as a staple of classic rock radio, the album is thick with forgotten contrasts in the dark, foreboding "21st Century Schizoid Man (Including Mirrors)," the folksy balladry of "I Talk to the Wind," the simultaneously aggressive and restrained "Epitaph Including March for No Reason and Tomorrow and Tomorrow," and the light and spritey "Moonchild (Including the Dream and the Illusion)." With the shortest song on the album coming in at over six minutes, King Crimson joined art-rock lords Pink Floyd and Frank Zappa in pushing radio-rock boundaries with the long-song form as well as a heavy dose of electronic experimentation in the studio.

King Crimson would help their contemporaries the Moody Blues and Yes to popularize the progressive sound in the 1970s, spawning numerous imitators and, eventually, detractors. "King Crimson will probably be condemned by some for pompousness," John Morthland wrote of *In the Court of the Crimson King* in *Rolling Stone* in 1969, foreshadowing the criticism that would haunt the entire genre of progressive rock through the 1970s. "But that criticism isn't really valid. They have combined aspects of many musical forms to create a surreal work of force and originality."[22]

The band's adventurous spirit would not only bring a new attention to the incorporation of jazz and classical elements in rock, but would challenge rock's basic structure as a blues-based art form. Such an arduous task makes the album itself challenging to listen to at some points, but a post-*Sgt. Pepper's* world was ready for just about anything, and the heretofore unheard pretentiousness struck a chord (a loud, overbearing chord) with rock audiences, elevating the album to No. 5 on the U.K. charts and No. 28 in the United States.

Fripp immediately joined the ranks of pop music's genius innovators—Frank Zappa, Pete Townshend, Miles Davis, Brian Wilson—and like many of them, his vision was often indecipherable to his colleagues. McDonald and Miles, frustrated with the direction the band was taking, left after *In the Court of the Crimson King*, and Fripp was the only remaining original member after the band's second album, 1970's *In the Wake of Poseidon*, with Greg Lake going on to form the massively successful prog-rock group Emerson, Lake and Palmer, and Ian McDonald joining one of the most successful rock acts of the late 1970s and early 1980s, Foreigner. But Fripp maintained the band through several incarnations with artists who would become notable in later acts, including Bill Bruford (Yes), John Wetton (Uriah Heep, Roxy Music), Boz Burrell (Bad Company), and Adrian Belew (David Bowie, Frank Zappa and the Mothers of Invention).

Fripp dissolved the band in 1974, later declaring "King Crimson ceased to exist in September 1974, which was when all English bands in that genre should have ceased to exist. But since the rock and roll dinosaur likes anything which has gone before, most of them are still churning away, repeating what they did years ago without going off in any new direction."[23] Despite his distaste for progressive acts that overstay their welcome, Fripp would reform King Crimson for several albums over the next two decades, though none of them reaching the musical sophistication and groundbreaking arrangements of *In the Court of the Crimson King*.

Album Title: *Trout Mask Replica*
Artist: Captain Beefheart and His Magic Band
Recorded: April 1969, at Whitney Studios in Los Angeles
U.S. release: November 1969 (Straight)
Producer: Frank Zappa

"A man just too creative, too human for the 20th century," is how a reporter for *Creem* described Don Van Vliet—better known as Captain Beefheart—shortly after his 1969 release *Trout Mask Replica*.[24] One of the most disputed works of art in the American musical canon, *Trout Mask Replica* is, to some, a staggering work of genius, and to others, a pretentious experiment too postmodern for its own good.

To understand *Trout Mask Replica*, we have to understand Van Vliet, a free-spirited experimentalist even by the standards of late-1960s rock music. Interested in the arts since he was a child, Van Vliet won a scholarship to study art in Europe when he was just thirteen-years old. His parents, however, maintained a dim view of the art world, and rather than allowing him to take the scholarship, they moved to Lancaster, California in the sunshine state's desolate backcountry. The plan backfired somewhat,

Captain Beefheart's 1969 *Trout Mask Replica*, one of the most avant-garde and heavily debated albums in the American musical canon. *Courtesy of Photofest.*

as it was there at Lancaster High School that Van Vliet met a man who would become rock's ultimate freak-out king, Frank Zappa. The adolescent duo spent entire evenings listening to records, and though they would part ways after high school, their musical relationship would be rekindled years later after a chance meeting at a fast food restaurant.

Van Vliet had attempted to make a career in sculpture, but found the form limited, and instead devoted himself to music. His earliest outings were a raw Delta blues, reflecting his appreciation for unusual sounds. "I've always liked human noises," he commented about his early musical attempts, "like animal noises and things like that, natural sounds. I got a more natural feeling out of say, country blues, field hollers, and things like that and progressive stuff. I was looking for something that extended rather than caged."[25] His first few incarnations of the Magic Band (containing no less a talent than future guitar legend Ry Cooder) attempted work that stretched the limits of blues-based rock—a few singles for A&M, followed by their 1967 release for Buddah Records *Safe as Milk*, then a 1968 album for Blue Thumb Records, *Strictly Personal*. But Van Vliet's visions were always one step ahead of his band and two steps ahead of his labels, and those who did not understand his music tinkered with it, much to Van Vliet's dismay. Dismal sales led the Captain to lose most of his group after each album, and 1968 found him frustrated and alone. Van Vliet gave up and returned to Lancaster, where he was lucky enough to spot Frank Zappa at a Colonel Sanders restaurant. Zappa had been doing well with his band, the Mothers of Invention, and invited Van Vliet to record in his studio. The collaboration would yield one of the most bizarre albums of the decade.

Zappa gave Van Vliet complete creative freedom—a considerable show of trust considering what he did with it. The legend goes that Van Vliet assembled a new Magic Band partly composed of nonmusicians, friends from the artistic community that joined Van Vliet on bass clarinet, tenor sax, soprano sax, and vocals, plus the musicians Zoot Horn Rollo (Bill Harkleroad) playing glass-finger guitar and flute, Antennae Jimmy Semens (Jeff Cotton) on steel appendage guitar, The Mascara Snake (Victor Hayden) on bass clarinet and vocals, Rockette Morton (Mark Boston) on bass, and Drumbo (John French) playing percussion. "The thing is that I found out that I couldn't use anybody that was a musician," said Van Vliet. "I tried to school them in sculpting, you see, by letting them school themselves as far as I could without going over into that form."[26] The truth is that Van Vliet was the most amateur musician of the bunch, often assigning pieces for band members to work on by humming his ideas into a tape recorder. Much of the musical foundation was laid by drummer John French, who transcribed Van Vliet's ideas into musical notation for the others.

"The band was shut up in the house for weeks on end, with no contact with the outside world," recalled a Beefheart chronicler who was close to the action. "Don had persuaded them that chicks and sex would interfere with their music, and so they played day and night, day and night. Unfortunately there was no money either and they starved, came down with illnesses, and were found wandering in search of food—one of them in a woman's dress, boots and a helmet, a crazed look in his eyes. Eventually they all left, some to return, but most to find food and recuperate and maybe even find a job with a band that made just a little money."[27]

When rehearsals were over, the group recorded the entire session in four and a half hours, playing straight through each cut until they had a double album on their hands. The result was a melange of off-beat vocals, unusual noises, and wandering instruments that seemed to be a stab at the complete deconstruction of music itself—Van Vliet is even heard to comment on one of the tracks, "How did that harmony get in there?" After the tracks were laid down, Van Vliet sang vocals in another studio without wearing headphones, lending an odd, off-rhythm theme to an album already weird enough with song titles like "The Dust Blows Forward N' the Dust Blows Back," "Neon Meate Dream of a Octafish," "Hobo Chang Ba," and "My Human Gets Me Blues."

Fans of Captain Beefheart claim that those who do not understand (or at least, cannot tolerate) *Trout Mask Replica* are simply too straight to participate in Van Vliet's vision. Esteemed rock critic Lester Bangs, who often liked things more because others liked them less, called Van Vliet "The only true dadaist in rock."[28] But one gets the sense that even among Captain Beefheart's fans (as it often is in the world of the avant-garde), everyone wants to "get it" more than everyone else. "Even those who term the music 'dada-rock' are hiding behind a classification, and totally miss the point," claimed one reviewer, calling the album "a delightful practice that defies categorization. What seems like chaos is merely non-structure, what seems like no direction is no direction. The bass and drums are not relegated to simple beatkeeping apparatus, but are free to make their own distinctive contributions. The guitars construct, and then harshly bend and rupture, rhythms and progressions seemingly without design. The music works as a whole, yet each band member is allowed to express himself in a very individual manner. And because the Magic Band is not composed of professional musicians, there is always that marvelous factor of discovery involved."[29]

The world surrounding *Trout Mask Replica* is as much a mystery as the indecipherable album itself. Zappa, Van Vliet, and other participants have given contradictory facts on how the album came about, and those who received it well were criticized by others who also received it well, but differently. Though one cannot draw a direct stylistic lineage from this album as one can from other monumental releases of the era, many later punk, new wave, and alternative bands have credited Captain Beefheart and *Trout Mask Replica*—whether as a matter of fact or just to appear ultrahip—with influencing their own musical experiments. Still it seems the debate will never end as to the merits of *Trout Mask Replica* as its own work of art. Detractors will always detract, and fans will always lay it on thick: "[*Trout Mask Replica's*] importance reaches far beyond rock, and it is doubtful that as paramount an achievement has been equaled in any genre. But, in leaving the musical public so far behind, Beefheart has once again victimized himself; a full appreciation of *Trout Mask* will undoubtedly be a long time coming."[30]

Album Title: *Sweet Baby James*
Artist: James Taylor
Recorded: December 1969, at Sunset Sound in Los Angeles
U.S. release: February 1970 (Warner Bros.)
Producer: Peter Asher

"Understated, personal, and tranquilizing," is how James Taylor's early career was later summed up by one critic. "Taylor's records offered a soothing antidote to heads ringing with the electrified political anthems of the 1960s . . . [capturing] a generation's transition from the frustrating tumult of radical politics to a preoccupation with the self."[31] It was this transition from the community-centered rock of the late 1960s to the ego- and relationship-centered rock of the 1970s that most typified the sound of the next decade, which traded in peace signs and jam sessions for couples therapy and deeply personal lyrics. As communal-style living began to disappear, the women's independence movement started to take hold, and the divorce rate escalated rapidly (nearly doubling by the end of the decade), a spotlight was cast on the individual as a single being, prompting an army of acoustic-oriented artists to pen confessional tales of lost or unrequited love for an audience of lonely people—solo artists writing for audiences made up of solo listeners.

Taylor was at the forefront of this singer-songwriter movement, featured on the March 1971 cover of *Time* magazine with the subtitle: "The New Rock: Bittersweet and Low," an article in which he was credited for the "cooling of America."[32] A native of Boston, Massachusetts, Taylor recorded his first album with the Beatles' Apple Records in London in 1968, a self-titled debut that met little success (despite help from George Harrison and Paul McCartney) and drove Taylor further into his already troubling heroin-fueled depression. After Taylor returned to the United States, his manager,

Peter Asher, parlayed a gig at the Newport Folk Festival into a record deal with Warner Bros., bringing about the now legendary album *Sweet Baby James* and Taylor's signature song, "Fire and Rain." "Understated" was an adjective bandied about by many critics, both about Taylor and *Sweet Baby James*. "Taylor's work has a marvelous capacity for growth," *Fusion* critic Ben Edmonds wrote in a review of the album. "When William Congreve said "music hath alarums to calm the savage beast," he must have been talking about James Taylor.... Time will undoubtedly prove James Taylor to be the most important young singer/songwriter to emerge in the latter '60s."

Sweet Baby James is one of a trio of albums that launched the singer-songwriter movement, followed the next year by Joni Mitchell's *Blue* and Carole King's *Tapestry* (see p. 82). These albums brought a new intimacy to rock, sparsely arranged with acoustic instruments and a focus on the lyrics and the artist's soothing voice. Taylor's album is thick with tropes of solitude—the secluded cowboy in the title track whose "horse and his cattle are his only companions"; the isolation of walking unbeaten paths on "Country Road"; the friendless character of Sunny Skies who "weeps in the evening" on "Sunny Skies"; and, of course, the all-consuming loneliness of "Fire and Rain," Taylor's stark autobiography of mental instability, lost friends, and heroin addiction that finds his dreams and hopes for the future "in pieces on the ground."

"It is very strange making a living out of being yourself," said Taylor once, referring to the singer-songwriter technique of laying one's soul bare to the audience.[33] Besides moving on from the loud political strains of 1960s rock, the softer rock of the 1970s also sought to escape the "rock star as untouchable idol" phenomenon that was embodied by acts such as Led Zeppelin, the Rolling Stones, and Rod Stewart, preferring instead to make personal connections with the audience. With the exception of soft-rock acts like Fleetwood Mac and the Eagles, it was in these two directions that rock split in the early 1970s—overbearing, noise-driven bands that filled stadiums (this includes the emerging genre of progressive rock from bands like ELO, Yes, and Pink Floyd with their massive stage sets and overwhelming waves of sound) and lyric-oriented singer-songwriters who filled smaller venues and attempted to make a connection with each listener.

Sweet Baby James would open the door for a slew of guitar-wielding troubadours, attempting to play the heart strings of the average American. In the 1960s, acts such as Bob Dylan, the Byrds, Buffalo Springfield, Simon and Garfunkel, and Crosby, Stills and Nash created the genre of "folk-rock" to bring a new sentimentality to rock music. Often the personal touch was added by early singer-songwriters such as Phil Ochs, Joan Baez, and Tom Paxton to further political causes as their folk-rock counterparts were doing. Taylor's success helped further the careers of his brother and sister folkies who had been playing longer than him and paved the way for a slew of memorable albums over the next two years, including Joni Mitchell's *Blue*, Carole King's *Tapestry*, Don McLean's *American Pie*, Cat Stevens' *Teaser and the Firecat*, Jim Croce's *You Don't Mess Around with Jim*,

Neil Young's *After the Gold Rush*, and Carly Simon's (who Taylor would later marry) *Anticipation*.

Of course, many of these artists (and many other uncredited) had a hand in furthering the singer-songwriter movement, but Taylor was the singer-songwriter's first superstar and one of the most beloved solo acts of the 1970s. Within a year of *Sweet Baby James'* release, *Time, Newsweek*, and *The New York Times Magazine* ran features on Taylor proclaiming him the king of the new movement. A later profile in *Rolling Stone* claimed that Taylor "pretty much wrote the book for the singer/songwriters of the Seventies. That may be a dubious distinction but Taylor's early work, characterized by subdued singing and restrained, clean backings, was also marked by an undercurrent of extreme agitation and angst. It was this sense of powerful emotions barely held in check that gave Taylor's music its dramatic tension."[34]

In January 1971, he was able to pack the traditionally hard-rock venue Fillmore East, the more posh and reserved Lincoln Center, and the stadium-like Madison Square Garden—three very different venues all within blocks of each other in midtown Manhattan—a testimonial to the widespread appeal *Sweet Baby James* had earned him and the countless singer-songwriters who were his contemporaries or followed in his wake.

Album Title: *Bitches Brew*
Artist: Miles Davis
Recorded: August 19–August 21, 1969, in New York City
U.S. release: April 1970 (Columbia)
Producer: Teo Macero

"After we finished we walked out of the studio...and while we were standing in the hallway John came over and whispered to me, 'Can I ask you a question?' I answered, 'Sure'. He then said, 'Herbie, I can't tell...was that any good what we did? I mean, what did we do? I can't tell what's going on!' So I told him, 'John, welcome to a Miles Davis session. Your guess is as good as mine. I have no idea, but somehow when the records come out, they end up sounding good.'"[35]

This exchange between two of the giants of jazz fusion—pianist Herbie Hancock and guitarist John McLaughlin—illustrates the power of Miles Davis' musical vision and his ability to lead his collaborators into musical territory they likely would not have discovered on their own. These sessions with Davis, Hancock, McLaughlin, saxophonist Wayne Shorter, keyboardists Chick Corea and Joe Zawinul, bassist Dave Holland, and drummer Tony Williams would bring about Davis' compelling 1969 album *In a Silent Way*, the jazz great's initial foray into fusion. Only six months later, Davis and an extended roster would break out of traditional jazz in a not-so-silent-way with *Bitches Brew*, the first full-on jazz-fusion album, and considered by many the greatest—or at least the most revolutionary—jazz album of all time.

By the time *Bitches Brew* was released, Miles Davis was already a legend for pioneering both the "cool jazz" movement with his 1957 album *Birth of the Cool* (see p. 7), and the "modal jazz" genre with his 1959 release *Kind of Blue* (see p. 12). With *Bitches Brew*, Davis almost seemed to have jumped the jazz ship entirely, inspired by no less a rock god than Jimi Hendrix to escape the smooth, mellow tones he was known for by embracing an electric, heavily produced wall of sound that seemed geared more toward the massive psychedelic audience than the reserved jazz world (a theory supported by the unusually surreal artwork on the album cover, painted by Mati Klarwein, who also produced work for Jimi Hendrix and Santana). Particularly on the twenty-six-minute title track and the overwhelming "Miles Runs the Voodoo Down," the listener can hear the powerful rock and funk that was coming out of 1960s' acts like James Brown and Sly and the Family Stone.

As was often the case with Davis, his own genius was only half the story, as he had an innate ability to gather extraordinary talent together and bring out their best work. Davis' sidemen would often go on to noteworthy careers of their own, expanding the vocabulary of music based on what they took away from sessions with Davis. *Bitches Brew* was no exception—rock fusion exploded as a musical genre through the 1970s, largely thanks to Davis' colleagues on the album [guitarist John McLaughlin and drummer Billy Cobham went on to form the Mahavishnu Orchestra; saxophonist Wayne Shorter, percussionist Airto Moreira, and pianist Joe Zawinul founded Weather Report; clarinetist Bennie Maupin and keyboardist Herbie Hancock (who played with Davis throughout the 1960s) created the Mwandishi Band and later the Headhunters; and Chick Corea and Lenny White set up shop with Return to Forever, which borrowed Airto Moreira from Weather Report].

In addition to the extraordinary instrumental talent that came together on *Bitches Brew*, producer Teo Macero followed the footsteps of Jimi Hendrix and Beatles producer George Martin in using the studio itself as an instrument. What sounds like an extended jam session centered on key grooves and phrases is actually a work of editing genius by Macero and Davis. Macero's editing gave *Bitches Brew* a wholly unique sound with the use of tape loops, delays, reverb, and echo, with many elements later reproduced on stage by the band. "Teo Macero added mid-20th century studio trickery, a 19th century classical music awareness of musical structure, and a way of looking at music as abstract blocks of sound, which he freely cut and moved around. In other words, the two most heavily edited tracks on *Bitches Brew* were hybrids of "figurative" and "abstract" art. They combined, respectively, the traditional musical line of something akin to a sonata form with the cut and paste ideas that had come out of musique concrète, serial music, and studio technology. Add to this the strongly chromatic improvising of the keyboard players, which has echoes of classical atonal music, and it is clear that an impressive amount of influences went into the making of *Bitches Brew*. This is no doubt one of the major reasons for the recording's immense success and influence. Virtually anyone willing to listen to it with an open mind is able to recognize something familiar in the music, despite the fact that it contains few easily identifiable melodies, hooks, or vamps."[36]

There is an ongoing debate in jazz circles as to whether *Bitches Brew* or Davis' 1959 album *Kind of Blue* was the best-selling jazz record ever (and for that matter, which was Davis' greatest achievement), but it was definitely *Bitches Brew* that made Miles Davis a household name. Despite the fact that many jazz fans turned their backs on Davis after *Bitches Brew* for what they saw as an aberration (though many of these fans would later return), Davis gained a new, larger audience of rock fans that elevated him from the small clubs to some of rock's great stages, including the Fillmore venues in San Francisco and New York, and the 1970 Isle of Wight rock festival in the United Kingdom. "It's hard to overstate the importance of *Bitches Brew*. It is one of the seminal albums that shaped Western music culture in the second half of the 20th century, dividing it into a 'time before' and a 'time after'. It crossed musical boundaries and influenced musicians of all music traditions. It gave rise to a whole new genre of music: jazz-rock."[37]

Album Title: *Paranoid*
Artist: Black Sabbath
Recorded: July 1970, at Regent Sound and Island Studios in London
U.S. release: January 7, 1971 (Warner Bros.)
Producer: Rodger Bain

"Black Sabbath are ten times cruder than Grand Funk," said rock critic Metal Mike Saunders, referring to reigning hard-blues band Grand Funk Railroad, who dominated America's high-volume rock market in the early 1970s. "[Black Sabbath's] music is based on the same formula great rock'n'roll has always risen from (from Little Richard to the Stones to the Stooges), that of crude, unrefined street clatter." *Crude* and *unrefined* were among the nicer adjectives used to describe the strained vocals and shrieking guitar riffs from this British powerhouse, but some critics and a legion of devoted fans saw the birth of a powerful new force in music, leading Saunders to label Black Sabbath "the most valid group ever to rise out of the genre of heavy rock."[38] This is high praise coming from the man who was the first to use the term "heavy metal"—in *Creem* magazine in 1971—as a musical genre.

Sabbath is rivaled only by Led Zeppelin and Deep Purple as the most important early metal act, but Zeppelin incorporated a great deal of folk and blues into their songs and Deep Purple was as much progressive rock as it was metal, leaving Sabbath as the first pure-metal band, with every song thunderous, weighty, and bordering on chaos. The band got their unique, heavy sound from guitarist Tony Iommi's unusual tuning method. Iommi had lost the tips of two fingers in an accident while working at a sheet-metal factory. With his fingertips too tender to manage the fretboard (he tried fashioning prosthetic tips from plastic bottle caps), Iommi lowered his guitar tuning from C to E#. The resulting slack made it easier to play, but also brought the band a heavier sound, with bassist Terry "Geezer" Butler lowering his instrument to match Iommi's tuning. This method of "downtuning" became such standard practice in heavy metal that it has come to define the sound as much as the guitar's distortion and the volume at which the songs are meant to be played.

Originally known as Earth, the group became tired of being confused with another band of the same name, and changed their name to Black Sabbath after seeing the title on a poster for a Boris Karloff horror film. With Iommi on guitar, Butler on bass, Bill Ward on drums, and Ozzy Osbourne on vocals, the band issued a dizzying onslaught of distortion and bass-heavy power chords that prompted one reviewer to credit them with the "sophistication of four Cro-Magnon hunters who've stumbled on a rock band's equipment."[39] While impolite, the remark was not without merit. Black Sabbath brought a new, primeval rawness to rock, an unrelenting push of bass and beat that got fans' heads bobbing as passionately as Little Richard had gotten feet tapping and Elvis had gotten pelvis' swinging. When they held practices in a barn in Wales, they would rock so hard that the roof shingles would crack and fall off the building. "It's all about raw, musical energy," Mike Saunders opined in a later article. "And if Sabbath's music also happens to be a shade more vengeful and violent than any previous rock, it's because they mean what they say about releasing the tension in their audiences. With few of the trappings and affectations common to all too many groups, Black Sabbath deliver."[40]

Another element of heavy metal that Sabbath brought to the table was provoking lyrics that seemed to beg for parental outcry. Many of the songs on *Paranoid* carry dark themes such as mental instability ("Paranoid"), nuclear war ("Electric Funeral"), drug abuse ("Hand of Doom"), and the end of the world ("Iron Man"). Their honest, confrontational lyrics and drastic appearance would inspire their followers to create an entire wardrobe of black leather, heavy jewelry, and brooding complexions that would come to define the world-weary posture of heavy-metal fandom. Such dark trappings earned the group no end of criticism from all corners as the band overshadowed even Led Zeppelin in their use of occult themes. Osbourne would become famous for biting the heads off of (allegedly) live animals such as bats and doves, and the band would quickly be vilified as devil rockers.

"We've never done anything really devilish," Osbourne once quipped to an interviewer. "Perhaps Tony has sacrificed a few too many virgins in his time, but nothing you could really call wrong."[41] With heavy metal still in its infancy, darker themes were uncommon even in hard rock, and the band's controversial lyrics often overshadowed their enviable talent. Iommi was an accomplished-enough musician that one reviewer had to call and apologize to him after he mistakenly credited Eric Clapton as guitarist on the band's first album. Osbourne would eventually be respected as one of rock's great showmen and the father of heavy metal.

Paranoid was originally called *War Pigs*, after its memorable opening track, and was meant as a protest to Britain's involvement in the Vietnam War. But even though the record company changed the name in fear of reprisal from prowar consumers, the message was still transmitted through the album's cover art—a charging, pink-spandex-clad warrior donning a tinfoil sabre—and the overwhelming opening of "War Pigs," with its heavy, droning power chords and air-raid sirens warning rock fans of a new force gathering beyond the horizon. Tighter and more focused than their debut album, *Paranoid* translated Black Sabbath's influences—1960s hard-blues rockers like Cream, the Yardbirds, and the Jimi Hendrix Experience—into not only a new sound for the 1970s, but a new way of listening to rock. The record only took a few days to produce, with the title track taking all of ten minutes to record, but its impact reverberated throughout the next three decades, inspiring and influencing acts such as Aerosmith, Alice Cooper, Metallica, Pearl Jam, Nirvana, Ice-T, and many of the thrash-metal bands of the 1980s.

It is only fair to say that Sabbath's first three albums—1970's *Black Sabbath*, 1971's *Paranoid*, and 1971's *Master of Reality*—all deserve credit for contributing to the growth of metal in the United States. Though *Black Sabbath* came first and *Master of Reality* charted the highest, *Paranoid* is seen in retrospect as not only the band's best release, but a foundation album for the harder, faster metal that would dominate rock in the 1970s and 1980s.

Album Title: *Tapestry*
Artist: Carole King
Recorded: 1971, at A&M Recording Studios in Hollywood
U.S. release: March 1971 (Ode)
Producer: Lou Adler

Carole King began playing piano at age four, and essentially never stopped. Though her own career as a recording artist would not blossom until the 1970s, she made a name for herself as a composer of catchy, endearing melodies from the time she was a teenager. Growing up as Carole Klein, a Jewish girl in Brooklyn's public school system, King played piano and sang for a vocal quartet before entering the professional music world while still in her teens.

King and her songwriting partner, Gerry Goffin, met at Queens College in New York City (where she also hung out with future songwriting greats Neil Sedaka and Paul Simon—Sedaka's 1959 hit "Oh! Carole" was penned for King, who was also his high school girlfriend). The songwriting duo of Goffin and King (they would later marry) took up residence in cubicles at New York's famous Brill building, where songwriters penned hit after hit for artists who were serious about climbing the *Billboard* charts. By the late

1960s, their songwriting partnership was one of the most productive in the business, writing hits for a range of artists including the Shirelles ("Will You Still Love Me Tomorrow"—King's first hit at nineteen years of age), Bobby Vee ("Take Good Care of My Baby"), Little Eva ("The Loco-Motion"), Aretha Franklin ["(You Make Me Feel Like) A Natural Woman"], the Chiffons ("One Fine Day"), the Monkees ("Pleasant Valley Sunday"), the Drifters ("Up on the Roof"), and the Crystals ["He Hit Me (And It Felt Like a Kiss)"].

But the kind of music coming out of the Brill building and similar "song factories" of the day were met with derision by the singer-songwriters' early 1960s equivalent: the folk artists. The shallow concerns of sixteen-year-olds seemed paltry compared with the important social commentary of the era's best protest songs, and when King dropped out of college to accept the job penning tunes at the Brill Building, her friend Paul Simon advised against it, for reasons King soon found to be valid. "Every day we squeezed into our respective cubby holes with just enough room for a piano, a bench, and maybe a chair for the lyricist if you were lucky," said King of her early adventures in the Brill Building. "You'd sit there and write and you could hear someone in the next cubby hole composing a song exactly like yours."[42]

Despite the fact that King placed more than 100 songs on the charts for other artists—making her the most successful female composer in pop music history—she was unable to get her own performing career off the ground, attempting and failing as a recording artist several times. In 1962, she released a single, "It Might as Well Rain Until September," originally written for Bobby Vee but released by King and reaching No. 22 on the charts, her only successful outing as a performer until *Tapestry* a decade later. After divorcing Goffin in the late 1960s, she recorded *Now That Everything's Been Said* with her band the City, and then in 1970 her solo debut *Writer*. Though both albums flopped commercially, King had become close friends with the new singer-songwriter wunderkind James Taylor, for whom King had played piano on his breakout 1970 album *Sweet Baby James*.

In the spring of 1971, Taylor invited King to open for him on a nationwide tour, just before *Tapestry* was ready for release. The same month that Taylor appeared on the cover of *Time* magazine in March 1971 as the crowned king of the new singer-songwriter movement, Ode Records released *Tapestry*, described by a later critic as "[T]he first great adult pop album: complicated, subtle, built on her subdued piano parts, lyrically concerned with the way people who've been living for a while relate to each other. King's music matured, too, giving up the simplicity of bubble gum for trickier, jazzier chords and letting her thin but mellow voice carry the songs. And it hits the mark over and over, because she didn't give up her Brill Building sense of hooks great and small."[43]

Within a month, *Tapestry* reached the No. 1 spot on the charts, where it remained for an amazing fifteen weeks, followed by another five-and-a-half years in the Top 200, making it the fifth most successful album of all time, in any genre, in terms of chart history. *Tapestry* was a landmark album in the transition from the ego and pomp of late 1960s rock music to the personal and confessional troubadour style of the 1970s. Many saw the singer-songwriter movement as a fad—one critic complained about King that "her record rarely gets past being an exceptionally good demonstration record for her songs. Unless you like your grown women to whine and wheedle at you. All the songs are written in the New York High School Secret Diary style, which works quite well with certain kinds of melodramatic overproduction, or with singers who sound truly innocent: Phil Spector and the Shirelles might have been able to come up with something. Unless you're a devotee of the Neil Young/James Taylor I'm-so-sorry-for-me club, you probably won't relate to Carole."[44]

Fortunately for King—and the rest of the singer-songwriter movement—people related in a big way. *Tapestry* earned Grammy awards for Album of the Year, Best Pop Vocal Performance (Female), and Record of the Year for "It's Too Late." Coincidentally, her song "You've Got a Friend" won Single of the Year—though King never released "You've Got a Friend" as a single; her friend Taylor took it to the top of the charts with his own rendition just four months after *Tapestry*'s release. King earned her own singles successes with "So Far Away," "I Feel the Earth Move," and "It's Too Late," the latter two spending five weeks at No. 1 as a flip-side single.

During her reign with Gerry Goffin in the Brill building, King generally wrote the melodies and left the lyrics to Goffin. But in her new incarnation as a singer, a songwriter, and a composer, King proved deft at all three, with her comforting vocals and jazz-tinged melodies smoothing the sharp emotional edges of her vivid and intimate lyrics. "Her total conception," said the *New York Times*' Don Heckman, "is what makes everything work: hard piano rhythms, chugging percussion and roving contrapuntal bass all combine to provide a pulsating and roving contrapuntal vehicle for her gospel-blues vocals."[45] Between *Tapestry* and James Taylor's *Sweet Baby James*, the stage was set for a host of singer-songwriters—Jim Croce, Harry Chapin, Joni Mitchell, Paul Simon, John Denver, Billy Joel, and Carly Simon among them—to vastly increase their audience base and find success through the 1970s.

Album Title: *What's Going On*
Artist: Marvin Gaye
Recorded: June 1970–April 1971, at Hitsville U.S.A. in Detroit
U.S. release: May 21, 1971 (Tamla/Motown)
Producer: Marvin Gaye

Praised by the *Rolling Stone Record Guide* as "perhaps the most underrated soul singer of the Sixties," Marvin Gaye was also the man that changed Motown. "He was by far the toughest and grittiest of all the male Motown singers," continues the *Guide*, "and he has influenced

Marvin Gaye's 1971 comeback *What's Going On*, which moved soul music to address urban social issues. *Courtesy of Photofest.*

everyone from Mick Jagger to Rod Stewart and Stevie Wonder."[46] But Motown's roster included many of the biggest soul stars of the 1960s and 1970s—Diana Ross, Smokey Robinson, Stevie Wonder, the Jackson 5—what made Marvin Gaye special?

It is difficult to appreciate the importance of *What's Going On* without understanding the circumstances that created it. Motown was the most successful label of the 1960s—approximately 65 percent of Motown's releases hit the Top 100, more than four times the success rate of any other label. The key to their phenomenal record was the factory assembly line method of producing songs. The label's founder, Berry Gordy Jr., employed one of the most prolific songwriting teams of the era—Brian Holland, his brother Eddie Holland, and Lamont Dozier—who penned forty-six Top 40 entries and twelve No. 1 hits between 1964 and 1966. The Holland/Dozier/Holland team and Motown's other songwriters would write songs on assignment, filling a need for a particular artist, or write a song and have it assigned to an artist by Gordy. After the song was written, the rhythm tracks would be laid down, then the artist would come in to sing the vocal tracks, then extra instrumentation would be laid down as required. When each song was complete, Gordy and a small cadre of executives would listen to the track and vote on whether or not it should be released.

This production-line approach (also practiced by Brill Building composers in New York City) made many of Motown's songs sound similar, a smooth, upbeat feel that was known as the "Detroit sound," which was a polished, watered-down version of the "Memphis sound," another dominant soul variation. "Berry [Gordy] wanted to make crossover music," said Smokey Robinson, who performed for Motown as a solo artist and with his band, the Miracles. "Crossover at that time meant the white people would buy your records. Berry's concept in starting Motown was to make music with a funky beat and great stories that would be crossover, that would not be blues. And that's what we did."[47]

Marvin Gaye was a session drummer and piano player before becoming a songwriter for Motown and then a solo artist. He was married to Berry's sister, Anna Gordy, and was an integral part of the Motown machine as one of its top-selling artists. Through the 1960s, he scored hit after hit for the label, charting thirty-four singles as a solo artist and fifteen more in duets. In 1967, his favorite duet partner, Tammi Terrell, collapsed onstage in his arms, later dying of a brain tumor in 1970. Gaye was devastated. Motown had also lost Holland/Dozier/Holland during this period, and its stock was on the decline, as their last No. 1 was Gaye's 1968 version of "Heard It through the Grapevine." After spending 1970 in relative seclusion, Gaye emerged from the studio with material that would lead to one of the most powerful soul albums ever produced.

What's Going On was a new direction for soul, and a complete about-face for Motown. Though retaining a pleasantly soothing sound, Gaye's songs flowed into and out of each other, incorporating jazz riffs and background chatter to aid in song transitions that gave the album a fluid, casual feel. More noticeably, Gaye's lyrics (which he co-wrote with several friends) abandoned the Motown penchant for poppy ditties in favor of addressing social issues such as poverty, faith, drug abuse, war, and the environment. No longer bound by themes of romance, Gaye's songs stood up and took notice.

When Gaye first handed over the title track to Gordy, Gordy refused to release it, protesting its lack of commercial potential. Gaye stood his ground and refused to record for Motown anymore unless "What's Going On" was released as a single. Though he was certain it would flop, Gordy relented and issued the cut. The song leaped onto the Hot 100, reaching No. 1 in the soul category and No. 2 on the pop charts. Gordy swallowed his pride and ask Gaye to come up with an accompanying album, which brought about two more hit singles—"Mercy Mercy Me" and "Inner City Blues"—shining a welcome spotlight on the reality of inner city life for black Americans. With the Civil Rights movement in full swing, Gaye found a receptive audience in a black community eager to realize their fair share of the American dream. Rather than trying to distract blacks from their problems with traditional Motown ear candy, Gaye got right up in the face of his audience, letting them know that their problems would not disappear if they were ignored. There is no question mark on the album for a reason—*What's Going On* was not a question. If anything, it required an exclamation point.

After its release, the album eventually became one of Motown's all-time biggest sellers, and established Gaye as the conscience of his community. Though he would not return to the political heat of *What's Going On* with future releases, Gaye would strike gold again in 1973 with his sultry album *Let's Get It On*, and would continue as a prominent artist through the remainder of the decade. But his powerful statement of independence and musical forthrightness would prove crucial to the careers of other Motown artists such as Stevie Wonder and Michael Jackson, both of whom won a great deal of independence (and scored smash hits throughout the decade) following in Gaye's footprints. Some of the most enduring albums of the decade, including Curtis Mayfield's *Superfly* and Stevie Wonder's string of monumental works (from *Talking Book* to *Songs in the Key of Life*) would owe a debt to Gaye's bold release. Gaye, sadly, would fall victim to the social ills he tried to put a stop to. After decades of drug abuse and a period of mental instability, Gaye was killed in a confrontation with his father in 1984, lending a tragic irony to the "What's Going On" lyrics: "Father, father, we don't need to escalate/War is not the answer, for only love can conquer hate."

Album Title: *There's a Riot Goin' On*
Artist: Sly and the Family Stone
Recorded: 1971
U.S. release: November 20, 1971 (Epic)
Producer: Sly Stone

"It's easy to write off *There's a Riot Goin' On* as one of two things—Sly Stone's disgusted social commentary or the beginning of his slow descent into addiction," wrote one reviewer of Sly and the Family Stone's darkest album. "It's both of these things, of course.... This is idealism soured, as hope is slowly replaced by cynicism, joy by skepticism, enthusiasm by weariness, sex by pornography, thrills by narcotics."[48]

It was precisely the dour themes on *There's a Riot Goin' On* that made the album so memorable—not because there had not been dark albums before, but because Sly and the Family Stone were the epitome of upbeat, positive dance music in the late 1960s. When the San Francisco-based band debuted in 1967 with the appropriately titled *A Whole New Thing*, they were enthusiastically received by rock and soul fans both, playing gigs from San Francisco's hard-rocking Avalon to Harlem's soul mecca, the Apollo Theatre. After making a name for themselves with a stunning performance at Woodstock, the group put out three more albums over the next eighteen months, combining James Brown's energetic rhythms and the San Francisco psychedelic scene's trippy grooves to bring the rock and soul worlds together in juicy, irresistible arrangements.

Sly (born Sylvester Stewart) had been one of the most popular radio DJs in the bay area, and had worked as a producer for favorite local acts, such as the Great Society and the Beau Brummels, allowing him to develop his engineering skills that brought a smooth, tight texture to his work with the Family Stone. "When Sly makes a record, he makes sure he grabs you and never lets go," claimed one album reviewer. "[H]e lays down rhythms in layers, so when you get tired of shaking to one, you can slip into another. Let yourself go, and by the end all five are somehow making their separate impacts. Every song is a moral instruction, to us and to himself, and they all have arrangements so full that it's impossible to find a space for any other sound, yet never so cluttered that something could be dropped out and not missed. Sock it unto others, as you would have them sock it unto you."[49]

The band's 1969 album *Stand!* reigned on the charts the longest, and is considered their artistic peak with enduring singles like "I Want to Take

You Higher" and the No. 1 hit "Everyday People," from which we get the phrase "different strokes for different folks." Sly and the Family Stone were unusual among rock and soul bands for their racial and sexual integration, which they played up in their songs that called for peace and unity. The band were known for their upbeat, celebratory hits, and with a diverse group of family and friends on board, they lived what they played. Sly was a singer, multi-instrumentalist, and talented composer, aided by his brother Fred Stewart ("Freddie Stone") on guitar, Larry Graham on bass and vocals, Greg Errico on drums and vocals, Jerry Martini on saxophone, Cynthia Robinson on trumpet, and Sly's sister Rosie Stone on piano. With an infectious, energetic sound that many believe changed soul music forever, Sly and the Family Stone originated much of the funk grooves later utilized by 1970s acts such as the Temptations, the Jackson 5, and George Clinton's bands Parliament and Funkadelic (Clinton himself later testified that "it was Sly who first cracked the barrier between black and white rock").[50]

But along with the clichéd success of the rock and roll star comes the clichéd pitfalls that inevitably follow. After *Stand!*, Sly let his game slip away from him. He began missing shows or showing up late, offering blasé performances, and gradually slipping into a world of drugs and excess. Over the course of 1970 and 1971, more than one quarter of his shows were cancelled. Between the drug abuse, illnesses, management woes, contract disputes, and lack of new material, it looked as if Sly Stone and family were bound for a short career. At one point, Sly was even evicted from his plush Los Angeles home and took to living in a camper outside the studio, where he buried himself in his recording work. Defending Sly in a *Rolling Stone* interview, his manager David Kapralik stated, "Sylvester Stewart does not create 'product.' Sylvester Stewart is an innovator, a source of new fusions, new concepts. Ya don't turn them out like you turn out pizzas. They're life statements."[51]

Kapralik's assertion was prophetically accurate—*There's a Riot Goin' On* was a life statement writ large, both a product of Stone's rapid descent into rock-star hell and a social commentary on American life in the early 1970s, particularly from the viewpoint of urban blacks. The first single to precede the album was the hit "Family Affair," an honest look at the communal living that was common at the time. "Family Affair" rose to No. 1 and would be the band's last big hit, and although its generally upbeat vibes were reminiscent of the group's earlier work, the song did not prepare audiences for the pessimism and stark honesty of the rest of the album. With instrumental help from the likes of Ike Turner, Billy Preston, and Bobby Womack (largely overshadowing his own "family" on the release), Stone let fly an album of candid commentary that included the drug-induced coma of "Luv N' Haight," the tense but melodic "Just Like a Baby," and the murky political assertions of "Africa Talks to You 'The Asphalt Jungle' " and "Thank You For Talkin' to Me Africa," the latter a slower, more depressing remake of "Thank You (Falettinme Be Mice Elf Agin)" from *Stand!*

Though *Stand!* made a stab or two at the social order with offerings such as "Stand!" and "Don't Call Me Nigger, Whitey," the hopeful tone of the lyrics, the gospel-infused vocals, and the positive underlying groove resulted in a message that was generally empowering and unifying, setting the pattern for disco that would sweep the mid-1970s. The Sly Stone that made *There's a Riot Goin' On* was an angrier man, frustrated at his own loss of control and recognizing the similarities between the flagging health of his own career and the social health of his community. The original album cover—later replaced by a concert photo—was of a red, white, and black American flag with the stars replaced by bullet holes. Such contentious social commentary ran through *There's a Riot Goin' On* from its dark lyrics to its plodding electric pianos, making it a blueprint for urban commentary by 1970s acts such as War and many rap and hip-hop artists of the 1980s and 1990s.

Album Title: *The Inner Mounting Flame*
Artist: The Mahavishnu Orchestra
Recorded: August 14, 1971, in New York City
U.S. release: December 1971 (Columbia)
Producer: John McLaughlin

Depending on how you look at it (or listen to it), John McLaughlin could be considered either the Miles Davis of the rock world or the Eric Clapton of the jazz world, though there's no reason he cannot be called both. McLaughlin was the mastermind behind the Mahavishnu Orchestra— Mahavishnu being the spiritual name McLaughlin was given by his Hindu guru Sri Chinmoy. Second only to Miles Davis in creating a fusion between jazz and rock, McLaughlin and company targeted young rock fans with *The Inner Mounting Flame*, inspiring scores of imitators that never had a chance of topping McLaughlin and his collection of virtuoso musicians.

To understand the deep complexities of what McLaughlin brought to *The Inner Mounting Flame*, it is important to be familiar with his broad musical background. Given his upbringing, it seems only natural that the Yorkshire, England-raised McLaughlin would end up as a fusion artist, contributing not only to the jazz and hard-blues genres, but incorporating Indian raga and spacey art rock into his work as well. Growing up in a musical household with a violinist mother and three musically inclined older brothers, McLaughlin was raised on classical composers such as Beethoven and studied piano from the age of nine. At twelve, he began playing his brother's guitar, and immediately set about dousing himself in the blues greats: Muddy Waters, Leadbelly, Big Bill Broonzy, and Sonny Terry. By the time he was fifteen, he had added flamenco and other world-music genres to his repertoire, copying the fingering styles of Django Reinhardt, Tal Farlow, Oscar Peterson, and Jim Hall.

Then one day, he picked up Miles Davis' *Milestones* album and was forever changed. "That completely blew away my previous concepts of how to improvise," McLaughlin told a later interviewer. "I had been aware of two movements in jazz: The West Coast thing with [Stan] Getz, [Lennie] Tristano—a cool kind of thing; the East Coast was the hard bop movement. I'm sure it wasn't like this in America, but it was as far as I was concerned, in England."[52] While immersing himself in the works of John Coltrane and Miles Davis, he maintained his love of classical music and found a new appreciation for 20th-century composers such as Béla Bartók, Anton Webern, Igor Stravinsky, Maurice Ravel, and Claude Debussy. As if this were not enough variety, he struck up an interest in Indian raga music, which would eventually make him one of the most acclaimed raga musicians in the West.

For the next decade or so, McLaughlin would work as a respected sideman in a number of R&B, jazz, and avant-garde groups in England, honing his chops and constantly exposing himself to new types of music, eventually playing with skilled acts such as the Graham Bond Organization and Lifetime, and finally backing his mentor Miles Davis on a series of major albums, including 1969's *In a Silent Way*, 1970's *Bitches Brew* (see p. 78), and 1970's *A Tribute to Jack Johnson*. In 1970, he finally formed his own band, the Mahavishnu Orchestra, who recorded *The Inner Mounting Flame* after only two weeks of playing together at the Café Au Go Go in New York's Greenwich Village.

It seemed as though the world had finally learned what the volume knob was for. With John McLaughlin on guitar, Jerry Goodman on violin, Jan Hammer on keyboard and Moog synthesizer, Rick Laird on bass, and drummer Billy Cobham—who had played with McLaughlin in Miles Davis' group—*The Inner Mounting Flame* was a monument of speed, agility, and precision. It was rare to hear rock that was both furiously loud and meticulously fine. Inspired by the sonic experiments of Jimi Hendrix, McLaughlin's compositions on *The Inner Mounting Flame* reflected both the power of Hendrix's hard blues and the improvisational imagination of Hendrix and the great jazz artists (Miles Davis chief among them).

Though released only one year after Davis' landmark fusion album *Bitches Brew*, *The Inner Mounting Flame* advanced electric jazz a generation, popularizing the use of free-flowing jazz in progressive rock and demonstrating the power of precise scales played at incredible speeds. The extraordinary talent of the band's members provided a sense of wonderment for the listener, amazed not only to be hearing such genius from each musician, but to hear each musician's skills brought to the forefront so cleanly through McLaughlin's compositions. More than just speed demons, McLaughlin and his cohorts demonstrated the ability to out-rock the rock gods of the day with songs such as "Meeting of the Spirits" and "The Noonward Race," and then show a surprisingly mellow—but still deftly articulate—side with the acoustic prowess of "A Lotus on Irish Streams" and "Thousand Island Park." "It's music that people are made to shy away from," Billy Cobham commented to an interviewer about the album, "because it's too sincere and it represents life in its real form. The fact that everybody's living a lie on the street, drugged out, eating corn flakes and thinking they're vitamins, makes it hard to take in because the music is just the opposite of all that."[53]

The classical, blues, raga, and jazz music that McLaughlin had intently studied for the past two decades had paid off in a tight amalgam of these various genres, blending seamlessly into one masterwork. Though the mixing of genres was nothing new to pop music (country-rock, folk-rock, southern rock, heavy metal, art-rock, and progressive rock had all been created within the previous decade), McLaughlin's group accomplished their particular instrumental experiment with such deep knowledge of the various genres they were dipping in to, that *The Inner Mounting Flame* came off less as a recognizable mixing of different genre elements (as, for instance, the way one can parse the classical elements and rock elements in Procol Harum's work or the folk elements and the pop elements in the Byrds' albums) and more as an actual blending of genres into a cohesive whole. This is true fusion.

The Inner Mounting Flame was unusually popular for an instrumental album. McLaughlin soon became a household name and would be known for his ability to play complex rhythms in odd time signatures with resolute passion. "The joy of music is like the joy a runner gets from running," McLaughlin later said, "and, musically, I'm running. If music doesn't carry any deep emotion, then what's it for?"[54]

NOTES

1. Bud Scoppa, "The Moody Blues: Gentle, Smooth, and Nice," *Circus*, August 1970.

2. Keith Altham, "Moody Blues: Saints or Sinners?" *New Musical Express*, October 20, 1973.

3. Scoppa, August 1970.

4. Steve Turner, "The Moody Blues: Justin Time for the Moodies," *Beat Instrumental*, June 1971.

5. Dave Laing et al., *The Electric Muse: The Story of Folk into Rock*. London: Methuen, 1975, 70.

6. Dave Marsh and John Swenson, *The New Rolling Stone Record Guide*. New York: Random House, 1983 (1979), 26.

7. Al Kooper, "The Band: *Music from Big Pink*," *Rolling Stone*, August 10, 1968.

8. Steve Turner, "Byrds Eye View," *Beat Instrumental*, June 1971.

9. David Szatmary, *A Time to Rock: A Social History of Rock And Roll*. New York: Schirmer, 1996 (1987).

10. David Dalton and Lenny Kaye, *Rock 100*. New York: Putnam, 1977.

11. Paul Friedlander, *Rock and Roll: A Social History*. Boulder, CO: Westview, 1996, 237.

12. Marsh and Swenson, 1983, 291.

13. Friedlander, 1996, 242–243.

14. Linda Martin and Kerry Segrave, *Anti-Rock: The Opposition to Rock 'n' Roll*. Hamden, CT: Archon, 1988, 261.

15. http://makemyday.free.fr/chic.htm.

16. Pam Brent, "MC5 Live at the Crow's Nest," *Creem*, March 1969.

17. Friedlander, 1996, 127.

18. Ibid., 128.

19. Ibid.

20. Lindsay Planer, www.allmusic.com.

21. Sylvie Simmons, "King Crimson," *Rolling Stone*, 1995.

22. John Morthland, "King Crimson: *In the Court of the Crimson King*," *Rolling Stone*, December 27, 1969.

23. Edward Macan, *Rocking the Classics: English Progressive Rock and the Counterculture*. New York: Oxford University Press, 1997, 179.

24. Miles, "Captain Beefheart is Alive in Hollywood," *ZigZag*, October 1969.

25. Ben Edmonds, "Captain Beefheart," *ZigZag*, August 1970.

26. Ibid.

27. Miles, October 1969.

28. Lester Bangs, "Captain Beefheart: *Trout Mask Replica*," *Rolling Stone*, July 26, 1969.

29. Edmonds, August 1970.

30. Ibid.

31. Chris Smith, *The Greenwood Encyclopedia of Rock History: The Rise of Album Rock, 1967–1973*. Westport, CT: Greenwood, 2005a, 121.

32. *Time*, March 1, 1971, cover.

33. Laing, 1975, 66.

34. Bud Scoppa, "James Taylor: *Gorilla*," *Rolling Stone*, July 17, 1975.

35. Paul Tingen, *Miles Beyond: The Electric Explorations of Miles Davis*. New York: Watson Guptill, 2001, chapter 4.

36. Ibid., chapter 5.

37. Paul Tingen, "The Making of *The Complete Bitches Brew Sessions*," 1999.

38. Metal Mike Saunders, "Black Sabbath: *Master of Reality*," The Rag, September 20, 1971.

39. Halfin, 1982, 5.

40. Metal Mike Saunders, "A Dorito and 7-Up Picnic with Black Sabbath," *Circular*, September 25, 1972.

41. *Beat Instrumental*, November 1970.

42. Simon Frith, *The Sociology of Rock*. London: Constable and Company, 1978, 83.

43. Douglas Wolk, "The Finest Children's Album Ever Made," *Salon.com*, May 25, 1999.

44. Charlie Gillett, "Joy of Cooking: *Joy of Cooking*, and Carole King: *Tapestry*," *Ink*, June 12, 1970.

45. David Ewen, *All the Years of American Popular Music*. London: Prentice-Hall, 1977, 713.

46. Marsh and Swenson, 1983, 193.

47. Friedlander, 1996, 174.

48. Stephen Thomas Erlewine, www.allmusic.com.

49. Charlie Gillett, "Soul Reviews," *Record Mirror*, 1971.

50. Szatmary, 1996, 242.

51. Fred Bronson, *The Billboard Book of Number One Hits*. New York: Billboard, 1985, 303.

52. Steven Rosen, "Mahavishnu John McLaughlin," *Guitar Player*, Feburary 1975.

53. Patrick Snyder-Scumpy, "John McLaughlin," *Crawdaddy*, November 1973.

54. Rosen, February 1975.

4
TAKE IT TO THE LIMIT, 1972–1976

In July, 1972, the rock musical *Hair* closed on Broadway after 1,741 performances that made it one of the most successful productions in Broadway history. *Hair* was the first rock musical, spawning numerous imitators and cultural battles straight out of the 1960s hippie songbook. By the time the play closed, the good vibes of 1967 San Francisco seemed like a distant memory as harder drugs, skyrocketing divorce rates, and the distancing of rock stars from their audiences brought about a schizophrenic battle between the intimate and the universal in American music. The former found a home in the massive popularity of sensitive singer-songwriters such as James Taylor, Carly Simon, and Joni Mitchell, while the latter was represented by an L. A. Memorial Coliseum concert in November 1972 (ushering in the age of stadium rock) and the Watkins Glen, New York concert in July 1973, which set records with 600,000 fans in attendance.

The largest battle in music personified this split between the corporate and the personal. The enormous popularity of progressive rock and heavy metal—with their elaborate stage productions, instrumental virtuosi, and complex, over-the-top studio concoctions—influenced landmark releases such as David Bowie's **The Rise and Fall of Ziggy Stardust and the Spiders from Mars (1972)** and 1973's *Aladdin Sane*, Jethro Tull's 1972 *Thick as a Brick*, Elton John's 1972 *Honky Chateau*, and Led Zeppelin's 1975 *Physical Graffiti*. These British releases, which continued a decade-long trend of U.K. domination on the U.S. music charts, were met with a counterattack by fresh voices demonstrating the range of promise in the American musical community, from the east-coast magic of Bruce Springsteen's **Born to Run (1975)** and Aerosmith's **Toys in the Attic (1975)** to the west-coast rock of Linda Ronstadt's **Heart Like a Wheel (1974)** and the Eagles' 1973 *Desperado*, 1976 *Hotel California*, and 1976 *Their Greatest Hits (1971–1975)*, which would eventually become the best-selling album (domestically) in all of American music.

Both live and studio technology was growing by leaps and bounds every year, and bands that proved adept at over-the-top theatricality on stage managed to bring a live feel to their recorded work, releasing live albums and double albums like the Grateful Dead's 1972 *Europe '72*, Deep Purple's 1973 *Made in Japan*, KISS' ***Alive!*** (1975), Peter Frampton's 1976 *Frampton Comes Alive!*, and Iggy and the Stooges' 1976 *Metallic K.O.* On the other end of the spectrum, studio wizardry brought some bands worldwide fame and pushed the frontiers of recorded sound with Pink Floyd's ***The Dark Side of the Moon*** (1973), Queen's ***A Night at the Opera*** (1975), Herbie Hancock's ***Head Hunters*** (1973), and Boston's ***Boston*** (1976). Lesser fame, but equal respect, found artists who were not afraid of being uncommercial, as electronica found an American audience with Kraftwerk's ***Autobahn*** (1974) and Brian Eno's ***Discreet Music*** (1975).

While studio genius was fine for carrying the ideas of the established rock gods and pioneering technical magicians, poor kids with little access had to take a different route. In August 1975, Johnny Rotten was recruited into the Sex Pistols fold when he showed up at their home base wearing an "I Hate Pink Floyd" t-shirt. This famous anecdote symbolized the frustration that disenfranchised youth felt as the gulf widened between them and their distant rock idols, leading to a string of groundbreaking punk albums kickstarted by the heavily influential garage-rock compilation ***Nuggets: Original Artyfacts from the First Psychedelic Era, 1965–1968*** (1972). Soon New York and other major cities were alight with the strains of passionate, underproduced, mostly amateurish noise like the New York Dolls' ***New York Dolls*** (1973), Iggy and the Stooges' ***Raw Power*** (1973), Patti Smith's ***Horses*** (1975), and the Ramones' ***Ramones*** (1976).

On the R&B front, Stevie Wonder turned twenty-one and won his artistic independence, keeping an ailing Motown on life support between 1972 and 1976 with arguably the greatest string of soul albums ever: *Music of My Mind, Talking Book, Innervisions, Fulfillingness' First Finale*, and *Songs in the Key of Life*. Much more elaborate and otherworldly soul techniques inspired by Sly Stone, Frank Zappa, and James Brown finally brought George Clinton's funkateers into the mainstream with Parliament's ***Mothership Connection*** (1976), and the outlaw country movement brought country-album sales a much needed boost with Willie Nelson's 1974 *Phases and Stages* and 1975 *Red Headed Stranger*, Waylon Jennings' 1972 *Ladies Love Outlaws* and 1973 *Lonesome, On'ry and Mean*, and the collaboration by Jennings, Nelson, Jessi Colter, and Tompall Glaser, ***Wanted! The Outlaws*** (1976).

Album Title: *Nuggets: Original Artyfacts from the First Psychedelic Era, 1965–1968*
Artist: Various Artists
Recorded: 1965–1968
U.S. release: 1972 (Elektra)
Producer: Jac Holzman, Lenny Kaye

So fast were the changes in pop music in the late 1960s and early 1970s that albums often seemed dated within months of their release. Every artist and band wanted to be the next Beatles or Bob Dylan or the Byrds—not stylistically, but in the sense that musical revolution was everywhere and everyone wanted to get credit for it.

In the midst of these changes, one man looked backward rather than forward. Jac Holzman, founder and president of Elektra Records, hit upon the idea to troll the waters of 1960s' psychedelic music and see what he could fish up from the deep. In a decade of greatest hits packages, throwing together a compilation of Top 10 songs was almost cliché. But Holzman was not looking for hits. He was looking for the obscure, the esoteric, the arcane garage-band tunes of the late 1960s that barely made it out of the garage and onto vinyl, but had a lasting effect on the more appreciated acts. The most successful among his selection were one-hit wonders—with the highest honors going to the No. 5 hit "Psychotic Reaction" by Count Five. The most invisible tracks, among them "Don't Look Back" by the Remains, "Let's Talk about Girls" by the Chocolate Watchband, and "An Invitation to Cry" by the Magicians completely slipped beneath the rock radar without ever seeing the charts.

With the assistance of rock historian Lenny Kaye—and by "assistance," I mean Kaye is generally credited as the primary architect of the release—*Nuggets* was ultimately whittled down to twenty-seven tracks that were meant to epitomize the garage-band ethos of the late 1960s. From somewhat-remembered bands like the Seeds, the Electric Prunes, and the Amboy Dukes, to nearly forgotten acts like the Mojo Men, Third Rail, and the Cryan' Shames, the featured bands were experimental punk and bubble-gum pop, Texas acid-rock and Long Island soul, national stars and local failures.

What they had in common, however, was their inventive contributions to the late 1960s garage-rock sound, what one critic described as "the sound of mid-'60s white, male, suburban America trying to break down the doors."[1] In the 1970s, these strains found a steady national audience in acts like the Patti Smith Group (for whom Lenny Kaye played guitar) and Talking Heads, but the style had been around for at least a decade in these local-hero bands that never achieved lasting acclaim, but influenced many of the acts that did. Caught between the cracks of the wildly popular late-1960s pop genres—folk-rock, surf music, San Francisco psychedelia, Detroit Motown, and of course, the British blues-rock invasion—the garage bands were powering local scenes and making brief appearances on the national stage to move popular music ahead one song at a time.

Hailed by one reviewer as "a wondrous double-album compilation of the sort we'd not seen before," "executed to perfection," and "visionary scholarship dressed up as great trashy fun," *Nuggets* captured the amateurish anyone-can-do-it style of early garage rock.[2] With appearances by future rock legends—Todd Rundgren in the Nazz, Ted Nugent strumming for the Amboy Dukes, and the soon to be Creedence Clearwater Revival appearing in an earlier incarnation as the Golliwogs—the album also captured the adventurous spirit that leads unknown wanna-be's to become enduring pop legends. Accompanying liner notes gave a brief biography of each band, placing them in the context of the larger mainstream movements, and helped coin the term "punk" to replace "garage" as the de-facto label describing all things loud, amateurish, and gutter-pure.

Nuggets is often placed alongside Iggy Pop and the Velvet Underground's early releases as the most important forebears to punk, new wave, and everything that came after, and is credited with almost single-handedly launching the punk movement in the 1970s. Ultimately, the album would be regarded by some of the most important bands of the 1970s and 1980s— among them R.E.M., the Ramones, Talking Heads, and the Patti Smith Group—as a major influence. Originally released by Elektra Records in 1972 and reissued by Sire Records in 1976, the album eventually found its way onto many "top albums" lists and spawned a number of similar releases with titles like *Pebbles*, *Rubble*, and *Back from the Grave*. In 1998, Rhino Records re-released the original double album on CD as part of a well-received four-CD box set that included an additional ninety-one songs from the era. The album was followed in 2001 by *Nuggets, Vol. 2: Original Artyfacts from the British Empire & Beyond*, capturing unheralded U.K. bands like the Small Faces and the Pretty Things as well as a selection of acts from countries like Brazil, Japan, and Iceland. In 2005, Rhino released *Children of Nuggets: Original Artyfacts from the Second Psychedelic Era, 1976–1995*, by this time just one of many small-label retrospectives attempting to chronicle forgotten but important contributors to the growth of popular music.

Album Title: *The Rise and Fall of Ziggy Stardust and the Spiders from Mars*
Artist: David Bowie
Recorded: September 9, 1971–January 18, 1972, at Trident Studios in London
U.S. release: September 1, 1972 (RCA)
Producer: David Bowie, Ken Scott

There was a time when musicians were not required to explain themselves. David Bowie, however, never really considered himself a musician— or at least he considered his music secondary to his "performance." With an extensive background in theater and mime, Bowie brought all of his considerable dramatic talents to bear in the early 1970s when he made glam rock an international phenomenon. There was "theater" in rock before Bowie—the Beatles' bizarre outfits and stage sets during their trippiest days, Frank Zappa's absurd displays of contempt for the audience, Alice Cooper's nightmarish visions—but they were always secondary to the music. Bowie, or at least the Bowie unleashed upon the world in the early 1970s, saw the musical performance as an avenue to get down to some really serious theater.

"Bowie is paradoxically the most facile and the most profound of rock actors," wrote one reviewer shortly after the release of *Ziggy Stardust*. "He incorporates the kosmic kuteness of Marc Bolan, the working class narrowness of spirit of Rod Stewart, the strutting sexual versatility of Mick Jagger, the deliberate destructive perversity of Alice Cooper, and the pained self-imposed alienation of "non-actors" such as Cat Stevens and James Taylor, all seemingly undercut by the popular staginess of a matinee idol in the mold of Anthony Newley. Bowie is as Hollywood as the Byrds, Jackie Curtis, or Gloria Swanson, as didactic as an eighteen century essayist, as concerned with mutability as the greatest of British myth-makers, Edmund Spencer, and as compassionately observant of middle-class "tragedy" as the James Joyce of *The Dubliners*. David Bowie, his pedigree aside, is one bitch of a rocker."[3]

As a struggling folk musician and cabaret artist in the 1960s, Bowie developed an ability to remove himself from the performance, thinking of the man on stage as a character rather than a performer. His performance method gave rise to character-driven songs, scoring his first major hit in 1969 with "Major Tom," an astronaut looking down on his home planet and asking questions about his place in the greater scheme of things. This sense of alienation, or the "outsider-looking-in" trope, became a significant element in Bowie's music, garnering him status as a cult favorite with the "outsider" set long before he began making waves in mainstream pop.

After a period reinventing himself in 1970, Bowie emerged at the end of the year with an album that marked the beginning of "classic Bowie"—an uber-alienation document called *The Man Who Sold the World*, replete with tales of perversion, insanity, and isolation. Followed closely by *Hunky Dory*, which revealed a more accessible but still chameleon-like figure in Bowie, the two albums launched him into the British spotlight, fueling the advent of his most over-the-top character, Ziggy Stardust.

Bowie had finally stopped performing as himself altogether. On January 29, 1972, he began his first tour as Ziggy, a science fiction anti-hero pop star who has foreseen the end of the world and has come from Mars (along with his band, the Spiders from Mars) to tell us about it. Bowie's ability to create such an elaborate persona—through both his songwriting and his performances—gave rise to unending speculation about "what it all means." "[Bowie has] absorbed himself in most of the avant-garde philosophies and beliefs which are bubbling beneath the surface of contemporary youth culture. Bisexuality, astral projection, magic, insanity, reincarnation, the apocalypse and ... rock 'n roll superstardom—they've all been photocopied and then put together in a collage called David Bowie. That's how the character sprung up. You are what you eat."[4]

Ziggy quickly found a home on vinyl with *The Rise and Fall of Ziggy Stardust and the Spiders from Mars*, which rocketed to No. 5 on the British charts, and made the Top 100 in the United States with no tour support. Up to this point, Bowie's success had been limited to the United Kingdom, but after American audiences became intrigued by Ziggy, Bowie's label reissued his first four albums in America, making glam-rock a viable genre in the U.S. market, and making Bowie a pop superstar.

However, it was *The Rise and Fall of Ziggy Stardust and the Spiders from Mars* that had pushed the envelope past the tipping point, bringing an entirely new level of theatricality to pop music. Its emotive melodrama and cinematic style pried open the listener's imagination in ways that songs about cars and girlfriends never had. From the desperate, doomsayer opening track "Five Years," to the cathartic mod hit "Starman"—evoking, according to one critic, Dorothy's "Somewhere Over the Rainbow"—to the final anguish of "Rock and Roll Suicide," the album is a bizarre journey for Ziggy, both introspective and world conscious, on the level of Carroll's *Alice in Wonderland* or Baum's *Wizard of Oz*, ending with the only possible, doomed conclusion for a messiah figure.

"Ziggy is a compelling droogie," claimed one review, "ultimately and almost tragically effete, but endlessly tantalizing as a manifestation of teen ego run amuck, an end in itself, justifiable, if you want it to be, in light of the imminent end of all. He is impossible, definitely an ineffectual sop against the full comprehension of man's final lost opportunity."[5] Such postmodern and hyperbolic musings seemed the only way to critique Bowie's Ziggy-era work. Bowie had combined the energy of proto-punk (Iggy Pop especially) with the world weariness of the Velvet Underground's avant-garde and the thick chords of folk and early glam to create an otherworldly sound that influenced every new genre that followed, establishing Bowie himself as a hero of punk, new wave, heavy metal, progressive rock, and avant-garde music for decades to come.

Album Title: *Raw Power*
Artist: Iggy and the Stooges
Recorded: September 10–October 6, 1972, at CBS Studios in London
U.S. release: February 1973 (Columbia)
Producer: Iggy Pop

"Nobody does it better, nobody does it worse, nobody does it, period. Others tiptoe around the edges, make little running starts and half-hearted passes; but when you're talking about the O mind, the very central eye of the universe that opens up like a huge, gaping, suckling maw, step aside for the Stooges."[6] These were the words of rock critic Lenny Kaye—himself a future punk legend as guitarist for the Patti Smith Group—just a few months after *Raw Power* was released in 1973. The album was a surprise, not just for the high caliber of its proto-punk caterwauling ("Raw Power" is the perfect title), but because it was released at all.

James Jewel Osterberg, better known as Iggy Pop, formed the Psychedelic Stooges in 1967 for a Halloween party at the University of Michigan. Over the next two years, they toured relentlessly through the Midwest, achieving notoriety for their wild performances, which often featured such antics as a shirtless Iggy smeared in peanut butter or his own blood and crawling or diving into the audience. With Dave Alexander on bass and brothers Ron and Scott Asheton on guitar and drums, the band forewent all rock-star pretensions in favor of primal instrument-thumping, completely abandoning the blues and swing roots of contemporary rock. They were, in most reflective accounts, the first true punk band.

What Lou Reed and John Cale brought to the garage-rock table with the Velvet Underground's introspective, cerebral yin, Iggy Pop's Stooges complemented with their extroverted yang, too wild even for rock, and their fans, though rabid, were too small to propel the group beyond minor cult status. In 1968, the band were signed to Elektra Records when a talent scout spotted them in Detroit opening for future-fellow punk legends MC5. Their first two albums, 1969's *The Stooges* and 1970's *Fun House*, though largely panned or ignored, vastly increased their status as cult figures, and by the time *Fun House* saw the light of day, they were minor underground gods. "Iggy transcended not only vaudevillians like Alice Cooper and his friend David Bowie but sham shamans like Jagger and Jim Morrison because his attitude was one of pure abandon. He became the one true subhuman archangel of Punk, defining it as essentially a cartoon-style death trip. This was rock's excess and exhibitionism carried over the borders of sanity."[7]

A little too predictably, however, the unruliness and drug abuse that contributed to their wild performances dragged the band's career down to the point where they could barely function. It was a minor miracle that Iggy could even keep the band together after *Fun House*, and after two years went by, many doubted the group would ever release again. But in 1972, David Bowie entered the picture as his own star was rising in the pop world. Bowie had been a long-time fan of the Stooges, and offered to take the group under his wing (in the form of his management team, MainMan) and helped them land a deal with Columbia Records for a third album.

For *Raw Power*, Dave Alexander was removed from the picture and Ron Asheton demoted to bass to make room for James Williamson, a blistering demon of a guitarist who co-wrote all eight tracks on the album. Naturally this made *Raw Power* more guitar driven than the Stooges' previous releases, but the collaboration between Pop and Williamson brought about a tighter focus, and Iggy's efforts to kick his heroin habit (or perhaps a recognition that this might be his last chance to make his band work) seemed to give him a new lease on his music as his vocals reached an unprecedented level of passion. With brash, disturbing tracks like "Search and Destroy," "Your Pretty Face is Going to Hell," and "Penetration," *Raw Power* was, well, raw and powerful, ultimately seen as a template for the revolution to come.

However, there was trouble in punk paradise as MainMan disliked Pop's production, and the album's release was halted. Pop agreed to let Bowie remix the album, which Bowie reportedly did in a cheap studio in one day, and the results—a thin, tinny, treble-heavy mix—have been both decried as ruining a great album and hailed as kick-starting punk. Bootleg versions of

Pop's original mix circulated for years, and Iggy remixed the album again decades later to—pardon the pun—mixed reviews.

Raw Power is considered the apex of the Stooges' work and a major force in the development of the early, amateurish, white-suburban garage sound that became punk. "By any formal criteria, they are a retrogressive group, a pale copy of the early Rolling Stones," wrote Lenny Kaye in a review of the band's first album. "Their music revolves around one modified Bo Diddley chord progression, and neither the singing nor musicianship on their album attains any memorable level of competence. But like the Velvet Underground...or the Seeds, or a select number of other bands, any formal criteria here become basically irrelevant in the face of what is actually happening within the music. All the above factors, negative though they seem, ultimately become necessary to the success of the Stooges, to the emotional set of moods they are trying to portray and, in consequence, they all work within the context the group members have set out for themselves. The world of the Stooges, simply, revolves around boredom."

Like the Velvet Underground before them, Iggy and the Stooges sent hundreds—perhaps thousands—of bored suburban teenagers into the dark recesses of their garage searching for dad's old drum kit, or to the pawn shop on the corner in search of a cheap electric guitar (the tuning did not matter, as long as it was *loud*), ultimately yielding a new generation of angst-ridden amateurs who vented their malaise from the top of their lungs.

Album Title: *The Dark Side of the Moon*
Artist: Pink Floyd

Recorded: June 1972–January 1973, at Abbey Road Studios in London
U.S. release: March 24, 1973 (Harvest)
Producer: Pink Floyd

"If you'd played this to an average record-company executive at the beginning of '73 and told him it would become the year's best-selling rock LP and carry off the majority of the poll-awards in its class, he'd have laughed in your face."[9] These words were written almost a year after the release of *The Dark Side of the Moon*, capturing the surprise at Pink Floyd's sudden emergence into mainstream popularity. It's not that the Floyd—as their fans called them—had "sold out." *The Dark Side of the Moon* was their ninth album, and its sophisticated aural landscape was as full of bizarrities as their previous LPs. But *Dark Side* was one of those rarities in American music that truly deserved the title "instant classic."

Most albums that reach the sacred peak of the *Billboard* charts do so in one (or several) of three ways: on the strength of one (or several) hit single; through an expensive mass-marketing campaign (aided by radio saturation which brings about those hit singles); or simply on the strength of the group's name, as an ardent fan base rushes out to buy the next album the day it is released, no matter how uneven its contents (also known as "the Rolling Stones effect"). Pink Floyd had none of these things in *Dark Side*.

The album's one hit single, "Money," reached No. 13 on the charts, but could hardly account for the album's immense popularity or its stamina as an enduring masterpiece.

Throughout the late 1960s and early 1970s, Pink Floyd were about as popular as a band could get while still being considered an underground act. They were the lead astronauts in the universe of space-rock, and while their distinct London-psychedelic sound brought synesthetic joy to legions of British fans, they barely cracked the American Top 100 with four of their pre-*Dark Side* albums. The band was, in fact, believed to be doomed at several points in their career, particularly after their resident unpredictable genius Syd Barrett was kindly booted from the group in 1968 just as they were making a splash on the London scene, leaving bassist Roger Waters, guitarist David Gilmour, drummer Nick Mason, and keyboardist Rick Wright to soldier on as best they could. But the group's first post-Barrett albums, 1968's *Saucerful of Secrets* and 1969's *Ummagumma*, were surprisingly listenable, and began to earn the band considerable concert draw as new genius was discovered in the songwriting and compositional talents of all four members. Between 1970 and 1972, their albums *Atom Heart Mother* and *Meddle* and their soundtrack *Obscured by Clouds* made small waves across the ocean, but had no major or lasting impact on the American market.

With *Dark Side*, however, the band managed to construct a sturdy bridge between the blues-based psychedelia of their forebears, the avant-garde experimentation of their earlier works, and the cutting-edge electronica that was sweeping progressive bands to new levels of pomposity. Taking approximately eight months to record and mix, *Dark Side* seemed to gather together all of the wandering bits of brilliance from their previous efforts— particularly *Ummagumma* and *Meddle*—and, using the most sophisticated studio equipment available, focus them into an incredibly tight and smooth series of songs that stood up as individual efforts and as a cohesive whole, often regarded as one of the greatest concept albums ever produced. With the use of modern studio techniques—including an echo chamber, double tracking, tape splicing, synthesizers, altered instruments, ambient noise, and brilliantly executed musique concrète (cash registers, tearing paper, adding machines, bits of chatter, and an imaginary roomful of perfectly timed clocks)—*Dark Side* dove into an abyss of aural and lyrical sophistication, tackling mature and philosophical themes of death, violence, and the fleeting moments of one's existence. "*Dark Side* is the ultimate space-rock album, a musical journey of madness, alienation, and age that includes powerful minimalist uses of space and pauses interrupted by ticking clocks and maniacal laughter. The album opens and ends with a lone heartbeat, and between the two, the universe is splayed out before the listener in long, slow beats; snippets of conversation; odd tempos and measures; Waters' brilliant songwriting; and Gilmour's captivating guitar work."[10]

Lush and thickly layered without being overbearing, the album captured the imagination of a post-60s pop audience that began to demand more from their artists. "*The Dark Side of the Moon* is a fine album with a textural and conceptual richness that not only invites, but demands involvement," claimed the LP's review in *Rolling Stone*. "There is a certain grandeur here that exceeds mere musical melodramatics and is rarely attempted in rock."[11]

The grandeur of *Dark Side* was also a touchstone for a new critical engagement with popular music by a burgeoning legion of music journalists that were not content with the simplistic notion that popular music was mere entertainment for the masses, undeserving of academic speculation. "It's a passively compassionate view of the world as seen by the British post-acid youth generation carefully linked to the bourgeois origins of that same generation," rambled one critic. "It's to do with the time/space dis-locations, of being a modern rock-star as a metaphor for the dislocation of meaning in modern society. It's to do with social insanity and our blitzed-out generation being so impotently laid-back and scared of believing in itself (and not some imported beamer from Bengal) that it can't get it to-gether to change things." [12]On the other hand, *Dark Side* and its progres-sive contemporaries helped launch the antisophistication of the punk movement, most famously sported by Sex Pistols singer Johnny Rotten and his "I Hate Pink Floyd" t-shirt.

But the most famous legacy of *The Dark Side of the Moon* is its en-durance. After only one week in the No. 1 spot, the album slipped at an almost imperceptibly slow rate down the charts, ultimately racking up 741 weeks (more than fourteen years—the first 591 weeks were consecutive) in the Top 200, a record unmatched (and practically unmatchable) in chart history. By comparison, the runner-up in terms of chart longevity was Carole King's *Tapestry* at 302 weeks on the charts, followed by Led Zep-pelin's untitled fourth album at 259 weeks. More than three decades since its release, the album still sells several hundred thousand copies a year, and is one of the twenty bestselling LPs of all time. It is estimated that one in every fourteen Americans under fifty years of age owns a copy of the album.

Despite the stellar material released by Pink Floyd throughout the 1970s, including the astonishing 1979 bestseller *The Wall*, Roger Waters claimed in a later interview that "*Dark Side Of The Moon* finished the Pink Floyd off once and for all. To be that successful is the aim of every group. And once you've cracked it, it's all over. In hindsight, I think the Pink Floyd was finished as long ago as that."[13]

Album Title: *New York Dolls*
Artist: The New York Dolls
Recorded: 1973 at the Record Plant in New York City
U.S. release: July 1973 (Mercury)
Producer: Todd Rundgren

In March of 1973, Pink Floyd's pioneering album *The Dark Side of the Moon* exploded all notions of musical limitation. It was a masterpiece of sophistication, an instant benchmark of erudite aural soundscape against which all sonic experimentation, before and since, would be measured. Three months later, the New York Dolls released *New York Dolls*. It pretty much had the opposite effect.

In an age of sweat-drenched rock gods, pompously orchestrated progressive outfits, soul-baring singer-songwriters, and west-coast country-rock harmonies, the New York Dolls decided to scrub clean the musical sophistication that had piled layer-by-layer on popular music over the previous decade and start from scratch. Talent, of course, was the first thing to go— they were a terrible, terrible band, "amateur musicians in an age of guitar prodigies, populists in a time of distant celebrities, minimal talents with maximum appetites. The New York Dolls were a garage band in search of a garage. They did not perform for the audience but performed for themselves, doing whatever they wished on stage, and if they weren't getting the sound they wanted, the solution was to turn up the volume. Anyone that desired to be a fan had to pay the price of actually listening to the music."[14]

If this credo sounds suspiciously like punk rock, there's a reason for that. Along with Iggy Pop and MC5, the New York Dolls are credited with bringing a raw, Pink-Floyd-hating amateurism to vinyl several years before the Ramones learned those three chords they played over and over and the Sex Pistols fired their bassist for having too much talent. Unlike Iggy Pop and MC5, the New York Dolls were almost completely without musical competence, and cared little for the opinions of others since commercial success seemed so unobtainable anyway. Instead they played for themselves, mocking the glittering rock stars by dressing as trashy women and strangling blues chords that had so often been used to create rather than critique. "It's a fact that LA soft rock has been stomped on by glittering lurid day-glo platform shoes worn by a female impersonating, posturing hard-rock singer," wrote one critic reviewing a New York Dolls performance in 1972. "Faggot rock, the music of total drop out."[15]

The Dolls spoke to a pent-up frustration with the increasing gap between artist and audience. Despite their lack of musicality, they attracted bohemian New York audiences to the run-down Mercer Arts Center in SoHo for the fantastic show they put on, an outrageous spoof of rock-celebrity that "got New Yorkers off their asses and on the floor, some of them hating the Dolls but loving the times they were having. The Dolls had become a symbol for hundreds of kids, one or two years out of school, chained to jobs as delivery boys or shop girls or just plain street people and hustlers, longing for some kind of communion with rock and roll heroes like Mick Jagger, Marc Bolan, and David Bowie. And then suddenly, there were the Dolls, so new and so much more real and present-time than those distant stars."[16] The Dolls were suddenly dim stars themselves, casting a smaller light but warming those who felt they had been left out in the cold. Vocalist Johnny Thunders, bassist Arthur Kane, guitarist/keyboardist Sylvain Sylvain, and drummer Billy Murcia bathed in their own light reflected off the appreciative audiences, and in 1972 headed for a low-budget tour of Europe.

Bored rock journalists latched onto the band, speaking about them as if they were rock's saviors, while deftly avoiding praise of the music itself (one can imagine them writing with one hand and trying to plug both ears with the other). After Billy Murcia drowned in a bathtub during their U.K. tour, the group's stock rose even more, hailed by one reviewer as "the best critics of rock and roll pop music has ever produced."[17] The Dolls parlayed their new-found fame (after adding Jerry Nolan on drums) into their self-titled 1973 debut, which poetically earned the group two of *Creem* magazine's most coveted readers-choice awards: "Best New Group of the Year" and "Worst New Group of the Year." Ads for the album called the Dolls "The Band You Love to Hate," and the album itself carried the tagline "A band you're gonna like whether you like it or not."

Despite unyielding praise from the tragically hip—legendary rock scribe Robert Christgau hailed the "careening screech of their music" and called them "the most exciting hard rock band in the country and maybe the world"—it was the *New York Dolls* statement rather than the album's music that got the feet jumping and the ink running.[18] Not since Frank Zappa's cutting insight on pop culture had a band made so many people stand up and exclaim, "Yeah . . . what he said!" Part Rolling Stones swagger, part David Bowie theater, part '60s girl-group pop, and part annoying teenage garage band next door, the New York Dolls gave 1970s rock a jolt that shook pop music from its mooring and allowed it to chart a new chorus through the 1970s, influencing such luminaries as the Sex Pistols, KISS, the Ramones, Guns N' Roses, the Damned, and the Smiths (whose lead singer Morrisey was reportedly once head of the New York Dolls fan club and in 2004 organized a reunion show of the band's surviving members). "Until the *New York Dolls* a hangover from the sixties had permeated the music scene," claimed a 1977 reissue of the LP. "That album was where a new decade began, where a contemporary vision of the essence of rock 'n' roll emerged to kick out the tired old men and clear the way for the New Order."[19]

Album Title: *Head Hunters*
Artist: Herbie Hancock

Recorded: 1973, at Wally Heider Studios and Different Fur Trading Co. in San Francisco
U.S. release: October 13, 1973 (Columbia)
Producer: Dave Rubinson, Herbie Hancock

If Miles Davis' own output does not already make him one of the most important figures in American musical history—he has three albums in this Top 100 list—then a look at those who went on to change music after learning from Davis should seal the deal. Davis' sidemen in the 1960s included Chick Corea, who broke new ground through the 1970s with his band Return to Forever; John McLaughlin, who brought world music into jazz and rock with his band the Mahavishnu Orchestra (see p. 89); and

Herbie Hancock, who occupies two spaces in this volume a decade apart: 1983's proto-hip-hop album *Future Shock* (see p. 170) and 1973's jazz-fusion landmark *Head Hunters*.

Though Hancock did not grow up in a musical family, he began studying classical music at seven years of age, ultimately finding influence in composers such as Stravinsky, Mahler, Ravel, and Debussy. Soon he found himself also grooving to the great jazz pianists like George Shearing, Oscar Peterson, and Erroll Garner. By the late 1950s when Hancock was studying electrical engineering at Grinnell College, he was an accomplished classical pianist as well as a learned jazz and R&B musician. Though his days were spent in the classroom studying circuits and breakers, evenings found him behind the keyboards at Chicago's great jazz clubs, where he played with stars like Coleman Hawkins and Donald Byrd.

Hancock left the engineering field for music before graduating, but his studies would later play an important role as he delved into electronic production techniques in the 1970s. "I showed interest in science even before I showed interest in music when I was a kid. So it's always kind of been in me. My first major in college, I chose electrical engineering because I was afraid of choosing music for practical purposes. I thought, 'What are the chances of me surviving as a musician compared to me surviving as an engineer?' During the middle of my second year in college, one day I looked in the mirror and said 'Look, who are you trying to kid?' you know? It just became so apparent to me that I had no choice but to be a musician."[20]

In 1962, Hancock released his debut with the legendary Blue Note label. Originally intended as a collection of cover songs, the label founder Alfred Lions was so impressed with Hancock's own compositions that he allowed him to debut without covers, making Hancock's 1962 *Takin' Off* the first Blue Note album to feature all original material. Hancock became one of Blue Note's favorite artists in the 1960s and was soon invited to join the famed Miles Davis quintet, which heavily influenced Hancock's jazz-fusion experiments. With Davis, Hancock moved on to electric keyboards, and was soon in the company of Joe Zawinul and Chick Corea (both of whom were regular Davis collaborators) as jazz's top electric keyboard players.

It was with Davis that Hancock became interested in electronic and experimental jazz, playing on Davis' renowned *In a Silent Way* while continuing to record dozens of highly regarded sessions for Blue Note. After leaving Davis and Blue Note in 1969, Hancock founded Mwandishi, a fusion ensemble that released three experimental albums between 1971 and 1973: *Mwandishi*, *Crossings*, and *Sextant*. Despite their critical acclaim, none of these albums sold well, but they provided the groundwork for his next adventure with a new ensemble called the Headhunters.

Though Hancock was by this time considered one of the great jazz musicians of the period, he also desired commercial acceptance, and began seeking a new way to tackle his music. In 1972, he began to seriously immerse himself in the study of Buddhism, which he claims guided him to success. "I started chanting for the answer to what kind of music did I want to do next. I just knew that I didn't want to do what I had been doing before that, and it occurred to me that I like James Brown and Sly Stone . . . and I thought about it, 'What would it be like if I did an album that was totally funk-based?' "[21]

For *Head Hunters*, Hancock assembled an entirely new outfit, retaining only Bennie Maupin on woodwinds for his fresh ensemble. He immersed himself in the heavy funk of Sly Stone and James Brown, seeking a more grounded approach than what he had taken before. "I began to feel that I had been spending so much time exploring the upper atmosphere of music and the more ethereal kind of far-out spacey stuff. Now there was this need to take some more of the earth and to feel a little more tethered; a connection to the earth. . . . I was beginning to feel that we (the sextet) were playing this heavy kind of music, and I was tired of everything being heavy. I wanted to play something lighter."[22]

In addition to Bennie Maupin, Paul Jackson on electric bass and marimbula, and Harvey Mason on drums, Hancock recruited ethnic percussionist Bill Summers to give the album an African vibe, incorporating exotic instruments such as congas, shekere, balafon, agogo, cabasa, hindewho, tambourine, log drum, surdo, gankoqui, and a beer bottle (used for the opening on the second track "Watermelon Man"). Hancock himself played electric piano and synthesizers on the album, and in lieu of a guitar, incorporated a clavinet, which largely defines the LP's sound.

Though Hancock was attempting a pure funk album, he could not escape his jazz background, and the record became a pivotal point in the evolution of jazz-rock fusion. From the fifteen-minute opening track "Chameleon," to a major reworking of his earlier hit "Watermelon Man" (borrowed from his 1962 Blue Note debut *Takin' Off*), to the hard-funk of "Sly," to the surprisingly mellow lounge of "Vein Melter," the album was a driving, danceable, percussion-heavy assemblage that found a large crossover audience, reaching No. 13 on the pop charts and becoming one of the best-selling jazz albums of all time until the new-age jazz of Kenny G swept the market years later. Though initially panned by jazz critics, who accused Hancock of selling out, *Head Hunters* stood the test of time to be regarded as one of the key documents of jazz fusion, influencing not only jazz and rock musicians but later rap, soul, and hip-hop artists who found a touchstone in Hancock's rich blend of jazz and funk.

Album Title: *Autobahn*
Artist: Kraftwerk
Recorded: 1974, at Conny Plank's personal studio in Cologne, Germany
U.S. release: November 1974 (Vertigo)
Producer: Conny Plank

"Kraftwerk have become one of the most important new acts to be released so far this year," wrote a *Circus* reviewer shortly after the issuing of Kraftwerk's *Autobahn* in the United States. "It's simple electronic music, totally in control, unemotional and detached. It's the kind of music you can put on in the background and forget about. I would imagine it would be an excellent cure for insomnia, as it sends you off into a lovely dreaming trance." Though it hardly makes one want to run out and buy the album, this review was representative of the notice *Autobahn* generated among music critics when it took American listeners—and the charts—by surprise.

Autobahn was not music to dance to like much of 1960s and 1970s pop, it was music to listen to, music that supposedly had some profound statement to make about man's relationship with his growing army of machines (machines that, ironically, made it possible to create this musical statement in the first place). Such cerebral engagement invited no end of flexing from journalists eager to show off their analytical muscle. "It is more than just a record," claimed Lester Bangs, "it is an indictment. An indictment of all those who would resist the bloodless iron will and order of the ineluctable dawn of the Machine Age."[24] In the 1960s, many subgenres of pop music were trying to give away answers. But early 1970s acts like Kraftwerk, the New York Dolls, and David Bowie were much more interested in posing questions, and with their postindustrial technology-based method of music making, Kraftwerk opened up a whole new conversation.

Founded by Ralf Hütter and Florian Schneider, who met as classmates at Düsseldorf Conservatory, Kraftwerk were one of the premiere "krautrock" bands, a term applied by the U.S. and U.K. press to the "kosmiche" music coming out of Germany in the early 1970s. "Kosmiche"—or "cosmic"— music came about through Germany's unique drive toward the progressive and avant-garde as the country attempted to move on from the cultural devastation of World War II. Along with contemporary acts such as Can, Faust, and Neu!, Kraftwerk (the name means "power station") set on a path toward postmodern artistic engagement by embracing technology as a source for music rather than just a means with which one could produce music. "The beauty of Kraftwerk, misunderstood and ignored by so many, lies in the fact that the unique rhythms and textures, the timeless melodies, are the faultless execution of a thoroughly radical ideology," wrote one *Autobahn* reviewer. "The snapshot simplicity of their pop portraits is the culmination of rigorous analysis and investigation. Mentally and sonically decades ahead of their contemporaries, Kraftwerk's work was underpinned by an embracing (not glorification or vilification) of technology. Born into the ecologically mobilized generation of post-war politicized Germans, they realized that retreating to the countryside was futile, and absorbed and harnessed what their contemporaries feared. They turned the sounds of car engines and factories into symphonies, and made the computers of state oppression sing harmlessly."[25]

Kraftwerk went through several band members and several albums before recording *Autobahn* in 1974 with Hütter and Schneider on vocals, keyboards, and synthesizers; Wolfgang Flür on electronic percussion; and Klaus Roeder on guitar and electric violin (with Schneider also adding a bit of flute to the proceedings and producer Conny Plank creating much of the band's trademark trance in the studio). The twenty-two-minute opening title track, which makes up more than half the album, is a steady, hypnotic adventure in minimalism, just predictable enough to be catchy, but not so repetitive as to bore the listener. The track is meant to be a musical representation of driving on the autobahn, with electronic swooshes and clicks layered over the synthesizers and keyboards, and the occasional repeating phrase "Wir fahren fahren fahren auf der autobahn"—often misheard by non-Germans as "fun fun fun on the autobahn," invoking the specter of the Beach Boys car surfing over endless highways. "Fahren" actually means "driving" rather than "fun," but the misheard lyrics do not substantially alter the intent of the song. "That is wrong, but it works," claimed percussionist Flür. "Driving is fun. We had no speed limit on the autobahn, we could race through the highways, through the Alps, so yes, fahren fahren fahren, fun fun fun ... We used to drive a lot, we used to listen to the sound of driving, the wind, passing cars and lorries, the rain, every moment the sounds around you are changing, and the idea was to rebuild those sounds on the synth."[26]

In late 1974, the musical road trip found its way onto American highways via thousands of car radios playing a severely edited three-minute version of the song. Some radio stations even played the entire twenty-two-minute version from the album, helping propel the song to No. 25 on the U.S. charts and the album to No. 5, a remarkable feat for an unknown, foreign band playing a bizarre synth-pop in a time when Americana jams, singer-songwriter ballads, and power-chord-driven hard rock ruled the airwaves. In concert, the band were even more removed, dressing in matching suits and standing still in front of identical synthesizer units with nary a head bob or bootie shake between them. But with the release of *Autobahn*, the band became the top group in Germany and opened American ears to an entire world of electronica, paving the way for acts like Brian Eno and Tangerine Dream to imagine sonic possibilities that would lead to ambient, house, techno, synth-pop, and new age music throughout the next few decades.

Album Title: *Heart Like a Wheel*
Artist: Linda Ronstadt
Recorded: June–September 1974, at the Sound Factory in Los Angeles
U.S. release: November 1974 (Capitol)
Producer: Peter Asher

Of all the transformations in popular music in the late 1960s and early 1970s, the genre of country-rock was among the most unexpected. Country music and folk had enjoyed their heydays throughout the century, and indeed had been major influences on the rockabilly of the 1950s and the psychedelic revolution of the 1960s. But country and western music never took off as a sweeping, consumer-driven market until its rural sounds were blended with 1960s rock by bands such as Poco, the Byrds, the Band, and the

Flying Burrito Brothers. "It was hard singing country music a few years back because the kids just didn't know what to make of it," claimed Linda Ronstadt in 1974. "I remember playing in New York and people would want to dance: they'd hear fiddles and would wanna stomp their feet but they were afraid it would be uncool. Now, country music is hip."[27]

Ronstadt was one of the major reasons country became hip, as she spent the early 1970s interpreting a wide range of rock, folk, soul, and country material with a distinctively smooth, urban twang, a style that came to be known as the "California sound" because of the many Los Angeles musicians that churned it out. Throughout the 1970s, some of the most successful bands of the decade achieved enormous popularity with variations on this sound, including chart toppers like Fleetwood Mac, the Band, Crosby, Stills, Nash and Young, and the Eagles, who had begun life as Ronstadt's touring band in 1971.

With her powerful soprano voice, Ronstadt seemed able to convincingly attack any genre. In the mid-1960s, her folk group the Stone Poneys were a favorite on the California circuit, scoring the Top 20 hit "Different Drum" before Ronstadt went solo in 1968. Initially, her work was uneven or unfairly overlooked—her third solo effort, 1972's *Linda Ronstadt*, barely made the charts at No. 163, but contained excellent covers of songs by Johnny Cash, Jackson Browne, J. D. Souther, and Neil Young, with backing by a talented session band that would soon become the Eagles. Her next outing, 1973's *Don't Cry Now*, slowly crept up to No. 45 on the charts, but honed her ability to shape a unique country-rock sound without the overshadowing blues tinge embedded in the voices of many of her female contemporaries. Ronstadt was an interpreter rather than a singer-songwriter, engaging both standards and new material by unknown writers. "Ronstadt fulfilled the same role for California singer/songwriters in the mid-Seventies that Judy Collins did for East Coast writer/performers in the late Sixties," claimed Dave Marsh in the *Rolling Stone Record Guide*. "Indeed, it can be argued that Ronstadt's most important artistic contribution has been giving exposure of such new songwriting talents as [Anna] McGarrigle, Karla Bonoff, and Warren Zevon to a wider public."[28]

For her follow-up to *Don't Cry Now*, Ronstadt teamed with Peter Asher, who had found fame in the 1960s as half of the English folk duo Peter and Gordon. Asher became Ronstadt's manager and producer, helping her bring about a focused country-rock sound on *Heart Like a Wheel*, her 1974 No. 1 release that launched her career as one of the most successful artists of the decade. Powered by the smash singles "You're No Good" (a No. 1 hit) and "When Will I Be Loved" (charting at No. 2), *Heart Like a Wheel* brought Ronstadt into her own with powerful readings of oldies from the Everly Brothers and Hank Williams coupled with new songs by the likes of Anna McGarrigle and James Taylor. Much of the credit for the album's engrossing sound has been attributed to producer Asher, who deftly combined Ronstadt's energy and vocal muscle with sensitive theme matter to create an album of power-ballads, as invigorating as they were tender. "All my other albums, I've stood over everyone like a vulture while they did every little bit of work on it," said Ronstadt. "But I actually got to trust Peter! About halfway through the album, I said to myself, 'Hey, he's okay'...he's an incredibly creative producer. Most of the vocals were done live over the tracks, which always makes a lot of difference. The last album I did took about a year and a half, and it was just really hard. So this one was relatively easy."[29] Part of the credit also goes to Andrew Gold, a multi-instrumentalist that Asher brought in for the album. Gold replaced some of the lackadaisical instrumentation from Ronstadt's earlier albums with original, emotive guitar, piano, and percussion, complementing Ronstadt's strong voice with robust accompaniment.

Throughout her career, Ronstadt was often regarded as a sex object first and a musician second, a view brought about by her very open sexuality and indiscreet stage outfits. With *Heart Like a Wheel*, however, she was able to assert her musical talents as a prime mover of the album rather than taking directions from others. "For the first time, everybody's sexpot shows confidence in her own intelligence," claimed rock critic Robert Christau of the album. "As a result, she relates to these songs instead of just singing them."[30] Ronstadt credited Asher with helping her to realize her vision after she had felt restricted by other producers. "Peter was the first person willing to work with me as an equal, even though his abilities were far superior to mine," she told *Rolling Stone*. "I didn't have to fight for my ideas....All of a sudden making records became so much more fun."[31] Between Ronstadt, Asher, and Gold, a landmark album brought about a wave of popularity for country-rock and the California sound, helping the Eagles, Fleetwood Mac, and Ronstadt herself to rank among the most successful acts of the 1970s.

Album Title: *Toys in the Attic*
Artist: Aerosmith
Recorded: January–February 1975, at the Record Plant in New York City
U.S. release: April 1975 (Columbia)
Producer: Jack Douglas

They called it the "British Invasion" for a reason. The first wave brought the Beatles, the Kinks, and the Rolling Stones. Eric Clapton contributed with a string of outfits, including the Yardbirds, Cream, Blind Faith, and Derek and the Dominoes. By the early 1970s, British domination of the American charts expanded with the overwhelming force of Led Zeppelin, the post-Beatles momentum of a solo George Harrison and Paul McCartney's Wings, the catchy new work of Elton John, and a host of genre benders that included Pink Floyd, Yes, David Bowie, Queen, Bad Company, Black Sabbath, the Who, Traffic...the list goes on. American acts were unable to match the sheer variety of talent imported from England and its environs, and while headway was made with San Francisco psychedelia, L.A.-based soft rock, some late Motown discoveries, and the new singer-songwriter movement, hard blues was firmly the domain of our neighbors to the east, the simplistic party rock of Grand Funk Railroad and Canadian band Bachman-Turner Overdrive notwithstanding.

Then along came Aerosmith. Sure, they looked and sounded a lot like the Rolling Stones, but the Stones themselves were little more than a composite of their forebears, yet managed to create a large catalog of catchy riffs that came to embody hard blues in the minds of every American teen up to this point. *Toys in the Attic*, Aerosmith's third album, was an announcement that hometown heroes had been found to challenge the U.K. domination of hard blues in the United States. "By the time it was recorded, the band's sound had developed into a sleek, hard-driving hard rock powered by simple, almost brutal, blues-based riffs. Many critics at the time labeled the group as punk rockers, and it's easy to see why—instead of adhering to the world-music pretentions of Led Zeppelin or the prolonged gloomy mysticism of Black Sabbath, Aerosmith stripped heavy metal to its basic core, spitting out spare riffs that not only rocked, but rolled. Steven Tyler's lyrics were filled with double entendres and clever jokes and the entire band had a streetwise charisma that separated them from the heavy, lumbering arena rockers of the era."[32]

Vocalist Tyler and guitarist Joe Perry soon tired of comparisons (both visual and aural) to the Stones' Mick Jagger and Keith Richards, preferring to accentuate Tyler's own clever lyrics and Perry's raw, catchy guitar hooks. With Brad Whitford on rhythm guitar, Tom Hamilton on bass, and Joey Kramer on drums, the fivesome combined Led Zeppelin's lively chops with the Stones' bloozy swagger and their own brand of gritty wordplay and guitar hooks to create a more playful hard blues that would largely define American rock over the next decade. Joe Perry—a big fan of former Yardbird Jeff Beck—modeled his guitar playing on the Yardbirds and his showmanship on the New York Dolls, who he felt encapsulated the independence and explosiveness a live band should.

Perry and Tyler had met in a New Hampshire ice cream parlor in 1970, and with Tom Hamilton they formed a power trio featuring Tyler on drums. By the end of the year, the trio became a quintet and moved to Boston with Tyler taking over vocals full time. Endless touring and rehearsal refined their sharp edges and earned them minor chart positions with their first two albums, 1973's *Aerosmith* and 1974's *Get Your Wings*. Finally, in 1975, *Toys in the Attic* found them in top form with a coarse, spirited style that appealed to the wild and confused hormone-influenced tastes of the American teenage market—in short, they sang about sex. From a cover of the dirty-blues classic "Big Ten Inch Record" to the less-than-subtle "Uncle Salty" and "Adam's Apple" to the album's most enduring hits "Walk This Way" and "Sweet Emotion," the band had found a unique formula that paired Perry's catchy, sleazy riffs with Tyler's equally catchy, sleazy lyrics and vocals, capturing the raw power of the British blues, but replacing its self-aware weightiness with an energetic party vibe more often found in southern rock and Philadelphia soul.

Not terribly dissimilar from their fellow '70s superstars KISS (though the latter band got more mileage from their love of theatricality), the two groups ignited the decade's party-rock scene. "Although their eponymous debut albums were released within a year of each other (*Aerosmith* in 1973, *KISS* in '74), by the time both bands were running at full speed in '76, Aerosmith's knack for punching out fast and greasy, riff-driven rockers with equal measures of punkish élan and Stones-inspired grit and swagger made them the band of choice for America's "cooler" older brothers (and sisters). By comparison, KISS, lunchboxes and comic books in tow, was for kids."[33]

Toys in the Attic launched Aerosmith from the barroom corner to the arena stage, bringing America its own version of the Yardbirds, less than a decade later but an entire generation of listeners different, a generation that had little respect for purity of genre or for honoring musical roots. Aerosmith was here-and-now music, punchy, raw, and fun to bob your head to. Publicly, the band made themselves generally unavailable to the press, saddling themselves with a reputation as having the same bad-boy attitude attributed to the early Rolling Stones (though much less the media whores, Aerosmith did little to dissuade the notion). But while the Stones' arrogance was largely calculated media fodder to offset the lovable Beatles, Aerosmith were dirty through and through, lyrics, riffs, and lifestyle, and their fans loved them for it. Much of their bad-boy press came about from frustrated journalists who were not satisfied with mundane answers to their mundane questions. But more in-depth coverage revealed the band to be rock fans as much as rock stars, as excited to be in the pit watching a show as they were being the show. The band simply loved playing together, never worrying too much about "making it big," a joy of performance captured on *Toys in the Attic*. An interviewer once wrapped up a Q&A with Perry—who had quickly become a guitar idol to thousands of teenage fans—with the question, "What do you tell somebody who wants to be a good guitar player?" Perry answered: "I don't know—go ask a good guitar player."[34] Such modesty flew in the face of their public image as conceited rock stars, but belied the focus they achieved on *Toys in the Attic*, a heavily skilled but intentionally raw hard-blues act that were genuinely concerned that their audience was having a good time.

Album Title: *Born to Run*
Artist: Bruce Springsteen
Recorded: 1975, at the Record Plant in New York City and 914 Sound Studio in Blauvelt, New York
U.S. release: August 25, 1975 (Columbia)
Producer: Bruce Springsteen, Jon Landau, Mike Appel

"Is Springsteen the new Dylan?" The question lingered in music publications and average living rooms throughout the mid-1970s. It had been asked before, with a host of names inserted in Springsteen's place—Kris

Kristofferson, John Prine, Loudon Wainwright III—all talented artists who just could not live up to the weighty albatross slung about their neck. Would Springsteen be the next "almost was"?

Steve Turner took a different approach. In a 1973 article in *New Musical Express*—two years before Springsteen charted a single album—Turner asked his audience, "Was Bob Dylan the Previous Bruce Springsteen?" "Springsteen's a hungry, scrawny-looking guy," noticed Turner. "There's definitely something very Dylany about his whole being, about his curly licking hair and his scrub beard... and, I must say it, about his songs. It's a comparison a lot of people are going to draw because of the connections with Hammond, the looks, and the highly influenced style of writing. [Springsteen] himself must be regretting the resemblances because the surest way of killing a man these days is to liken him to the late Bob. Too many people have been primed to walk in to those boots only to find they didn't fit."

Turner's mocking of Dylan as "the late Bob" is intentional and telling. Dylan's albums over the previous few years had been less than stellar, and his comeback opus *Blood on the Tracks* was still two years in the future, leaving a blue-collar-hero-sized gap in the pop music world. Despite the career-killing hype, Springsteen was just what audiences needed—a fresh face with a guy-next-door persona who sang about common people with their common hopes and fears. "The other fault with PBDs (potential Bob Dylans)," Turner continued, "is that people choose them on looks and sound alone, thinking that's what made BD into BD. It wasn't. BD filled the psychological need of a generation. Where there isn't a psychological need there'll be no BD or indeed no PBD."[35]

Springsteen didn't just fill a psychological need, he filled it with raw, powerful lyrics as stirring as anything Dylan had ever concocted in his heyday as the voice of the everyman. Springsteen was the new everyman for a new decade, replacing Dylan's universal "Masters of War" and "Subterranean Homesick Blues" with the more intimate strains of "Thunder Road" and "Born to Run." Not that Dylan was not also a master of the personal, but Springsteen's passionate, almost desperate tales of loss and hope, of desire and promise, were perfectly suited for the directionless, self-absorbed audiences of the 1970s that were still reeling from the broken promises of the 1960s. "I saw rock and roll's future," gushed well-known music critic Jon Landau in 1974, "and its name is Bruce Springsteen."[36]

Landau was so impressed with Springsteen—still playing small clubs around the Northeast—that he signed on to his management team and helped produce the breakthrough *Born to Run* the following year, launching Springsteen onto the national stage with the kind of awe and might that Jimi Hendrix got out of *Are You Experienced* in 1967 and Nirvana would get out of *Nevermind* in 1991. *Born to Run* was an explosive album, not only showcasing a tremendously talented newcomer to the pop-icon set, but introducing the first singer-songwriter with the energy and propulsion of a rock star. Springsteen's previous albums, 1973's *Greetings from Asbury*

Park, N.J. and *The Wild, the Innocent and the E Street Shuffle*, failed to chart before *Born to Run* was released, and though fine albums in their own right, neither captured the exhausting live performances Springsteen and his polished entourage were becoming famous for. "What a band," gushed Bud Scoppa reviewing a performance shortly after *Born to Run* hit the shelves. "Even without the boss they'd be one of the best in the business; with him they're practically unrivalled. A magically balanced coupling of the rough-neck and the refined, of the cocky and the charming, of gutter-raunch and purple majesty, they're right there with Springsteen at every turn, in every sense. In an instant, they can recreate summer of '68 on the Jersey Shore, or 1935 on 125th Street, or they can drop the bottom out and suddenly you're alone in a bedroom with a lover or in an alley with a shadow. You don't think of words like 'resonance' or 'majesty' while it's happening in front of you—you think, 'Man, this is fun, and I'm really happy, and I don't ever want it to end.'"[37]

Landau's 1974 performance review fueled the hype surrounding Springsteen, and the eagerly awaited *Born to Run* did not disappoint, soaring to No. 3 and remaining on the charts for more than two years. So keenly anticipated was *Born to Run* that it pushed both of Springsteen's previous albums onto the charts at No. 59 and 60—two months before *Born to Run* was even released. With a string of follow-up albums over the next decade, all of them charting in the Top 5, Springsteen became the undisputed poet laureate of the working class, as well as a monumental influence on nearly every songwriter of note that followed in his wake. "Bruce Springsteen is just a prisoner of his dreams," wrote one reviewer in 1975 as the Boss was on the brink of stardom, "honest and aware enough to accurately depict the dilemmas facing someone growing up in these times, sensitive enough to capture their emotional quandaries in attempting to deal with them. . . . It works because Springsteen has lived and sings of experiences and fantasies common to all: joining the circus, hanging out in amusement parks and pinball arcades, cruising in the summer looking for love, skipping school and acting cool, staying out all night. The effect is galvanizing on vinyl; live, with the E Street Band playing like a jungle fire behind him, Springsteen's impact is riveting. If rock'n'roll has ever struck a responsive chord in your soul, this man will affect you.[38]

Album Title: *Alive!*
Artist: KISS
Recorded: March–June 1975 (on tour)
U.S. release: September 10, 1975 (Casablanca)
Producer: Eddie Kramer

Hey, twelve-year-olds need heroes too. In the middle of the 1970s, teenagers had their Led Zeppelin and Alice Cooper, young adults had their Rolling Stones and Elton John, grown-ups had James Taylor and Wings, and

KISS' 1975 live album *Alive!*, which launched the band's career and created a form of heavy metal that teeny-boppers could enjoy. *Courtesy of Universal Music Enterprises.*

everyone pretty much shared Pink Floyd. But what of the wee ones? Who could they look up to?

Enter KISS, one of the most successful and derided, unusual and predictable, hardcore and comical bands of the decade. "Kiss have the ability to make an energetic single, utterly disposable and totally entertaining," wrote one reviewer shortly before their fourth album, *Alive!*, launched the band toward stardom. "Granted that you may not walk around humming Kiss songs to yourself, and you probably don't even know most of the titles either. The lyrics won't be quoted, and you couldn't possibly care who wrote or played what. But Kiss have a solidity, direction and stance which has to rate them as one of the most significant bands around today. They probably won't be around for many years to come, but who cares—they're here right now, and that's all that counts."[39]

Taking advantage of the escapist 1970s (divorce rates skyrocketing, hard drugs replacing marijuana, the '60s dream dead or dying), KISS indulged in pure theater, the same over-the-top comic surrealism that drove the *Rocky Horror Picture Show* phenomenon. David Bowie had already brought theater to rock with his Ziggy Stardust and Aladdin Sane characters, and Alice Cooper came to the Halloween party dressed as himself, but KISS did not bother with the cerebral social commentary of the former or the pointed wit of the latter. With studded leather outfits, seven-inch-high platform boots, and heavy makeup, guitarist and singer Paul Stanley ("the Starchild"), guitarist Ace Frehley ("the Spaceman"), bassist Gene Simmons ("the Demon"), and drummer Peter Criss ("the Catman") took rock to a new extreme, creating music that was not something to listen to as much as it was something to unite over. No one old enough to have a driver's license really took the band seriously (particularly the critics), but most agreed it was fun while it lasted.

To everyone's surprise, it lasted quite a while. Before their breakthrough live double-album *Alive!* in late 1975, the band had already released three LPs over the previous 18 months to limited success and excessive ridicule, but built a considerable reputation as a dominating opening act, so much so that some headliners refused to play with them for fear of being over-shadowed. By mid-1975, KISS was in the red from lackluster reception of their first three albums, sometimes touring on the strength their manager's American Express limit. By the time *Alive!* was released, the band had been thoroughly flogged by the press, and they were several hundred thousand dollars in debt. It is fitting that their breakthrough LP was a live album, capturing the energy and party atmosphere of their sets, best encapsulated by their immortal No. 12 hit "Rock and Roll All Nite."

"Kiss are one of the few groups fighting against the trend of understand-able rock and roll, which is precisely why they have succeeded. Too many bands these days want to be understood and accepted by the mass media outside of traditional rock scenarios. That's exactly what killed rock and roll since 1968. It killed the Stones. It killed Alice Cooper. It killed David Bowie. Once rock gets too serious or moves outside its milieu onto the pages of *Time* or onto the stage of the Metropolitan Opera, it's lost."[40] While it is true KISS did not care too much about being understood, their formula was not exactly hard to decipher. Teenyboppers picked up on it quickly, and with a string of successful follow-up albums through the 1970s, their audience got younger and younger. The band latched on to the bicycle-and-curfew set with an astounding array of products—from KISS bubblegum cards to KISS toys to KISS lunchboxes to KISS comic books—creating one of the most devoted fan bases in all of rock, dubbed the "KISS Army" (albeit an army whose parents had to drive them to the concerts) that numbered more than 100,000. As the band's popularity increased, their shows became more elaborate and entertaining—including massive pyro-technic displays, fire-breathing, blood-spitting, flaming guitars, and Peter Criss' famous levitating drums—until the band resembled an amusement park ride more that a rock outfit.

KISS elevated rock theater to its most extreme, taking the urban glam of the New York Dolls and setting it on fire (literally as well as figuratively), and influencing a whole generation of pop-metal that would dominate the 1980s. Amazingly, the band survived (with occasional lineup changes) through the next two decades with regular comeback albums and publicity-oriented stunts and tours (including a reunion of the original lineup in 1996 that became one of the highest-grossing tours of the year). If it were not for 1975's *Alive!*, the band may have been a footnote in rock history, as they were deeply in debt and their label, Casablanca, was on the verge of bankruptcy. But by bringing their live show to vinyl, the group established themselves as one of the most potent bands in rock, and proved that a thick layer of showmanship can adequately cover a thin layer of material. "Kiss have always worked outside the normal framework of rock and roll," wrote a reviewer at the height of KISS's fame in 1977. "Not for them the mundane life of bands like the Rolling Stones. They've never done anything so pe-destrian as to get up onstage, play good music and send the audience home satisfied."[41]

Album Title: *Horses*
Artist: Patti Smith
Recorded: 1975, at Electric Lady Studios in New York City
U.S. release: November 1975 (Arista)
Producer: John Cale

Patti Smith's 1975 debut *Horses*, which became a touchstone for 1970s' punk and new-wave acts. *Courtesy of Photofest.*

Rock stars, being rock stars, are often little else. Like the professional athlete or super-model who have little to fall back on when their career ends on a mis-timed step, the rock star is a specialist rather than a dilettante, a professional entertainer whose role changes little with the occasional leap to the screen or the political arena.

Patti Smith was more than an exception to the rule, she was a new kind of pop icon, an anti-rock-star operating simultaneously as an entertainer and a critic, predating (and heavily influencing) the new-wave and punk genres that exploded across the latter 1970s in a fit of collective scorn for all things pretentiously virtuosic. Before becoming queen of the New York underground in 1974 and releasing her debut album *Horses* in 1975, Smith had already established herself among the bohemian intelligentsia as a brainy and energetic purveyor and critic of the arts world.

Growing up in working-class New Jersey in the late 1950s and 1960s, Smith claimed she always felt like an outsider, and the experiences of her late teens—a factory job, an unexpected pregnancy, and expulsion from the local community college—seemed to doom her to a life of general insignificance. After a move to New York City in 1967, Smith befriended the hippest of the Village avant-garde, including playwright Sam Shepard, with whom she co-wrote the play *Cowboy Mouth*, rock critic Lenny Kaye, who provided a musical bedrock for Smith's poetry [and was chief architect of the landmark compilation album *Nuggets: Original Artyfacts from the First Psychedelic Era* (see p. 96)], and erotic photographer Robert Mapplethorpe, with whom Smith shared a tiny apartment in the Chelsea Hotel, an artist haven that had housed everyone from Bob Dylan to Dylan Thomas.

Smith immersed herself in New York's art and counterculture scene, and by 1974 had earned respect for her self-published poetry, as a lyricist for emerging metal band Blue Öyster Cult, and as a critic for rock's hippest magazines. Kaye and Smith had been irregularly performing together (Kaye's rhythm guitar backing up Smith's poetry) since 1971, and with the addition of keyboardist Richard Sohl and later guitarist/bassist Ivan Kral, the group began playing a mix of spoken word, avant-garde experiments, and rock oldies at Max's Kansas City and the newly opened CBGB, often performing alongside the band Television and helping form New York's post-Velvet Underground punk scene.

Smith and Kaye's experiments were risky and geared toward the appreciative, unconventional audiences that sought out music's darker corners, and Smith proved to be a Svengali-like performer as well as a highly skilled wordsmith. "Patti Smith has an aura that'd probably show up under ultra violet-light," claimed notable rock critic Charles Shaar Murray, reviewing a pre-*Horses* performance at CBGB. "She can generate more intensity with a single movement of one hand than most rock performers can produce in an entire set. . . . She stands there machine-gunning out her lines, singing a bit and talking a bit, in total control, riding it and steering it with a twist of a shoulder here, a flick of a wrist there—scaled down bird-like movements that carry an almost unbelievable degree of power, an instinctive grasp of the principles of mime that teach that the quality and timing of a gesture is infinitely more important than its size. . . . For the duration of her set that night, Patti Smith embodied and equalled everybody that I've ever dug on a rock and roll stage."[42]

In 1975, Arista Records president Clive Davis offered Smith a record deal, flying in Velvet Underground legend John Cale to produce her debut album. *Horses* became a landmark for both punk and new wave, inspiring a raw, almost amateurish energy for the former and a critical, engaging reflexivity for the latter. With tracks ranging from a hungry interpretation of the '60s garage gem "Gloria" to the literate and terrifying "Land of a Thousand Dances," *Horses* opened the door to a new world of rock that was simultaneously crude and sophisticated. Smith as a figurehead almost overwhelmed her own work, earning the title "punk rock's poet laureate" and opening the door for strong, intelligent women in pop music who can entertain both men and women as an artist rather than as a prisoner of gender. The album cover for *Horses* is one of the most appreciated in popular music, a simple black and white photo of Smith—looking as simultaneously erotic and androgynous as David Bowie ever did—taken by Robert Mapplethorpe. With almost no airplay, the album cracked the Top 50 on the *Billboard* charts, paving the way for commercial success for a host of punk and new-wave acts.

"For some of us, Patti Smith is the girl of our rock and roll dreams," wrote one scribe several months after *Horses* hit the shelves. "As a performer she doesn't merely flirt with danger, she seduces it, trying at the same time to be both audacious and ingratiating, to challenge an audience and win it over. Of course, there's never been a rock star that mattered who didn't provoke some hostility, and she passes that qualification with ease. . . . Patti Smith is a rampage, fairly bursting with a talent that scatters fragments in all possible directions, and whatever her failures, they are certainly not failures of nerve. She wants it all."[43]

Album Title: *Discreet Music*
Artist: Brian Eno
Recorded: May 9–September 12, 1975, at Brian Eno's private studio
and Trident Studios in London
U.S. release: December 1975 (EG Records)
Producer: Brian Eno

Ambient music was born in a hospital bed. In early 1975, Brian Eno was injured in an automobile accident from which he spent several months recuperating. One night, while lying incapacitated in bed, a storm moved in and the rain grew loud outside his open window. Eno was irritated that he could barely hear the 18th-century harp music from his stereo above the din, and unable to turn up the volume, he resigned himself to the annoyance. "I drifted into this kind of fitful sleep, a mixture of painkillers and tiredness," recalled Eno. "And I started hearing this music as if I'd never heard music before. It was a really beautiful experience. I got the feelings of icebergs. I would occasionally just hear the loudest parts of the music, get a little flurry of notes coming out above the sound of the rain . . . and then it would drift away again."[44]

The experience changed Eno's understanding of music, but in a sense it was an inevitable progression of Eno's interest in avant-garde sounds. Brian Peter George St. John le Baptiste de la Salle Eno has been a pivotal figure in the development of electronica since the 1960s, pioneering the use of the studio as an instrument in itself rather than as a tool to process traditional instruments. "I can't play any instruments in any technically viable sense at all," said Eno in 1974 just as his studio experiments were beginning to receive critical respect. "And it's one of my strengths, I think, actually. Simply because I believe technique is as much a barrier as a way of opening something up."[45]

Like many figures from the 1970s musical avant-garde, Eno was an art school alum who drew on mediums such as painting and sculpture to enhance his understanding of the musical process. One of the first artists to delve into the recently invented tape recorder as a creative instrument, Eno engaged in all sorts of nontraditional musical endeavors in the late 1960s and early 1970s, including work with the art troupe Merchant Taylor's Simultaneous Cabinet, the improv-rock outfit Maxwell Demon, and the avant-garde musical ensembles Cardew's Scratch Orchestra and the Portsmouth Sinfonia. Eno's public cache took off when he joined Bryan Ferry's glam-rock band Roxy Music in 1971, where he manned a synthesizer and electronically "treated" the band's sound. Reportedly the critical attention lavished on Eno created a rift between he and frontman Ferry, and Eno left the group after stamping his signature on the band's first two albums, 1972's *Roxy Music* and 1973's highly regarded *For Your Pleasure.*

Free from the bonds of subordination and enjoying a surge of outside interest in his experiments, Eno embarked on a string of projects that provided a foundation for electronica and studio-generated music for decades to come. His 1973 collaboration with King Crimson alum Robert Fripp resulted in the album *No Pussyfooting*, for which the duo developed a tape-delay system (dubbed "Frippertronics") that brought an entirely new sound out of Fripp's guitar. After several highly acclaimed solo albums on which Eno showed an increasing mastery of studio technology—1974's *Here Come the Warm Jets*, 1974's *Taking Tiger Mountain (By Strategy)*, and 1975's *Another Green World*—Eno released *Discreet Music*, his first full realization of generative music and a touchstone for all ambient music to follow.

Generative music takes a minimal amount of input from the composer and uses studio technology to apply a system of algorithms that alter the realization of the music beyond the composer's control, leaving much of the resulting product to chance. "Some very basic forms of generative music have existed for a long time, but as marginal curiosities," recalled Eno in a later autobiography. "Wind chimes are an example, but the only compositional control you have over the music they produce is in the original choice of notes that the chimes will sound. . . . Until 100 years ago, every musical event was unique: music was ephemeral and unrepeatable and even classical scoring couldn't guarantee precise duplication. Then came the gramophone record, which captured particular performances and made it possible to hear them identically over and over again. But now there are three alternatives: live music, recorded music and generative music. Generative music enjoys some of the benefits of both its ancestors. Like live music it is always different. Like recorded music it is free of time-and-place limitations—you can hear it when and where you want. I really think it is possible that our grandchildren will look at us in wonder and say: "you mean you used to listen to exactly the same thing over and over again?"'"[46]

For *Discreet Music*, Eno employed dual reel-to-reel machines to create a thirty-one-minute title track consisting of two layered melodic lines. The melodies were fed through a long-delay echo system and their timbre altered by synthesizer to create serene, ambient sounds. For the album's remaining tracks, Eno had musicians play Pachelbel's Canon in D Major, but with predetermined systematic changes that heavily altered the composition's sound. "Since I have always preferred making plans to executing them, I have gravitated towards situations and systems that, once set into operation, could create music with little or no intervention on my part," claimed Eno in the album's liner notes. "That is to say, I tend towards the roles of the planner and programmer, and then become an audience to the results. I was trying to make a piece that could be listened to and yet could be ignored . . . perhaps in the spirit of [experimental composer Erik] Satie who wanted to make music that could "mingle with the sound of the knives and forks at dinner."''[47]

The resulting album was Eno's first full engagement with ambient music, generating a whole series of later work meant to "mingle" with ambient sounds, including works specifically created to be played in places like airports and hospitals, and ultimately influencing genres as diverse as new age and hip-hop. Eno also continued his work in the pop medium, becoming one of popular music's most sought-after producers and influencing a generation of new wave and power-pop through his collaborations with David Bowie, Talking Heads, and U2. "Some bands went to art school," claimed U2's lead singer Bono. "We went to Brian Eno."[48]

Album Title: *A Night at the Opera*
Artist: Queen
Recorded: August–November 1975, at Sarm Studios, Roundhouse Studios, Olympic Studios, Scorpio Studios, and Landsdowne Studios in London and Rockfield Studios in Wales
U.S. release: December 2, 1975 (Elektra)
Producer: Queen, Roy Thomas Baker

The parallels between Queen and Led Zeppelin are too obvious to ignore. Both bands exploded onto the scene (five years apart) with an exciting, hard-driving rock that blew audiences away. Both bands produced an epic song on a signature album that more or less defined them for decades to come (Led Zeppelin's "Stairway to Heaven" on their untitled fourth album, and Queen's "Bohemian Rhapsody" on *A Night at the Opera*). Both bands featured a powerful, grounding rhythm duo that supported an extraordinarily skilled guitarist and an over-the-top vocalist. Both bands were dismissed by critics—particularly *Rolling Stone*—as pompous, overblown no-talents who would be quickly forgotten. And both bands proved the critics wrong.

With a five-year head start, Led Zeppelin were the band to beat, and Queen spent their first thee albums not only living in the mighty Zep's shadow but also competing with the band's continuing high-quality output. But Queen were never a group to settle for second place, and the quartet's hard-driven members—Freddie Mercury on vocals, Brian May on guitar, John Deacon on bass, and Roger Taylor on drums—soon proved themselves worthy of respect, ultimately earning honors ahead of Zeppelin in all-time British popularity (although they were runners-up behind the Beatles—not bad as far as second place goes).

In the mid-late 1970s, when many rock acts were either preening, sexualized idols or campy, trenchant new wavers, Queen seemed to be both, a collection of puffed up virtuosos with a sharp wit pointed squarely at their own genre. "The great thing about Queen," wrote a *Melody Maker* critic, "is that they make one's critical barbs thoroughly redundant, so hell-bent are they on self-parody."[49] And yet such barbs kept coming, from all corners through their first three albums, and from select critics even after Queen established themselves as one of the biggest acts in the world. "Whatever its claims, Queen isn't here just to entertain," wrote *Rolling Stone*'s resident fussbudget Dave Marsh. "This group has come to make it clear exactly who is superior and who is inferior. Its anthem, "We Will Rock You," is a marching order: you *will not* rock us, we *will* rock you. Indeed, Queen may be the first truly fascist rock band. The whole thing makes me wonder why anyone would indulge these creeps and their polluting ideas."[50]

Marsh, however, neglects any mention of the band's musical talent, like many journalists focusing on his personal distaste for the band's presence rather than critical engagement of their material. But critics who appreciated Queen's tongue-in-cheek pomp complained about their overabundance of talent rather than their lack of it. "With a little concentration these geezers could become the best English group in Britain," wrote *Phonograph Record* in 1975 as the band teetered on the brink of stardom. "At the moment, though, they've got a disastrously cock-eyed view of their own strengths. The production effects they pile on with so little restraint and their apparent phobic dread of ever over-dubbing fewer than thirty-five guitar parts on anything combine to smother the actual songs, to which they seem to be paying less and less attention. For instance, were May to spend as much time composing lead vocal lines as he does constructing harmonies for his guitar leads, he might, one suspects, come up with a lot more memorable songs. I mean I adore the heavily-produced English sound as much as any man on earth, but Queen have just gone overboard."[51]

Overboard was what Queen was all about. A band of overachievers—Deacon had a master's degree in acoustics and vibration technology; May was completing his PhD in astronomy; Taylor had reportedly turned down a job as drummer for Genesis; and Mercury had one of the most powerful and dextrous voices outside the opera set—the group were even more critical of their own work than the rock scribes were. "If there was ever an equally divided quartet, this is it," claimed Freddie Mercury. "We need that kind of blend where each one's got to contribute just about evenly. Just because I'm out front doesn't necessarily mean I'm any kind of leader. We all have strong characters and we row constantly. It's healthy, because then you get the cream, the good product. We're very fussy, very meticulous, and have numerous battles to get the right sound."[52]

The band achieved the right sound—by outsiders' standards—with their fourth outing, the overwhelming *A Night at the Opera*, breaking them out in the United States where they had had limited success. By the standards of the time, the album was very expensive to produce, costing in the neighborhood of £35,000, recorded in a half-dozen studios over four months, and sometimes being engineered in three studios at once. The album's centerpiece, "Bohemian Rhapsody," went down in history as one of the grandest productions in rock, channeling characters ranging from Beelzebub to Galileo, covering genres from heavy metal to a capella, and featuring 180 vocal overdubs at its climax—the vocal harmonies alone reportedly took eighty-four hours of studio time. "Bohemian Rhapsody" camped in the United Kingdom's No. 1

spot for nine weeks and reached No. 9 in the United States (seventeen years later it re-climbed the American charts to No. 2 following the death of Freddie Mercury and the song's use in a famous scene in the film *Wayne's World*). The album reached No. 1 in Britain and No. 4 in the United States, remaining on the American charts for more than a year. Critics, perhaps feeling guilty for missing the boat, called the LP the "greatest single long-playing achievement since Sgt. Pepper" and "the most important record album ever made."[53] Whether the album deserves such hyperbolic acclaim is up for debate, but with *A Night at the Opera* Queen set a new standard for theater-rock that was imitated by dozens of bands that sought to combine the excitement of KISS with the virtuosity of Cream. "If it's hard to love, it's hard not to admire," wrote a slightly more sympathetic *Rolling Stone* reviewer. "This band is skilled, after all, and it dares."[54]

Album Title: *Wanted! The Outlaws*
Artists: Waylon Jennings, Willie Nelson, Jessi Colter, Tompall Glaser
Recorded: 1975
U.S. release: January 12, 1976 (RCA)
Producer: Waylon Jennings, Richie Albright

Few artists have had as much impact on modern country music as Waylon Jennings. By the time he broke into the mainstream as leader of the "outlaw country" movement in the 1970s, he had already been a working musician for nearly two decades, starting out as a bass player for Buddy Holly in the late 1950s. Following Holly's tragic death in an airplane crash in 1959 (Jennings gave up his seat on the plane to the Big Bopper at the last minute), Jennings embarked on a path exploring rockabilly, rock, folk, and country in Texas, Arizona, Los Angeles, and Nashville, developing a unique style that made him one of the biggest names in 1970s country.

Oddly, it was Jennings' messy breakup with the country establishment that made him one of their brightest stars. For years, Nashville maintained a stranglehold on the production and distribution of country music. If it was not a direct descendent of Hank Williams or Jimmie Rodgers, it was not considered country, and artists that sought to stray from the pre-approved musical vocabulary suffered the wrath of their corporate overlords.

But the vastly expanded vocabulary of 1960s rock had spilled over into the country market with landmark crossovers like Bob Dylan's *Nashville Skyline* and the Byrds' *Sweetheart of the Rodeo* (see p. 61) and *The Notorious Byrd Brothers*, followed by a swarm of easy-goin' country-rock in the 1970s with acts like Linda Ronstadt, the Band, and the Eagles. On the other end of the genre spectrum, respected songwriters like Waylon Jennings and Willie Nelson were challenging the Nashville establishment by experimenting with pop and rock techniques and changing their physical appearance to adopt more of an outlaw rocker look. Jennings already had long had a reputation as something of a rebel, and through the turn of the decade had fought for greater and greater control of his albums, from choosing his own material to using his touring band in the studio (many labels required their artists to use payroll studio musicians). Willie Nelson left Nashville altogether, returning to Texas to set up shop in Austin in 1972, which had been growing as a hotbed of "progressive country" (also known as "redneck rock" and "hip hillbilly")—a unique combination of established country music audiences and the hippie youth at the University of Texas mingling night after night in Austin's many venues.

Nelson and Jennings' increasing forays into honky-tonk, rock, dated pop, and odd experiments earned them larger and larger crossover audiences with Nelson's 1974 *Phases and Stages* and 1975 *Red Headed Stranger* and Jennings' 1972 *Ladies Love Outlaws*, 1973 *Lonesome, On'ry and Mean*, and 1973 *Honky Tonk Heroes*. Jennings' albums in particular massively increased his fan base and established the genre of "outlaw country," which sold so well that soon other Nashville artists were adopting the "outlaw" brand and riding a wave of commercial acceptance—oddly enough, helping the country market by breaking out of pure country forms. "The ultimate irony of the Outlaws may be that, while drawing upon a diverse array of musical sources and reaching out to new audiences, they did more to preserve a distinct identity for country music than most of their contemporaries who wore the 'country' label."[55] Finally, it seemed, the Nashville labels and their independence-seeking artists had found a language they could both speak: money.

The success of the "outlaw country" movement prompted the industry to jump on board, with RCA releasing a collection of previously recorded songs by some of country's most notorious "outlaws"—Waylon Jennings, Willie Nelson, Tompall Glaser, and Jessi Colter (who was also Jennings' wife)—in 1976. *Wanted! The Outlaws* was a massive success by country standards, the first country album to go platinum and a watershed moment in the popularization of country music, which had always been something of a niche market but would slowly grow from this point to be the most popular genre in America by the 1990s. The right mix of covers and originals sung by some of Texas' hottest commodities sent *Wanted* to the Top 10 of the pop charts, with songs like "My Heroes Have Always Been Cowboys" and "Good Hearted Woman" finding comfortable homes in the pop and country canon. "It's unfortunate that there still has to be a sampler, or primer, or golden book," wrote *Rolling Stone* editor Chet Flippo in the album's liner notes, "but apparently not everyone has gotten the message yet. Maybe this album can introduce you to some people you would have liked to have known sooner, but just didn't have the opportunity to meet.... They've been waiting in the wings for years, too many years, to assume their proper places in the structure of American music. Call them outlaws, call them innovators, call them revolutionaries, call them what you will, they're just some damned fine people who are also some of the most gifted songwriters and singers anywhere."[56]

Wanted! The Outlaws moved Jennings and Nelson into the highest pantheon of country artists (also spawning a series of enormously successful collaborations between the two), and advanced the careers of a number of their close friends and occasional collaborators—such as songwriters Billy Joe Shaver and Kris Kristofferson—merely by association. Though there was never an official group in this company named "The Outlaws," the foursome featured on the album profited greatly by the popular belief that they were actually a band—a notion they had no reason to dissuade. "They're the cutting edge of a brand of American music that I find the most satisfying development in popular music in the past decade," wrote Flippo. "It's not country and it's not country-rock, but there's no real need to worry about labeling it. It's just damned good music that's true and honest and you can't ask for more than that."[57]

Album Title: *Mothership Connection*
Artist: Parliament
Recorded: 1975, at Limited Sound in Detroit, Michigan and
Hollywood Sound in Hollywood
U.S. release: February 1976 (Casablanca)
Producer: George Clinton

"Parliament-funkadelic, P-Funk, The P—Specially designed afronauts capable of funketizing entire galaxies. Their mothership long ago made its terrestrial connection and they are amongst us even now. Cloned by a race of super-intelligent beings, represented in Clintonian mythology by the cosmic pimp Dr Funkenstein, they are the earthly sentinels for a returning alien civilization: The guardians of the secrets of the pyramids: The true and original saviours of the Funk—and funk is getting ready to roll."[58]

If you think the reviews are bizarre, you should check out the music. Not since Frank Zappa's Mothers of Invention has a band been so weird that reviewers just did not know how to write about them, often choosing to imitate their weirdness (poorly) rather than critically engage the material at hand. More than a single, cohesive act, Parliament was a wandering cocktail party hosted by George Clinton, the heir-apparent to James Brown's danceable soul. In the 1970s, Clinton was ringleader in a circus of incredibly funky music mainly split between his two bands Parliament and Funkadelic, collectively known as "P-Funk." It was often unclear which band was which, as the two shared many regular members and at times had more than fifty musicians moving back and forth between Clinton's studio albums and live performances.

Clinton founded the Parliaments in the 1960s out of his Plainfield, New Jersey barber shop. Although they started as a doo-wop group, the quintet soon developed a unique sound framed by very unusual lyrics that Clinton and his entourage would become famous for—one reviewer described Clinton's singing as "a miscellany of shuck and jive, inconsequential bullshit and honed-to-the bone philosophy, thoughts, fantasies, truths and monologues. He's irreverent, freaky, sometimes even romantic, and good God, hit me, and y'all can bump 'n' grind a mite too."[59]

In the early 1970s, with psychedelic rock on the way out and disco on the way in, Clinton reached backward and forward to create a bizarre hybrid of the two, drawing on the energy and originality of Sly Stone, Jimi Hendrix, and Frank Zappa to create acid rock that you could groove to. (Besides active imaginations, Zappa and Clinton also shared in common enormously prolific outputs and an ability to bring together talented collaborators— Clinton could easily be described as the Frank Zappa of urban soul.)

The combined releases of Parliament and Funkadelic marked a significant development in the progression of black music in the United States. For the first time, artists like Clinton, Stevie Wonder, and Marvin Gaye were addressing the daily problems of urban blacks head-on, bringing a new awareness to 1970s soul music and laying the groundwork for the rap and hip-hop to come. Clinton's genius was in creating an entire mythology through his music, with characters that reoccured from album to album and an outer-space themed storyline drawn from 1950s' and 1960s' science fiction. "All this shit is connected," claimed Clinton, highlighting the central theme of universal togetherness that wove through the band's music. "Ain't no one mafunker can do this shit. And no one species...no one state...no one nothin'. 'Cause it's all the One. I mean I am not one. I am *part* of one. We are all part of one."[60]

Of course, no amount of off-the-wall storytelling would make an audience boogie without the proper musical accompaniment, and like his influences James Brown and Frank Zappa, George Clinton had a knack for recruiting the best and getting the best work out of them. Among the Parliament and Funkadelic rosters were brothers Bootsy Collins and Catfish Collins, who had held down the rhythm section of James Brown's backing band before moving on to Clinton's group in 1972, where Bootsy earned fame for his powerful and otherwordly bass playing. But the centerpiece of Clinton's sound lay in his Julliard- and Conservatory-trained keyboardist Bernie Worrell, who not only helped arrange and produce much of the P-Funk canon in the 1970s, but gave the band its signature space-funk sound with his creative synthesizer work.

Many of Parliament's albums in the 1970s were key documents in the evolution of funk, particularly 1974's *Up for the Downstroke* and 1975's *Chocolate City* (predated by Funkadelic's groove masterpieces in 1970 and 1971: *Free Your Mind...and Your Ass Will Follow*, *Funkadelic*, and *Maggot Brain*). But it was Parliament's 1976 opus *Mothership Connection* that broke the outfit into the mainstream, featuring horn aces Maceo Parker and Fred Wesley, also alumni of James Brown's revue. The combination of Parker and Wesley's horns with Worrell's brilliant synthesizer work, Bootsy's space bass, and Clinton's imaginative writing and production elevated the group's sound beyond the advanced R&B they had been doing into a whole new realm of futuristic urban boogie, as important to the later development of rap and hip-hop as Iggy and the Stooges were to punk rock. Climbing to No. 13 on the pop charts, *Mothership Connection* brought Clinton before a wide-ranging pop audience for the first time, allowing him to increase his output to include side projects and elaborate stage productions through the latter 1970s, taking his small circus and expanding it into, as one review called it, "a Space Age Mardi Gras."[61]

Album Title: *Ramones*
Artist: The Ramones
Recorded: February 2–19, 1976, at Plaza Sound Studios in New York City
U.S. release: April 23, 1976 (Sire)
Producer: Craig Leon, Tommy Ramone

"[M]y theory has always been that good rock and roll should damn well make you uneasy," noted rock critic Robert Christgau in a review of the Ramones' self-titled debut album, "and the sheer pleasure of this stuff—which of course elicits howls of pain from the good old rock and roll crowd—is undeniable. For me, it blows everything else off the radio: it's clean the way the Dolls never were, sprightly the way the Velvets never were, and just plain listenable the way Black Sabbath never was."[62]

Or, as Tommy Ramone put it a bit less eloquently to *Punk* magazine in 1976: "Rock 'n' roll, man, just rock 'n' roll. The way it should be—entertaining, a lot of fun, sexy, dynamic, exciting. Ah, y'know, everything that everyone seems to have missed the point on. Further, we believe in songs . . . not in, uh, boogying and, uh, improvisation and stuff like that, y'know?"[63]

The Ramones were the first true punk band. Earlier groups contributed to what would become the punk aesthetic—the Kinks' fuzzed-out power chords, Iggy Pop's primitive stage antics, the Velvet Underground's minimalism, MC5's raw politicking, the New York Dolls' amateurism—but the Ramones were the tipping point in 1970s New York City, pounding basic chords, repetitive lyrics, and fast tempos into short songs (rarely more than three minutes long) that gave a fresh start to the overbearing complexity rock had recently achieved through its progressive acts. Though the Ramones cited "everything" as an influence, the real drive behind their music was the fact that they didn't like anything they were hearing on the radio.

Most of the band members grew up in the middle-class neighborhood of Forest Hills in Queens, New York, taking up rock and roll out of sheer suburban boredom. When they teamed up to form the Ramones in 1974, each member adopted a band name that ended in "Ramone" (an homage to Beatle Paul McCartney, who often checked into hotels under the alias "Paul Ramon" or "Paul Ramone"). Originally a trio with Johnny Ramone (John Cummings) on guitar, Dee Dee Ramone (Douglas Colvin) on bass, and Joey Ramone (Jeffrey Hyman) on drums, the group soon added Tommy Ramone (Thomas Erdelyi) on drums so Joey could concentrate on vocals.

By the end of 1974, they had earned a cult following at the recently opened CBGB in Manhattan's lower east side, widely considered the club where punk and new wave were born with the Ramones, Blondie, Television, and Patti Smith in 1974 and 1975. Their shows were as primitive and raw as anything in music up to that point, and since their songs were so short, their sets followed suit—when they were asked to play a longer set, they would just play their existing repertoire twice. "[T]heir idea of playing is to plug in with the amps juiced to maximum level and don't let nothin' come in the way of their fingers and your ears," wrote one performance review. "They perform so it hurts. Ramone rock forbids the audience to pass pleasantries while it goes down. In return Johnny Ramone leaves the stage with gore-soaked hands most nights, flesh cut to ribbons for the sake of taking your lobes somewhere they were never intended to go."[64]

Little changed when the band committed their tunes to vinyl on their 1976 debut *Ramones*, recorded in a week for a mere $6,400. The same stripped-down, four-chord simplicity that carried their sets onstage moved the album quickly from song to song, none of the tunes lasting much more than two-and-a-half minutes, and many far less. The group's bouncy, goofy melodies and inane lyrics—starting with the first chords of album opener "Blitzkrieg Bop" and its immortal starter lyrics "Hey, ho, let's go"—opened a whole new world of garage rock for those fed up with the excesses of existing rock gods. The band earned critical kudos in some corners and scorn in others, often praised by one reviewer for the same techniques that earned them condemnation from another. "Thing about The Ramones is you either take them in the intended spirit, or you go home," wrote one London journal following the band's immortal performance on July 4, 1976, which ignited the British punk movement. "The appeal is purely negative, based on their not being able to play a shit or give a shit. The thinking process involved in evaluating their performance is non-existent; it's first step moronorock strung across a selection of imbecilic adolescent ditties whose sole variation lies in the shuffling of three chords into some semblance of order."[65]

Imbecilic or not (it was certainly adolescent), *Ramones* set fire to the underground in the United States and England, inspiring future bands from the Sex Pistols to Green Day to rally bored suburban teenagers with high-energy, fast-paced garage rock. Though largely unappreciated when they were laying punk rock's foundation in the 1970s, the group managed to stay together relatively intact for twenty-two years (a truly amazing feat for a garage band), long enough to be worshipped and surpassed by the acts they influenced. Their earliest albums—1976's *Ramones*, 1977's *Leave Home* and *Rocket to Russia*, and 1978's *Road to Ruin*—are considered classics of the genre, varying little in content or quality, establishing the Ramones as arguably the most important act in punk-rock history and influencing many dozens of alternative and mainstream bands over the following three decades.

Album Title: *Boston*
Artist: Boston
Recorded: October 1975–April 1976, at Foxglove Studios in Massachusetts, Capitol Records in Hollywood, and the Record Plant in Los Angeles
U.S. release: August 25, 1976 (Epic)
Producer: John Boylan, Tom Scholz

Many albums feature heavy contributions from all corners—musicians, songwriters, engineers, mixers, producers, label execs, graphic artists, backup singers, and even roadies—to create an enduring masterwork; the Beatles' *Sgt. Pepper's Lonely Hearts Club Band* comes to mind, and Pink Floyd's *The Dark Side of the Moon*. Then there are albums that are largely the work of a single creative genius with a good deal of support behind him—Brian Wilson's work on the Beach Boys' *Pet Sounds* for instance, or Pete Townshend's magnum opus with the Who, *Tommy*. But rarely has a lone innovator almost single-handedly created a smash album and gotten so little public recognition for it than in the case of the 1976 LP *Boston*.

Boston, the debut album of the eponymous band, was not the product of Boston the group, but of an MIT graduate named Tom Scholz. Through the early 1970s, Scholz worked as an engineer at Polaroid by day, played keyboards in local bands in the evenings, and hovered over a jumble of recording equipment in his makeshift basement studio at night. Between 1972 and 1975, Scholz, with help from local singer Brad Delp, recorded three sets of demos and sent them out to dozens of record companies without a single bite. Finally in 1976, with the help of an outside management team, the band was given a name and signed by Epic Records, which released *Boston* to little fanfare that August.

There were two fairly remarkable things about the album. The first was the degree to which *Boston* was an individual effort by Scholz—though there is some disagreement as to just how much some members of the group contributed, Scholz wrote, arranged, produced, and played guitar and keyboards on the release, with the other members—Brad Delp, Barry Gordreau, Fran Sheehan, and John Hashian—assembled to fill in on certain instruments and prepare for a tour. Delp, whose clear, wailing voice largely defined the band's sound to the public ear, is credited with writing or cowriting two songs and performing several instruments, but the album is overwhelmingly the brainchild of Scholz whose perfectionist engineering made the demos so crisp and polished that almost no mixing was done by the label, and the final product varied little in quality from the demo tapes.

The second amazing feat was the enormous and entirely unexpected sales figures. An album by a completely unknown new band, with nary a marquee name in the group, with zero buzz and almost no advertising, playing an entirely new kind of rock, managed to pull off the impossible. *Boston* jumped to No. 3 on the charts, producing massive sales week after week. By week seven it had gone gold, by week eleven platinum, and by the time it fell off the charts two years later, it was the biggest-selling debut album in history. "I would like to say that we made a colossal executive decision to make them this big," said CBS Records Group President Walter Yetnikoff. "But we did not. The album took off immediately, all by itself. I didn't even hear the first album until it was platinum."[66]

More than an individual success, *Boston* was the blueprint for a new wave of massively popular music dubbed corporate rock, a catch-all term for music featuring soaring vocals, interchangeable guitar solos, heavily layered, but very cleanly mixed instruments, utterly vapid lyrics, and practically anonymous band members. "A typical tune will start with a strong melodic hook—sometimes tough, sometimes close to lilting," claimed an analysis of Boston's formula in *Time* magazine, "then build in volume and intensity, the instruments laying under and layering on one another until the song shatters around your ears like a sheet of glass falling off a fast-moving truck. This is heavy-metal music with easy-listening inflections, rock fierce enough for the FM stations, flighty enough to fit right into Top 40 AM radio."[67]

Boston's extraordinary debut opened the floodgates for some of the most successful bands of the late 1970s and early 1980s—among them Foreigner, Journey, Styx, and REO Speedwagon—many of whom had been around for years before Boston, but had been largely ignored by the public and their labels. In the long run, corporate rock came to be used as a term of disdain for generic, soulless, overly hyped rock balladry. "Boston has so little rock 'n' roll coursing through its veins—Scholz is the kind of musician you suspect of never listening to pre-Sgt. Pepper rock; his songs betray no prior influence—that they're more depressing than uplifting," wrote one reviewer. "It is test tube rock, and all too rarely does the emotional motivation seem genuine."[68]

Nevertheless, Scholz' pop craftsmanship touched millions of listeners and launched an entirely new direction for blues-based rock, heavily influencing the progression of pop music in the 1980s with later bands like Def Leppard, Bon Jovi, and Guns N' Roses. Scholz' perfectionist tendencies led to long periods between subsequent albums, with *Don't Look Back* released two years later (only because pressure from the label forced Scholz to release it half finished), and *Third Stage* taking another eight years, with both albums finding their way to the top of the charts. Despite Scholz' production virtuosity and the degree to which Boston resurrected classic rock as disco and punk seemed to be taking over, critics have been less than kind with his output, blaming him for a sea-change that injured what little soul was left in pop. "Boston makes cold, computerized music that's antithetical to everything venturesome and vital about rock 'n' roll," wrote one critic in a review of Boston's second album, *Don't Look Back*, "and if they sell 20 million of this one, they still couldn't make me care."[69]

NOTES

1. "*Nuggets: Original Artyfacts from the First Psychedelic Era 1965–1968*," *Q*, August 1999, 139.

2. Ben Edmonds, "*Nuggets: Original Artyfacts from the First Psychedelic Era 1965–1968*," *Mojo*, September 1998.

3. Ron Ross, "David Bowie: Phallus in Pigtails, or the Music of the Sphere Considered as Cosmic Boogie," *Words and Music*, July 1972.

4. Steve Turner, "The Rise and Rise of David Bowie," *Beat Instrumental*, August 1972.

5. Ross, July 1972.

6. Lenny Kaye, "Iggy Pop: *Raw Power*," *Rolling Stone*, May 10, 1973.

7. Barney Hoskyns, "Iggy Pop: Animal God off the Street," *New Musical Express*, October 1986.

8. Lenny Kaye, "The Stooges: *The Stooges*," *Fusion*, September 19, 1969.

9. Ian MacDonald, "Pink Floyd: *Dark Side of the Moon*," *New Musical Express*, February 23, 1974.

10. Chris Smith, *The Greenwood Encyclopedia of Rock History: From Arenas to the Underground, 1974–1980*. Westport, CT: Greenwood, 2005b, 126.

11. Loyd Grossman, "Pink Floyd: *The Dark Side of the Moon*," *Rolling Stone*, May 24, 1973.

12. MacDonald, February 23, 1974.

13. Chris Salewicz, "An Interview with Roger Waters," *Q*, June 1987.

14. Chris Smith, *The Greenwood Encyclopedia of Rock History: The Rise of Album Rock, 1967–1973*. Westport, CT: Greenwood, 2005a, 65–66.

15. Miles, "They Simper at Times," *New York Dolls/Glam Rock*, 1972.

16. Ron Ross, "The New York Dolls: An Insider's View," *Phonograph Record*, October 1973.

17. Ibid.

18. Robert Christgau, *Creem*, November 1973, 62.

19. *New York Dolls* reissue, 1977, Mercury/Polygram.

20. *Jazz Profiles* from NPR, Herbie Hancock, www.npr.org.

21. Ibid.

22. *Head Hunters* reissue, 1997, Columbia.

23. Janis Schact, *Circus*, June 1975.

24. Lester Bangs, *Psychotic Reactions and Carburetor Dung*. New York: Anchor Books, 2003, 154.

25. Simon Witter, "Kraftwerk: *Autobahn*," *New Musical Express*, July 6, 1985.

26. Dave Thompson, www.allmusic.com.

27. Barbara Charone, "Linda Ronstadt: Ronstadt Country," *New Musical Express*, February 16, 1974.

28. Dave Marsh and John Swenson, *The New Rolling Stone Record Guide*. New York: Random House, 1983 (1979), 434–435.

29. Tom Nolan, "The Linda Ronstadt Coverup!" *Phonograph Record*, November 1974.

30. Robert Christgau, www.robertchristgau.com.

31. Fred Bronson, *The Billboard Book of Number One Hits*. New York: Billboard, 1985, 393.

32. Stephen Thomas Erlewine, www.allmusic.com.

33. Smith, 2005b, 63.

34. Ira Robbins, "Joe Perry Meets the Press," *Trouser Press*, November 1978.

35. Steve Turner, "Was Bob Dylan the Previous Bruce Springsteen," *New Musical Express*, October 6, 1973.

36. Jon Landau, "Bruce Springsteen," *The Real Paper*, May 22, 1974.

37. Bud Scoppa, "Bruce Springsteen: at the Roxy, Los Angeles," *Phonograph Record*, November 1975.

38. Don Snowden, "Bruce Springsteen: Hustling for Rock's Record Machines," *Pasadena Guardian*, September 24, 1975.

39. Alan Betrock, "Kiss: *Hotter Than Hell*," *Phonograph Record*, February 1975.

40. Ibid.

41. Mick Farren, "Pinocchio Reversed," *New Musical Express*, July 16, 1977.

42. Charles Shaar Murray, "Down in the Scuzz with the Heavy Cult Figures," *New Musical Express*, June 7, 1975.

43. Mitchell Cohen, "Patti Smith: Avery Fisher Hall, NYC," *Phonograph Record*, May 1976.

44. Paul Morley, *Words and Music: A History of Pop in the Shape of a City*. Athens: University of Georgia Press, 2005, 165.

45. Cynthia Dagnal, "Eno and the Jets: Controlled Chaos," *Rolling Stone*, September 12, 1974.

46. Brian Eno, *A Year with Swollen Appendices: Brian Eno's Diary*. London: Faber & Faber, 1996.

47. Brian Eno, *Discreet Music* liner notes, 1975.

48. Ron Sarig, *The Secret History of Rock: The Most Influential Bands You've Never Heard*. New York: Billboard Books, 1998, 128.

49. Steve Lake, "Queen's Gambit," *Melody Maker*, September 22, 1984.

50. Dave Marsh, "Queen: *Jazz*," *Rolling Stone*, February 8, 1979.

51. John Mendelssohn, "Queen: *Sheer Heart Attack*," *Phonograph Record*, March 1975.

52. Mitchell Cohen, "Queen: The New British Invasion," *Phonograph Record*, March 1976.

53. Jon Tiven, "Queen Swings Both Ways," *Circus*, April 8, 1975.

54. Bud Scoppa, "Queen: *Sheer Heart Attack*," *Rolling Stone*, May 8, 1975.

55. Bill C. Malone, *Country Music, U.S.A.* Austin: University of Texas, 2002, 404–405.

56. Chet Flippo, *Wanted! The Outlaws* liner notes, 1976.

57. Ibid.

58. Frank Broughton, "George Clinton at 54," *i-D*, 1994.

59. Cliff White, "It's a PARLIAFUNKADELIC-BOOTSYMENT THANG!!," *New Musical Express*, August 21, 1976.

60. Smith, 2005b, 11.

61. Ibid., 10.

62. Christgau, www.robertchristgau.com.

63. Mary Harron, "The Ramones," *Punk*, January 1976.

64. Max Bell, "The Ramones: 'Waitin' for World War III Blues'," *New Musical Express*, July 17, 1976.

65. Max Bell, "Flamin' Groovies/The Ramones/The Stranglers: Roundhouse, London," *New Musical Express*, July 10, 1976.

66. Cameron Crowe, "Boston: The Band from the Platinum Basement," *Rolling Stone*, August 10, 1978.

67. Jay Cocks, "Boston's Sonic Mystery Tour," *Time*, September 28, 1978.

68. Mitchell Cohen, "Boston: *Don't Look Back*," *Creem*, November 1978.

69. Ibid.

5

THE MODERN DANCE, 1977–1985

In October 1977, the Sex Pistols released their only studio album after going through three different labels: ***Never Mind the Bollocks, Here's the Sex Pistols* (1977)**. The LP touched off a wave of controversy, including a lawsuit over the use of the profanity "bollocks," a refusal to work by employees at the record plant, and a boycott by radio stations and record stores. The album still went to No. 1 on the U.K. charts and almost breached the Top 100 in the United States. Three months later, the band broke up after a disastrous two-week tour of the American south, during which members of the group were repeatedly beaten up by their audiences. Later in the year, bassist Sid Vicious was arrested for murder after his girlfriend was found stabbed to death in their New York City hotel room. Four months after that, Vicious died of a heroin overdose the night before his hearing.

The period surrounding the turn of the 1980s was marked with such extremes—revolutionary album releases, tragic events, sudden endings, and just as sudden new beginnings. On August 16, 1977, Elvis Presley died of a heart attack at his Graceland mansion, marking, in more ways than one, the final death of rock and roll and the ascension of his many subgenre stepchildren to their various thrones. Presley was followed to the grave by a litany of important musical figures—glam-rock pioneer Marc Bolan and three members of southern-rock legends Lynyrd Skynyrd later that year; Who drummer Keith Moon and Carter Family matriarch Maybelle Carter in 1978; Sid Vicious, jazz great Charles Mingus, and musical theater legend Richard Rogers in 1979; and New Orleans pianist Professor Longhair, AC/DC singer Bon Scott, Joy Division singer Ian Curtis, Marshall Tucker Band founder Tommy Caldwell, Germs singer Darby Crash, and Led Zeppelin drummer John Bonham in 1980, a sad year for music that ended in the assassination of John Lennon. Three weeks after his death, Lennon's first release in five years, "(Just Like) Starting Over," reached the top of the charts, a tragically ironic song to mark his end, but appropriate to mark a new beginning for American music.

Among the genres with short life spans, punk rock and disco burned too brightly and were quickly eclipsed by more commercial and less vapid forms. Punk's reign was brought down by one of its own, as the Clash's *London Calling* (1980) brought political acumen and smart arrangements to punk rock, continuing an evolution already begun by punk and new-wave releases such as Television's *Marquee Moon* (1977), Talking Heads' 1977 *Talking Heads: 77* and 1978 *More Songs About Buildings and Food*, Blondie's 1977 re-release *Blondie*, Elvis Costello and the Attractions' 1978 *This Year's Model*, and Pere Ubu's *The Modern Dance* (1978). Punk's harsher side was kept alive through its influence on America's interior and west coast (particularly Los Angeles) with albums like X's 1980 *Los Angeles*, Black Flag's 1981 *Damaged*, Hüsker Dü's *Zen Arcade* (1984), and Metallica's *Kill 'em All* (1983). Overseas imports like AC/DC's 1979 *Highway to Hell* and *Back in Black* (1980) and Def Leppard's *Pyromania* (1983) helped move loud, aggressive punk-influenced metal to the higher reaches of the charts, while Van Halen's *Van Halen* (1978) made speed and technical expertise a valuable commodity in heavy metal.

Disco, which had slowly developed as an underground phenomenon through the 1970s and seemed destined to stay that way, suddenly hit the mainstream with the film soundtrack *Saturday Night Fever* (1977), making megastars out of the Bee Gees with their contributions to the album and their follow-ups *Spirits Having Flown* and *Greatest Hits* in 1979. Though disco hit a wall as soon as it reach 120 mph, its technical beats and infectious groove found homes in popular music with albums like Blondie's 1978 *Parallel Lines*, the Cars' 1978 *The Cars*, and Prince's 1980 *Dirty Mind*, 1982 *1999*, and *Purple Rain* (1984). The more bootie-shakin' elements of the disco beat would return with a vengeance as Michael Jackson brought dance pop to a whole new level with his 1979 *Off the Wall* and *Thriller* (1982), followed by his female counterpart Madonna's *Like a Virgin* (1984), whose single "Material Girl" perfectly encapsulated the politically conservative gluttony of the Reagan era that pervaded American culture throughout the decade.

As much as artists like Madonna and Michael Jackson had an immediate, massive impact on popular culture—influencing everything from musical styles to movies to fashion—more understated cult figures maintained a grip on the underground and grew to influence popular music years later through their impact on college radio and other bands. One of the few successful acts in this category, Neil Young blended his folk-rock leanings with punk rock's commercial disgust on *Rust Never Sleeps* (1979). Iggy Pop, who was already considered punk's godfather, showed a more personal side with his solo efforts in 1977's *The Idiot* and *Lust for Life*, which were joined by releases such as Joy Division's 1980 *Closer* and R.E.M.'s *Murmur* (1983) in bringing about a slow, steady sea change in the development of alternative music.

The understatement of such unconventional releases was complemented by a number of emotive and original epics that kept music exciting and kept audiences guessing. Albums such as Meatloaf's 1977 *Bat Out of Hell*, Pink Floyd's 1977 *Animals* and 1979 *The Wall*, the Pretenders' 1980 *The Pretenders*, and Kate Bush's 1982 *The Dreaming* found fresh and imaginative ways to constantly push the boundaries of rock. While the Clash's *London Calling* is the most lauded political release of the period, socially introspective snapshots of humanity abounded in the worlds of R&B, blue-collar rock, and rock-related imports such as Funkadelic's **One Nation Under a Groove** (**1978**), John Cougar's 1982 *American Fool*, U2's **War** (**1983**), Bruce Springsteen's 1982 *Nebraska* and **Born in the U.S.A.** (**1984**), and Bob Marley and the Wailers' **Exodus** (**1977**) and 1984 hit *Legend*. Marley's releases introduced reggae to a wider American audience, just as Stevie Ray Vaughan and Double Trouble's **Texas Flood** (**1983**) would return blues to the forefront of popular music and Herbie Hancock's **Future Shock** (**1983**) would resurrect a widespread interest in jazz.

Album Title: *Marquee Moon*
Artist: Television
Recorded: 1976–1977, at A&R Studios in New York City
U.S. release: May 1977 (Elektra)
Producer: Andy Johns, Tom Verlaine

Among the mix of notable personalities that changed the course of popular music in the 1970s—Bruce Springsteen's working-class mettle, Johnny Rotten's provoking sneers, Patti Smith's cerebral poetics—Tom Verlaine's contributions have been largely (and unfairly) forgotten. It was Verlaine that convinced bar-owner Hilly Kristal in 1974 to allow unsigned local bands to play at his 315 Bowery bar, CBGB, after the Mercer Arts Center closed down. It was Verlaine's band, Television, that launched the punk and new-wave scenes in New York when they played their first gig at CBGB on March 31, 1974 (reportedly the band members physically built the venue's stage). It was Verlaine that foresaw the export of a whole new breed of music from New York City after Patti Smith, the Heartbreakers, the Ramones, and Blondie followed Television's performances at CBGB and began reaching out to a wider audience (Patti Smith wrote Television's first press review, and Verlaine played guitar on Smith's first single). And it was Verlaine that anchored Television's sound with his deft, melodic guitar rhythms, the occasional solo, warbling singing, and piercing, post-punk lyrics on their debut album *Marquee Moon*, considered one of the crucial foundation documents of 1970s new wave.

"With the bands that are coming out of New York, some of them can play and some of them can't," remarked Verlaine in 1977 as the new-wave phenomenon was starting to take hold. "But there definitely is something new about them—an electricity that doesn't exist in bands in any other part of America." In a reversal of the British Invasion of the mid-1960s, many of New York's unsigned bands earned recognition through tours of England in 1976 and 1977, heavily influencing the emerging British punk and new-wave sounds before finding wide acceptance in their home nation. Of particular importance to the nascent punk scene in London was an article written in England's *New Musical Express* in 1975 about the CBGB scene, focusing on Patti Smith and Television in particular. "Television are a total product of New York, but like the Feelgoods they embody both the traditional and the revolutionary, and they represent an escape from the roller-coaster to oblivion into which rock is currently strait-jacketed—i.e., an imaginative return to basics—and what they lose to the Feelgoods in energy and pacing, they gain in imagination."[1]

Standing at the forefront of the new-wave revolution, Television embodied a world-weary punk aesthetic (their initial lead singer, Richard Hell, was the first to sport the ripped and safety-pinned clothing—soon copied by the Sex Pistols—that would become the punk uniform), complemented by a postured ennui that was the hallmark of new-wave bands. "He's the kid in the back of every high school classroom," wrote one music critic about Tom Verlaine, "the one you never thought could talk. . . . You'd least expect to find him a rock cult hero, purveying terminal romanticism to an amplified beat. But Tom Verlaine isn't your run-of-the-mill rock hero. He refuses to swagger; he couldn't strike a pose if he tried. If he's the Jesus of Cool, it's because, as he says, 'I don't care.'"[2]

Richard Hell started out as Verlaine's equal in the band, but sensing his waning influence at the hands of Verlaine, he left Television in 1975 to form the Heartbreakers with refugees of the New York Dolls, months later moving on again to form the Voidoids. Soon after Hell's departure, Verlaine recorded *Marquee Moon* with bandmates Billy Ficca on drums, former Blondie bassist Fred Smith replacing Richard Hell, and guitarist Richard Lloyd, who shared guitar duties with Verlaine, each weaving tight leads around Verlaine's imaginatively penned rhythms. Verlaine, who composed every song on the album, demonstrated a particular affinity for mid-1960s psychedelic jam bands like Moby Grape and the Grateful Dead, but with a strong Velvet Underground influence that only a New York band could muster, reaching for a "small and dry" sound that anticipated future groups ranging from Talking Heads to Sonic Youth. "Where their predecessors in the New York punk scene, most notably the Velvet Underground, had fused blues structures with avant-garde flourishes, Television completely strip away any sense of swing or groove, even when they are playing standard three-chord changes," wrote one later retrospective account. "*Marquee Moon* is comprised entirely of tense garage rockers that spiral into heady intellectual territory, which is achieved through the group's long, interweaving instrumental sections, not through Verlaine's words. That alone made *Marquee Moon* a trailblazing album—it's impossible to imagine post-punk soundscapes without it."[3]

When released in 1977, *Marquee Moon* sent shivers down the spine of Television's fans, music critics, and the underground music scene.

"Forget everything you've heard about Television," wrote one New York journal reviewing the album. "Forget punk, forget New York, forget CBGB's...hell, forget rock and roll—this is the real item." The wider public, trapped in the mighty hypnotic clutches of Boston, Led Zeppelin, the Eagles, Wings, and Elton John, ignored the LP completely. Though the album failed to chart, its potent and expertly crafted mix of prepunk garage and postpunk melancholy laid the groundwork for a new generation of sounds. The rock journal *Crawdaddy!* praised Television's fusing of New York energy and California experimentation, claiming the band's debut album "firmly established Television's spirit...an album which definitely rocked, but which presented a unique sound and vision which, though not 'commercial,' at least approached rock unselfconsciously as popular music."[4]

Album Title: *Exodus*
Artist: Bob Marley and the Wailers
Recorded: January–April 1977, at Harry J's in Kingston, Jamaica and Island Studios in London
U.S. release: June 3, 1977 (Tuff Gong/Island)
Producer: Bob Marley and the Wailers

Bob Marley and the Wailers' 1977 album *Exodus*, which exposed a large American audience to reggae for the first time. *Courtesy of Universal Music Enterprises.*

Claiming *Exodus* as Bob Marley and the Wailers' most important album—particularly since it is the only reggae album featured in this list—is just asking for trouble. To be honest, it was a toss-up between Marley's 1974 *Natty Dread* (arguably the greatest reggae album of all time) and his 1984 posthumous Greatest Hits package *Legend* (inarguably the bestselling reggae album of all time).

At issue here is the matter of audience. This book is about American music, or more accurately, the albums that shaped American music and in the process American culture. Many of the Wailers' releases were important for one reason or another. Their early singles and albums—notably mid-1960s singles like "Simmer Down," "Rude Boy," and "Soul Rebel" and the 1970s' Lee "Scratch" Perry-produced *Soul Rebels*, *Rasta Revolution*, and *African*

Herbsman—were rarely heard outside Jamaica, but were powerful mixes of R&B, soul, ska, and rocksteady that laid the foundations for reggae in Jamaica and presaged dub music.

From its inception, reggae was essentially the music of the poor and disenfranchised in Jamaica in the 1960s and 1970s. Approximately one-third of the residents of Jamaica's capital, Kingston, were unemployed in the 1960s and crying out for a better life. Bob Marley, Peter Tosh, and Bunny Livingston—the core trio of the early Wailers—found their voice in the early 1960s as they sang on street corners in the slums of Trenchtown in West Kingston. Soon the trio adopted the beliefs of Rastafarianism, a Jamaican religion that regarded the Ethiopian King Haile Selassie as a prophet and prince of God (Jah), and their music reflected their beliefs. "Reggae, the word," explained Tosh, means "king's music," and I play the King's music. The King put many princes on earth, and the music is given to those who praise Him. You have to be spiritually inclined to deal with this kind of talent."[5]

The spiritual roots of reggae brought Marley fame well beyond the average earthly celebrity. Marley and his crew quickly took on a mythic proportion, and as their legend grew the strains of the Wailers and other burgeoning reggae acts—Toots and the Maytals, Burning Spear, Black Uhuru, and Steel Pulse—came to embody the cry of the downtrodden, replacing westernized calypso as the sound of Jamaica.

In 1973, the group released their first international LP with Island Records, *Catch a Fire*, an excellent album that earned them worldwide recognition, but still failed to ignite American audiences. As their international audience grew, the Wailers moved toward a more easy-going, commercial sound, slowly letting up on the angry militancy and social commentary that fueled their early releases (which is why no self-respecting Rastafarian would regard the toned-down collection on *Legend* as representative of Marley's music). Their live and studio albums over the next three years—*Live!*, *Natty Dread* (featuring their timeless classic "No Woman, No Cry"), *Rasta Revolution*, *Burnin'* (with the Eric Clapton-covered "I Shot the Sheriff"), and *Rastaman Vibration*—caught the band at their peak and earned them increasing critical recognition and commercial acceptance. Their influence was especially felt in the United Kingdom, as a large antiracism movement began developing in the mid-1970s. Early new-wave and punk acts adopted Jamaican ska and reggae as the universal sound of the oppressed and began importing the music into their own forms of anticapitalist garage rock. British bands, including the Selectors, the Specials, Madness, and the English Beat soon began bringing Jamaican sounds into western pop music.

In late 1976, Marley survived an assassination attempt two days before a politically charged music festival. While recuperating in London, he recorded *Exodus*, a major hit in the United Kingdom and a Top 20 in the United States. *Exodus* featured some of Marley's most enduring songs, including the title track, "Jamming," "Waiting in Vain," and the immortal

"One Love/People Get Ready," which was an extensive reworking of a Curtis Mayfield song. *Exodus* put Marley and the Wailers over the top in Britain and America, and was followed by a surge of reggae-infused punk bands in the United Kingdom. By the time Marley died from cancer five years later, he was nearly as well known in America as he was in Britain.

In 1984, three years after Marley's death, Island Records and the Wailers' label Tuff Gong released *Legend: The Best of Bob Marley and the Wailers*. An extraordinarily popular album in the United States, it came to define Marley's music and reggae in general for Americans, spending more than two years on the charts and embedding all fourteen of its songs in the brain patterns of anyone who ever kicked a hackey sack or threw a frisbee. The album's collection of "good vibrations" material in lieu of the Wailers' more political output made it a favorite leisure album, or a "defanged selection" as one later writer put it. "Listening to *Legend* to understand Marley is like reading *Bridget Jones's Diary* to get Jane Austen."[6] Nonetheless, for most Americans, *Legend* is the first and often only exposure they will ever have to Marley, and it is better than no exposure at all. But in terms of influence, it was *Exodus* that finally cracked open the door to the American market, an LP eventually hailed by *Time* magazine as the best album of the 20th century.

Album Title: *Saturday Night Fever*
Artist: Various Artists
Recorded: 1977
U.S. release: November 1977 (RSO)
Producer: Arif Mardin

"Every so often, a piece of music comes along that defines a moment in popular culture history: Johann Strauss' operetta *Die Fledermaus* did this in Vienna in the 1870s; Jerome Kern's *Show Boat* did it for Broadway musicals of the 1920s; and the Beatles' *Sgt. Pepper's Lonely Hearts Club Band* album served this purpose for the era of psychedelic music in the 1960s. *Saturday Night Fever*, although hardly as prodigious an artistic achievement as those precursors, was precisely that kind of musical phenomenon for the second half of the 1970s."[7]

The question begs to be asked: was disco really all that important? In the grand scheme of things, perhaps not. Compared with the blues, folk, jazz, punk, soul, and even classical genres that have informed popular tastes over the past century, each feeding into future developments in music, the influence of disco has largely fallen by the wayside, and many of its more enduring qualities were already present in the R&B and soul of Motown years before DJ Rick Dees took his embarrassingly comical "Disco Duck" to the top of the charts.

And yet, how many of us instantly recognize the opening riff to "Stayin' Alive," maybe produce a little head-bob when it unexpectedly appears on the radio, even absentmindedly sing those initial lyrics in our best Bee-Gee voice,

The soundtrack for the film *Saturday Night Fever*, which almost single-handedly turned disco from niche entertainment to national sensation. *Courtesy of Universal Music Enterprises.*

"Well you can tell by the way I use my walk..." and for those of us old enough to remember, transport ourselves for an instant to a very specific period of the late 1970s when bell bottoms and giant collars were the height of fashion? More than any other American genre, disco bookmarks a precise—and very small—period of popular music and its cultural backdrop, and more than any other album, the soundtrack to the film *Saturday Night Fever* bookmarks that genre.

The movie *Saturday Night Fever* came along at an opportune time. Starting in the late 1960s, pop music took on an increasingly central role in film. There had always been musicals whose soundtracks scored high on the charts, but the songs were written specifically for the film and carried elements of the movie's plot, and whatever impact they made on the wider culture was specifically because of their association with the film. But as rock and roll and its associated genres increasingly took control of the airwaves, films like 1967's *The Graduate*, 1969's *Easy Rider*, 1973's *American Graffiti*, and 1973's *Mean Streets* incorporated certain types of extant music to bring an associative edge to the movie (try to imagine *Easy Rider* without the Steppenwolf song "Born to be Wild," or *The Graduate* without Simon and Garfunkel's unique coming-of-age compositions).

In the 1970s, music graduated beyond soundtrack material to become the basis for the stories themselves. "More than two decades of rock and roll had expanded the music's audience enormously," claimed uber-critic Greil Marcus. "Events in rock history could now be taken, by filmmakers and by a broad, mass audience, as historical events pure and simple. No special audience or genre premise was needed to justify rock as subject matter."[8] Rock music's increasing omnipresence in American culture led to an explosion of movies in the mid–late 1970s, including rock musicals (*Tommy*, *Grease*, *Sgt. Pepper's Lonely Hearts Club Band*, *The Wiz*, and *Hair*), concert films (*The Blank Generation*, *The Last Waltz*, and *Good to See You Again, Alice Cooper*), rockumentaries (*Jimi Hendrix*, *Janis*, *The Kids Are Alright*, *Renaldo and Clara*, and *Journey Through the Past*), and music-themed films (*The Rose*, *American Hot Wax*, *The Buddy Holly Story*, *I Wanna Hold Your Hand*, and *Rock and Roll High School*).

Saturday Night Fever belonged to this latter category, feature films that used music as a central element in the plot. Disco had already been around for several years, largely a short-lived European phenomenon that had spread to gay and black clubs in the United States and, at the time, seemed on its way out. After a writer for *New York* magazine penned a feature on disco in Brooklyn, the article found its way into the hands of Robert Stigwood, a British (by way of Australia) producer who was behind the film adaptation of the Who album *Tommy* (and would later go on to produce the movies *Grease* and *Sgt. Pepper's Lonely Hearts Club Band*).

When *Saturday Night Fever* and its accompanying soundtrack were released in 1977, both far exceeded expectations. In addition to producing the film, Stigwood was the manager of the Bee Gees, whose songs permeate the movie and provided then-unknown star John Travolta with his own personal theme music. The combination of Travolta and the Bee Gees made the movie one of the biggest blockbusters up to that point, grossing more than fifteen times the expected $20 million at the box office.

The soundtrack, meanwhile, won a Grammy for album of the year and spent an incredible twenty-four weeks in the No. 1 spot—more than the combined total of every Rolling Stones album up to that point—making it the bestselling soundtrack of all time and one of the biggest albums in any genre. The Bee Gees were already a very popular band worldwide, but after scoring several No. 1 singles off the soundtrack, they were disco legends, producing two more chart-topping albums before the disco craze fizzled out as fast as it had ignited. But in those intervening two years the country went disco-mad, as dance floors, roller discos, disco cruises, and all-disco radio stations sprang up around the nation like some very groovy alien fungus. Never before had a single album had such an impact on its genre, and while disco itself may have been short-lived, the *Saturday Night Fever* soundtrack has survived as a one-stop nostalgia boutique for a very weird and fashion-challenged period of the latter 1970s.

Album Title: *Never Mind the Bollocks, Here's the Sex Pistols*
Artist: The Sex Pistols

Recorded: October 1976–August 1977, at Wessex Studios in London
U.S. release: November 10, 1977 (Warner Bros.)
Producer: Chris Thomas, Bill Price

It is unusual that the two most visible members of a band are the two least talented. But in mid–late-1970s punk rock—which was founded on the frustrations of youth who felt abandoned by their virtuosic rock heroes—the sincerest adoration was ladled on those who best embodied that frustration. And in a band like the Sex Pistols, which fired their original bassist for being a little too clean and talented, the two members who had no prior musical skills or training were bound to be the most adored.

"Enter Johnny Rotten," wrote one reviewer during the Pistols' first year as a cohesive group. "Not content to feel frustrated, bored and betrayed, he and the Sex Pistols...have decided to ignore what they believe to be the elitist pretensions of their heroes, who no longer play the music they want to hear. The Pistols are playing the music they want to hear. They are the tip of an iceberg."[9] Although lead singer Johnny Rotten (originally John Lydon) and replacement bassist Sid Vicious (John Ritchie) were not original members of the band, they have come to symbolize the energy, angst, and choreographed rebellion of mid-1970s London punk.

The pre-Rotten Sex Pistols were measurably less offensive, playing songs from the Who and the Small Faces' catalogs, but generally getting nowhere until they asked Malcolm McLaren to manage them. McLaren ran a risque London clothing store called SEX, and had spent a brief period managing the influential New York Dolls in the United States. Unimpressed by vocalist Steve Jones' showmanship, McLaren convinced Jones to learn guitar and replaced him on vocals with Rotten, a local truant who habited McLaren's shop.

What Rotten lacked in singing ability—and "lacked" does not even begin to cover it—he made up for in presence and attitude, screaming lyrics *at* the audience rather than to them, picking fights with fans from the stage, and confronting the pretension of pop music with headline-making comments and antics at every opportunity. "I hate shit," Rotten told a reporter during one of his first interviews only four months after joining the group. "I hate hippies and what they stand for. I hate long hair. I hate pub bands...I'm against people who just complain about Top Of The Pops and don't do anything. I want people to go out and start something, to see us and start something, or else I'm just wasting my time."[10]

Throughout 1976, the band built a loyal following at about the same rate they built controversy, as half their gigs turned into brawls and the other half were cancelled by local authorities. Between the Pistols' bad-boy behavior and McLaren's clever publicity stunts to capitalize on this image, the band took center stage in the unfolding drama of London punk, even though many of their contemporaries—the Clash, the Jam, the Damned, Buzzcocks—broke that ground first or were more skilled musicians. Built on the foundation laid in New York over the previous few years by the New York Dolls, the Ramones, and Television, punk music attracted a growing legion of young fans in London, "People sick of nostalgia," according to a 1976 Pistols performance review, "People wanting forward motion. People wanting rock and roll that is relevant to 1976. At the moment that criteria is best embodied in the Sex Pistols...They are loud. They are fast. They are energetic. They are great. Coming on like a Lockheed Starlighter is more important to them than virtuosity and sounding immaculate. This quartet has no time for a pretty song with a nice melody."[11]

In early 1977, Glen Matlock was kicked out of the group (over the years, explanations have ranged from an overabundance of skill to an overabundance of bathing, but his constant confrontations with Rotten almost certainly had a hand in it). Matlock was replaced by Sid Vicious on bass, a fan of the Pistols who matched Rotten's punk aesthetic and attitude to a T, but was so bad on his instrument that they kept his amplifier unplugged during many of their performances. The Pistols continued to aggravate proper Englanders with their mix of social diatribes and political baiting, releasing four singles (three of them charting in the U.K. Top 10) before finally issuing their only studio album (after being picked up and dropped by several labels) in late 1977, *Never Mind the Bollocks, Here's the Sex Pistols*, a top-of-the-lungs rant at capitalism, the British monarchy, and the oppression that kept down the working class.

The album continued the furor the band had been causing in England for nearly two years, setting off a lawsuit over the title ("bollocks" was considered an obscene word), inciting workers at the pressing plant to refuse to work on the LP, and provoking record stores and radio stations to ignore the release altogether. Nevertheless, the importance of the Sex Pistols in the punk revolution was confirmed when the album went to No. 1 on the British charts and ultimately became one of the decade's most important recordings. "*Never Mind the Bollocks* perfectly articulated the frustration, rage, and dissatisfaction of the British working class with the establishment, a spirit quick to translate itself to strictly rock & roll terms. The Pistols paved the way for countless other bands to make similarly rebellious statements, but arguably none were as daring or effective."[12] Though the album only reached No. 106 on the American charts and the band broke up two months later, the Sex Pistols took on mythical proportions in their homeland and the United States, fueling the emergence of punk on America's west coast and influencing a wide swath of alternative acts over the next two decades.

Album Title: *The Modern Dance*
Artist: Pere Ubu

Recorded: October 1976–November 1977, at Cleveland Recording in Cleveland, Ohio and SUMA in Painesville, Ohio
U.S. release: January 1978 (Blank)
Producer: Pere Ubu, Ken Hamann

"What we are not is pretty," Pere Ubu singer David Thomas told England's *New Musical Express* shortly before the band's debut album *The Modern Dance* was released in early 1978.[13] Much like the quintet's hometown of Cleveland, Ohio, Pere Ubu's avant-garde punk in the latter 1970s was remote and unattractive, but contained a strong sense of individuality and purpose. "It's hard for us to talk about what that is," Thomas continued. "We put the unit together with the idea that what we do would be different, but I don't know why it sounds like that....I suppose, though that it has something to do with Cleveland. There's this relationship between machines and flesh in Cleveland that is very strange....Cleveland is a giant, blown-out factory town...steel mills going flat out all day and all night, and it's just a half-mile away from where all the people live. This gives them the feeling that there's no future for somebody here, and all the musicians seem to be in love with that fact. In Cleveland nobody's going to pay any attention to you. The bands all know there's no future in a commercial sense for them, so they all say we're going to do what we goddamn want. All I can say is whatever you feel from the music is what it feels like to be here."

Music is always informed to some degree by a sense of place (where the act is from, where the album is recorded, what locales are particularly muse-like to a composer), and this was especially true at the advent of punk rock in the 1970s. The Sex Pistols based their entire repertoire on working-class oppression in London. Patti Smith's early work reeks of urban New Jersey and Manhattan's bohemian district. The Ramones drew the blueprint for bored-suburban-teenager rock. And just as the punk-rock noise and attitude began infiltrating the American musical tradition, industrial Ohio played a larger-than-expected role in punk's more avant-garde frontiers, largely thanks to Pere Ubu.

After leaving the well-known Cleveland proto-punk outfit Rocket from the Tombs in 1975, singer David Thomas and guitarist Peter Laughner put together Pere Ubu with guitarist Tom Herman, bassist Tim Wright, drummer Scott Krauss, and synthesizer player Allen Ravenstine. Though Thomas fronted the group with his eccentric lyrics and high-pitched caterwauling, Ravenstine provided the band with a unique sound by giving synthesizers a whole new role—not to mimic other instruments, as synths were traditionally used (hence the name), but to create entirely new, otherworldly sounds by playing the synthesizer as an original instrument.

The group's self-produced debut single, "30 Seconds over Tokyo," followed by "Final Solution" and "Street Waves" in 1976, announced to an appreciative underground that the new avant-garde revolution would not be coming out of New York this time around. The band's pulsating rhythms, regularly punctured by Thomas' nearly unlistenable vocals and occasional odd sound effects, built on the hypnotic and soothing krautrock and art-rock that came before, but added elements of disturbing urban decay that made their rhythmic charms seem like a decoy to entice listeners in so the anguished punctuations would be that much more effective.

In 1976 (after a minor lineup change), Mercury Records financed the group's debut album through Blank Records, an imprint made especially for Pere Ubu. "Built to last!" claimed a review in *Sounds*, praising the album's cutting-edge experimentation while deftly avoiding its utter lack of commercial appeal—or, for that matter, easy accessibility. "Ubu's world is often eerie, rarely comfortable, full of the space beyond the electric light and what it does to people, but always direct and unwavering. And courageous—or plain realistic: these days the two are getting synonymous: they see the collapse around them, the gap between reality and people's attitudes and face them squarely...."[14]

Like many avant-punk bands (as the critics called the new wave of screeching experimentation coming out of America's hinterland), Pere Ubu were better received in the United Kingdom than in the United States, failing to make a dent on the American charts, but earning kudos from a distance in London's insightful and widely read music journals. "Every week a new version of the future, every other week a new soundtrack of the times," wrote an album review in England's *New Musical Express*. "Seems like the race is on to see who can coin the most potent version of the world as we experience it now.... What counts is that the document reflects that mood of the times in a way that relates to and that can paradoxically offer both relief from and instruction on those times.... Pere Ubu offer neither relief nor instruction...they just simply experience things. They experience the human condition as it presently stands and, aside from a moment of Zen resolve in the final cut, find little or nothing to be joyful about."[15]

Pere Ubu followed *The Modern Dance* the next year with the equally groundbreaking *Dub Housing*, and taking their regular breakups, roster changes, and reunifications in stride, continued producing a unique blend of garage-rock, musique concrète, and offbeat experiments into the following decades. Though managing more than a dozen albums without ever cracking the charts—Thomas has famously called Pere Ubu "the longest-lasting, most disastrous commercial outfit to ever appear in rock 'n' roll"—the band's adventurous meanderings into bleak territory influenced countless new-wave and alternative acts in the 1980s and 1990s, including landmark groups such as the Pixies, Hüsker Dü, and Nine Inch Nails.

Album Title: *Van Halen*
Artist: Van Halen
Recorded: December 1977, at Sunset Sound in Hollywood
U.S. release: February 10, 1978 (Warner Bros.)
Producer: Ted Templeman

Until 1978, heavy metal approximated the sound of its own name: thick, powerful, weighty guitar riffs and bass lines with punishing percussion and dark themes of youthful angst, drugs, insanity, and the occult. It was music taken seriously by its earliest practitioners—Deep Purple, Alice Cooper, Black Sabbath, Blue Cheer—and even more so by its fans, who huddled together under the metal umbrella and found community among like-minded outsiders.

Then the party showed up. Out of nowhere—also known as Pasadena, California—the self-titled Van Halen debut album rose to No. 19 on the pop charts in early 1978. Within three months, it was gold. Within six months, it was platinum. Within two years, *Van Halen* would be appreciated as a landmark release, bringing heavy metal into popular music territory, infusing it with a positive energy that appealed to the rocker and the partier inside music fans, who could now experience the power and energy of metal without its gloom-and-doom themes. "We celebrate all the sex and violence of the television, all the rockin' on the radio, the movies, the cars and everything about being young or semi-young or young at heart," claimed lead singer David Lee Roth soon after the band's vinyl debut. "That's Van Halen."[16]

From the beginning, Van Halen was a balancing act between David Lee Roth's promises and guitarist Eddie Van Halen's delivery. Eddie Van Halen and his brother Alex Van Halen studied classical piano from a young age. In their early teens (Alex was two years older), Eddie took up drums, while Alex studied guitar. The story goes that Alex played Eddie's drums while Eddie worked his paper route to pay for them. When Alex's drumming skills surpassed his own, a dismayed Eddie took up the guitar and became addicted to it, sometimes skipping school to practice, and by fourteen he had learned every Cream lick laid down by his hero, Eric Clapton.

Shortly after high school, the Van Halen brothers teamed up with singer David Lee Roth and bassist Michael Anthony after all four members had stints with other bands, and the quartet began playing the Los Angeles scene. Their ability to cover material from bands such as Bad Company, Aerosmith, ZZ Top, and Led Zeppelin—as good as or better than the originals—earned them a respectable local following, and by the time they began working their own material into their sets, they were one of the biggest bands in the Los Angeles rock scene, headlining venues along the Sunset Strip like the famous Whisky-A-Go-Go. In 1976, KISS bassist Gene Simmons saw one of these shows and offered to pay for a set of demo tapes for the band, ultimately resulting in a record deal with Warner Bros. and their debut release in 1978.

Eddie Van Halen's classical training paid off enormously, as he opened the door to a new way of thinking about rock guitar, expanding the instrument beyond its blues roots and into a classically informed format. His blinding arpeggios, heavy use of vibrato, and a unique tapping technique using both hands on the fretboard (applying "hammer-ons" and "pull offs" that allowed him to play the guitar like a keyboard at unbelievable speeds) were blueprints for a new generation of six-string slingers. After the release of *Van Halen*, every guitarist wanted to be Eddie, who would win *Guitar Player*'s annual "Best Rock Guitarist" award for the next five years.

The most successful rock bands have always been the ones who could exhibit not only musical virtuosity, but a degree of showmanship to draw the crowds. Although David Lee Roth was a merely adequate singer, his ability to whip a crowd into a frenzy with his acrobatic leaps, party-rock vocals, and hypnotic presence contributed to what Roth called "entertainment delivered at maximum impact."[17] The man dripped rock-star charm, and grounded by Alex Van Halen's clever drumming and Michael Anthony's more-than-competent bass, Roth's showmanship and Eddie's furious licks rained down on the rock scene like radio-friendly *deus ex machina*. From the first notes—which are actually sampled car horns—on the opening track "Runnin' with the Devil," to the banshee screams on the closer "On Fire," *Van Halen* put its listeners in a headlock and demanded their attention. Eddie's dizzying fretboard display on "Eruption" became his most famous composition, required imitating by every teenage air guitarist for years to come (all the more remarkable given that the song was actually just one of Eddie's warm-up exercises). Without a stage from which to charm listeners, Roth found his vinyl persona through a sense of play—almost as if he were singing metal out of pure irony—best encapsulated in one of the two covers on the album, the Elmore James/John Brim song "Ice Cream Man," which features yet another mind-bending solo by Eddie. These tracks have joined every other song on the album—"You Really Got Me," "Ain't Talkin' 'bout Love," "I'm the One," "Jamie's Cryin'," "Atomic Punk," "Feel Your Love Tonight," and "Little Dreamer"—as classic rock radio staples, making the LP one of the most enduring albums in the metal canon, and paving the way for Van Halen to become one of the biggest bands of the 1980s, with every one of their eleven studio albums breaking the Top 10 over the next two decades.

The release of *Van Halen* has been marked as the advent of "pop metal," also called "hair metal" and "glam metal" for all the . . . hairy, glamorous acts that followed in its wake. Up to this point, London had been the epicenter of the heavy-metal universe, producing the overwhelming majority of metal acts in the decade or so since it had come into its own as a distinct genre. The advent of *Van Halen* sparked an explosion of California-based pop metal that would ring through the 1980s with bands like Guns N' Roses, Mötley Crüe, Ratt, Metallica, and Quiet Riot, suddenly giving rock and roll a new home base in Los Angeles and marking a sea change in the sound of American popular music.

Album Title: *One Nation Under a Groove*
Artist: Funkadelic
Recorded: April 15, 1978, at the Monroe Civic Center in Monroe, Louisiana, and United Sound in Detroit, Michigan
U.S. release: September 1978 (Priority)
Producer: George Clinton

The history and mythology behind George Clinton's 1970s funk circus is far too complicated and involved to relate in detail here. In summary, a series of complex legal issues in the late 1960s and early 1970s resulted in Clinton and his entourage recording for several different labels under several different names, though always drawing from the same pool of musicians. Sometimes the musicians worked anonymously or under adopted names of funk alter-egos, which helped prevent contract issues with the labels. Clinton had learned from his negative label experiences with his first band, the Parliaments, and his clever skirting of industry contracts led to the creation of the P-Funk spectacle, a combination of his two major outfits Parliament and Funkadelic, both of which were landmark funk bands in the 1970s sharing more than fifty musicians between them (see Parliament's album *Mothership Connection* on p. 127).

By 1978, Clinton's troops had amassed an arsenal of powerful, forward-looking soul and funk, releasing as many as a half-dozen albums a year, including groundbreaking LPs such as Parliament's *Up for the Downstroke*, *Chocolate City*, and *Mothership Connection*, and Funkadelic's *Free Your*

Mind...And Your Ass Will Follow, Funkadelic, and *Maggot Brain*. A decade before hip-hop made its first inroads into popular music, Clinton and company rivaled Sly Stone and James Brown as masters of party funk, jive rap, and energetic R&B.

In the process, Clinton became a skilled bandleader, applying the lessons he learned about dealing with the music industry through unconventional means to his music, encouraging his collaborators to break free from traditional expectations of how music is "supposed" to sound. "Funkadelic is an attitude to whatever it takes," Clinton told *New Musical Express* in 1978. "You can get away with so much when you haven't got to think about structures or constructions and can leave yourself to your instincts and know that it's cool and all the musicians know it that way. Then the possibilities are unlimited....Even now the music scares us sometimes, like 'Wow! Did you hear that?' So think what we might eventually achieve. At the same time we know it just ain't us; it's something coming through us.... What I mean is we've learned how to relax and play and be inspired by one another, and by being crazy all along we don't have to go by no rules."[18]

The main difference between the sounds coming out of Parliament and Funkadelic was the predominance of horns in the former and guitars in the latter. Though both were based on the soul and psychedelia of the 1960s, Parliament owed more to James Brown, while Funkadelic was deeply in debt to Frank Zappa and Jimi Hendrix. Through the mid-1970s, Parliament took the lead on the pop charts, often cracking the Top 40 and Top 20, while the less-accessible Funkadelic hovered around the unfashionable end of the Top 100.

That changed when George Clinton recruited the brilliant Junie Morrison in 1977 to join his assembly as keyboardist and music director. Morrison had already found some fame with the Ohio Players in the early 1970s, with whom he wrote the 1971 hit "Funky Worm." Although *One Nation Under a Groove* was Morrison's debut with Funkadelic, the album is soaked with his presence, from his smooth, upbeat keyboards to his lyrical contributions. Also moving to the forefront of the band's sound was Michael Hampton, who started playing with Clinton while he was a teenage guitar prodigy, but fully comes into his own on this album with the authority of Jimi Hendrix playing hip-hop. Funkadelic already had a notable list of artists on their roster—including Bootsy Collins, who provided the backbone to the P-Funk sound with his authoritative bass playing, and the Julliard-trained Bernie Worrell, whose arrangements and inventive synthesizer work gave both bands a space-funk feel. With such a skilled group of musicians and a prolific output, Clinton guided the P-Funk family to the top of the R&B kingdom in the late 1970s.

Funkadelic had taken a backseat to Parliament on the charts in recent years, but *One Nation Under a Groove* brought them into their own, providing the band with their first platinum album and their most popular release, appearing at No. 16 on the pop charts. More accessible than their earlier albums, *One Nation Under a Groove*—surrounded by a series of hit singles on the R&B charts—opened up the commercial possibilities of the band without sacrificing the groundbreaking experimentation the outfit had become known for. While earlier releases tested a wide range of urban black tropes, sometimes bordering on the militant, *One Nation Under a Groove* elevated Funkadelic's constantly changing themes to a joyous celebration of community and free-thinking, particularly through the first three mesmerizing tracks "One Nation Under a Groove," "Groovallegiance," and the aptly named "Who Says a Funk Band Can't Play Rock?" The album received lofty praise upon its release, and has become widely accepted as the pinnacle of funk-rock and one of the greatest R&B releases of all time. Its influence on the new music of the 1980s and 1990s is almost without peer, with future hip-hop artists like Dr. Dre, Snoop Dogg, and Ice Cube borrowing directly from the album, and pop acts ranging from the Red Hot Chili Peppers to De La Soul to Talking Heads incorporating the unique Clintonian funk into their own influential work.

Album Title: *Rust Never Sleeps*
Artist: Neil Young
Recorded: 1978 and 1979
U.S. release: July 1979 (Reprise)
Producer: Neil Young and Crazy Horse, Tim Mulligan, David Briggs

Neil Young is something of a paradox, and has been since he first rose to fame with Buffalo Springfield in the late 1960s. More than most artists, Young represents a range of styles that has made him hard to pigeonhole, exploring hard rock, folk-rock, country-rock, punk rock, and grunge with varying degrees of success, but always with his uniquely brooding lyrics and from-the-gut delivery that has earned him both praise and derision over the decades, but mostly it has earned him enduring respect as one of rock's truly original icons. "I don't know if I can be classed as a contemporary songwriter," said Young between his punk and grunge periods in the early 1980s. "I'm like a dinosaur with a large tail—I'm so big I have to keep eating all the time. I look around, there's not many dinosaurs left, just a lot of smaller animals moving very fast. And it's their vibrant energy that I need to stay alive. Sometimes I think I might have to cut off my tail because I can't afford to keep feeding myself."[19] The smaller, swifter animals in the late 1970s were the purveyors of punk rock, a genre suited to Young's general distaste for and distrust of the music industry, but a genre seemingly incompatible with the aging blues-rock and vulnerable singer-songwriter material that had made Young famous.

A Canadian by birth, Young moved to Los Angeles in his early twenties and found success partnering with Stephen Stills in the early folk-rock act Buffalo Springfield, whose Stills-penned hit "For What It's Worth" provided an anthem for antiauthority activists in the late 1960s. Following Buffalo Springfield's breakup, Young juggled a budding solo career and a stint with the trio Crosby, Stills and Nash, forming CSN&Y, one of the most popular and enduring west-coast rock groups of the early 1970s. Between CSN&Y's two No. 1 albums (1971's *Deju vu* and 1972's *4 Way Street*) and his own Top 10 LPs (1970's *After the Gold Rush* and 1972's *Harvest*), Young was at the top of his game, respected as one of America's most stirring lyricists. But as Young straddled the rock and the singer-songwriter worlds, he also faced commercial success with a wary eye, referring to his 1972 breakthrough No. 1 single "Heart of Gold," as the song that "put me in the middle of the road." However, after a fair taste of success, he decided the middle of the road was a good place to get run over. "Traveling there soon became a bore so I headed for the ditch. A rougher ride, but I saw more interesting people there."[20]

His follow-up releases would be known as his "ditch albums," taking him further from commercial success, but leading to some interesting collaborations through the 1970s with artists like Stephen Stills, Emmylou Harris, and Linda Ronstadt, and more notably, an enduring relationship with his back-up band Crazy Horse. With his 1978 album *Comes a Time* and 1979's *Rust Never Sleeps*, Young experienced a sudden resurgence in popularity, not because he had given in to mass tastes, but because his musical interests and the course of rock and roll had merged again in the form of punk music.

Young's material had always exhibited a degree of the individuality that marked punk rock—eschewing technical virtuosity and pretentious lyrics for simple melodies and common-man themes. The collision between Young's earthy lyricism and punk's rebellious energy marks *Rust Never Sleeps*, a partially live release featuring acoustic tracks on one side and electric on the other. Largely remembered for its opening and closing tracks—the acoustic "My My, Hey Hey (Out of the Blue)" and the electric rework "Hey Hey, My My (Into the Black)"—which highlight Sex Pistols singer Johnny Rotten as a symbol of rock's evolution, the album has been hailed in retrospect as the bedrock of the grunge movement that would appear more than a decade later. "*Rust Never Sleeps* is an album borne of the decade that saw Vietnam, environmental disasters, and other events of global change, and ends up being one of the most direct and coherent statements about the punk movement ever put to vinyl," claimed a later reviewer. "This is the story of Johnny Rotten," Young sings, and you know he sees Rotten as the ambassador to an irresistible driving force in popular music at the time. This only serves to reinforce the grunge connection, with that later (and almost exclusively North American) phenomenon being a fruitful (if somewhat overdue) offspring of the union between punk and rock music."[21]

Although Young was highly respected during his heyday in the 1970s, it would be another decade before his mingling of punk and straight-up blues rock was appreciated by a new generation of alternative musicians such as Sonic Youth, Nirvana, and Pearl Jam, whose moody tales of teen agony further influenced Young's work in the 1990s and beyond. To what degree Young and *Rust Never Sleeps* were directly responsible for the grunge movement that changed the course of music in the 1990s has been debated to death, but many of the 1990s' top Americana and grunge bands have cited him as an influence, and the suicide note of Kurt Cobain—the lead singer for Nirvana whose death was one of the most significant moments in 1990s music—contained Young's most famous lyric from *Rust Never Sleeps*: "It's better to burn out than fade away."

"For the decade's greatest rock and roller to come out with his greatest album in 1979 is no miracle in itself," claimed notable music critic Robert Christgau, "the Stones made *Exile* as grizzled veterans. The miracle is that Young doesn't sound much more grizzled now than he already did in 1969; he's wiser but not wearier, victor so far over the slow burnout his title warns of."[22]

Album Title: *London Calling*
Artist: The Clash
Recorded: August 1979, at Wessex Studios in London
U.S. release: January 1980 (Epic)
Producer: Guy Stevens

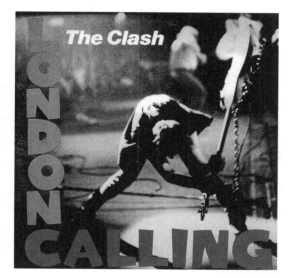

The Clash's 1980 double album *London Calling*, which brought focused politics to punk rock. *Courtesy of Photofest.*

"If the Sex Pistols were the promise of punk shattered soon after leaving the starting gate, the Clash were punk rock's potential fulfilled both musically and commercially."[23] Comparing the Clash to the Sex Pistols has become the de facto method of defining the Clash within the complicated rubric of late-1970s punk music, as well as a favorite metaphor among music journalists for punk rock's lifespan in the United Kingdom. The Sex Pistols were one of London's first punk bands and the most infamous, serving both as an inspiration to other acts and as a voice for the frustrated, disenfranchised youth from working-class families. The Clash expanded punk's role both musically—creating much more sophisticated and engaging songs than the Sex Pistols were capable of—and socially, extending the Pistols' anticapitalist angst to the world stage.

It was in early 1976 when singer, songwriter, and guitarist Joe Strummer saw the Sex Pistols perform, opening his eyes to the future of British music and inspiring him to quit his group the 101ers. Teaming up with guitarist Mick Jones, bassist Paul Simonon, drummer Terry Chimes, and guitarist Keith Levene, Strummer became the frontman for the Clash, playing their first gig on July 10, 1976, as the opening act for the Pistols (the Clash manager, Bernie Rhodes, had once worked for Sex Pistols manager Malcolm McLaren, creating an instant image for the Clash as the Pistols' successor).

By the end of the year (with minor lineup changes), the Clash had signed with CBS Records and released their self-titled debut album the following summer, beating the Pistols to vinyl as the Pistols had been signed and dropped by several labels already, only managing to get one single out of the studio. The Clash quickly took their place as top new stars among pace-setting U.K. punk bands like the Damned, the Buzzcocks, the Boomtown Rats, and the Stranglers, and soon the Clash and the Pistols came to define British punk for international audiences. The Clash, however, invited criticism from some corners as sellouts, as their world-music influences and their desire to extend punk rock beyond its limited confines of ama-teurish, open-ended rebellion brought them commercial recognition and critical appreciation unseemly for a punk outfit. "Whereas the Pistols stayed within a limited musical framework, the Clash were consciously assimilating influences from external styles and rapidly expanding their musical boundaries. The Clash, through lyrics and social deeds, chose to present their criticism of imperialism, racism, and an abusive economic system in concrete personal and political terms, as opposed to the uncon-scious, undirected rage of the Pistols' shocking stories and situations. The Pistols were content to strike out and expose; the Clash wanted to have some impact on their audience."[24]

The Clash's debut album was not initially released in the United States, but soon became the bestselling import of all time, leading to its release in America (in an altered form) two years later alongside the band's second album, 1978's *Give 'em Enough Rope*. Critical approval in the States and increasing admiration in the United Kingdom set the stage for two U.S. tours in 1979, helping the band build an appreciable fan base to make the group's opus, the sprawling double album *London Calling*, the first punk LP to break the Top 40 in America, and one of the most important releases since Patti Smith's *Horses* in 1975 and the Ramones' *Ramones* in 1976.

London Calling is regarded in some corners as the death of punk rock, owing to its sophistication that steps well beyond the accepted limits of punk amateurism. The Clash reached past the U.K.-centric garage rock of the Sex Pistols to include a wide range of styles, from rockabilly to pop to R&B to hard rock, surprising listeners with a sincere and studied sampling of rock's complex web of subgenres. And yet, despite the competent mu-sicianship and far-reaching influences that earned the Clash categorization as a new-wave band, their music retained all the fury and frustration of punk's most snarling activists, expanding working-class aggravation be-yond London's poorer districts to speak for injustice everywhere. The Clash notably incorporated the Jamaican sounds and attitudes of ska, rocksteady, and reggae to their music—as had some of their contemporaries such as the Specials, the Selector, Madness, the Police, and the English Beat—elevating Jamaican dissident music to a language that represented resistance to universal oppression.

The reach of *London Calling* was much wider than their previous two albums, both stylistically and commercially, earning the band tremendous respect in both the United States and in England. With themes reaching from drug addiction to British politics to American folklore to the Spanish Civil War, *London Calling* was a masterwork of political insight and social awareness, delivered with equal degrees of musical erudition and virtuous outrage, charting an energetic, engaged direction for punk and new wave. From its opening political diatribe "London Calling" to its infectious pop closer "Train in Vain"—both songs earning permanent spots in the punk-rock canon—the album encapsulated the paradox of punk's anticommercial agenda and its commercial potential. This paradox carried over on the famous album cover—a fuzzy photograph of Paul Simonon smashing his bass onstage, with the album titles imitating Elvis Presley's debut LP—summarizing the violent sounds of punk within the framework of classic pop and rock influences.

Although the double album consisted of more than an hour of music spread over nineteen tracks, the band insisted it be sold as cheaply as possible—priced at five pounds in London—so their target audience could afford it, which only added to the group's reputation as true voices for the poor and oppressed. *London Calling* has earned an enduring reputation as a landmark precursor to the "alternative" rock that would emerge through the next two decades, finding a spot on many "best album" lists and considered by many the most revolutionary release of the 1980s.

Album Title: *Back in Black*
Artist: AC/DC
Recorded: April–May 1980, at Compass Point Studios in the Bahamas
U.S. release: July 25, 1980 (ATCO)
Producer: Robert John "Mutt" Lange

"[I]t is rather inspired...that the undisputed idol of the HM [heavy metal] scene should be not a godlike space warrior but a hypnotically grotesque brat who appears to be having a permanent epileptic fit....His performance is a form of possession, and the audience becomes merely an extension of the guitar's emissions, gasping between its repeated stabs. Angus Young is what happens when—out of desperation and frustration—the youth once more call for the monster of Metal to rescue them from reality."[25]

As the guitarist for Australian heavy-metal band AC/DC, Angus Young did more than rescue teenagers from reality. With a little help from his bandmates, he rescued heavy metal too. In 1980, at a time when metal dinosaurs like Deep Purple and Black Sabbath were losing their touch (as well as their audiences), and newcomers like Van Halen and Ted Nugent were hard to take seriously (a case of intentional playfulness with the former and comical overkill with the latter), AC/DC struck out for America' shores to remind everybody what heavy metal was all about: alienated teenagers bobbing their heads in unison to crunchy power chords, banshee screams, and a thundering rhythm section. No vain posturing as in the rapidly fading phenomenon of disco, no angry politics like the self-imploding punk genre, no ironic social awareness like the trendsetting new wavers, and no heavily polished arena filler like the overproduced corporate groups that were hijacking America's radios. Just loud rock played with wild abandon. "They've got a strong rock'n'roll/boogie following, dedicated to guitarmanship, high energy and raw power," summarized a live review in San Francisco on the band's first tour of America's west coast in 1977. "AC/DC doesn't use safety pins, never went to art school, and they sure don't limit themselves to 2 or 3 chords, but if new wave is a reaffirmation of rock'n'roll's traditional values, this band is an important part of it."[26]

It took AC/DC five albums in three years to break through in the United States (several of their LPs were not released in America), and along the way they were classified as both punk and new wave, finally giving way to the heavy-metal label under the weight of Angus Young's maniacal guitar solos and lead singer Bon Scott's distinctive shrieks. Founded in Melbourne in 1973 by Scottish brothers Angus and Malcolm Young (both guitarists), the group went through several members before eventually stabilizing around singer Ron Belford "Bon" Scott (originally the band's chauffer), bassist Mark Evans, and drummer Phil Rudd. Only fifteen years old when the band formed, Angus wore his school uniform onstage (reportedly a suggestion made by his sister), an image that became an enduring trademark for the group as they spent the mid-1970s working to become one of Australia's top musical acts.

With their initial albums in 1977 and 1978, the group tasted success at home and in the United Kingdom, finally cracking the American Top 20 with their 1979 hit *Highway to Hell* when producer Robert John "Mutt" Lange was brought on board, giving the band a meatier sound. Suddenly experiencing a wave of popularity in U.S. heavy-metal circles, the group continued gathering stateside support through a series of tours with smoking live performances. "AC/DC operates on the musical principle that the best way to an audience's heart is to hammer it into submission with a collection of hoary, heavy-rock cliches," wrote one reviewer in Los Angeles just as the band teetered on the brink of stardom. "Concepts like subtlety, refinement and dynamics don't exist in its musical dictionary.... All the songs are built around short, choppy guitar riffs supported by a throbbing, elementary rhythm and topped by Scott's hoarse screeching and macho breast beating. AC/DC's dedication to the primeval stomp sustained my interest for about 20 minutes, but the utter lack of variety and Angus' increasingly excessive guitar solos ultimately registered as boring in the extreme."[27]

But what was boring to sophisticated music journalists was cathartic to fans of tear-the-walls-down heavy metal. The band set out to record their breakthrough album in early 1980, but were stopped suddenly by Bon Scott's untimely death from an overindulgence in alcohol. Angus Young was the band's image, but Scott's throat-shredding vocals were a large part of their sound, and the group appeared doomed on the eve of superstardom. The band members soon agreed that Scott would have wanted the act to continue, and hired Brian Johnson—singer for the British band Geordie, of whom Scott had been a fan—to replace him. Johnson's screeching vocal style was amazingly similar to Scott's, and when *Back in Black* was released only six months after Scott's death (ostensibly as a tribute album), it was as if the band had barely missed a beat—some reviews even mistook Johnson's vocals for Scott's, giving Scott postmortem kudos for a world-shaking release.

Back in Black shot to No. 4 in the United States, remaining on the charts for nearly three years, ultimately becoming the fifth highest selling album of all time in America and one of the bestselling albums in the world. Buoyed by immortal tracks like "Back in Black," "Hell's Bells," "You Shook Me All Night Long," and "Rock and Roll Ain't Noise Pollution," the album was the first heavy-metal release in years to find wide acceptance, helping to fuel the genre to massive sales in the 1980s. AC/DC fans were devoted to the band in a way that could be described as cultish, had there not been so many thousands of them, and seeing the group live became a right of passage for any self-respecting metal-head. "From the sanctuary of the soundman's enclosure on the balcony they looked like...a jar of maggots seething and squirming in the crush to be an inch or three closer to the stage," a live reviewer claimed upon noticing the fans' fanatical eagerness. "They must have been just about as uncomfortable as any human being could be outside of trench warfare and yet they were very happy too....It's an instinctive flesh and blood volcano. Compress and compress the energy, and soon it must erupt."[28]

Album Title: *Thriller*
Artist: Michael Jackson
Recorded: April–November 1982, at Westlake Audio in Los Angeles
U.S. release: December 1, 1982 (Epic)
Producer: Quincy Jones

In the minds of some, Michael Jackson's legacy is that of tabloid fodder, a bizarre, overly hyped has-been, whose strange habits and uncomfortably sincere love of children make the rest of us feel a little more normal. To his fans, he is a misunderstood genius, so unbelievably famous that all avenues of normality are closed to him, and so unbelievably gifted that his role as artist-savant allows his behavior to extend beyond the limits of mere mortals. "His fame fascinates because it is total," wrote Barney Hoskyns in 1983 at Jackson's absolute peak of stardom. "Seemingly withdrawn from it, in fact it

Michael Jackson's 1982 album *Thriller*, which would become the bestselling album in the world by the end of the century. *Courtesy of Photofest.*

cocoons him. Like Howard Hughes, he doesn't have a public relationship with fame but abstractly embodies it. So when he starts saying things that sound completely mad, like "if I could, I would sleep onstage," he is simply stating a logical implication."[29] But before the paparazzi, before the "Entertainment Tonight" exclusives, before the Elephant Man's bones, the pet monkey, the private amusement park, the plastic surgeries, the oxygen tent, the endless parade of prying noses into every crevice of his life, Michael Jackson was music.

And what music it was. Jackson was not just the king of pop, he was the essence of it. Inasmuch as "pop" is a definable genre, Jackson's smooth delivery and catchy phrases defined popular music in the 1980s, and became the yardstick for universally accessible sound. Jackson's mastery of pop (as well as his unusual behavior) can be attributed to the fact that he has never known life outside the spotlight, starting his career before his sixth birthday as lead singer for his family group the Jackson 5, later billed as the Jacksons after they moved to the Epic label in 1976. One of Motown's marquee groups in the early 1970s, the Jackson 5 brought Michael's voice to the forefront of pop and R&B with No. 1 hits like "I'll Be There," "ABC," "I Want You Back," and "The Love You Save," paving the way for future success for several of the siblings. Michael began a solo career when the Jackson 5 were still on top, scoring hits with "Rockin' Robin" and "Ben" in 1972, the latter a very unusual love song dedicated to a pet rat. Though he waded through several medicore recordings in the 1970s with R&B greats Brian Holland and Berry Gordy Jr. alternating in the production role, Jackson did not find his voice until he began recording his own compositions under the guidance of uber-producer Quincy Jones. Jones and Jackson had met during production of the film *The Wiz*, for which Jackson played the scarecrow and Jones produced the soundtrack. The two teamed up to give Jackson a sound that would distinguish him from his Jackson 5 days. With the album *Off the Wall* in 1979, Jackson came into his own as a solo performer and changed the face of pop forever.

Off the Wall was itself a monumental release, and were it not for the phenomenal impact of the follow-up *Thriller*, would be featured among these listings on its own merits. With *Off the Wall*, Jackson became the first solo artist to chart four singles in the Top 10 off of one album—"Don't Stop 'Til You Get Enough," "Off the Wall," "Rock With You," and "She's Out of My Life"—a feat that had only been accomplished by Fleetwood Mac and two soundtrack recordings before. Jackson wrote two songs for the album, including the No. 1 "Don't Stop 'Til You Get Enough," opening a new door for himself as an intelligent pop craftsman rather than merely an interpreter of other people's visions. The more Jackson invested in his own talents, the brighter his star shone, despite his unusual modesty. "I wake up from dreams and go 'Wow, put *this* down on paper'," Jackson told *Rolling Stone* about his songwriting process. "The whole thing is strange. You hear the words, everything is right there in front of your face. . . . And that's why I hate to take credit for the songs I've written. I feel that somewhere, someplace, it's been done and I'm just a courier bringing it into the world."[30]

Michael's shy, sensitive persona seemed like some kind of secret identity when stacked next to the pop superhero that emerged onstage, and when it took three years for him to release his next album *Thriller*, the anticipation had built to the point that the album was expected to save the world. The truth was not far off—*Thriller* spent thirty-seven weeks at No. 1 and nearly a year and a half in the Top 10, the second-highest charting album in history next to the 1962 soundtrack for *West Side Story*. At its peak, it sold one million copies per week. Its status as the bestselling album in American history was eventually toppled by the unusual lifespan of the Eagles' *Greatest Hits 1971–1975*, but worldwide it has never been equaled, with international sales estimated at nearly 60 million copies, more than the combined solo domestic catalogs of all four Beatles. Jackson also smashed his previous record set by *Off the Wall* by placing seven singles from *Thriller* in the Top 10—"Thriller," "Billy Jean," "The Girl is Mine," "Wanna Be Startin' Somethin'," "Human Nature," "P.Y.T. (Pretty Young Thing)," and "Beat It"—with both *Thriller* and "Billie Jean" simultaneously topping the charts in both America and in England.

More than moving Jackson to the highest echelon of pop stardom, *Thriller* broke barriers for black artists on mainstream radio and on MTV. Jackson became one of MTV's biggest stars, allowing him to show off his trendsetting moves that were praised by dance legends Bob Fosse, Gene Kelly, and Fred Astaire. Eddie Van Halen, another one of pop's biggest names, played guitar on "Beat It" for free, one of several crossover collaborations for Jackson that included memorable duos with Paul McCartney. The music video for "Thriller" was highly anticipated, and endures as perhaps MTV's most legendary feature. Ultimately *Thriller* reached platinum status or higher in at least fourteen countries, and its unbelievable sales, crossover appeal, and role in popularizing music videos made it one of the most important albums in the American musical canon, and Michael Jackson the world's best-known pop icon. "He's taken us right up there where we belong," Quincy Jones told *Time* magazine in a cover story on the artist. "Black music had to play second fiddle for a long time, but its spirit is the whole motor of pop. Michael has connected with every soul in the world."[31]

Album Title: *Pyromania*
Artist: Def Leppard
Recorded: 1982, at Park Gates Studios in Sussex, England and Battery Studios in London
U.S. release: January 20, 1983 (Mercury)
Producer: Robert John "Mutt" Lange

Def Leppard's 1983 breakout *Pyromania*, which led the charge of pop-metal through the 1980s. *Courtesy of Photofest.*

They called it the "new wave of heavy metal," and some even went so far as to use the acronym "NWOHM" (or "NWOBHM," since much of it came out of Britain). It's not that there was anything wrong with the old heavy metal, but as Van Halen opened the door to a slew of new American groups like Mötley Crüe and Quiet Riot, threatening to recenter heavy metal in Los Angeles, the United Kingdom countered with a surge of slick pop-metal bands that focused on loud, fast, and entertaining rock. And they came by the truck full—an estimated thousand or so metal acts trying to take over England between 1978 and 1982—helping reinvigorate the waning heavy-metal scene in both the United States and the United Kingdom, and with a more formulaic touch than their predecessors, make the genre more accessible to mainstream audiences. "Have there ever been so many heavy bands getting signed," asked a *Village Voice* reporter in 1983, "breaking onto play-lists, and appearing bad, live, and nationwide on triple bills around the world? So many shag haircuts? So much loud abysmal dreck?"[32]

The formula was simple: Start with a solid, easy to memorize song about love, rock and roll, or other tropes important to teenage boys (occasionally a reference to the occult or other dark themes thrown in to give the band an edge, but couched in much more positive terms than earlier metal acts). Pin the song on catchy hooks and guitar riffs, highlighting an impossible-to-forget refrain, usually sung at the top of one's voice and with the pinky and index finger jutting defiantly into the air. Inflate the song to maximum thickness with punishing drums and rhythm guitars and a heavy dose of background vocals, and when the mood strikes, garnish with a lead guitar solo. Bake between three and four minutes—any longer and the audience will catch on to the simple recipe.

Formulaic or not, many bands from British metal's new wave rocked hard, with Judas Priest, Iron Maiden, and Def Leppard leading the invasion in the United States. But where the former two were pigeonholed into the metal category (largely by Christian groups who misunderstood some of their lyrics as Satanic, or more often simply believed they were without actually listening to them), Def Leppard managed to dodge most controversy by avoiding darker themes, maintaining a surprisingly clean and disciplined air of professionalism in their work, and by virtue of being young and wholesome, attracting enough girls to their fold to make them purveyors of well-rounded pop-metal.

"Def Leppard typify the 'new' metal—or the 'new' hard rock—because their product is not, like the 'old' metal, based on an attempt to utilize modern technology to express, reinvent, or just psychedelicize the blues," wrote one reviewer. "In fact, the 'new' heavy metal isn't based on much except a market for the regurgitation of the old. Like just about every other 'new' heavy band (and every other 'old' heavy band, too), Def Leppard have very little to tell us except they think it's rock and roll and they like it."[33]

Def Leppard's simplistic pop metal (meaning only that it had a simple sound—the band became known for putting a tremendous amount of work into their music, so the effort itself was by no means simple) earned them derision in the United Kingdom, where they were accused of pandering to American audiences. Although true, the disparagement stung the group until they were finally accepted commercially in England in the latter 1980s. Meanwhile, the band focused on the United States, where their first two albums reached the Top 60 on the charts before 1983's *Pyromania* swept the country with the help of several popular music videos. *Pyromania* reached No. 2 in America—held back by the astounding success of Michael Jackson's *Thriller*—and buoyed by the hit singles "Foolin,'" "Photograph," and "Rock of Ages," made the band an arena-rock attraction and one of the first pop-metal bands to receive heavy airplay on MTV, which would find a massive audience for the genre through the 1980s.

Pyromania sold six million copies in the United States its first year alone, opening the door for many successful (but limited) imitations in the 1980s, including Bon Jovi, Poison, Warrant, Slaughter, and Cinderella. Though Bon Jovi rivaled Def Leppard in popularity and at least approached them in terms of talent, most of their imitators were flashy, hair-metal acts with more hair than metal, seriously watering down the metal genre but attracting younger and younger crowds into the fold. The band's follow-up, 1987's *Hysteria*, was itself a watered-down version of *Pyromania*, but spent six weeks on top of the U.S. charts, and made Def Leppard one of only five bands in history to have two albums surpass the ten million mark in sales.

"Perhaps Def Leppard's youth and energy make their stance an honest and convincing one, at least for the time being," wrote the *Village Voice*. "Their best songs—'Rock! Rock! (Till You Drop)', 'Action! Not Words', 'Rock of Ages'—capture the arena-rock experience and the arena rock and roll fantasy in a way few bands—young or old—ever really do, and 'Photograph' is rock and roll fantasy, adolescent fantasy, and fantasy fantasy in a single snap."[34]

As couriers of the teenage rock fantasy in the early 1980s, Def Leppard had few peers, helping rescue harder rock and roll from the bankrupt promises of the punk revolution, the soulless soul of the dusty disco floor, and the removed ennui of the new wave. Following the road paved by L.A.'s Van Halen and Australia's AC/DC (with whom Def Leppard shared the formidable hitmaking talents of producer Robert John "Mutt" Lange), *Pyromania* brought metal's more commercial aspects to the fore and set the tone for the next decade of hard pop.

Album Title: *War*
Artist: U2
Recorded: 1982, at Windmill Lane Studios in Dublin, Ireland
U.S. release: February 28, 1983 (Island)
Producer: Steve Lillywhite, Bill Whelan

U2's 1983 *War*, which married politics and passion to launch the career of the decade's hottest band. *Courtesy of Universal Music Enterprises.*

It would be difficult to argue that U2 was in any way a limited band in terms of imagination or success. Constantly reinventing themselves over their two-decade-plus career, each album was refreshing yet familiar, taking listeners down a new road, but always accompanied by Paul "Bono Vox" Hewson's stirring, soulful voice, Adam Clayton's percussive bass, Dave "The Edge" Evans' harmonic-infused guitar, and Larry Mullen's martial drumming. Fully half their catalog deserves serious consideration for this list, and I cautiously await letters from fanatical fans (of which there are many), condemning the absence of *Boy*, *Under a Blood Red Sky*, *The Joshua Tree*, *Achtung Baby*, and *Zooropa* among these selections.

Instead, we have *War*, the 1983 masterpiece that served as the band's tipping point in the United States, and revealed the power this incredible foursome could let loose on their fans when their musical skills caught up to their passionate sermons. From the beginning, U2 were a formidable act, outshining more technically proficient bands with their fiery performances. Influenced by the mid-1970s New York City new wave of Patti Smith and Television, U2 fashioned an energetic pop sound with all the combustion of London punk. The defining difference between U2 and the more talented of the punk and new-wave set had to do with attitude. Eschewing punk's nihilistic outlook and new wave's bored posturing, U2 made an effort to be uplifting, partly informed by the Christian faith shared by most of the band. "I don't like music unless it has a healing effect," Bono declared early in the band's career. "I want people to leave our concerts feeling positive, a bit more free."[35]

And yet, for a band that quickly earned a reputation for energizing music and inspiring live performances, they didn't seem to have a problem finding bullies to pick fights with. They were a band "informed by the spirit of the punk revolution of the mid-1970s," claimed *Rolling Stone* editor John Swenson, "but inspired by the heroic gestures of the 1960s who tried to make rock the medium for the self-realization and spiritual growth of a generation."[36] Exhibiting a political awareness unseen—with the exception of the Clash, with whom they were frequently compared—since the anti-war movement in Vietnam-era America, U2 were one of the few 1980s' acts that still believed music could change the world. Although the occasional risk-free social cause still rallied other musical troops to aid their fellow man, U2 were not afraid to mix it up and get bloody. "If people come along expecting the world from U2 then they're gonna get it," claimed a confident Bono when their first album, *Boy*, was freshly in the sleeve in 1981. "I'm not afraid we won't be able to give it to them."

The world was exactly what U2 began delivering to its growing legion of fans through their 1980s' albums—or at least a fresh, disturbing look at the chaotic state of the world through the band's empathetic eyes. Following their powerful, emotive debut *Boy* in 1981 and the confused but still impressive sequel *October* later in the year, U2 went for the jugular with *War*, their first album to crack the Top 20 on the American charts, where it remained for more than three years. *War* found the band more competent and focused without losing any of their passion, pounding out the political ("Sunday Bloody Sunday") and the personal ("Two Hearts Beat as One") with equal fervor, even managing to incorporate both in their first Top 20 hit in the United Kingdom, "New Year's Day." The album set the world on its ear, establishing the group a fan base that would become as loyal and massive as any in rock.

But, as is often the case, what sets one apart from peers is what sets one up for ridicule. Critics believed the band used social causes to prop up their own image, and dismissed their music as "hapless, dated Clash style agit-pop" and "blank liberal awareness." Reviewing *War*, a *New Musical*

Express critic claimed the album "over-reaches itself.... Who, forgodsake, gives a damn? Rock music as a naive communal 'we can change the world' pursuit went *rigor mortis* when the Stones played Altamont and the three Js (Janis, Jimi and Jim) topped themselves. If it's to be stirred to life again, it will be through spontaneous action—not calculated manifestoes from the soap box...In spite of itself *War* is another example of rock music's impotence and decay."[37]

Critics have been wrong before, but perhaps never on a scale that reached so far beyond the immediate album. *War* set U2 up as the undeniable leaders of a new social and political awareness in pop music, while simultaneously announcing a fresh sound that would make them the biggest band of the century's last twenty years. Like ascending dominoes, each subsequent album pushed the next to new heights. *War* was followed later in the year by their live *Under a Blood Red Sky*, containing the ultimate rendition of their most famous political anthem "Sunday Bloody Sunday," which recalled the 1972 massacre of unarmed civilians by British troops in U2's home country of Ireland. In 1984 came *The Unforgettable Fire* with its stirring Martin Luther King Jr. tribute "Pride (In the Name of Love)." With 1987's opus *The Joshua Tree*, the band finally topped the American charts—for nine weeks—scoring their first two No. 1 singles with "I Still Haven't Found What I'm Looking For" and "With or Without You." As their fame grew to staggering proportions, accusations of using causes to prop up the band withered—the band, in fact, became deft at using their fame to prop up a wide variety of social causes, leading a resurgence in rock music as antidote for society's woes. Though U2's most devout fans will always argue over which album was the best or which had the greatest impact, it was the brutal, focused, and inspiring *War* that broke the band out in the States and demonstrated the musical potential of one of pop's all-time biggest bands.

Album Title: *Murmur*
Artist: R.E.M.
Recorded: January 6–February 23, 1983, at Reflection Studios
in Charlotte, North Carolina
U.S. release: April 1983 (I.R.S.)
Producer: Mitch Easter, Don Dixon

The members of R.E.M. never planned on being professional musicians. None of them considered themselves more than mediocre talents, none of them had written songs before, and even after making a splash on the American underground with their first few albums, they wondered aloud what kind of jobs they would have five years down the line. But their unique bright-but-distant sound that came to be known as "jangly pop" and "college rock" pushed them to the forefront of the alternative rock movement in the mid-1980s, providing an escape from post-punk depression, new-wave ennui, and the shallow glitter of corporate rock and pop-metal.

"It's not that we're so original," lead singer Michael Stipe told an interviewer after their debut EP *Chronic Town* took the music world by surprise in 1983. "We're not doing anything new. I mean, everything's pretty much been done. But I can't really find a word that replaces it. The closest than any of us have come is "folk rock", and that's so undefineable in 1982 that it probably works."[38] R.E.M. based their reputation on this undefineable quality, combining images and sounds (intentionally and otherwise) from 1960s' garage rock (the Searchers), British merseybeat (early Beatles), cerebral experiments (Dylan's first electric outings and the Velvet Underground), 1970s postpsychedelia (the Soft Boys), and the Rickenbacker clatter of America's folk-rock godfathers, the Byrds, to whom they were often compared. But to many fans and appreciative critics in the mid-1980s, the lack of a clearly discernable set of easily classified influences made the band seem to appear out of nowhere, earning them early recognition as true originals. "R.E.M. outshines the competition because they use that garage sound only as a launching pad, and not as something to be slavishly emulated," gushed *Creem*'s review of *Murmur* in 1983. "[W]hen I listen to the other groups rooted in the mid-'60s, I hear none of the bursting-out that their models represented. Instead, I hear those unpredictable shrieks and yowls of freedom being reduced to conventions, to a set of rules that are to be followed and mastered. R.E.M. uses those same conventions to destroy the rules, or at least to get out past them, and that counts for plenty."[39]

At the heart of their sound—complemented by simple, wandering bass lines and arpeggio-heavy acoustic guitar (chords played slowly enough that each string can be heard distinctly)—was Stipe's cryptic lyrics, even more mysterious for his mumbling (lack of) articulation, making *Murmur* the perfect title for their commercial debut. "These songs are like taking a picture of your bedroom," claimed guitarist Peter Buck. "It may not make much sense to anyone else, but to you it's all the things in your life. We're certainly not setting out to be deliberately obscure, but you have to short-circuit the whole idea that literal language is what things are, because literal language is just codes for what happens. Without wanting to sound too arty about it, to bypass actions and go straight to the results is what we're trying to do, to make people feel moved."[40] Stipe even claimed that three quarters of his lyrics came from overheard conversations, giving the band's songs an airy quality that made them difficult to grasp, reducing Stipe's vocals to the level of an added instrument rather than a conveyor of eloquent, well-shaped ideas.

After forming in Athens, Georgia, in January of 1980 to play a friend's birthday party, R.E.M. spent many months touring throughout the south, eventually dropping out of the University of Georgia to take a chance on their music. Their first single, "Radio Free Europe," and their five-song EP *Chronic Town* earned them critical kudos from the underground, encouraging them to pursue a full release through I.R.S. Records, resulting in their debut LP *Murmur*. Unlike many acts that sought a mainstream audience or targeted followers of a specific subgenre, R.E.M. floated around the eclectic airwaves of college radio. Despite *Murmur* being named Album of the Year by *Rolling Stone* and finding an unexpected Top 40 chart appearance, it was this college radio market that helped the band the most. Album after album found the group hovering outside the Top 20—never remaining on the charts for long—but constant touring and college-radio appreciation earned them a steadily expanding audience and a legion of imitators who reveled in the band's ambiguity.

"I initially saw this group, this Radical Electric Magic, 18 months ago in their own locale of Atlanta, Georgia," claimed an early critic, "but I guess I was too drunk to take in just how much was being proposed, how many of rock's assumptions shaken down....from a nexus of close, coarse chording...they spin a web of hooks and harmonies that so radically reshuffle the standard-issue blocks of rock you feel you're at the onset of a new musical dimension. Quite possibly you are."[41] Though R.E.M. experimented with different approaches from album to album, always seeking to expand their music with songs that ranged from the mellow and murky to the clean and upbeat, the fragile but insistent sound and obscure lyrics found on *Murmur* remained their trademark, influencing dozens of alternative acts and providing a transition from art-rock and post-punk to college rock and alternative rock that dominated the late 1980s and early 1990s. "When I get to heaven, the angels will be playing not harps but Rickenbackers," claimed a particularly adoring reviewer. "And they will be playing songs by R.E.M."[42]

Album Title: *Texas Flood*
Artist: Stevie Ray Vaughan and Double Trouble
Recorded: November 1982, at Down Town Studio in Los Angeles
U.S. release: June 13, 1983 (Epic)
Producer: Stevie Ray Vaughan, Richard Mullen, Timothy White, Double Trouble

If there was ever a second coming of Jimi Hendrix—a man born to play guitar, with a resonance so unique and brutally honest that his heroes would flock to see him play, a man obsessed with finding the perfect sound, a man who could rightfully claim to own the electric blues in his time—that man would be Stevie Ray Vaughan. "Stevie was one of three or four artists who I heard and had to know who it was, right then," declared Eric Clapton, one of the all-time great white bluesmen. "I was driving and 'Let's Dance' came on the radio. I stopped my car and said, 'I have to know who this guitar player is today. Not tomorrow, but today.'"[43] Such accolades pepper nearly every article ever written about Vaughan. His genius and innovation were undeniable, and where many of the great albums of American music were impressive and important for many different reasons and brought about by many different people, Vaughan's monumental impact, largely through his debut album *Texas Flood*, was simply the story of a man and his guitar.

A teenage prodigy along with his older brother Jimmy Vaughan (who would earn fame in the 1980s playing for the Fabulous Thunderbirds), Stevie was by all accounts shy, funny, charming, and absolutely devoted to his guitar. As a young teenager, he constantly pestered Jimmy to teach him new licks, and before he was twenty, he blew away every blues lover who happened upon his performances. Stevie focused intently on the great blues masters, soaking up the deep-hearted playing of guitarists like Chuck Berry, Albert King, B.B. King, Jeff Beck, Jimi Hendrix, Buddy Guy, and Lonnie Mack. "He was probably the most fierce of the bluesmen I've ever heard," asserted blues legend Bonnie Raitt, a close friend and devoted fan of Stevie. "He had a furnace in his heart, and was the epitome of all that is dark and sexy, brooding and passionate. The most extreme emotions of the blues and of life were in every breath he took. . . . He was playing as if his life depended on it, and it did."[44]

After playing in and out of bands through the 1970s, Dallas native Stevie formed Double Trouble with drummer Chris Layton and bassist Jackie Newhouse (replaced by Tommy Shannon in 1981). Double Trouble was a new incarnation of Triple Threat, which featured Lou Ann Barton on vocals, but after Barton left in 1978, Stevie took the lead on vocals as well as guitar, and the group soon wrapped itself around his unique and passionate delivery of the blues, with Stevie coaxing every possible tone out of every single note. Stevie's obsession with milking a pure tone from his instrument gave him an immediately identifiable sound, and many of his professional opportunities came from people walking right up to him after seeing him play and offering to help advance his career.

After seeing Double Trouble play at the Montreux Festival in 1982—one of their first major gigs—heavyweights David Bowie and Jackson Browne both approached Vaughan about future collaboration, and Browne offered the band free recording time in his Los Angeles studio, Down Town. Stevie called Browne that fall to take him up on the offer, and Browne gave them three days in his studio to pump out a demo. On Thanksgiving weekend, 1982, Vaughan and company showed up in Los Angeles, ready to record a demo they could use to find a record deal. Seventy-two hours and ten songs later, the group—much to their surprise—had cut an entire album, recording over Browne's own demo tapes for his hit single "Lawyers in Love." "That whole recording was just so pure," remembered drummer Chris Layton, "the whole experience couldn't have been more innocent or naive. We were just playing. If we had known what was going to happen with it all, we might have screwed up. We just went in there and did it. The magic was there and it came through on the tape."[45]

Still without a record deal, however, another opportunity threatened to break the band up. After recording their demos, Vaughan went to New York to play on Bowie's album *Let's Dance*, and Bowie asked him to join his band for a year-long tour. With Double Trouble still unknown and unsigned, Vaughan agreed, planning on saving the money from Bowie's tour to finance Double Trouble upon his return. But just before the tour was to begin, Vaughan decided it was better to struggle with music he loved than to be well paid supporting someone else's vision. He remained with Double Trouble, whose momentum continued to accelerate when Stevie's playing on *Let's Dance* and Double Trouble's demo tapes earned them an industry buzz. Within a few months, Epic Records released the demo as *Texas Flood*, announcing to the music world a new beginning for the blues.

"When I heard 'Pride and Joy' on the radio, I said 'Hallelujah,'" claimed Allman Brothers star Dickey Betts, referring to one of Double Trouble's most memorable tracks from *Texas Flood*. "Stevie Ray Vaughan single-handedly brought guitar- and blues-oriented music back to the marketplace. He was just so good and strong that he would not be denied.... Playing blues rock suddenly didn't seem like a commercial dead end."[46] Many legends of blues-based rock rejoiced with Betts, recognizing the rebirth of a genre all but silenced by the punk, disco, new wave, pop-metal, and corporate rock that had choked the blues out of mainstream tastes. While his contemporaries were focusing on a swinging groove and advanced proficiency, Stevie dug deep to find the fire and passion that elevated the blues beyond mere technique, reigniting blues-based rock and opening the door for a resurgence of the genre's popularity. Mirroring the material that he played, Stevie's decade in the sun was both triumphant and tragic, earning critical acclaim as an artist, but sinking into a quicksand of alcohol and drug abuse, then coming clean in 1986, only to die four years later in a helicopter crash as his star was continuing to rise.

Appreciation of Vaughan's contributions to music continued to grow after his death, with two postmortem albums outcharting the five albums released when he was alive. Of these, only his last, *In Step*—which found a clean and sober Stevie returned to the top of his game a year before his death—measured up to the power, passion, and virtuosity of *Texas Flood*.

Album Title: *Kill 'em All*
Artist: Metallica
Recorded: May 1983, at Music America in Rochester, New York
U.S. release: July 1983 (Megaforce)
Producer: Paul Curcio

If you could boil Metallica down to one word, that word might be "power." From their muscular, driving guitars to their thundering rhythm section to James Hetfield's hungry vocals to their weighty lyrical themes of violence, death, and all of human nature's darker elements, Metallica counteracted the thinning sound of heavy metal in the early 1980s with the most powerful and frightening noise since American metal was born on March 9, 1968 (the day that Iron Butterfly and Blue Cheer first hit the charts with their debut albums *Heavy* and *Vincebus Eruptum*).

Kill 'em All, Metallica's first full-length release, was a foundation album for thrash metal, an outgrowth of what had been termed the New Wave of British Heavy Metal in the early 1980s. When blue-collar Californian James Hetfield and Danish tennis prodigy Lars Ulrich started Metallica in 1981, they combined the power and depth of metal bands like AC/DC and Judas Priest with the relentless speed of punk/metal acts like the Misfits, Motörhead, and Diamond Head, creating an entirely new sound that earned them an immediate following on the American underground metal scene. "Well, in heavy metal you have all the different aspects, from the AC/DC steady blues-metal to Iron Maiden, sort of semi-progressive metal, to Rush, full-progressive, to Judas Priest, all leather and stuff," explained Ulrich to *Creem* magazine. "Metallica, when we first started, it was like a new branch of the tree. There had never been anything like we were doing in America. The closest was we had obvious ties with Motörhead back then, with the energy and the sort of obnoxiousness, but we were playing fast, I think, in a different way. We were adding aspects of Diamond Head and how they wrote their songs, how they looked at each song as being completely different from the next one, and they had really long songs. We fused it together, threw in the odd 'X' factor, and it's Metallica. I think we've done our bit for metal!"[47]

After going through several guitar and bass players, the band settled into their classic lineup with Hetfield on rhythm guitar and vocals, Ulrich on drums, Cliff Burton on bass, and Kirk Hammet on lead guitar. Though the group had built a considerable following in California, where their demo tape *No Life 'Til Leather* had taken on a life of its own as an underground classic, the ensemble moved to New York to record their debut album for Megaforce Records. Originally called *Metal Up Your Ass*, the label pleaded with the band to change the title so as not to upset distributors, who became the target of the somehow less offensive *Kill 'em All*. Though the album failed to chart, it was critically lauded by the metal scenesters. The band's loud, fast, and heavy sound immediately defined thrash metal and was quickly imitated by other top thrash bands like Slayer, Anthrax, and Megadeth (whose founder, Dave Mustaine, was Metallica's original lead guitarist).

Although *Kill 'em All* lacked the subtlety and sophistication that would soon distinguish Metallica from their peers, its driving, forceful delivery was a welcome return-to-basics for fans that had been swept away by the watered-down metal of acts like Van Halen and Def Leppard that employed theatricality and lighter themes at the cost of deeply serious music. Suddenly there was an American response to the New Wave of British Heavy Metal, with California continuing its rise as the heart of metal and post-Sex-Pistols punk in the United States. As Metallica grew in popularity and sophistication, they began to reach beyond their early influences of Motörhead, Deep Purple, Saxon, and Iron Maiden, making their subsequent releases, *Ride the Lightning* in 1984 and *Master of Puppets* in 1986, more complex and accessible to mainstream audiences while still expanding their base of hardcore metal fans. "We like playing fast, we like playing slow, we like being melodic once in a while, we like being unmelodic, we like to throw a little bit of intelligence in there," the band told *Creem* as their star was on the rise. "I think we try and avoid as many obvious things as we can, because that's a lot more of a challenge for us."[48]

With few initial videos and little commercial airplay, Metallica slowly grew to become the most popular metal band in history and one of the world's top acts by the mid-1990s. Their ability to pen metal ballads that conveyed a seriousness every bit as engaging as their most ferocious thrash work earned them the respect of critics and an army of fans from all corners of the rock world. *Kill 'em All* wrote a new chapter in the book of hard rock, using the speed and ruthlessness of punk to elevate heavy metal's adrenaline level and introduce to the masses one of America's hardest-rocking bands.

Album Title: *Future Shock*
Artist: Herbie Hancock
Recorded: 1982, at OAO Studio in New York City
U.S. release: August 1983 (Columbia)
Producer: Herbie Hancock, Bill Laswell, Material

Herbie Hancock's *Future Shock* is perhaps one of the most unappreciated albums in this entire selection. Often landmark albums that are derided by critics upon their release—such as Led Zeppelin's self-titled debut, Queen's *A Night at the Opera*, and Hancock's own *Head Hunters*—are seen in retrospect as pioneering or at least humbly reappreciated LPs. *Future Shock*, unfortunately, has not even earned the honor of a critical mea culpa. In some estimations, it continues to occupy the forgettable region of the Hancock catalog. Obviously, I do not agree.

Throughout his career, Herbie Hancock built a well-deserved reputation as an excellent sideman, largely living in the shadow of Miles Davis, for whom Hancock played keyboards in the 1960s, notably on Davis' legendary 1969 album *In a Silent Way*. Hancock joined other Davis sidemen such as Chick Corea and John McLaughlin in taking Davis' visions a step further after leaving his quintet, pioneering jazz fusion in the 1970s through Corea's band Return to Forever, McLaughlin's outfit the Mahavishnu Orchestra, and Hancock's short-lived ensemble the Headhunters.

Hancock was traditionally a piano player with both classical and jazz backgrounds, influenced by the bebop of Wynton Kelly and Bud Powell, the classical works of Debussy and Ravel, and the popular jazz of George Shearing and Oscar Peterson. Though he originally studied to be an electric engineer, it took a bit of trickery on Miles Davis' part to move Hancock into the realm of electronic music. "I walked into the studio one day and...I couldn't see the piano," Hancock related in a retrospective interview. "The only thing that was in the room, off in a corner, was a Fender Rhodes electric piano, but I didn't play that. I asked Miles, 'Miles what do you want me to play?' Miles said, 'Play that,' and he pointed to the Fender Rhodes. I said, 'Really?' and I'm thinking, 'What, that toy?' So we pulled it over, plugged it in, turned it on, and then I played a chord on it, and it sounded pretty! It had a nice mellow, guitar-like sound to it, and I said, 'Oh, okay . . .' and then I turned the volume up and it could get loud! I was shocked."[49]

Hancock dove headlong into the electric keyboards, soon earning a reputation as one of the hottest electric keyboard players in jazz. Already having made a name for himself as a proficient solo artist with Blue Note Records, he continued pioneering different jazz forms with various ensembles through the 1970s on albums such as 1973's fusion-heavy *Head Hunters* (see p. 106), 1977's bop-tinged acoustic jazz album *V.S.O.P.*, and the 1980 electronic adventure *Mr. Hands*. To be fair, plenty of Hancock's work during this period was easily forgettable, better off dismissed as disco-infected experiments that sadly clouded critical listening of Hancock's better efforts. But Hancock endured in his quest to find new ways of uniting pop and jazz. "I get a lot of negative criticism from some reviewers," Hancock claimed shortly before the release of *Future Shock*. "They want me to play what they want. I just ignore it. Both areas [pop and jazz] challenge me—so I feel I have to do them. Unless I'm going to be a real flake and kowtow to what's expected of me. . . . I couldn't sleep nights if I did that!"[50]

In 1982, Hancock took a major leap forward when he brought bassist Bill Laswell aboard to help him create a new sound, relying heavily on electronic orchestration and putting jazz in the back seat for the landmark *Future Shock*. Laswell was the mastermind behind the seminal underground proto-hip-hop group Material in the early 1980s, and helped infuse *Future Shock* with a funky electronic fusion that honored the album's title. *Future Shock* was, in a sense, jazz for the streets, applying invigorating drum machine beats, space-funk synthesizers, and techno rhythms to catchy pop formulas to create an addicting, danceable soundscape. Its most daring feat, however, was the incorporation of turntable scratching, a hip-hop technique that had not reached mainstream audiences yet. Hancock recruited respected scratcher Grandmaster D.ST for the album's hit single, "Rockit," which rode high on the dance charts and breached the Top 100 on the pop charts—an unusual accomplishment for an instrumental.

But radio play and album sales were beginning to feel the impact of music videos, which had been quickly gaining momentum as a method of distribution with the advent of MTV in 1981, whose subscriber base grew to 16.2 million by the end of 1983. The music video for "Rockit"—featuring stop-motion break-dancing mannequins—proved extremely popular, helping spread the hip-hop sound and introducing millions of suburban white audiences (MTV's bread and butter at the time) to the technique of scratching, one of hip-hop's most basic building blocks. The Sugarhill Gang had brought the street party known as hip-hop to the broader American public in 1979 with their hit single "Rapper's Delight," marking the beginning of hip-hop's slow ascent into mainstream music. *Future Shock* not only helped flesh out the funk, jazz, and electronic elements of hip-hop, but expanded its audience crossculturally and helped bring the sounds of the street into mainstream pop.

Album Title: *Born in the U.S.A.*
Artist: Bruce Springsteen
Recorded: 1984, at the Power Station and the Hit Factory in New York City
U.S. release: June 4, 1984 (Columbia)
Producer: Bruce Springsteen, Jon Landau, Chuck Plotkin,
Steven Van Zandt

"What I heard in the Drifters, in all that great radio music, was the promise of something else," Bruce Springsteen once claimed. "Not a politician's promise, y'know, that everything is gonna be alright...that would be a false promise anyway. I mean the promise of possibilities: the promise that the search and the struggle matter, that they affirm your life. That was the original spirit of rock'n'roll. And that's what I hope we carry on, a message that no one, nothing has the right to tell you you gotta forfeit your hopes and your dreams."[51] To his fans, this is Bruce Springsteen in a nutshell. More than one of America's greatest poets, more than the best live show around in the 1970s and 1980s, more than a gazillionaire with solid blue-collar appeal, Bruce is the rock star everyone is on a first-name basis with, the conscience of the nation, Mr. Smith, Pete Seeger, and Martin Luther King Jr. all rolled into one, an iconic heartland hero who takes his role very seriously as Protector of the American Dream.

After bursting onto the national stage in 1975 with his epic third album *Born to Run* (see p. 114), Bruce spent the first decade of his career trying to live down comparisons to Bob Dylan, all the while producing consistently high-quality recordings and earning hyperbolic reactions to his marathon three- and four-hour concerts. "It was like rock 'n' roll and a gospel meeting and a party and the World Series rolled into one," wrote one adoring reviewer.[52] Certainly some of the credit goes to his E Street Band, centered around saxophonist Clarence Clemons, guitarist Steve Van Zandt, and drummer Max Weinberg, one of the tightest lineups rock and roll had ever seen. But Springsteen, already appreciated as an insightful and gifted writer, jumped the tracks in 1982 with the risky *Nebraska*, an album recorded on a four-track in the bedroom of his New Jersey farmhouse. His darkest album yet, *Nebraska* found the celebrated rock star returning to his singer-songwriter roots. The LP, originally recorded as a demo, was released with no further production elements, Springsteen and his management believing that the thin, amateur recording value enhanced the brooding, rural tone of the songs. The gamble paid off in critical appreciation, elevating Bruce's status as a man who is more concerned with serving the song than serving his own commercial interests.

Two years later, Springsteen was back in force with his band on their most immortal release, *Born in the U.S.A.*, a gutsy, passionate album with powerful lyrics relating the frustrations and resilience of the everyman.

Like no artist before him, Springsteen tapped into the magic of nostalgia to produce a litany of songs that simultaneously criticized the treatment of working-class heroes and glorified their ability to continue the struggle in the face of overwhelming odds. Lyrically, *Born in the U.S.A.* was as dark and desperate as *Nebraska*, but the energy of the E Street Band brought the songs such power that many mistook the album—and the title track in particular—as a celebration of patriotism devoid of any critical commentary. Such two-dimensional reading was particularly apparent in the political arena, where the 1984 reelection campaign for Ronald Reagan had mentioned Springsteen as emblematic of core American values and sought an endorsement from him, even though many of the songs from *Nebraska* and *Born in the U.S.A.* tended toward chastising the government for decades of working-class oppression. The title track to the album became Bruce's best-known and most misunderstood song, often played by prowar demonstrators at rallies during the Persian Gulf conflict in 1991 and the Iraq war in 2003, even though the song explicitly decries the horror and futility of armed conflict.

Although Springsteen was already one of the most popular entertainers in America, *Born in the U.S.A.* touched off a wave of "Bossomania" (referring to Springsteen's nickname "The Boss"), with advertisements, political speeches, and the like latching on to the wave of patriotic sentimentality the album brought about (it should be noted here that although the album was critical of blind nationalism, it could nonetheless be deemed "patriotic" in that the free expression of dissent is the very heart of the American spirit). The Chrysler corporation offered Springsteen several million dollars to use the song in an advertisement. When Springsteen declined, his essence was nonetheless captured in the new Chrysler slogan, "The Pride is Back."

Critically, *Born in the U.S.A.* elevated Springsteen to the highest level of American musical icon, as a fawning editorial in the top rock journal *Creem* confirmed: "[W]e consider him not only to the '80s what Elvis was to the '50s and Dylan was to the '60s, but the greatest of the three. And thus the pre-eminent figure in the history of American rock'n'roll.... His songs bulge with heart and soul. Utterly predictable though his music may be, he can make the simplest chord change imaginable seen absolutely thrilling.... By turns thrilling, touching, and hilarious, he puts on the best live show in rock'n'roll.... He's not only compassionate and generous himself, but encourages his audiences to be likewise. In this age of W.A.S.P. and MTV, of brazen sham, arrogant artifice and shameless pandering, he can single-handedly make you proud to still love rock'n'roll."[53]

Though Springsteen and his band continued making memorable albums through the following decades, 1975's *Born to Run* and 1984's *Born in the U.S.A.* bookended the first stage of their career as the booming voice of the common man, with neither album feeling dated twenty and thirty years after their release. *Born in the U.S.A.* would become Bruce's all-time bestseller and one of the bestselling albums in the American musical canon—a truly remarkable feat considering Springsteen never forgot his roots or got lost in the blinding spotlight that rarely left his side. "I believe that the life of a rock and roll band will last as long as you look down into the audience and can see yourself, and your audience looks up at you and can see themselves," Springsteen once claimed. "The biggest gift your fans can give you is just treatin' you like a human being because anything else dehumanizes you."[54]

Album Title: *Purple Rain*
Artist: Prince
Recorded: 1983, at the First Avenue Club in Minneapolis, Minnesota, an unnamed warehouse in Eden Prairie, Minnesota, Sunset Sound in Hollywood, and the Record Plant in New York City
U.S. release: June 25, 1984 (Warner Bros.)
Producer: Prince and the Revolution

If Prince's music seemed to come out of nowhere, there was a good reason for that. Though his mother and father were members of a jazz combo (the Prince Roger Trio, hence Prince's full name "Prince Rogers Nelson"), his father left the family when Prince was seven years old, and growing up in Minneapolis, Minnesota, Prince claimed there was simply never any good music to be heard. "Listening to the radio there," he said in an early interview, "really turned me off to a lot of things that were supposedly going on. If they did pick up on something they'd just play it to death, and you'd end up totally disliking it. So I missed out on a lot of groups."[55]

Although his musical career would take him out of Minnesota for long periods of time, Prince never truly left, eventually building his Paisley Park Studios in Minneapolis in 1987. The lack of a dominant influence is central to Prince's musical identity, and though bits and pieces of other artists have crept into his music over the years (covering a surprisingly wide range of genres), Prince spent his first few albums in the late 1970s searching for an identity of his own. What he found turned out to be one of the widest-reaching and yet most distinguishable sounds in all of 1980s' music.

After taking up piano when his father left the family behind, Prince excelled at music and taught himself a variety of instruments, playing in bands throughout high school. Lucking into an astute agent (a cousin's husband) when he was nineteen years old, Prince scored a deal with Warner Bros. in 1977. The label offered the artist complete control of his music for his first album, making him the youngest producer ever to get such a deal. His lack of stage and recording experience led to tepid critical and commercial acceptance of his first two albums, which found a talented but novice artist struggling to carve a place for himself in the world of funk-pop.

But from the beginning, Prince established a reputation for independence. On his 1978 debut release *For You*, Prince is credited with playing twenty-seven instruments, and the liner notes carry the citation that would almost become a slogan on his albums: "Produced, Arranged, Composed, and Performed by Prince." Though he used a backup band for tours, his studio work was usually a solo effort with just the engineer on the other side of the glass for company. "He doesn't make records like other people," said Peggy McCreary, one of the engineers for *Purple Rain*. "He doesn't have any set hours and he doesn't have any set way of doing things. Nothing is normal."[56]

In 1980, Prince released his third album, *Dirty Mind*, an unprecedented erotic romp through bedroom themes ranging from oral sex to threesomes to incest. Complemented by a creative blend of funk, new wave, and pop, *Dirty Mind* was the first album to fully demonstrate Prince's potential for groundbreaking work, from the cutting-edge pop experiments that brought him the respect of the musical community to the scandalous lyrics that earned him a reputation as a social deviant. His pop craftsmanship would grow through his follow-up albums (including his synthesizer-drenched double album *1999*, which spawned the hit singles "Little Red Corvette," "1999," and "Delirious"), but it was not until 1984's *Purple Rain* that Prince would graduate from trend to icon.

Purple Rain was the soundtrack album to the eponymous movie, which was co-written by and starred—you guessed it—Prince, ostensibly a (highly dramatized) account of his rise to stardom. Though the film was generally panned by critics, both the movie and the soundtrack were a commercial smash, with the album spending twenty-four weeks in the No. 1 spot, second only to Michael Jackson's *Thriller* for the highest charting album of the decade. The title track reached No. 2 on the charts, and the singles "When Doves Cry" and "Let's Go Crazy" both reached the top spot. At one point, Prince held the No. 1 movie, album, and single all at the same time.

But if sales figures alone made an album important, this would be a very different book. *Purple Rain* was a stunning artistic achievement, considered by many to be among the greatest albums of all time. Rather than wallow in predictable pop configurations, Prince takes on a remarkable range of genres from song to song without ever making a track feel like it does not belong. From the electronic flourishes of "When Doves Cry" to the metal guitar work on "Let's Go Crazy" to the anthemic soul of "Purple Rain," Prince simply outdoes himself—and just about every other pop artist before and since. Unwittingly, Prince would create a powerful enemy with the sexually charged song "Darling Nikki" from the album, which reportedly prompted future Second Lady Tipper Gore to create the Parents Music Resource Center in 1985, which successfully manipulated the Recording Industry Association of America into requiring warning labels on albums with sexually explicit lyrics, and listed "Darling Nikki" as the No. 1 track on their "Filthy Fifteen" list. Despite the negative consequences brought about by its detractors, *Purple Rain* broke barriers in both content and artistry and set a new standard for what was possible in experimental pop.

Album Title: *Zen Arcade*
Artist: Hüsker Dü
Recorded: October 1983, at Total Access in Redondo Beach, California
U.S. release: July 1984 (SST)
Producer: Hüsker Dü, Spot

There were many reasons to regard Hüsker Dü as just another aggressive ensemble in an emerging lineup of hardcore punk bands in the early 1980s. Following the export of the Ramones to the United Kingdom in the mid-1970s and the Sex Pistols to California a few years later, the American west coast (with nearby Vancouver thrown in to boot) was soon overrun with a speed-and-volume hungry barrage of young men in black t-shirts fronting bands called X, Black Flag, the Dead Kennedys, D.O.A., and other anxiety-inducing monikers.

A world away, buried deep within America's heartland, the Minneapolis trio Hüsker Dü attempted to join the fast and the furious set by criss-crossing the country in their van, playing alongside many west-coast bands in every dive that would book them. With the exception of Bob Dylan's memory and Prince's possible futures, Minnesota had no national attention to speak of in music circles, and along with their local distant cousins, the Replacements, Hüsker Dü guitarist Bob Mould, drummer Grant Hart, and bassist Greg Norton set out to deafen their audiences with fuming speed, volume, and distortion.

Formed as a quartet in 1979, the band (whose name comes from a popular Danish board game and means "Do you remember?") reportedly dropped their keyboardist during their first gig, when a friend of the group unplugged his instrument and nobody objected. One of the hottest hardcore punk bands at the time was Los Angeles' Black Flag, who took a liking to Hüsker Dü and signed them to guitarist Greg Ginn's independent label SST, leading to their first release, the live *Land Speed Record* in 1981. Both *Land Speed Record* and its studio follow-up *Everything Falls Apart* in 1982 were little more than punishing assaults on the ears, each song falling into the next with little discernable pause, transition, or variation, described by one critic as sounding "much like a vacuum cleaner."[57] With only the subtlest hints at the richness that lay beneath the surface of their music, Hüsker Dü earned a reputation as one of the fastest hardcore punk bands in America, gunning through one of their songs at 360 beats per minute. "It's just straight energy," claimed guitarist Mould in one of the band's first interviews. "I don't know what the world view is, or what the implications of it are. To me, it's just that I get up there, and I just get wired as hell. That's what I want to do. I get my enjoyment out of playing at that speed, because I'm pushing myself to a point where I'm almost passing out because I'm trying so hard."[58]

After five years of exhausting tours and single, EP, and LP releases, Hüsker Dü committed hardcore punk treason by accentuating their subtleties in the landmark release *Zen Arcade* in 1984. Retaining the band's powerhouse formula of fury and feedback, the double album dips its toes into nearly every rock subgenre available, from acoustic experiments to psychedelic musings to electronic swirls, without ever letting go of its seething hardcore base. "They are playing this earth's most magnificent rock," wrote one live reviewer shortly after the release of *Zen Arcade*. "It's not, as I had glancingly feared, heavy metal for sophisticats. True, they have discovered an amazing blend of the primitive and the progressive—they are like bludgeoning, deranged cavemen in calm command of technical resource. Yet the exhaustive ferocity of the music comes in a language that's poetry, an expression that runs in colours.... This bitter metal howl is a sound that seems to literally pour over the ears, a glittering river of savage harmony."[59]

The seemingly incompatible blend of harmonic vocals and punk-metal attack—complemented by a considerable leap forward in lyrical talent by both Mould and Hart—gave the band a unique sound that was part ferocious punk and part west-coast rock melody. The extension of punk and metal energy into pop territory garnered the group sudden critical acclaim and so many new fans that the tiny SST label could not press the albums fast enough to keep up with demand. Harcore purists, however, screamed "sellout," particularly after the band's jump to the giant Warner Bros. label in 1986, costing the group their credibility as a hardcore act. "To me, hardcore music, whether it was hardcore jazz, or hardcore industrial, or hardcore rock'n'roll, was no rules involved," said Mould, defending his band's advances in sound, "you could do anything you wanted to, it was the intensity you put it across with that made it what it was. The hardcore punk thing got to have a lot of rules, and when we stopped being associated with those rules...we were immediately on the out. You grow up, you change your perspective. You're not always 18-years-old, drunk, with a mohawk, driving around screaming and hollering about anarchy—you don't do that all your life."[60]

Despite the distancing between the band and their original fans, Hüsker Dü more than survived with their legacy intact, producing one of the most influential albums of the next two decades in *Zen Arcade*. Notwithstanding the group's assertion that they never really thought they were doing anything new, *Zen Arcade* and Hüsker Dü have been credited by nearly every alternative band of note—including Nirvana, Green Day, the Foo Fighters, the Pixies, the Dead Milkmen, and their Minneapolis brethren Sonic Youth—as a major influence, rivaled only by R.E.M. as pioneers in the formation of the alternative sound that would dominate pop toward the end of the century.

Album Title: *Like a Virgin*
Artist: Madonna
Recorded: 1984
U.S. release: November 14, 1984 (Sire)
Producer: Nile Rodgers

Perhaps more than any other artist in the history of popular music, Madonna Louise Veronica Ciccone manipulated her image beyond the limits of music's traditional media, and in doing so extended her reach as a musical artist to that of near-legendary cultural phenomenon. "Unlike [Michael] Jackson, Madonna's popularity reflected less her particular synthesis of disco, funk, and hip-hop than how she challenged the mainstream on issues of race, gender, sexual activity, sexual orientation, and power. Like Jackson, Madonna understood the power of creative music video to promote both product and artist. And through the creative and intelligent use of video, radio, television, magazines, movies, and books, Madonna presented the world with such a spectrum of images that she was able to appeal to different audiences."[61]

Before she was MADONNA!, the future pop diva was simply Madonna Ciccone, a struggling dancer from the Detroit suburbs who longed for stardom. After a brief appearance at the University of Michigan on a dance scholarship, she decided to take a chance on herself, and in 1977 landed in New York City with $35 in her pocket. For several years she studied dance, modeled, and worked low-paying jobs, barely surviving until friends convinced her that she had a pleasant singing voice, leading to experiments with disco and pop that caught the ear of a disco DJ who helped land her a deal with Sire Records in 1982. Sire reportedly paid Madonna $5,000 per song for several singles, which found moderate popularity on dance and R&B stations, leading many to believe she was a black artist and convincing the record company to finance a full LP. "My inspiration is simply that I love to dance," Madonna said of her first release, *Madonna*, in 1983. "All I wanted to do was make a record that I would want to dance to, and I did. Then I wanted to go one step further and make a record that people would listen to on the radio."[62]

Madonna was more than just a record to dance to. With the sour taste of disco still lingering on the mass palate, *Madonna* and Michael Jackson's recently released *Thriller* salvaged disco's catchier elements and brought the dance back to pop. *Madonna* spawned three Top 40 hits with the No. 16 "Holiday," the No. 10 "Borderline," and the No. 4 "Lucky Star," successfully launching her music career and marking a sea change in dance-pop. But much like Michael Jackson's pre-*Thriller* triumph *Off the Wall*, the album *Madonna*, brilliant and important though it was, was overshadowed the following year by the monumental *Like a Virgin*, which not only spent three weeks at No. 1 and made Madonna into an international sensation almost overnight, but brought the full weight of Madonna's forceful personality to bear on an unsuspecting and unprepared public.

"On this album, dedicated to 'the virgins of the world,' Madonna finds the fifth-dimensional spaces where dance clubs and malls meet," claimed a later retrospective of Madonna's first ten years. "*Like a Virgin* became not a second album so much as another debut. The title cut, with its built-in shock operatta and rigid live drums, matches erotic and innocent impulses in a single shot....it's hard to imagine how insane this record sounded when it came out. It's Madonna's world now, with Power Radio Crossover mixes non-stop, but back in 1984 the lusty positivity of songs like 'Dress You Up' was so forward it was almost embarrassing. From that embarrassment a whole generation of girls and boys found a way to be."[63]

It was with *Like a Virgin* that Madonna stole the spotlight, asserting her sexuality as only male rock stars had done before, moving well beyond the limited confines of pop artist to eventually become a focal point for nationwide discussions of power relationships in the areas of sex, race, gender, religion, and other divisive social topics. Featured on the cover of *Time* magazine in 1985—in which she was accurately described as "an outrageous blend of Little Orphan Annie, Margaret Thatcher and Mae West"—Madonna became a national lightning rod for both criticism by conservative groups and imitation by scores of teenage girls, who began sporting her coquettish blend of lace, leather, and iconic jewelry.

At the center of her new image lie the themes embedded in her two most memorable songs from the album, the No. 2 "Material Girl" and the title track, which straddled the top of the charts for six weeks and became an international blockbuster. With the tongue-in-cheek "Material Girl," Madonna mocked the money-hungry consumer culture of the 1980s, creating a memorable video in which she recreated Marilyn Monroe's rendition of "Diamonds Are a Girl's Best Friend" in the film *Gentlemen Prefer Blondes.* Though the song and video certainly helped her fame, it backfired on her personally, as the whimsical nature of the lyrics were lost on the media, who dubbed Madonna "Material Girl" from that point on.

"Like a Virgin" created far more powerful shockwaves, not particularly dirty (at least not as dirty as hundreds of songs by male artists had been before, particularly her rival Prince whose recent material made Madonna look like an 18th-century school marm by comparison), but suggestive enough to push the right cultural buttons and make Madonna realize that pursuing forbidden themes of sexuality (and other controversial topics) would define her as an artist. Her performance of the song at the first MTV Video Awards in 1984 became one of pop music's most historic moments, as she writhed on stage in mock masturbation, shocking and delighting crowds and starting a trend for herself as public spectacle and controversial gadfly. Though initially dismissed in critical circles as a temporary phenom with no real talent, Madonna demonstrated a keen understanding of presentation and media manipulation to become one of the hottest acts of the decade, and eventually the most successful female artist of all time, selling more than 100 million albums internationally by the end of the century and cementing her place in history as one of pop music's most enduring icons.

NOTES

1. Charles Shaar Murray, "Down in the Scuzz with the Heavy Cult Figures," *New Musical Express*, June 7, 1975.

2. Deborah Frost, "Knock, Knock, Knocking: Television's *Adventure*," *Boston Phoenix*, June 6, 1978.

3. Stephen Thomas Erlewine, www.allmusic.com.

4. Dave Shulps, "Television: *Adventure*," *Crawdaddy!*, June 1978.

5. David Szatmary, *A Time to Rock: A Social History of Rock And Roll*. New York: Schirmer, 1996 (1987), 263.

6. Field Maloney, "Free Bob Marley!" *Slate*, February 22, 2006.

7. Bruce Eder, www.allmusic.com.

8. Jim Miller, *Rolling Stone Illustrated History of Rock and Roll*. New York: Random House, 1980, 398.

9. Caroline Coon, "Punk Rock: Rebels Against the System," *Melody Maker*, August 7, 1976.

10. Jonh Ingham, "The Sex Pistols Are Four Months Old," *Sounds*, April 24, 1976.

11. Ibid.

12. Steve Huey, www.allmusic.com.

13. Paul Rambali, "Pere Ubu: Weird City Robomen," *New Musical Express*, January 7, 1978.

14. Jon Savage, "Pere Ubu: *The Modern Dance*," *Sounds*, February 11, 1978.

15. Paul Rambali, "Wreckless Ubu: Waiting for the End," *New Musical Express*, March 11, 1978.

16. Phast Freddie Patterson, "Van Halen's Back Door Rock 'n' Roll," *Waxpaper*, 1978.

17. Szatmary, 1996, 290.

18. Cliff White, "Funkadelic: The Noble Art of Rhythm 'n' Biz," *New Musical Express*, November 18, 1978.

19. Richard Cook, "Neil Young: When Does a Dinosaur Cut Off Its Tail?" *New Musical Express*, October 9, 1982.

20. Neil Young, *Decades* liner notes.

21. Richard Dubourg, "Rust Never Sleeps," *Funhouse!*, October 20, 1994.

22. Robert Christgau, www.robertchristgau.com.

23. Chris Smith, *The Greenwood Encyclopedia of Rock History: From Arenas to the Underground, 1974–1980*. Westport, CT: Greenwood, 2005b, 149.

24. Paul Friedlander, *Rock And Roll: A Social History*. Boulder, CO: Westview, 1996, 257.

25. Barney Hoskyns, "Fantasy Castle: Monsters of Rock!" *New Musical Express*, July 1981.

26. Howie Klein, "AC/DC Hit California," *New York Rocker*, 1977.

27. Don Snowden, "AC/DC Plugs into Primitivism," *Los Angeles Times*, September 12, 1979.

28. Phil Sutcliffe, "AC/DC: Sex, Sweat, Snot, and School Kids," *Sounds*, October 29, 1977.

29. Barney Hoskyns, "Michael Jackson," *New Musical Express*, September 17, 1983.

30. Fred Bronson, *The Billboard Book Of Number One Hits*. New York: Billboard, 1985, 511.

31. Ibid., 569.

32. Deborah Frost, "Def Leppard: What's 'New'?" *Village Voice*, November 1, 1983.

33. Ibid.

34. Ibid.

35. Steve Turner, "Songs of Praise: Fire and Fervour from Ireland's U2," *The History of Rock*, 1984.

36. Hank Bordowitz, *The U2 Reader: A Quarter Century of Commentary, Criticism, and Reviews*. Milwaukee, WI: Hal Leonard, 2003, xvii.

37. Gavin Martin, "U2: *War*," *New Musical Express*, February 26, 1983.

38. Blake Gumprecht, "R.E.M.," *Alternative America*, Winter 1983.

39. John Morthland, "R.E.M.: *Murmurs*," *Creem*, July 1983.

40. Barney Hoskyns, "Four Guys Working for the Sainthood," *New Musical Express*, April 21, 1984.

41. Barney Hoskyns, "R.E.M.: Marquee, London," *New Musical Express*, November 1983.

42. Mat Snow, "American Paradise Regained: R.E.M.'s *Reckoning*," *New Musical Express*, 1984.

43. Alan Paul, "Blue Smoke: The Life and Death of Stevie Ray Vaughan," *Guitar World*, April 1999.

44. Ibid.

45. Ibid.

46. Ibid.

47. Sylvie Simmons, "I Confronted Metallica on Their Own Terms," *Creem*, October 1986.

48. Ibid.

49. *Jazz Profiles* from NPR, Herbie Hancock, www.npr.org.

50. Richard Cook, "Herbie Goes Lite-weight," *New Musical Express*, June 19, 1982.

51. Cynthia Rose, "Out in the Street: Bruce Springsteen, Tom Petty, and the Simple Truths of Blue-Collar Rock," *The History of Rock*, 1984.

52. Glenn O'Brien, "Bruce Springsteen," *Spin*, 1985.

53. John Mendelssohn, "The Year of the Boss," *Creem*, 1986.

54. Maryann Janosik, *The Greenwood Encyclopedia of Rock History: The Video Generation, 1981–1990*. Westport, CT: Greenwood, 2005, 39.

55. Chris Salewicz, "Prince: Strutting With the New Soul Monarch," *New Musical Express*, June 6, 1981.

56. Bronson, 1985, 591.

57. Janosik, 2005, 68.

58. Blake Gumprecht, "Hüsker Dü," *Alternative America*, Winter 1983.

59. Richard Cook, "Hüsker Dü: Camden Palace, London," *New Musical Express*, May 25, 1985.

60. Andy Gill, "Hüsker Dü: The Trash Aesthetic," *New Musical Express*, June 8, 1985.

61. Friedlander, 1996, 269.

62. Barney Hoskyns, "Cheek to Cheatham: Madonna/Oliver Cheatham," *New Musical Express*, November 5, 1983.

63. Danny (Shredder) Weizmann, "A Madonna Discography: The First Decade," *L.A. Weekly*, 1990.

6

WELCOME TO THE JUNGLE, 1986–1990

By the mid-1980s, the album format was pushing forty, rock and roll began graying around the temples, and music journalism had graduated college and was finally moving out of its parents' basement. American popular music that had been centered around the LP had matured to the point that it seemed to serve largely as a reflection of its own past—much of what was hailed as new was actually a rediscovery of what had been forgotten or had gone unappreciated for too long. Jazz had long since loosed itself from the moorings of scales and modes and sailed on to meet new genres; the blues had been electrified, amplified, abandoned, and then welcomed home; the magic of electronica had been watered down to harmless new-age music or simplistic dance-pop; country had finally broken free of the Nashville system and was discovering itself in Austin; and rock and roll had found gospel with Elvis, folk with Dylan, psychedelia with the Beatles, metal with Zeppelin, art with Pink Floyd, antiart with the Ramones, and ironic self-mockery with everything that came after—a string of short marriages that were not meant to last, but left behind memories both good and bad and many bastard children too numerous to recount.

The heroes had done their jobs, now was the time for well-deserved monuments. In the late 1980s the Rock and Roll Hall of Fame inducted its first class of honorees: Chuck Berry, James Brown, Ray Charles, Sam Cooke, Fats Domino, the Everly Brothers, Buddy Holly, Jerry Lee Lewis, Little Richard, and Elvis Presley. The Monkees were honored by MTV with a twenty-two-hour marathon, and the band reunited for a 20th-anniversary tour. U2 honored the Beatles by reenacting their famous rooftop performance. The Byrds honored Roy Orbison by reuniting after twenty-five years for a tribute concert. Milli Vanilli honored themselves when they claimed to be more talented than Bob Dylan, Paul McCartney, and Mick Jagger. The Recording Academy honored Milli Vanilli by revoking their Grammy after the duo admitted to lip-synching their material. James Brown, Tommy Lee, and Ike Turner were honored by government authorities with jail time. The Parents Music Resource Center honored American popular music by filing lawsuits against bands they deemed offensive. Sonny Bono, Alice Cooper, and Tiny Tim honored their hometowns by launching campaigns for mayor of Palm Springs, governor of Arizona, and mayor of New York City, respectively. And in the spirit of establishing monuments, the California Raisins wrote an epitaph on music's gravestone when their interpretation of "I Heard it through the Grapevine" broke into the Top 100.

But, as they say, God never closes a door without opening a window. A breath of fresh air blew in from the streets when hip-hop emerged from block-party novelty to MTV airplay with the rock/rap hybrids **Raising Hell (1986)** by Run-D.M.C. and **Licensed to Ill (1986)** by the Beastie Boys. Following close on their heels were Public Enemy's political **It Takes a Nation of Millions to Hold Us Back (1988)** and 1990's *Fear of a Black Planet*, N.W.A's gangsta **Straight Outta Compton (1989)**, and De La Soul's hippy-hop **3 Feet High and Rising (1989)**, all of them forcing listeners to acknowledge the "everyman" forgotten in Springsteen's *Nebraska*, the Band's *Music from Big Pink*, and the collections of Harry Smith and Woody Guthrie.

Those rural common men were remembered by others, however, as Uncle Tupelo kicked off the 1990s Americana movement with their historic **No Depression (1990)**, once again giving voice to the streets of the small town as hip-hop bands were giving voice to the urban ghettos. Paul Simon suffered the slings and arrows of embargoed fortune when he traveled to South Africa to record **Graceland (1986)**, giving worldwide voice to the music of the indigenous majority when they had no voice at home, and along with Peter Gabriel's 1989 *Passion: Music for the Last Temptation of Christ*, opening the door for world musicians to find a welcoming audience in America. And not that Los Angeles needed to be heard any louder, but the volume knob was cranked to eleven with Guns N' Roses' **Appetite for Destruction (1987)**, L. A. Guns' 1988 *L.A. Guns*, the Red Hot Chili Peppers' 1989 *Mother's Milk*, and Mötley Crüe's 1989 *Dr. Feelgood*.

Quieter voices found willing ears as well, as albums like Suzanne Vega's **Solitude Standing (1987)**, Sinéad O'Connor's 1987 *The Lion and the Cobra*, Tracy Chapman's 1988 *Tracy Chapman*, and the Indigo Girls' 1989 *Indigo Girls* began a whole new era of success for female singer-songwriters and independent music. The growing number of independent labels moved many subgenres closer to the spotlight, as major labels picked up indie artists and college radio made listeners more keen to wander into unknown territory. Industrial, hardcore, and underground music benefited as much as the singer-songwriter set, with Bad Religion's 1987 *Suffer*, Sonic Youth's **Daydream Nation (1988)**, Ministry's 1988 *The Land of Rape and Honey*, Nine Inch Nails' **Pretty Hate Machine (1989)**, and Jane's Addiction's 1988 *Nothing's Shocking* and 1990 *Ritual de lo Habitual* all finding their way out of the underground and into the hands of eager listeners and respectable sales figures. Lastly, after years of struggle country music finally moved their sales figures beyond the merely respectable and into gargantuan territory with albums like Steve Earle's 1988 *Copperhead Road*, Clint Black's 1989 *Killin' Time*, and Garth Brooks' **No Fences** (**1990**).

Album Title: *Raising Hell*
Artist: Run-D.M.C.
Recorded: 1986, at Chung King House of Metal in New York City
U.S. release: June 1986 (Profile)
Producer: Russell Simmons, Rick Rubin

To be fair, Run-D.M.C.'s hip-hop touchstone *Raising Hell* has not aged well. That's not to say it is not still an enjoyable and hard-rocking masterpiece—most critics would argue that it is. But in the context of the directions hip-hop has taken since—both culturally, in terms of the often violent, misogynistic, and socially engaging lyrics, and artistically, in terms of the great strides made in sampling, complex rhyme schemes, and hybrids with other genres—*Raising Hell* is just so . . . 1986.

But in its time, *Raising Hell* was nothing short of stunning, both as an artistic endeavor and as a major catalyst in the popularization of hip-hop. "*Raising Hell* is the first great hip-hop album, a cohesive whole rather than a collection of a couple of hit singles plus filler," claimed *Rolling Stone* in a later homage to the album. "With *Raising Hell*, Run-D.M.C. also opened the doors for rappers and rockers who followed, from the audio assault of Public Enemy (as Chuck D once pointed out in song, "Run-D.M.C. first said a DJ could be a band") to the latter-day rap-metal fusion of artists like Limp Bizkit and beyond."[1]

Marking the transition from old-school rap to modern hip-hop, the two dance MCs known as "Run" (Joseph Simmons) and "D.M.C." (Darryl McDaniel) grew up surrounded by early rap in the New York City borough of Queens in the latter 1970s. Joseph's older brother, Russell, was one of the first major producers of rap, helping launch the career of Kurtis Blow and eventually co-founding Def Jam Records, later signing acts like L. L. Cool J and the Beastie Boys. Joseph and Darryl were friends as teenagers, both penning rhymes and following the scene from an early age, with Joseph apprenticing to Kurtis Blow when he went on tour. Russell promised the duo he would help them with their careers once they finished school, and sure enough after they had graduated he arranged gigs for them opening for bigger acts in the area.

In 1982 the pair brought on board their friend Jason Mizell, who adopted the moniker Jam Master Jay, to scratch turntables for them as they rapped. The trio's first singles were R&B hits out of the box, "It's Like That" and "Sucker M.C.'s," immediately earning the outfit a following for their distinctly harder beats, imaginative arrangements, and literate rhymes, considered by many the first recordings that moved old-school rap into new-school hip-hop territory. After their self-titled debut album in 1984 and the follow-up *King of Rock* in 1985 made the trio one of the biggest rap acts in the country, Run-D.M.C. kicked the legs out from under their audiences with the monumental *Raising Hell* in 1986, a powerful blend of hard rock and urban rhyming that sent white suburban teenagers into a tizzy and breathed mainstream life into underground rap culture. "Run DMC's third LP shatters atrophied dogmas," hailed one review of the album, "legislating against these ears taking the rap in the interim. *Raising Hell* scores both as a dance/noise fission, there to hotfoot fast reacting feet, and as a capsule of NY suburban Americana that satisfies desires for sassy backstreet culture that grates against mainstream homogeneity, while remaining impregnated with its flavour."[2]

Raising Hell was a new beginning for hip-hop as a mainstream musical force, the first rap album to go platinum, the first to reach No. 1 on the R&B charts, and the first to break the Top 10 on the pop charts, where it settled at No. 3, spawning the hits "You Be Illin'" and "It's Tricky." But the biggest success from the album was the mini-revolution "Walk This Way," a collaboration with the greasy hard-rock band Aerosmith on which Run-D.M.C. laid their funky beats and hip-hop articulation over the old standard that was a No. 10 hit for Aerosmith in 1975. Starting in the late 1970s, Aerosmith had seen their popularity steadily slide, and were bound for obscurity until this remake collaboration with Run-D.M.C. gave both acts a No. 4 hit and relaunched Aerosmith's star in one of the greatest comebacks in rock history. The video for the song was played in heavy rotation on MTV, opening the door for rap artists who up to this point were completely absent from the music network.

The true power of *Raising Hell*, however, was in the creative fusion of rock and rap that moved hip-hop forward from street-party dance music to a powerful social force, partially thanks to the producing talents of Rick Rubin, who knew how to mix the two genres in ways no one had even considered before (such as borrowing from the 1979 Knack hit "My Sharona" to give a familiar beat to *Raising Hell*'s "It's Tricky"). Within a few years, acts ranging from the Beastie Boys to Public Enemy to N.W.A to Ice T were moving the genre forward into deeper social and political territory, surpassing Run-D.M.C. in terms of style and sales, as Joseph and Darryl began to sink beneath the weight of personal issues, leaving *Raising Hell* as the highlight of their legacy. But what a legacy it was, fueling a massive surge in popularity in hip-hop and making the genre one of the most pervasive forces in music through the remainder of the century.

Album Title: *Graceland*
Artist: Paul Simon
Recorded: February 1985, in Johannesburg, South Africa (with later over-dubs at studios in London, Los Angeles, New York City, and New Orleans)
U.S. release: August 1986 (Warner Bros.)
Producer: Paul Simon

Long before his 1986 album *Graceland* fell from the sky like *deus ex musica*, Paul Simon was one of American music's most revered poets. His early work with Art Garfunkel in the 1960s was straight out of the folk-rock songbook and promised little in the way of commercial success, causing the two to split up and remain unknown quantities in the popular music equation. That was, however, until an enterprising engineer added a few rock-and-roll flourishes to their 1965 single "The Sounds of Silence," unexpectedly sending it to No. 1 on the charts. The duo hastily reunited, and over the next five years became one of the most successful folk-rock partnerships in music, placing three albums at the top of the charts for a combined twenty-six weeks.

Despite several years of relative solo success for both artists after they split up in 1970, Garfunkel soon faded into obscurity, and Simon's output, though often brilliant, was sporadic and always seemed of its own era—whether listeners would allow themselves to step into Simon's personal time frame was pretty much a hit-or-miss proposition. Though his style dipped into a variety of pop, jazz, folk, and international configurations, his solid songwriting was always the bedrock of his compositions, managing to convey both the deeply personal and the deeply universal through masterful storytelling.

In the early 1980s, a number of musicians got a bandwagon rolling in the fight against apartheid in South Africa. Bruce Springsteen's guitarist Steve Van Zandt led the charge with his organization Artists United Against Apartheid, pulling together powerful names like Springsteen, Pete Townshend, Bob Dylan, Keith Richards, Lou Reed, U2, Peter Gabriel, and Ringo Starr to advance civil rights on the world stage. Musically, producer and musician Brian Eno worked with Talking Heads frontman David Byrne to incorporate African and Middle Eastern sounds on 1981's *My Life in the Bush of Ghosts* and African polyrhythms on 1980's landmark *Remain in Light*. Such artistic and political involvement in the music of other cultures was not without precedent, but was accompanied by a surge of interest in social causes for Third-World countries (including the massive collaborations U.S.A. for Africa and Live Aid) and the rural sounds of Asian, African, and Latin American countries.

In 1984 a friend of Simon gave him a compilation album featuring African sounds that sparked his imagination, particularly the little-heard South African style of mbaqanga that reminded him of the positive energy of early rock and roll and R&B. Soon after participating in U.S.A. for Africa's "We Are the World" sessions in January 1985, Simon violated a cultural boycott of South Africa by Western countries when he traveled to Johannesburg to record with a number of local musicians, notably the group Ladysmith Black Mambazo. Though Simon had long held interest in international sounds, experimenting with disparate styles such as salsa, reggae, zydeco, and norteño music over his long career, his involvement with mbaqanga was wholehearted. The recordings—later overdubbed with rock highlights featuring Adrian Belew's seamless guitar work—resulted in the extraordinary mbaqanga/rock hybrid *Graceland* in 1986, which simultaneously earned Simon disdain for participating in a South African enterprise and kudos for celebrating the musical language of the country's oppressed majority. "In the most moving track, the a capella "Homeless," Simon's soft, ageless voice harmonizes with the vocal group Ladysmith Black Mambazo in a way that suggests a natural link with doo-wop," read the *Rolling Stone* album review. "The unity of their voices expresses beauty, strength and endurance, despite the song's grim subject. Simon's goal is not to rouse further conflict over apartheid but to provide a hopeful tonic."[3]

Intentional or not, Simon's collaboration with South African musicians was inherently political, bringing new-found attention to the struggles of South African blacks and eventually helping to end apartheid in the country. Artistically, *Graceland* was hailed by many as Paul Simon's greatest work—no small praise for the artist who created a soundtrack for the early 1970s with compositions like "Bridge Over Troubled Water," "The Boxer," and "Mrs. Robinson." A departure from his linear storytelling, Simon moved into the abstract on *Graceland* without letting go of his masterful phrasing, marrying straightforward lines such as "There is a girl in New York City that calls herself the human trampoline" with fanciful departures that skip off the tongue like "we're bouncing into Graceland." The album's lyrical balance between the concrete and the intangible perfectly matched its equilibrium of South African rhythms and rock-and-roll trimmings, leading to critical and commercial acclaim and making it the longest-charting album of Simon's career. "*Graceland* is the Promised Land, built on landfill," read the album review in *Spin* magazine. "It's the end of the rainbow, a pot of gold grown from the wise investment of chump change. It's a great beauty built from the eyes of a million beholders. It's a distraction turned into a quest. It's the search for the grail as an excuse for a joy ride."[4] Besides standing the test of time as one of the decade's most lauded releases, *Graceland* elevated the public's and the musical community's interest in world music to unprecedented levels, leading to a major influx of international styles into American music over the following decades.

Album Title: *Licensed to Ill*
Artist: The Beastie Boys
Recorded: 1986, at Chung King House of Metal in New York City
U.S. release: November 1986 (Def Jam)
Producer: Rick Rubin, the Beastie Boys

It is more than a little ironic that one of the biggest acts of the nascent hip-hop scene in the mid-1980s was made up of three wealthy, white, Jewish kids from Brooklyn and Manhattan. The irony lies only partially in the fact that they were white—it is not terribly surprising that it took the participation of white artists for hip-hop to fully infiltrate the living rooms of suburban teenagers (as was already witnessed by the fact that the first major rap crossover hit, "Walk This Way," was a collaboration between rap lords Run-D.M.C. and the established white rock group Aerosmith). The larger irony comes from the fact that the Beastie Boys were a punk-rock outfit adopted by hip-hop mastermind Rick Rubin, and their debut LP, 1986's *Licensed to Ill* [particularly the hit single "(You Gotta) Fight for Your Right (to Party)"] was a tongue-in-cheek rap/rock hybrid that largely satirized the white frat-boy audience that made the album such a big hit. "As born aesthetes, they grabbed onto rap's musical quality and potential," claimed one critic, "as reflexive rebels, they celebrated its unacceptability in the punk subculture and the world outside."[5]

Founded by Mike Diamond and Adam Yauch in 1981 as a punk outfit with Kate Schellenbach on drums and John Berry on guitar, the group schlepped around the New York underground scene until Schellenbach and Berry left and Adam Horovitz joined, taking the remaining trio in a new direction with rap rhymes layered over rock guitars. After minor success in the New York underground, the Beasties were signed to the fledgling Def Jam Records, who would be responsible for most of the rap hits of the decade. Opening act duties on Madonna's *Like a Virgin* tour and Run-D.M.C.'s *Raising Hell* tour, coupled with some minor R&B/dance hits, earned the group enough exposure (both positive and negative) to justify the release of their full-length debut, *Licensed to Ill*, a surprise smash that spent seven weeks at the top of the pop charts—the first rap album to reach No. 1—ultimately becoming the best-selling rap LP of the decade.

The success of *Licensed to Ill* was completely unexpected, fueled in large part by the brain-dead single "(You Gotta) Fight for Your Right (to Party)," which received heavy airplay on MTV, bringing hordes of suburban teens into the rap-music fold and suddenly launching the group to the top of the genre. Completely dismissed by critics as frat-boy rock, criticized by other rappers as genre pirating, and denounced by conservatives for ungodly lyrics and lewd performances, the Beastie Boys earned a much smaller amount of respect than their sales seemed to indicate. Only in retrospect, after the release of the stunningly forward-thinking *Paul's Boutique* in 1989 and *Check Your Head* in 1992 did critics look back on *License to Ill* as a laudable artistic achievement. "There hasn't been a funnier, more infectious record in pop music than this," wrote a later reviewer, "and it's not because the group is mocking rappers (in all honesty, the truly twisted barbs are hurled at frat boys and lager lads), but because they've already created their own universe and points of reference, where it's as funny to spit out absurdist rhymes and pound out "Fight for Your Right (To Party)" as it is to send up street-corner doo wop with "Girls." Then, there is the overpowering loudness of the record—operating from the axis of where metal, punk, and rap meet, there never has been a record this heavy and nimble, drunk on its own power yet giddy with what they're getting away with."[6]

Though "(You Gotta) Fight for Your Right (to Party)" became the album's most successful anthem, other memorable tracks such as "Girls," "Brass Monkey," "Hold It Now, Hit It," and "No Sleep Til Brooklyn" earned limited airplay and belated respect as exploratory punk/rap hybrids.

Rubin had already successfully merged hip-hop and metal with Run-D.M.C.'s *Raising Hell* months earlier, but the Beastie Boys brought the element of snotty punk into the mix, summoning the force of commonality between punk and hip-hop as music of the young and bored, while at the same time adding an element of playfulness that was severely lacking in the music of the status-conscious eighties. Though poorly received out of the gate by critics, the album's massive crossover appeal helped bring audiences to diverse rap acts such as LL Cool J and Public Enemy, and influenced 1990s rap-metal acts (identified by the band as "goatee metal rap" in one of their later songs) like Korn and Limp Bizkit. "There is a sense of genuine discovery, of creating new music, that remains years later, after countless plays, countless misinterpretations, countless rip-off acts, even countless apologies from the Beasties, who seemed guilty by how intoxicating the sound of it is, how it makes beer-soaked hedonism sound like the apogee of human experience," claimed later critic Stephen Thomas Erlewine. "And maybe it is, maybe it isn't, but in either case, *Licensed to Ill* reigns tall among the greatest records of its time."[7]

Album Title: *Solitude Standing*
Artist: Suzanne Vega
Recorded: 1986–1987, at Bearsville Sound Studios in Bearsville, New York, A&M Recording Studios in Los Angeles, RPM Sound Studios, Clinton Recording Studios, Celestial Sound Studio, and Carnegie Hill Studios in New York City
U.S. release: April 1, 1987 (A&M)
Producer: Steve Addabbo, Lenny Kaye

It was the mid-1980s, and the seventies were long gone. Many were not sure they ever really happened. Hair metal, corporate rock, and slick pop ruled the airwaves, and hip-hop and alternative rock were threatening on the horizon. Missing in action were the acoustic solo artists of 1972, the Joni Mitchells, the James Taylors, the Carole Kings, the Don McLeans, the tender troubadours who wore their hearts on their sleeves, and nobody cared enough to send out a search party. Vulnerability was out, replaced by dazzling guitar solos, punishing bass grooves, and the Star Wars Missile Defense System.

"Acoustic music had gone from the public scene," recalled Suzanne Vega of her early years performing after she graduated from college in 1982 and devoted herself to the local folk arena, "but not from people's lives. People will always play it because all you need is a guitar. It's a very independent music and I'm a very independent person. I could just get on a Greyhound to any town, set up and sing."[8] The idea of signing an unknown singer-songwriter in 1985 was laughable, and Vega was rejected by every major record company before finally being signed by A&M (who had already turned her down twice). With her first album, *Suzanne Vega*, in 1985, Vega wowed the critics with her literate, unguarded songwriting and naked

Suzanne Vega's 1987 *Solitude Standing*, one of the first albums to mark the rise of female singer-songwriters over the next two decades. *Courtesy of Universal Music Enterprises.*

delivery, compared by many to her earliest influences Leonard Cohen, Paul Simon, and Joni Mitchell. Buoyed by the single "Marlene on the Wall," the album was well received in the United Kingdom and reached No. 91 on the U.S. charts, not a bad start for an unknown acoustic artist in the age of Reagonomics. "Every era needs its introspective romantics," declared the *London Guardian* in 1985, "preferably with a literate turn of phrase and a wry sense of humour. And it is true if a little facile to say that Suzanne Vega fills the current bill in much the same way as Joni Mitchell...did in previous times. The critical praise and superlatives heaped upon her in America are perhaps premature, but Vega is certainly good enough to make them sound like prophecy."[9]

Vega was not just good, she was about to lead a resurgence in the popularity of acoustic music and a whole new wave of female singer-songwriters. Taken aback by the 200,000 copies of her debut album sold, Vega struggled to complete a follow-up, eventually reaching back to songs she had written over the previous decade and putting together an eclectic sophomore effort *Solitude Standing*. As unlikely as it was, a song about child abuse stood out from the others as "Luka" shot to No. 3 in the United States and catapulted the album to No. 11 stateside and No. 1 in England. A lesser hit but more memorable tune, the a capella "Tom's Diner," infected listeners with its hypnotic groove and innocent charm and became the song with which Vega was most associated.

Vega's magic was something she inherited from Lou Reed, who impressed her so much during a performance in 1979 that it deeply affected her songwriting. Reed and Vega didn't alternate between uplifting and depressing tunes like many of their folk-rock forebears. They were more slice-of-life artists, capturing the subtler aspects of anticipation and denouement in a minute-by-minute existence. "I knew I wanted to be a folk-singer from the time I was 16, partly because it was the music I had been brought up on," Vega declared in an interview after her first album began capturing the attention of critics. "I remember being eight or nine years old and feeling this kind of climate of, oh, if we can just follow Joan Baez and sing 'We Shall Overcome' then we shall overcome. Then all of a sudden the '70s came and it was, like, that really wasn't good enough. You can sing 'Blowin' In The Wind'—and 'Blowin' In The Wind' is a great song—but it doesn't save you from your political situation, so a kind of cynicism crept in, a feeling of futility."[10]

Considering the period, the subject matter, and the genre, *Solitude Standing* was an astonishing success, marking Vega as a harbinger of change in the American musical scene. Record companies that wouldn't give Vega the time of day just two years earlier infiltrated every coffee house in Greenwich Village and beyond in search of soulful, introspective songwriters with pent-up emotions ready to be spilled onto vinyl. Within two years of *Solitude Standing*, a host of female songbirds—including Tracy Chapman, Shawn Colvin, Edie Brickell, the Indigo Girls, and Sinéad O'Connor—released albums on major labels, and unappreciated con- temporaries and predecessors of Vega such as Ferron, Emmylou Harris, and Michelle Shocked were commanding new-found respect. Within a decade, dozens of female acts (ranging from acoustic singer-songwriters to women- led and all-female bands) crowded the airwaves and concert halls, enough to spawn a successful women-oriented touring festival in 1997 called Lilith Fair. Though Vega would continue to make excellent music for decades, *Solitude Standing* would be the apex of her career—largely because she was a victim of her own influence, and had to compete with the many acts for whom she had paved the way—a bedrock album that created a market for independent women in a male-dominated music industry.

Album Title: *Appetite for Destruction*
Artist: Guns N' Roses
Recorded: 1986–1987, at Rumbo Studios in Canoga Park, California, Take One Studio in Burbank, California, and Can Am Studio in Tarzana, California
U.S. release: July 21, 1987 (Geffen)
Producer: Mike Clink

If anyone doubted the sway MTV held in the American music con- sciousness in the late 1980s, one would only have to see how close Guns N' Roses came to being just another L.A.-hair-metal band that could not quite pull it together. Though barely known outside Los Angeles, Guns N' Roses had attracted attention from several labels in 1986 after building a reputa- tion for furious performances on the west coast. The band eventually signed with Geffen Records after a long courting period with a number of A&R representatives—not an effort to get a better deal, but an attempt by the destitute band to get as many free dinners and drinks out of the labels as possible before committing.

The group had only recently graduated from strip clubs to the better Los Angeles venues, and after signing with Geffen built a small buzz with *Live ?!*@ Like A Suicide*, a four-song EP released on their own Uzi Suicide label but funded by Geffen. After a number of lineup changes over their first

Guns N' Roses' 1987 *Appetite for Destruction*, one of several albums that marked Los Angeles as the center of heavy metal in the 1980s. *Courtesy of Universal Music Enterprises.*

few years, they settled into recording their debut album with Axl Rose on vocals, Steven Adler on drums, Duff "Rose" McKagan on bass, and their signature interweaving guitars shared by Izzy Stradlin and Saul "Slash" Hudson. With the release of *Appetite for Destruction* in 1987, the band marked their entry into the hard-rock stratosphere as one of the most dangerous-sounding hair-metal acts of the decade, rivaling AC/DC, Metallica, and Def Leppard for sheer energy and explosiveness.

A combination of early Aerosmith garage rock and late Sex Pistols' attitude, Guns N' Roses were poised to take America by storm—if only they could get people to listen. When sales of *Appetite for Destruction* stalled at about 200,000 copies (a paltry number for potential glam-metal superstars), the label decided MTV was to blame. The network was afraid to air the band's videos because of the violent and misogynist nature of their material (less a moral stand on MTV's part than a fear of reprisal from cable companies). More than six months after the album's release, Geffen Records president David Geffen convinced MTV to play one video as a favor to him. To avoid controversy, the network aired one of the catchier songs, "Welcome to the Jungle," at 5 a.m. on a Sunday. Within twenty-four hours it was MTV's most requested video, setting into motion a string of events that would push the label to re-release several of the album's singles. Suddenly, a year after its release, the album catapulted into the No. 1 position, where it remained for five weeks, lingering on the charts for almost three years. The re-released singles "Welcome to the Jungle," "Paradise City," and "Sweet Child O' Mine" all broke the Top 10, with the latter nesting at the top.

"The one thing Guns N' Roses indisputably have is attitude, an asset no amount of money can buy," declared one critic as the band ascended to superstardom. "They leave nobody in any doubt that they really are the destructive, thrill-seeking brain dead yobbos they come across as. They may be thick, apolitical, old-fashioned spoilt rock brats, but somehow that's still more endearing than the posturing corporate yes-men who make up most of the current rock scene."[11] Guns N' Roses would make their name as interpreters of the Los Angeles lifestyle, singing about sex, drugs, and rock and roll that made up the Sunset Strip, prolonging the wave of interest in the L.A. hardcore scene that started with Van Halen in 1978 and was carried forward by Metallica and west-coast punk bands like Black Flag, X, and the Dead Kennedys.

But Guns N' Roses found inspiration in the alleys and gutters of Los Angeles like no band before them, channeling the untapped rage of the New York Dolls and the Ramones, and combining it with the passion of the Sex Pistols and Motörhead to create an image as the Rolling Stones of the 1980s, who by this time had become downright sleepy compared to their scandalous lyrics and activities in the mid-1960s. *Appetite for Destruction* was the perfect title for this city and this band, as was the opening track "Welcome to the Jungle," a paean to the city's seedy underbelly inspired by a homeless man who once screamed at a teenage Axl, "You know where you are? You're in the jungle baby. You're gonna die!" Rose adopted the words into the song's lyrics, creating one of the hardest-rocking tunes of the decade.

Surrounded by controversy at every turn for their drug abuse, destructive behavior, and offensive lyrics, Guns N' Roses did everything but shy away from confrontation, believing themselves to be the saviors of hard rock at a time when most metal (particularly hair metal) offered comparatively sanguine lyrics about partying it up sans the sleazier aspects of rock and roll. "[T]here's a lot of barriers that need to be broken down because people have got used to what they're supposed to hear," complained an outspoken Rose in defense of his band's material. "Look, even Judas Priest did it, they decide, okay, we're going to try selling out and see if that works, they toned their music down and tried to appease somebody else besides themselves and it cost them. But the public is conditioned on what they're allowed to like, and if something's too far out of the norm, even if it's cool, they won't—we want people to realise man, just play whatever the f**k you want to play, not what someone else thinks you should play, so that's what we've done."[12] Their defiant attitude made Guns N' Roses one of the most successful bands of the later 1980s, and until Nirvana's 1991 opus *Nevermind* redirected the flow of hard rock, *Appetite for Destruction* served as a reminder of what rock and roll sounds like when delivered from the gut.

Album Title: *It Takes a Nation of Millions to Hold Us Back*
Artist: Public Enemy

Recorded: 1987, at Greene Street Recording and Chung King House of Metal in New York City, Sabella Recording in Roslyn, New York, and Spectrum City Studios in Hempstead, New York
U.S. release: April 1988 (Def Jam)
Producer: Hank Shocklee, Carl Ryder

Music as a form of social protest was not exactly a revolutionary idea in 1988. Some of the most influential artists in American and British popular music—Bob Dylan, the Beatles, Pete Seeger, the Clash, Sly Stone—used their lyrics as a force for social change, often directly challenging extant political ideologies and gathering the collective power of disenfranchised youth to rally behind the revolution.

But in the late 1980s, as one commentator on Public Enemy's activist music put it, "Being young no longer guarantees identification with rebel rockers: these are notes from the front in a struggle that is likely to exclude many potential fans. . . . The subjective issue for record buyers is no longer just digging the sounds: the question of agreeing with (or at least tolerating) ideas must be faced. Where does this leave the ignorant and the impressionable? If the modern world is truly a terrordome, then kids who get their nutrition from fast food, culture from cartoons and education from TV might as well get their politics from a record."[13] The politics in question come from Public Enemy's attempts to unify blacks in America, and the records are a trio of radical LPs that made the band one of the most respected rap groups of all time and a major social force in the late century: 1991's *Apocalypse 91 . . . The Enemy Strikes Black*, 1990's *Fear of a Black Planet*, and 1988's *It Takes a Nation of Millions to Hold Us Back.*

It was this latter release that first captured the imagination of the black musical community and rewrote the rules of hip-hop. Describing their music as "the black CNN," Public Enemy used *It Takes a Nation* as a soapbox to address issues like police brutality, institutional racism, the overwhelming percentage of blacks in American prisons, and the hypocrisy of white government—matters that plagued the black community but got little attention from mainstream media. Preceded by their debut release *Yo! Bum Rush the Show*—a powerful album in its own right but lacking the focus and wide appeal of its successor—*It Takes a Nation* showcased the potential of rap music, in the words of frontman Chuck D, "to show that the black man can be just as intelligent as he is strong. . . . Never again will we allow our culture, language, God, whatever we choose as a base of our foundation, to be stripped from us in the same manner it has been in this world."[14]

Chuck D was the stage name of Carlton Ridenhour, a graphic design student at Adelphi University on Long Island who worked as a DJ at the student-run radio station. Teaming up with rapper William Drayton (who adopted the pseudonym "Flavor Flav"), the duo formed Public Enemy in 1982 with considerable production and DJing support from Professor Griff (Richard Griffin), Terminator X (Norman Rogers), DJ Lord (Lord Aswod), and "The Bomb Squad," a brilliant production team that Chuck D had met at the radio station and who provided the group with a sophisticated, hard-hitting blend of party sounds, musique concrète, and electric guitars.

After hearing Chuck D rap over a demo tape, producer Rick Rubin convinced him to sign with his fledgling Def Jam Records, which would soon have a hit with the revolutionary Run-D.M.C. album *Raising Hell* (see p. 185). Rubin had co-produced *Raising Hell* and reportedly came up with the idea of pairing Run-D.M.C. with Aerosmith for the album's smash hit "Walk This Way." Thanks in part to Rubin's signature blending of rap and heavy metal—a genre appreciated by Chuck D and The Bomb Squad—Public Enemy complemented their hard lyrical edge with the focus heavy metal had gained from two decades of commercial success. "In rap, groups are treated like they're disposable, and so they become disposable," claimed Chuck D. "Heavy metal groups are involved in how their music is presented, packaged, marketed. They have control of the merchandising and their logos, whereas the vast majority of rap groups have no control at all."[15]

Public Enemy's quest to bring more focus and control to rap music as a genre mirrored their social quest for a more organized and active black community, the resounding theme throughout *It Takes a Nation of Millions to Hold Us Back* and its follow-up albums. Though the band would face extensive criticism for charges of racism, militancy, and antisemitism (largely fueled by Griff's famous comment that Jews were responsible for "the majority of the wickedness that goes on across the globe"—he was later dismissed from the band), Public Enemy were unapologetic about their music and their message. Like Malcolm X fronting Run-D.M.C., the group spun intelligent, meaningful rhymes (a complex interplay between Chuck D.'s activism and Flavor Flav's comic foil) around dense, forceful rock. "One thing that Public Enemy's kind of rap shares with Anthrax and Metallica's kind of metal is an apocalyptic vibe. In righteous rap, as in doomsday thrash, the lyrics speak of chaos and imminent devastation, while the music embodies survivalist discipline in the face of that threat." Public Enemy were not the first to combine rap and metal, nor the first to use rap as a forum for social commentary, but their deft command of their medium and their widespread appeal continued hip-hop's development from New York street-party noise to the voice of millions.

Album Title: *Daydream Nation*
Artist: Sonic Youth
Recorded: July–August, 1988 at Greene Street Recording in New York City
U.S. release: October 1988 (Enigma)
Producer: Nick Sansano, Sonic Youth

The unlikely (eventual) ascent of Sonic Youth to major label stardom and the upper pantheon of alternative rock idols was due in part to their longevity, as many new-wave and no-wave acts to emerge from the arty postpunk scene in the early 1980s couldn't bare to remain unknown for more than a few years or a few albums, whichever came first. Underground appreciation carried its own rewards, but hardly the means to the rock-star lifestyle most post-punk bands secretly craved (artistic integrity be damned).

Sonic Youth were the exception—to many alt-rock fans, the finest exception, a highly respected anti-rock outfit that endured through seven years and as many albums before receiving their fair share of critical acclaim, and several more years before tasting the commercial success that accompanied it. Though surrounded by the macho posturing of heavy metal (thrash, pop, hardcore, lite, hair, and otherwise), the slick grooves of dance-pop, and the *Breakfast Club*-variety litany of Top-40 shuffles lifted straight out of a fourteen-year-old girl's diary, Sonic Youth were in it for the sound, reaching beyond scripted pop and rock constructs to create a blueprint for the alternative rock that would soon feed into mainstream taste. "We're talking about subterranean influence," claimed one analysis of the band's clatter, "the underground network of alert listeners and operatives who make up a tiny part of any given population, but—in the end—get everywhere."[16]

Formed in 1981 by guitarists Thurston Moore and Lee Ranaldo and bassist Kim Gordon, the band went through several drummers before settling on Steve Shelley in 1985. The early 1980s were a period of extreme sonic experimentation in New York City, with bands like Theoretical Girls, Swans, DNA, and Teenage Jesus and the Jerks marking the short-lived no-wave scene, a rejection of traditional rock structures and the commercial success of new wave in favor of anti-harmony and dissonance. Avant-garde heroes abounded, influenced by the raw architecture of Lou Reed and Iggy Pop and the electronic experiments of Brian Eno and company (Eno came to define the no-wave movement in the minds of many with his 1978 LP *No New York*, a compilation of four no-wave bands from the East Village).

Ranaldo, Moore, and Gordon had all collaborated to some degree with Glenn Branca, founder of Theoretical Girls and an influential avant-garde composer in New York City, influencing Sonic Youth's experimental sound. The band made its debut in the summer of 1981, when Moore put on a ten-day "Noise Festival," after which they recorded their self-titled debut EP to little attention. A series of EPs and LPs followed over the next five years, released on a number of indie labels and featuring a wild mix of guitar experiments, from alternate tunings to objects wedged under the fretboard to give the instrument an unusual sound. The band could only afford cheap guitars, and according to biographer Michael Azerrad, "cheap guitars sounded like cheap guitars. But with weird tunings or something jammed under a particular fret, those humble instruments could sound rather amazing—bang a drumstick on a cheap Japanese Stratocaster copy in the right tuning, crank the amplifier to within an inch of its life, and it will sound like church bells."[17] Sonic Youth's guitar experiments on their first few albums provided a link between New York's no-wave movement and the college rock that would follow, with Georgia's R.E.M. and Minneapolis' Hüsker Dü sharing duties with Sonic Youth as major influences on the formation of alternative music. *Village Voice* critic Robert Christgau termed the music of Sonic Youth and their New York contemporaries "pig fucker" music, referring to the abrasive, dissonant guitars that rattled the listener's brains.

After stints on several indie labels, Sonic Youth finally earned critical kudos for their albums pressed on the west-coast punk label SST, 1986's *EVOL* and 1987's *Sister*, both albums marking an evolution of their sonic experiments toward a more mainstream sound and earning the group high praise from the major rock journals. "When we started, we were being very reactionary, pulling against the norm at the time, which was this post-punk thing with bands like the Bongos and the Individuals, or bands with more traditionalist ideas like X," claimed Moore. "We were trying to bring back and update the elements we liked that came out of bands like the Stooges and the MC-5. Now there's a balance we like to have between formal songwriting and using sound elements, noise elements; it's akin to what Public Enemy's doing."[18]

But it was their 1988 double-album *Daydream Nation* that finally brought the band to the forefront of alternative rock with a roller-coaster ride of soundscapes that earned them immediate acclaim from all corners as a revolutionary album. In a characteristically muddled (but uncharacteristically fawning) review of the album, Christgau professes, "At a historical juncture we can only hope isn't a fissure . . . the anarchic doomshows of Our Antiheroes' static youth look moderately prophetic and sound better than they used to. But they don't sound anywhere near as good as the happy-go-lucky careerism and four-on-the-floor maturity Our Heroes are indulging now. Whatever exactly their lyrics are saying—not that I can't make them out, just that catch-phrases like "You've got it" and "Just say yes" and "It's total trash" and "You're so soft you make me hard" are all I need to know— their discordant never-let-up is a philosophical triumph. They're not peering into the fissure, they're barreling down the turnpike like the fissure ain't there."[19]

Unfortunately for Sonic Youth, the Enigma label fell on hard times and went into bankruptcy before having the chance to properly distribute the album, leading to poor sales and influencing Sonic Youth to finally sign with a major label (though some fans screamed "sellout," the group negotiated full creative control, and demonstrated on their highly praised next album, *Goo*, that they were still the masters of their own noise). It was with *Daydream Nation*, however, that the group fully realized the cross-breeding experiments and sonic chaos within listenable structures, establishing a home for no-wave influences in college radio and influencing a generation of alternative rock to come.

Album Title: *Straight Outta Compton*
Artist: N.W.A
Recorded: 1988, at Audio Achievements in Torrance, California
U.S. release: February 6, 1989 (Ruthless)
Producer: Dr. Dre, Yella

In the mid-1980s—more than a decade after DJ Kool Herc helped import Jamaican dub music to the streets of South Brooklyn and DJs Grandmaster Flash and Afrika Bambaataa elevated street-corner parties into a full-blown subculture—rap music found its way into the American mainstream. Following on the heels of the Sugarhill Gang's 1979 hit single "Rapper's

Delight," Russell Simmons and Rick Rubin founded the tiny Def Jam Records in 1984, and within a few years found themselves at the center of rap's popularity with three of the genre's most successful stars on their label: Run-D.M.C., the Beastie Boys, and LL Cool J. Meanwhile, on the other side of the country in Los Angeles' desperately poor neighborhood of Compton, two friends named Antoine Carraby and Andre Young decided to see what the fuss was all about. "When I was growing up, there was no hip-hop, just funk like George Clinton," recalled Carraby. "We'd seen a show with Run DMC for the first time. It was their first time in California. We sat back and looked at the show and it wasn't nothin'! It was two people rapping and a DJ! We said, 'That's it? We can do that!' "[20]

The two friends had been DJing in local clubs since they were teenagers under the names DJ Yella (Carraby) and Dr. Dre (Young), and (un)inspired by Run-D.M.C., turned their rap outfit the World Class Wreckin' Cru into a semipopular local attraction and one of the first west-coast hip-hop acts. Before long the duo teamed up with other Compton-based artists O'Shea Jackson (Ice Cube), Eric Wright (Eazy-E), Mik Lezan (Arabian Prince), and Tracy Lynn Curry (the D.O.C.) to form N.W.A—which stood for Niggaz with Attitude—one of hip-hop's most legendary acts and important pioneers of gangsta rap.

Although Public Enemy (also a Def Jam client) had already moved hip-hop forward from party music into the realm of social commentary, largely with their 1988 landmark release *It Takes a Nation of Millions to Hold Us Back* (see p. 194), N.W.A turned Public Enemy's work on its head, spinning violent, racist, misogynistic rhymes that mirrored and glorified the gangbanger lifestyle pervading their community. Philadelphia rapper Schoolly D (Jesse B. Weaver Jr.) and Californian Ice-T (Tracy Morrow) were two of the first hardcore rappers, but N.W.A took it nationwide with their sophomore hit *Straight Outta Compton*, a vicious, no-holds-barred celebration of dangerous day-to-day existence in one of America's poorest and most violent neighborhoods. Though the band was criticized for venerating black-on-black crime, their lyrics were a fascinating look for millions of white suburban youth (who were quickly becoming gangsta rap's main market) into the inner-city subculture they would otherwise never see. "I show white America about the black community," said Ice Cube, one of the band's most gifted writers, "and I hold a mirror up to the black community to show them about themselves."[21]

By the time *Straight Outta Compton* was released in early 1989 (following their 1987 effort *N.W.A. and the Posse*), bandleader Eazy-E had managed to parlay money accumulated from drug deals into his label Ruthless Records, bringing MC Ren (Lorenzo Patterson) into the fold and moving Arabian Prince and the D.O.C. onto the backburner as ghostwriters. It was MC Ren, Ice Cube, and Eazy-E (whose lyrical contributions have been questioned) that made the largest impact on *Straight Outta Compton* with the album's first three tracks, "Straight Outta Compton," "Fuck tha Police," and "Gangsta Gangsta," a legendary trio of songs that influenced every gangsta rapper to follow. "Fuck tha Police" was a particularly jolting track, resulting in a Fraternal Order of Police vote to not provide security at N.W.A concerts. The song sparked outrage among law enforcement agencies across the country, leading the public affairs department of the Federal Bureau of Investigation to send a warning letter to Ruthless Records: "Law enforcement officers dedicate their lives to the protection of our citizens, and recordings such as the one from N.W.A. are both discouraging and degrading to these brave, dedicated officers. Music plays a significant role in society, and I wanted you to be aware of the FBI's position relative to this song and its message. I believe my views reflect the opinion of the entire law enforcement community."

Despite the negative reaction to the album from conservative groups (and to some degree because of it), *Straight Outta Compton* went platinum within a few months with no radio or MTV airplay and very little publicity, establishing west-coast gangsta rap as the new bad boy in the hip-hop world. More significantly, the album launched the careers of Ice Cube and Dr. Dre, both of whom soon left the group under less than ideal circumstances. Nonetheless, the duo survived to become two of the most important gangsta rap figures in 1990s hip-hop, with Dr. Dre founding Death Row Records, releasing the groundbreaking album *The Chronic* in 1992 (see p. 220), and igniting the careers of rappers Snoop Doggy Dogg and Eminem. But it was *Straight Outta Compton* that gave gangsta rap a push into the mainstream and Compton's forgotten residents a voice of their own. "Like white working-class youth finding power in the heavy metal identity, it is easy to see how disenfranchised Black youth could concur with these macho expressions of power and bravado," wrote one historian. "It is also clear that rap's characterization of American society as oppressive and unfriendly found support across broad segments of the African-American community."[22]

Album Title: *3 Feet High and Rising*
Artist: De La Soul
Recorded: 1988, at Calliope in New York City
U.S. release: March 1989 (Tommy Boy)
Producer: Prince Paul

The boundaries of hip-hop expanded rapidly in the mid-late 1980s, partly fueled by the sudden acceptance of rap artists by consumers, partly because of MTV's increasing willingness to show videos by black artists (and the 1988 debut of their rap feature "Yo! MTV Raps"), and partly a result of the music industry recognizing rap's commercial potential after the heavy sales of Run-D.M.C.'s 1986 *Raising Hell* (see p. 185) and the Beastie Boys' *Licensed to Ill* (see p. 188) later that year.

Though it wasn't until these two albums fused hip-hop and rock (largely thanks to the talents of Rick Rubin, who produced both LPs) that audiences sat up and took notice. Rap music's roots ran more than a decade deep, and artists quickly emerged from the woodwork with their own versions of what they felt hip-hop should sound like. Since hip-hop was essentially music that interpreted the street, rap acts reflected their environment, as was especially evident with hardcore rappers such as Schoolly D (from West Philadelphia), Ice-T (from the Crenshaw area of Los Angeles), and N.W.A (from L.A.'s infamous Compton district). It was from these artists that gangta rap was born, highlighting the daily struggle of living in America's most dangerous neighborhoods.

But just as hardcore rap was sinking its teeth into the hip-hop community, three high-school friends from Long Island's middle-class suburbs came out of nowhere with a new direction for a genre that seemed to be getting darker by the day. Kelvin Mercer (Posdnuos), David Jolicoeur (Trugoy the Dove), and Vincent Mason (Pasemaster Mase) had submitted a demo tape, "Plug Tunin'," to local producer Prince Paul, who was working with an upbeat Brooklyn outfit called Stetsasonic. Prince Paul passed the tape around and eventually got De La Soul a contract with Tommy Boy Records, a nascent hip-hop label that had released Afrika Bombaataa's seminal hip-hop single "Planet Rock."

Hailed by one critic as "new wave to Public Enemy's punk,"[23] the trio's debut for the label, *3 Feet High and Rising*, signaled a new era for hip-hop, moving away from the popular hardcore rap in favor of positive, energetic vibes and lyrics that were both relaxed and clever. The album is loosely centered around a fictional game show, and from track to track the artists cover an amazing amount of ground, tackling themes that include ghetto life, teenage sex, body odor, fashion, drug abuse, poverty, and independent thinking. Most of the material conveys a positive message, earning the group the distinction of being labeled a "hippy-hop" outfit, a brand to which they took exception. "There's not one cut on 3 Feet High where we straight out said 'peace'," claimed an irked Posdnuos. "The 'hippy hop' thing was always something that the critics invented. 'Me Myself & I' was about not being like everybody else, 'Say No Go' was anti-drugs, 'Buddy' was about being with the one you want to be with. What happened was the critics saw the overall vibe and look of the album and said we was about peace."[24]

The band's objections notwithstanding, De La Soul were the first of a small cadre of rap outfits that found success with a playful, trippy style whose sense of humor stood in stark contrast to the violent and misogynistic egotism of gangsta rap (setting aside the Beastie Boys' *Licensed to Ill*, which was sarcastic and straightforward rather than clever and intricate). Complementing their sharp songwriting, the band introduced more sophisticated sampling techniques to hip-hop as well (with a great deal of help from Prince Paul, who would quickly become one of the most sought-after producers in the genre). Whereas up to now hip-hop DJs would rely heavily on samples to define the texture of a piece (often from established and identifiable R&B artists like James Brown and George Clinton), De La Soul sampled in short increments to provide a variety of interesting variations that greatly expanded the dimensions of the album. On this single LP, dozens of samples are used, including the music and spoken words of Ray Charles, Otis Redding, the Turtles, Liberace, Steely Dan, Michael Jackson, Richard Pryor, a French-language instruction tape, and even hardcore rappers Run-D.M.C. and Public Enemy. On the first song alone, the group borrows from Bill Cosby, Eddie Murphy, Led Zeppelin, Johnny Cash, and a Schoolhouse Rock tune.

"De La Soul has already mastered the three j's of postmodernism: juxtapose, juxtapose, juxtapose," claimed the album's review in *Rolling Stone*. "Welcome to the first psychedelic hip-hop record. . . . The uncanny sonic collages are as catchy as they are clever, and the mellow, bass-heavy grooves are tailor-made for blissful hip shaking. Lyrics range from social consciousness ("Ghetto Thang") to stream of consciousness ("I Can Do Anything"). One of the most original rap records ever to come down the pike, the inventive, playful *3 Feet High and Rising* stands staid rap conventions on their def ear."[25]

The "def ear"—itself a playful smack at the Beastie Boys and Run-D.M.C. label Def Jam—would soon face challenges from a host of R&B and dance acts that were more charming than aggressive, as groups like DJ Jazzy Jeff and Fresh Prince and Deee-Lite got R&B crowds grooving again. De La Soul's music also inspired a wave of positive, socially conscious groups like Jungle Brothers, Queen Latifah, A Tribe Called Quest, Monie Love, and Black Sheep, a collective that reinforced each others work and called themselves the Native Tongues Posse, providing rap audiences with an alternate view from the streets.

Album Title: *Pretty Hate Machine*
Artist: Nine Inch Nails
Recorded: 1989, at Right Track Studios in Cleveland, Ohio, Blackwing and Roundhouse Studios in London, Unique Studios in New York City, and Synchro Sound in Boston
U.S. release: October 20, 1989 (TVT)
Producer: Trent Reznor, Flood, Adrian Sherwood, Keith LeBlanc, John Fryer

Nine Inch Nails were one of those acts that moved music journalists to mine the darkest depths of their thesauri in search of appropriately evil descriptions: "Nine Inch Nails is the clammy warmth of psychosexual angst set against the detached cold of coarse rhythmic aggression."[26] "Branding Nine Inch Nails as merely a techno-pop band is akin to referring to an Uzi as a thing that could cause discomfort."[27] "Nine Inch Nails is an entrancing juxtaposition of imagery and energy built on a foundation of intermingled repulsion and desire."[28] And of course, the inevitable opening line damning the band's frontman with faint praise: "Trent Reznor doesn't *look* psychotic."[29]

Reznor was not just Nine Inch Nails' frontman, he was essentially the entire group, picking up backing musicians when he needed them for tours, but otherwise masterminding every detail of his music. Considering the

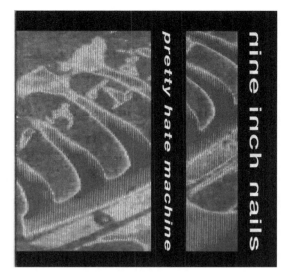

Nine Inch Nails' 1989 *Pretty Hate Machine*, which brought industrial music to mainstream audiences. *Courtesy of Universal Music Enterprises.*

exceedingly disturbing imagery that ran thick through his songs, it's no wonder so many reviews concentrated more on Reznor's state of mind than on his music. "I'm not the happiest guy in the world," Reznor (under)stated. "I'm not sure why. But I can't say, 'It's because someone stole my bike.'"[30]

Reznor hailed from Mercer, Pennsylvania, but spent his early career in Cleveland, Ohio, where he worked as a janitor at a local studio, saving money to purchase recording time. He had spent one year in college studying music and computers, and finding kindred spirits in the work of pioneering industrial acts like Ministry and Skinny Puppy, taught himself how to use synthesizers and computer applications to create synth-heavy songs with aggressive beats and crunchy guitars (he had been studying classical piano since he was a child, and parlayed his training into a postmodern decay of synth-work). While his angstier noise approximated his industrial forebears, his songs were more lyrically oriented and centered around catchier hooks, making them more accessible to audiences that weren't immersed in industrial culture—if only he could reach them.

After releasing *Pretty Hate Machine* in 1989 to scant attention, Reznor attempted to open up industrial music to larger audiences by touring as an opening band for the more mainstream acts Jesus and Mary Chain and Peter Murphy. A short stint opening for Skinny Puppy before *Pretty Hate Machine*'s release had earned him respect as an industrial artist, but more commercial acceptance—for both Reznor and industrial sounds—came from exposing himself to these larger audiences. Three months after *Pretty Hate Machine*, he began the larger tours, and one month later saw his debut slowly begin its climb up the charts where it rested at No. 75 (impressive for an industrial act, as no Skinny Puppy or Ministry albums had managed that kind of chart presence).

The moody, unpredictable anguish in Reznor's songs resonated with the tormented fans of gothic and synth-heavy groups like the Cure, Depeche Mode, and the Smiths, but with much harder beats and more vicious lyrics. "Trent Reznor isn't the kind of guy who moos about having his own personal Jesus or being a victim of love," wrote one reviewer mocking well-known lyrics of competing synth bands. "Granted, he does heap on the electronics but he also uses sweat and drums and bold guitars and not one damn tape recorder. Forget all about things gloomy with a touch of mascara; Reznor would rather slap you silly than give you a handkerchief."[31]

A delayed video of the album's first track, "Head Like a Hole," channeled MTV's massive teen audiences in Reznor's direction, generating radio play for the single and increasing his fan base that had been steadily growing just from word of mouth. Adolescent listeners that had been lulled to sleep by the saccharine pop of Madonna, Whitney Houston, Paula Abdul, Bon Jovi, and coming-of-age movie soundtracks suddenly woke up to the primal rage of *Pretty Hate Machine* singles "Head Like a Hole," "Down in It," and "Sin," and even industrial fans appreciated the teeth-gnashing balladry of "Something I Can Never Have," an almost romantic tune that still manages to balance on its toes at the very edge of fury.

Reznor's nonstop intensity and self-loathing persona that shone through on *Pretty Hate Machine* and in his fuming live performances made him a hero to the stereotypically wretched teen and a precursor to Nirvana's terminally depressed Kurt Cobain, to whom Reznor was often compared. "I'm not proud to say I hate myself and don't like what I am," he asserted, "but maybe there is real human communication that ends up positive even though everything being said is negative. . . . I have clarity, I've hit lows, but fortunately it has never involved putting a needle in my arm. My strategy is not to avoid [lows] but to explore them, to shed light on them."[32] A five-year period would pass before Reznor would release another full album, but in the meantime dozens of bands would imitate his fusion of pop structures, industrial noise, and brutal lyricism. When he returned with the 1992 EP *Broken*, his fan base had only grown, sending the release to No. 2 on the charts and earning a Grammy for the song "Wish." *Pretty Hate Machine* would eventually be certified triple platinum and credited with bringing industrial music into the mainstream without sacrificing its inherent ferocity.

Album Title: *No Depression*
Artist: Uncle Tupelo
Recorded: January 1990, at Fort Apache South, Boston
U.S. release: June 1990 (Rockville)
Producer: Paul Kolderie, Sean Slade

The great irony of the 1990s alternative country-movement—pointed out by pretty much every music journalist who was paying attention—involved the sudden leap of punk-rock oriented bands towards the emotional abyss of traditional material at a time when country acts were clawing their way out of the canyon and toward the slick, polished cliffs of mainstream pop. Leading the downward plunge were Chicago's Souled American and the influential Minnesota bands of the 1980s, the Jayhawks and Paul Westerberg's group the Replacements, but it was Uncle Tupelo's

1990 debut *No Depression* that is widely regarded as energizing the alternative-country movement that pervaded rock music in the 1990s.

One of the main themes in defining alternative-country is that you are not supposed to be able to define it, since it draws on so many traditions and so many of the acts that claim the genre (or have it claimed upon them) sound nothing alike. Though no one has yet provided an entirely pleasing classification, a good starting point would be its name, which invokes the spirit of 1980s alternative rock and the specter of rural American country. "It does draw from a number of rock and country influences creating a hybrid sound that is neither country or rock," claimed John Molinaro in his thesis *Urbane Cowboys: Alt.Country in the 1990s.* "To understand it fully, its influences, liminal artists from a wide spectrum of popular styles, need to be examined: Country artists like Johnny Cash or Willy (sic) Nelson who border on rock and/or folk; rock stars like REM (sic) and Bruce Springsteen that border on country-folk; punk bands like the Replacements or X who border on roots-rock.... Alt.country, while drawing from all these liminal styles, defies categorization. Both the artists and the audience recognize that this is something different."[33]

Though hardly a satisfying definition, this sampling of artists for possible inclusion speaks to alternative-country's wide-ranging roots, as well as the variety of names it has gone by: alt.country, alt-country, Americana, cowpunk, insurgent country, y'alternative, and No Depression, the latter directly lifted from the Uncle Tupelo album as if the band had single-handedly created an entirely new genre (which, at the time, many believed they had). Like most of bands that were called alt-country (let us settle on one name here), Uncle Tupelo combined the small-town nostalgia of country and Americana (Leadbelly, Hank Williams, the Flying Burrito Brothers) with the driving energy of punk rock (Hüsker Dü, the Minutemen, Black Flag).

Formed in 1987 in Belleville, Illinois, the trio of Jay Farrar, Jeff Tweedy, and Mike Heidorn were initially steeped in the garage bands of the 1960s. "Jeff and Jay knew where the good record stores were and turned me on to records by the Clash, Pretty Things, Standells, 13th Floor Elevators, The Seeds, Yardbirds, Sonics, Them, Ramones, Bob Dylan...all kinds of stuff," claimed drummer Heidorn, who was sixteen years old when he first started jamming with Tweedy and Farrar in 1984. Soon the band's tastes changed as they discovered the Gram-Parsons-infused country rock of the decade. "The records we were listening to a couple of years ago (i.e. '60s garage stuff) had morphed into the other side of the sixties: bands like the Byrds, Flying Burrito Brothers, Texas Tornadoes, The Band, Neil Young. Jeff always had Dylan tapes around and Jay always had a Johnny Cash song on hand, but now it seemed we wanted to branch away from doing just sixties covers."[34]

The group's sound was a resurgence of a kind of rebel folk-rock that had been seen before and occupies several spaces among this book's listings—the early honky-tonk of Hank Williams in the 1940s and 1950s; the Byrds album that found Gram Parsons at the helm in 1968, *Sweetheart of the*

Rodeo (see p. 61); the post-Byrds efforts of Parsons in the Flying Burrito Brothers' 1969 release *The Gilded Palace of Sin*; the outlaw country of Merle Haggard, Waylon Jennings, Willie Nelson, and company in the early 1970s that turned Austin, Texas into alt-Nashville, then exploded onto the national scene with the album *Wanted! The Outlaws* (see p. 125).

In 1990, Uncle Tupelo assembled in Boston for their first recording, *No Depression*, the title taken from a 1930s Carter Family song covered on the album, "No Depression in Heaven." Ten days and about $3,000 later, the group had their first LP, which was appreciated critically and by their word-of-mouth fan base, but failed to chart or win widespread appeal. The range of influences evident on the album, however, and the group's truly alternative sound at a time when everyone was looking for alternatives to alternatives in music, helped the album's appeal spread like a slow prairie fire, and before long dozens of bands were imitating their style (including three influential bands from the ashes of Uncle Tupelo's breakup in 1994—Jeff Tweedy's Wilco, Jay Farrar's Son Volt, and the Bottle Rockets, which was formed by former Uncle Tupelo roadie Brian Henneman). In 1995, *No Depression* magazine was founded to track the revitalized Americana movement, which has influenced acts from Beck to Gillian Welch to Nirvana in the subsequent decade. Between their *No Depression* debut and their breakup, Uncle Tupelo released three unique albums, each more highly praised than the last. Though Uncle Tupelo's influence since their debut has soaked American rock in alt-country to the point that most of the group's alumni distance themselves from the very term, there is no doubting the immense contribution the band made to rock's new sound in the 1990s and the particular influence of *No Depression* as the cornerstone of the decade's Americana movement.

Album Title: *No Fences*
Artist: Garth Brooks
Recorded: 1990, at Jack's Tracks in Nashville
U.S. release: August 27, 1990 (Capitol)
Producer: Allen Reynolds

Throughout the history of American recording, country music (and its associated genres of bluegrass, honky tonk, western swing, and so on) had always been a niche market. Legends abounded, of course—Hank Williams, Jimmie Rodgers, Roy Acuff, Johnny Cash, Waylon Jennings, to name just a few—but in terms of commercial sales, country artists always took a back seat to the crooners and the rock stars. Even popular country musicians had trouble eeking out a living from record sales alone, and as often as possible album releases were supplemented by extensive performing in small and medium-sized venues and any television opportunities that presented themselves. In the 1970s, country music hit a boom with the outlaw country movement, led by pioneer Waylon Jennings and a dozen or so of his cohort, leading to the first country album to sell more than one million copies, 1976's compilation *Wanted! The Outlaws* (see p. 125).

Wanted! sparked a slow but steady rise in the popularity of country music, and in the late 1980s country began to achieve respectable sales figures as aging baby boomers took to the genre's sounds that were easier on the ear than the glam-metal and dance-pop that dominated the airwaves. It was not until the early 1990s, however, that country music exploded in popularity. Between 1982 and 1992, the number of country albums that went gold rose almost threefold. In roughly the same period, the number of country-oriented radio stations in the United States grew by approximately 60 percent, and the country television network TNN multiplied its viewership by a factor of eight. The period surrounding 1991 was the real boom, however, with the sale of country albums rising a whopping 50 percent in one year.[35] At the center of this eruption stood one man, Garth Brooks, who could easily be called country music's first commercial superstar.

In the grand scheme of American music, Garth Brooks was one of many important artists. But within the context of his own style, he was an absolute giant, almost single-handedly causing the slow-growing country genre to leapfrog in popularity, becoming the most popular genre in the United States by the end of the decade. Brooks himself retired after little more than a decade of national exposure, during which time he had risen to become the third best selling artist of the 20th century behind Elvis Presley and the Beatles.

Amazingly, Brooks was a fan of rock music at least as much as country, growing up on sixties and seventies folk- and rock-flavored acts such as Townes Van Zandt, Janis Joplin, Bruce Springsteen, and Peter, Paul and Mary, as well as singer-songwriters like Arlo Guthrie, Tom Rush, Janis Ian, and James Taylor, who he worshipped. He told a reporter in 1992 that it was a Queen show that made him want to be the country music equivalent of a rock star, hoping to reproduce in the country genre "that seventies-arena-rock thing." "My ears are still ringin' from that concert," he said. "I was thinking, one day I'm going to feel this feeling—only it's gonna be me up there on that stage."[36]

It was his sophomore album *No Fences* that made that dream come true. His 1989 debut, *Garth Brooks*, reached No. 1 on the country charts and instantly established him as a major country performer, but he shared the spotlight with other rising young talents such as Clint Black, Alan Jackson, and Travis Tritt. 1990's *No Fences*, however, broke all records and expectations when it demonstrated true crossover appeal by reaching No. 3 on the pop charts and selling an extraordinary ten million copies within two years—a number absolutely unheard of in country music. The album spent twenty-three weeks on top of the country charts and spawned four No. 1 singles—the playful "Two of a Kind," the redneck anthem "Friends in Low Places," the tender "Unanswered Prayers," and the controversial "Thunder

Rolls,'' a disturbing story of domestic violence that hinted at Brooks' willingness to work outside of traditional country themes.

It was this keenness to expand the genre that earned Brooks such a massive audience and yet warranted ire from country purists, who did not appreciate Brooks' departures from the Nashville formula (much less his liberal leanings that would show up on future releases and cost him much of his conservative country audience). Besides the rock themes that Brooks displayed in his music, he also took on the rock trappings from the 1970s arena shows he emulated—including light shows, special effects, a wireless headset microphone that allowed him to dance around on stage, and even a harness that flew him over the crowds as he performed.

With his follow-up album *Ropin' the Wind* in 1991, Brooks completed his dreams of pop domination—the LP was not only the first country album ever to top the pop charts, but it remained on top for a staggering eighteen weeks, beating out megastars like Mariah Carey, Michael Jackson, and Guns N' Roses for America's top artist that year. Several of his subsequent albums sold nearly as well or better, making Brooks worldwide the biggest star of the decade, but it was *No Fences* that established him as a major force in mainstream pop and paved the way for dozens of other artists to incorporate rock themes and strategies into their albums, transforming country music from a niche market to the most popular genre of the decade.

NOTES

1. Mark Kemp, "Run-D.M.C.: *Raising Hell*," *Rolling Stone*, September 5, 2002.
2. Biba Kopf, "Run-D.M.C.: *Raising Hell* (Profile/London)," *New Musical Express*, July 19, 1986.
3. Rob Tannenbaum, "Paul Simon: *Graceland*," *Rolling Stone*, 1986.
4. Glenn O' Brien, "Paul Simon: *Graceland* (Warner Bros.)," *Spin*, 1986.
5. Robert Christgau, *Grown Up All Wrong: 75 Great Rock and Pop Artists from Vaudeville to Techno*. Cambridge: Harvard, 1998, 265.
6. Stephen Thomas Erlewine, www.allmusic.com.
7. Ibid.
8. www.suzannevega.com.
9. Mick Brown, "Suzanne Vega: Live at the LSE, London," *The Guardian*, 1985.
10. Mat Snow, "Suzanne Vega: Vaguely Seeking Suzanne," *New Musical Express*, October 5, 1985.
11. Simon Witter, "Guns N' Roses," *Sky*, 1991.
12. Sylvie Simmons, "Guns N' Roses: Colt Heroes," *Kerrang!*, June 1987.
13. Ira Robbins, "Public Enemy: Fear of a Black Planet," *Request*, April 15, 1990.
14. Ibid.
15. Simon Reynolds, "Public Enemy," *Melody Maker*, October 12, 1991.
16. Mark Sinker, "Sonic Youth: Super Sonic Sisterhood," *New Musical Express*, June 1987.
17. Michael Azerrad, *Our Band Could Be Your Life*. New York: Little Brown, 2001, 243.

18. Ted Drozdowski, "Sonic Youth: *Dirty*," *Boston Phoenix*, July 17, 1992.

19. Robert Christgau, www.robertchristgau.com.

20. "Yella Interview," *Prop$ Magazine*, 1996.

21. David Szatmary, *A Time to Rock: A Social History of Rock And Roll*. New York: Schirmer, 1996 (1987), 337.

22. Paul Friedlander, *Rock And Roll: A Social History*. Boulder, CO: Westview, 1996, 275.

23. Christgau, www.robertchristgau.com.

24. Simon Reynolds, "De La Soul: Malice in Wonderland," *Melody Maker*, May 25, 1991.

25. Michael Azerrad, "De La Soul: *3 Feet High and Rising*," *Rolling Stone*, 1989.

26. Steve Martin, "Nine Inch Nails," *Thrasher*, 1990.

27. Jason Pettigrew, "Branding Nine Inch Nails," *Rockflash*, 1990.

28. Martin, 1990.

29. Alan Di Perna and Mike Katzberg, "Machine Head," *Guitar World*, April 1994.

30. Robert Reinhardt, "Black Celebration/Flash," *Spin*, February 1990.

31. Pettigrew, 1990.

32. Edward Helmore, "Trent Reznor," *Mojo*, November 1994.

33. John Molinaro, *Urbane Cowboys: Alt.country in the 1990s*, University of Virginia, 1998.

34. Mike Heidorn, *No Depression* liner notes.

35. Szatmary, 1996, 311.

36. Ibid.

7

SMELLS LIKE TEEN SPIRIT, 1991–2000

It was 1991, and nobody cared. In May, Douglas Coupland's book *Generation X* opened its first chapter with the ominous words, "The Sun is Your Enemy," capturing the overwhelming weight of powerlessness felt by a stifled wave of young adults. In July, an unnamed character in Richard Linklater's film *Slacker* asked the immortal question, "Who's ever written a great work about the immense effort required in order not to create?" capturing the cynical response of these young adults to their suffocating cultural quagmire. When the levee broke, however, a cathartic growl erupted from the Pacific Northwest as albums like Pearl Jam's *Ten*, Nirvana's **Nevermind (1991)**, Soundgarden's *Badmotorfinger*, and Alice in Chains' *Dirt* railed against ubiquitous commodification at a level of controlled chaos that allowed listeners to release their pent up frustrations without actually having to do anything about them. Punk was back, and it was pissed.

The new punk was called "grunge," and despite its promise to deliver the youthful masses from the gaping maw of consumer culture, the genre became bogged down under the weight of its own commercial success. To actually rescue hungry listeners from the pop and rock stalemate took a string of imaginative works throughout the decade, including the Spin Doctors' 1991 *Pocket Full of Kryptonite*, Counting Crows' 1993 *August and Everything After*, Green Day's **Dookie (1994)**, Weezer's 1994 *Weezer*, and Beck's 1994 *Mellow Gold* and **Odelay (1996)**.

Hip-hop, meanwhile, slowly moved forward from fad to enduring mainstream genre as the gangsta rap of Los Angeles inspired scores of inner-city performers to try their hand at the big time and artists from other genres began to infuse their music with hip-hop's imaginative beats. Albums like the Red Hot Chili Peppers' **Blood Sugar Sex Magik (1991)** and Rage Against the Machine's 1992 *Rage Against the Machine* borrowed from the funk of Sly and the Family Stone and George Clinton, as well as hip-hop and rock from 1980s groups like Public Enemy and Faith No More to bring about the subgenres of rap core and nu-metal in popular bands such as Korn, Limp Bizkit, and Linkin Park. Two of the original innovators behind mainstream hip-hop took gangsta rap to a whole new level with Ice-T's *O. G. Original Gangster* (1991) and Dr. Dre's *The Chronic* (1992), while the Wu-Tang Clan's *Enter The Wu-Tang (36 Chambers)* (1993) extended hip-hop culture well beyond its musical element, Notorious B.I.G.'s 1994 *Ready to Die* and Tupac Shakur's 1996 *All Eyez on Me* fueled the east coast/west coast hip-hop war, and Eminem's *The Slim Shady LP* (1999) elevated rap's lyrical possibilities to a whole new level.

But it was the women who made the most remarkable strides, both artistically and professionally, in an industry historically dominated by a patriarchal power structure. Riding the wave of independence and outspoken attitude set in motion by artists like the Indigo Girls, Suzanne Vega, and Sinéad O'Connor, a whole new crop of singer-songwriters, riot grrls, and chart-topping sensations took the decade by storm. Albums such as Tori Amos' *Little Earthquakes* (1992), Bikini Kill's 1993 *Pussy Whipped*, Bratmobile's 1993 *Pottymouth*, and Liz Phair's *Exile in Guyville* (1993) tackled taboo subject matter and pushed the boundaries of "acceptable" themes by female acts. These artists, in turn, paved the way for a similar revolution in country music with the Dixie Chicks' *Wide Open Spaces* (1998), while from England a one-act invasion made the words "girl power" a national catch phrase with the Spice Girls' *Spice* (1997), and Ani Difranco's *Not a Pretty Girl* (1995) turned millions of eyes toward the power and future of the independent music that would saturate the market at the dawn of a new century.

Album Title: *O. G. Original Gangster*
Artist: Ice-T
Recorded: 1991, at Syndicate Studios West, Widetracks, Dodge City, and Fox Run Studios in Los Angeles
U.S. release: May 14, 1991 (Sire)
Producer: Bilal Bashir, Afrika Islam, Ice-T, DJ Aladdin

"There's a lot of admirable qualities in gang membership. A guy will look at you and say, 'If something happens to you I'll be the first one to die.' There's a lot of love."[1] This is not the kind of saccharine sentiment one often hears coming from South Central Los Angeles gang members, but Ice-T was not your everyday gangster. His raw, lyrical, intelligent tales of gang life in one of the nation's most dangerous neighborhoods provided the foundation for the massively popular gangsta rap in the 1990s, and with his 1991 album *O. G. Original Gangster*, he dispelled all notions of the genre as simplistic hedonism by revealing the complexities and challenges of ghetto life.

Born Tracy Morrow in Newark, New Jersey in 1958, Ice-T went to live with relatives in Los Angeles' crime-ridden Crenshaw district after his parents were killed in an automobile accident. While attending Crenshaw high school, he became fascinated with gang culture and rap music, reportedly joining a faction of the notorious Crips while immersing himself in the writings of Iceberg Slim, a pimp who wrote poetry and novels (and from whom Ice-T borrowed his name). Following high school, Ice-T pursued simultaneous careers as an actor and a musician, appearing in an episode of "Fame" and in the early hip-hop films *Rappin'*, *Breakin'*, and *Breakin' 2: Electric Boogaloo*.

After releasing several forgotten singles and composing for various low-budget projects in the early 1980s (including penning vocal arrangements for Mr. T in the 1984 children's motivational film *Be Somebody... Or Be Somebody's Fool!*), Ice-T saw his major-label release with 1987's *Rhyme Pays*, one of the first west-coast rap albums to fuse hip-hop with heavy metal. Rap had already experienced a fusion with rock music on the east coast the previous year through Def Jam's records *Raising Hell* by Run-D.M.C. (see p. 185) and *Licensed to Ill* by the Beastie Boys (see p. 188). But at the time, Los Angeles was positively drowning in the punk and heavy metal of Guns N' Roses, Metallica, Black Flag, X, and their many imitators, and Ice-T was among the earliest artists to bring hardcore metal into the rap idiom, even sampling Black Sabbath's song "War Pigs" on the title track to *Rhyme Pays*.

Ice-T found national exposure the next year with the title song to the movie *Colors*, a critically praised drama about gang life in South Central Los Angeles—a subject with which Ice-T was intimately familiar. More powerful and culturally engaged than his previous work, "Colors" foreshadowed his 1988 album *Power*, the first major-label album to take on the poverty and violence of South Central's ghettos. Though overshadowed by N.W.A's *Straight Outta Compton* (see p. 198) the following year, *Power* (along with Public Enemy's simultaneous *It Takes a Nation of Millions to Hold Us Back* (see p. 194)) elevated hip-hop from a form of entertainment to a vehicle for social discourse, bringing the character of the black urban male into popular culture. "If there wasn't rap, where would the voice of the eighteen-year-old black male be?" asked Morrow. "He would never be on TV, he ain't writin' no book. He is not in the movies."[2]

In the late 1980s, hip-hop continued its accelerated evolution with bands like Run-D.M.C., the Beastie Boys, N.W.A, Public Enemy, and De La Soul leading the way through a minefield of gangsta rap, rap-metal, and hippy-hop. But it was not until 1991 that the dominant form of gangsta rap reached its poetic apex with Ice-T's *O. G. Original Gangster*, a sweeping, complicated journey through the nightmarish streets of the ghetto. "There's perceptive social analysis, chilling violence, psychological storytelling, hair-trigger rage, pleas for solutions to ghetto misery, cautionary morality tales, and cheerfully crude humor in the depictions of sex and defenses of street language," wrote critic Steve Huey. "But with a few listens, it's possible to assimilate everything into a complex, detailed portrait of Ice-T's South Central L.A. roots—the album's contradictions reflect the complexities of real life."[3]

Like all gangsta rap, *O. G. Original Gangster* faced criticism for its portrayals of violence, drugs, and misogyny, but where gangsta rap up to this point largely glorified the lifestyle, Ice-T highlighted the contradictions of gangster life through erudite storytelling and complex narratives that ushered in a new age of socially conscious hip-hop. "On its own terms, *O. G. Original Gangster* serves as the 1991 equivalent of *There's a Riot Going On*," claimed *Rolling Stone's* review of the album. "It's a bleak, prophetic and savagely funny dispatch from the front lines of the war at home. Combining his own narrative approach to rapping with the freestyle boasting of New York's "old school," Ice-T has forged a flexible, hyperliterate style that sacrifices none of hip-hop's rhythmic momentum. In the frank manner of black pulp-paperback writers like Iceberg Slim and Donald Goines, his slice-of-street-life stories and badass parables offer a fascinating glimpse into a half-hidden world."[4] Besides marking an important literary evolution in gangsta rap, *O. G. Original Gangster* also advanced the fusion of hip-hop and heavy metal in the track "Body Count," which featured the debut of Ice-T's thrash metal band of the same name. Ice-T and Body Count would face notoriety two years later with the song "Cop Killer," which outraged police organizations across the country and got the band dropped from their label, but reinforced Ice-T's status as a central figure in the rapid evolution of hip-hop.

Album Title: *Nevermind*
Artist: Nirvana
Recorded: January–September 1990, at Sound City in Van Nuys, California
U.S. release: September 24, 1991 (Geffen)
Producer: Butch Vig, Nirvana

Since the dawn of punk rock, alternative artists have walked a fine line between commercial acceptance and artistic integrity. With the former comes inevitable intervention in the creative process from label representatives who want to make sure they are getting the most return on their investment dollar. With the latter comes a slippery slope of missed opportunities that more often than not lands one in the ditch of relative obscurity. Few punkish acts have managed to have their cake and eat it to—Patti Smith, the Sex Pistols, Sonic Youth, the Pixies, Jane's Addiction—and none have managed to stack both sides of the equation like the groundbreaking indie act Nirvana and their 1991 landmark release *Nevermind*.

"[O]n *Nevermind*, Nirvana's rage is mostly unspecific and apolitical, and at times verges on incoherent," read the album's review in the *New York Times*. "It provides a catch-all catharsis that fits in perfectly with the directionless disaffection of the 20something generation. 'Smells Like Teen Spirit' could be this generation's version of the Sex Pistols' 1976 single, 'Anarchy in the U.K.', if it weren't for the bitter irony that pervades its title. As Nirvana knows only too well, teen spirit is routinely bottled,

Nirvana's 1991 breakthrough *Nevermind*, which served as the tipping point for the grunge music that swept the 1990s. *Courtesy of Universal Music Enterprises.*

shrink-wrapped and sold. Mr. Cobain, acutely aware of the contradiction of operating in an industry that's glad to turn rebellion into money, rails against the passivity of today's youth with lyrics like "Here we are now, entertain us/How stupid and contagious." ... The song is an anthem for kids who don't know what they want, and probably wouldn't have the will power to get it even if they did."[5]

Much like the Richard Linklater film *Slacker* and the Douglas Coupland book *Generation X* (both of which came out the same antimagical summer as the Nirvana album), *Nevermind* defined a generation coming into adulthood at the turn of the 1990s, trapped in a constant state of corporate manipulation, disillusioned by the commodification of rebellion, and bored by the utter futility of getting up in the morning. The album was a tipping point for American youth, who soon abandoned the hair-metal train wreck that had carried them through the 1980s and adopted the angstier, more punkish grunge music coming out of Nirvana's home state of Washington.

Nirvana had gone through several incarnations before 1989 when they settled into their three-man lineup of Kurt Cobain on vocals and guitar, Chris Novoselic on bass, and Dave Grohl on drums, a furiously passionate trio of performers who capitalized on constant touring and the success of the band's first album, 1989's *Bleach* (sans Grohl), to land a record deal with David Geffen's label DGC. *Bleach* had brought the group to the attention of college radio and alternative music press, plus the admiration from established alternative bands like Dinosaur Jr., Sonic Youth, and Mudhoney (with whom Nirvana had shared the indie label Sub-Pop in Seattle). Contract in hand, Nirvana embarked on a tour of Europe supporting Sonic Youth before releasing *Nevermind* in September of 1991. By January, the album poetically knocked the slick Michael Jackson release *Dangerous* off the top of the charts, shooing away the 1980s like an annoying insect and establishing a new sound for a new decade.

Before long the Pacific Northwest had replaced Los Angeles as the center of American rock, with bands from Seattle, Portland, and Olympia finding national audiences in a hurry. The "grunge" sound (originally a derogatory term for the genre) brought greater public recognition to bands like Mudhoney, Pearl Jam, Soundgarden, and Alice in Chains—most of whom were around before Nirvana and eventually sold more albums once they reached stardom. Much of the dirty-punk sound of grunge music is attributed to Washington acts the Melvins and Green River, both of whom mined early metal like Black Sabbath and west-coast punk like Black Flag for inspiration. Nirvana built on these influences, as well as the early punk of Iggy and the Stooges and the experimental alternative of 1980s acts like the Pixies and Sonic Youth to construct a sound that constantly teetered on the brink of chaos, alternating from listenable melodies to sudden crashes of guitars and unrestrained emotional explosions.

Nevermind eventually sold more than ten million copies, landed in the Top 5 of nearly a dozen countries' charts, and by the end of the decade was near or at the top of every major list of the 1990s' most important releases. The album cover, featuring an underwater shot of a baby swimming after a dollar bill on a fishing hook, perfectly encapsulated the corporate-weary tone of the music and has achieved similar status as a lauded artistic statement. The album's first single, "Smells Like Teen Spirit," was made into a popular video of a teen pep rally run amok, which significantly helped push the album's sales. The song has since become something of an anthem for the 1990s, its somewhat indecipherable lyrics analyzed to death for hidden meanings, despite Cobain's claims that he was a lazy songwriter and most of his lyrics were pastiches of nonsensical poetry he often wrote at the last minute. Nonetheless, for many fans Cobain encapsulated the frustration of his generation, and *Nevermind* was the greatest articulation of the emptiness of consumer culture. "Nirvana's name is as much an ironic shot at middle American mindlessness as a statement of belief in the considerable redemptive power of what they do. They are a reaction—and a magnificently psychotic one at that—to the passivity of a rock culture whose only function is to be consumed."[6]

Album Title: *Blood Sugar Sex Magik*
Artist: The Red Hot Chili Peppers
Recorded: May–June 1991, in Los Angeles
U.S. release: September 24, 1991 (Warner Bros.)
Producer: Rick Rubin

It's not as if the world needed another rock and roll subgenre in the 1980s. The myriad of new styles that came about over the previous two decades, coupled with the crossover fusions that brought no end of hyphenated forms—country-rock, folk-rock, punk-metal, rap-metal, and so on—flooded the marketplace with choices that continued to expand the American musical palette. But Los Angeles, the city that dominated the decade with hair-metal and west-coast punk, found a new reason to crow when the Red Hot Chili Peppers emerged in the mid-1980s with an unusual blend of metal, punk, hip-hop, blues, and psychedelia in a mix often and most accurately described as "punk-funk."

Also labeled "funk-metal," "funk-n-roll," and other similar constructions, punk-funk was an upbeat and energetic mingling of 1970s' "dirty funk" and the driving guitars and percussion of punk rock and heavy metal. Originated by 1980s acts like the Red Hot Chili Peppers, Living Colour, Primus, Fishbone, and Faith No More, the sound gained much of its early press through the Peppers' domination of the Los Angeles rock scene, a group hailed by *Spin* magazine as "the greatest rock band in the world" in 1984—just after their vinyl debut and long before they ever made a dent in the charts. "The Chili Peppers' music is an unprecedented blend of styles," read the review, "mixing Hank Williams with rap, Led Zeppelinoid arpeggios with R & B chicken-scratch guitar; producing a sort of seamless fusion of hardcore, Delta Blues, hip hop and straight-ahead rock. They are very black, very white and never gray. Onstage, bare chests, arms and legs smeared with dayglo paint, wearing weird hats and masks, moving like pinballs or witch docs or barefoot on hot asphalt, they're as wild as Iggy and the Stooges or P-Funk or Zulus or Mardi Gras Injuns."[7]

The centerpiece of the Red Hot Chili Peppers sound was the rap-punk vocals of singer Anthony Kiedis and the gritty metal-funk of guitarist Michael Balzary, the only two members of the group who stuck it out from the beginning. Citing an array of influences as their sound developed over the 1980s—ranging from the psychedelic rock of Jimi Hendrix to the west-coast punk of Black Flag and the Germs to the dance R&B of the Ohio Players and Sly and the Family Stone to the sophisticated party funk of George Clinton—the Red Hot Chili Peppers quickly became the darlings of the Los Angeles club scene soon after their formation in 1983. Originally billed as Tony Flow and the Miraculously Majestic Masters of Mayhem, the Chili Peppers were mounting full-scale attacks in clubs along Sunset Strip within months of their formation, and by the end of the year secured a contract with EMI Records.

"Funky is about the most oblique description of the airtight jerky sound-splash mayhem they deliver," wrote a Los Angeles paper reviewing the group early in their career when they faced criticism for being an all-white band tackling sounds of black funk. "If they're the white-funk joke-band that they're being hyped and hipped as, then it's the most solid white-hot funk and the most deadly serious barrel-of-monkeys joke I've heard for two, maybe three millenniums."[8] Despite continued criticism from some racially-overaware corners, the Peppers gained serious credibility when funkmaster George Clinton agreed to produce their second album *Freaky Styley* (after their two-dimensional, self-titled debut release failed to capture the energy of their live sound). *Freaky Styley* was straight-up funk, a loose and more limber album than their debut, strengthening their industry cache and popular appeal that led to steadily increasing praise of their punkier follow-ups, 1987's *The Uplift Mofo Party Plan* and 1989's *Mother's Milk*, which first placed the band in the wider public spotlight with a modern remake of the Stevie Wonder classic "Higher Ground."

With the near-breakthrough success of *Mother's Milk*, the band rented a house in Los Angeles known as "the Mansion" (which had lodged acts like the Beatles, Mick Jagger, and David Bowie at one time or another, and many believed was haunted) to focus on what they knew would be their make-it-or-break-it sequel. The label brought in producer Rick Rubin, who had almost single-handedly pioneered the rap/rock fusion of the 1980s by co-founding Def Jam Records and guiding Run-D.M.C. and the Beastie Boys to stardom. Rubin's spare, uncluttered production technique was just what the band needed to open up their crowded sound and demonstrate how tight an act they could be.

After *Blood Sugar Sex Magik* debuted in September 1991, it took nearly a year for it to wind its way up the charts to the No. 3 spot, along the way finding airplay and critical lauds for funk powerhouse tunes such as "Suck My Kiss" and "Give It Away," as well as sensitive material with "Breaking the Girl" and the surprise No. 2 ballad "Under the Bridge." With *Blood Sugar Sex Magik* the group exhibited an impressive collision of influences and originality and revealed a more world-aware consciousness (poorly executed on earlier records) that would mark this release as their most accessible work. "The album title is an eloquent but abstract description of how we feel," explained Kiedis. "We live in a world packed with desensitising forces, that strip the world of magic. And music can help restore a sense of magic. The world is full of negativity, but we fight back with positivity. We're inspired by oceans, forests, animals, Marx Brothers films. We can't help but project uplifting vibrations, because we love each other so much and get off on playing together."[9]

Blood Sugar Sex Magik graduated the Red Hot Chili Peppers from a niche market band to a hot mainstream ticket, bringing punk-funk to a mass audience and influencing a string of softer and harder acts to follow—from the "nu metal" of Korn, Linkin Park, and Limp Bizkit, to the "rap-core" of Rage Against the Machine and 311, to the alternative rap-rock of Kid Rock and Incubus—securing a place for punk-funk as one of American music's driving forces at the dawn of the new century.

Album Title: *Little Earthquakes*
Artist: Tori Amos
Recorded: 1990–1991
U.S. release: February 1992 (Atlantic)
Producer: Tori Amos, Eric Rosse, Davitt Sigerson, Ian Stanley

In the late 1960s, American music was being broadcast through a megaphone. Rock and roll was creating new genres with practically every album, and most of them were loud: psychedelia, blues-rock, proto-punk, southern rock, glam, progressive, and of course heavy metal blared from car radios and hi-fi speakers in a mass cacophony of volume and power. Even the softer sounds of country-rock and folk-rock lacked a certain private connection with their listeners, personal revelations subdued to historical and universal tropes. That was, until the singer-songwriters took the stage at the turn of the decade. Led by artists such as James Taylor, Carole King, and Joni Mitchell, the solo acoustic performers took American music by hushed storm, baring their souls in displays of candid, unadorned intimacy, making one-on-one connections with their audiences and ushering in a decade of confessional songwriting that silenced louder concoctions with its openness and sincerity.

It may be cliché to insist that American trends repeat themselves every twenty years, as has often been claimed, but it's hard to ignore the coincidence. The late 1980s, like the late 1960s, rang the ears with a dizzying clatter. Los Angeles hair-metal bands ruled the airwaves and overblown dance pop dominated the charts, and even underground and alternative acts like Sonic Youth, the Pixies, and R.E.M. eschewed intimate connections in favor of sonic experimentation. The singer-songwriter club was about to take over again, re-ignited by artists like Suzanne Vega, Tracy Chapman, and the Indigo Girls, sharing well-crafted, character-driven stories that touched their audiences in forgotten, personal ways. But it was Tori Amos' debut solo album in 1992, *Little Earthquakes*, that really found America's heartstrings and opened up a new chapter in intimate revelations in music.

Hardly a magazine story was written of Amos' music that did not recount in detail her unusual upbringing and the incidents that fueled her uniquely autobiographical music. A child piano prodigy, Amos was the youngest person ever to be admitted to the prestigious Peabody Conservatory (at age five), then was kicked out at age eleven for her unconventional style. Her teens were spent playing Washington D.C.'s piano bars—escorted by her minister father—until she turned twenty-one and moved to Los Angeles, where she continued playing smaller venues, eventually landing a contract with Atlantic Records and releasing *Y Kant Tori Read* in 1988. The album was not only a dismal commercial fiasco, but completely failed to represent Amos' piano and songwriting skills, opting instead for hair-metal image with a loud and uninspired backing band. Amos was crushed, and shipped off to England by her record company, she lingered in relative obscurity until she found—or more appropriately, returned to—a style of performance that best displayed her talents: alone at a piano, pouring her heart out through her songs.

Amos' first release as a singer-songwriter found a small but dedicated audience in the United States and England. *Little Earthquakes* was nothing less than a bare-bones exploration of Amos' search for herself, more stark and confessional than nearly anything produced by her 1970s forebears. "To create anything approaching real art, there's a certain amount of nakedness involved," London writer Neil Gaiman said of the album. "The willingness to bare more of your soul than is comfortable for you or the audience. She allows herself to say things that most people wouldn't dare say."[10] Like James Taylor's single "Fire and Rain" from his 1970 album *Sweet Baby James*, Amos struck tender nerves with haunting tracks that waved her vulnerabilities like a banner, including "Silent All These Years,"

"Crucify," "Winter," and the heartbreaking "Me and a Gun," Amos' attempt to find closure after being raped several years earlier.

But her songs, as full of vulnerability as they were, were anything but weak. These were stories of a woman taking control, and Amos' powerful, determined keyboard prowess reinforced that notion. Amos didn't just confess her pain and regrets trough her music, she confronted them, and in doing so built a massive, fanatically devoted following among young females in America. Her songs were catharsis by proxy, addressing every young woman's insecurities without blame or excuse. Amos became a symbol for true female power—not the manipulative sexuality of Madonna that came years earlier or the empty rhetoric of the Spice Girls' "girl power" campaign that followed down the road, but true ownership of one's self esteem.

Even though Amos was on a major label, her widely publicized independent spirit and her deeply personal songs helped further the growth of the indie music community and its legions of female singer-songwriters trying to break into the mainstream, as well as returned the piano to its status as an acceptable instrument for rock music. *Little Earthquakes* was a watershed moment for women in music, inspiring countless female folkies to assert themselves and fueling the growing female presence in the music community. Within a few years self-assured artists like Sarah McLachlan, Sheryl Crow, Jewel, and Alanis Morissette would find stardom with their own versions of personal strength and authority, leading to the successful female-oriented music festival Lilith Fair, founded by McLachlan in 1996. Amos continued releasing similarly strong-minded albums throughout the decade and became an icon for independent women in music, finding a crossroads between vulnerability and strength that rang through "chick-rock" in the 1990s, but started with *Little Earthquakes*.

Album Title: *The Chronic*
Artist: Dr. Dre
Recorded: 1992, at Death Row Studios in Los Angeles
U.S. release: December 15, 1992 (Death Row)
Producer: Dr. Dre

By the time Andre Young—aka Dr. Dre—released his solo debut *The Chronic* at the tail end of 1992, he was already one of the better known personalities in the hip-hop community. His pioneering work with the west-coast hip-hop group N.W.A put gangsta rap on the map, and his producing, DJing, and songwriting skills were increasingly admired by the fast-growing hip-hop industry. As producer for the groundbreaking 1989 N.W.A release *Straight Outta Compton* (see p. 198) and its 1991 follow-up *Niggaz4life*, Dre's erudite sonic experiments were often buried beneath brutal lyrics and ego clashes among the band's members, but when he left N.W.A and the Ruthless label to pursue his own visions, his strengths as a producer took center stage.

Dr. Dre's 1992 solo debut *The Chronic*, the signature release by hip-hop's most respected producer. *Courtesy of Universal Music Enterprises.*

By the time Dre had left Ruthless, the departure of songwriter Ice Cube from N.W.A had crippled the band artistically and gangsta rap edged closer and closer to becoming a parody of its own genre, particularly as more intelligent and playful rap was evolving through acts like De La Soul and Queen Latifah. Dre was making his own plans to follow in Ice Cube's footsteps, but was unable to convince Ruthless to release him from his contract. According to widely-held belief, Dre's former bodyguard Suge Knight threatened N.W.A frontman Eazy-E and manager Jerry Heller with baseball bats (and possibly kidnapped Heller's mother) to secure Dre's independence (a fairly believable story since Knight's coldblooded disposition was legendary, and he spent much of the 1990s afoul of the law for similar business tactics).

In 1991, with Dre free from Ruthless, Dre and Knight teamed up to form Death Row Records, releasing the seminal album *The Chronic* the following year. "High-volume hypnotism, *The Chronic*, like the marijuana it's named for, alters the senses," claimed one review. "Mixing loping beats, smooth and gruff voices from South Central, giggles, snarls and reggae intonations, it updates the aural movies P-Funk (and psychedelia) once made. Its sounds are as raw and complex and real as life. The assaultive Dre and the more relaxed Snoop Doggy Dogg...may be, to put it mildly, problematic souls, and romanticizing criminal behavior sucks. This music, however, cannot be refuted or easily forgotten."[11]

For better or worse, *The Chronic* reinvigorated gangsta rap, and though its lyrics were as violent and misogynistic as its predecessors, Dre's production talents shone through in deft, complex soundscapes that influenced every rap release to follow. Pioneering a noise known as G-funk ("G" for "Ghetto" or "Gangsta," a play on George Clinton's legendary funk outfit P-funk), *The Chronic* moved gangsta rap into a slower, more bass-heavy groove, building on Clinton's formidable funk foundation with cleverly layered synthesizers and a slow, lazy lyrical drawl that simulated the articulations of a heavily medicated vocalist. One of the unique characteristics of G-funk was the use of portamento, a centuries-old technique of sliding from one pitch to another without a discrete break in frequency.

Dre gave G-funk a defining sound by using synthesizers to simulate portamento (which cannot be achieved on a traditional keyboard). G-funk would immediately make many rappers pale imitations of Dr. Dre and his colleague Snoop Doggy Dogg as the sound swept through the hip-hop community and gave a much needed boost to west-coast rap. Soon the LP reached the Top 10 on the pop charts and became one of the bestselling rap albums in history, starting a dynasty for Death Row as the top hip-hop label through most of the 1990s.

More than just pioneering a new sound, *The Chronic* introduced artists such as Snoop Doggy Dogg and Warren G (Dre's stepbrother) to a wide audience, launching their careers on subsequent albums. The 1993 Dre-produced debut for Snoop Doggy Dogg entitled *Doggy Style*—the first debut album in history to enter the charts at No. 1—was second only to *The Chronic* for influencing the G-funk fad, and although Warren G signed with New York's Def Jam rather than Death Row, his smash 1994 album *Regulate . . . G-Funk Era* thematically sat square in the west-coast gangsta camp.

Like many gangsta rap albums, *The Chronic* fueled as much controversy as it did praise. Gangsta rap had already earned the ire of parents and culture police for its glorification of the violence and misogyny in Los Angeles' most notorious neighborhoods where the genre got its start. Death Row Records became a target of activist groups and boycotters, and the pressure reportedly forced Time Warner to sell its subsidiary, Interscope Records, who were contracted to distribute Death Row albums.

There were also accusations of plagiarism by the Ruthless Records band Above the Law, whose 1993 release *Black Mafia Life* bore noticeable G-funk similarities to *The Chronic*. Dr. Dre had helped produce Above the Law when they shared the Ruthless Records label, and the band's frontman, Cold 187um (Greg Hutchinson), claimed that Dre stole some of his ideas that generated the G-funk sound. *Black Mafia Life* was released months after *The Chronic*, but it was supposedly in the works for two years, and it is possible that Dre simply beat the band to the punch. But regardless which producer originated the G-funk noise, it was Dre's *The Chronic* that brought it into the mainstream, breathing new life into gangsta rap and permanently changing the sound of hip-hop.

Album Title: *Exile in Guyville*
Artist: Liz Phair
Recorded: 1992, at Idful Studios in Chicago
U.S. release: June 24, 1993 (Matador)
Producer: Liz Phair, Brad Wood

No one expected Elizabeth Clark Phair's debut album to sell 200,000 copies, least of all Elizabeth Clark Phair. "I figured if we made it to 2,000 copies we might have a shot at re-pressing the thing," she told *Vogue* magazine a year after she became the hottest new commodity in indie rock. "I was just a neighbourhood kid who wanted to show the boys I could do it."[12]

"Showing the boys" became a theme for the album's unexpected mass appeal. When Liz Phair's *Exile in Guyville* was released in the summer of 1993, it struck a nerve with the indie rock community, particularly the riot grrl and feminist contingents. Alternative rock in America was beginning to take a turn toward the equitable, as female punk bands took advantage of the genre's candor and began addressing subjects that had been taboo for female artists, such as women-oriented politics, lesbian relationships, and good old fashioned sex. Groups like Bikini Kill, Bratmobile, and 7-Year Bitch were coming out of the woodwork to establish an anticorporate femi-punk movement, and solo artists like Tori Amos and Sinéad O'Connor were finding themselves role models to thousands of young women who identified with Amos' deeply personal ballads and O'Connor's fiery political rhetoric.

Then came Liz Phair. An average, art-inclined local songwriter from Chicago scored a minor deal with a minor label and hoped for the best, completely surprised when the best turned out to be exponentially better than she expected. Raised by wealthy, adoptive parents in a tony suburb of Chicago (her father was chief of infectious diseases at Northwestern Memorial Hospital, and her mother was a teacher at the Art Institute of Chicago), Phair was always encouraged to speak her mind and love what she does. While studying art at Oberlin College in Ohio, Phair became interested in the underground music scene, and after returning to Chicago began writing songs and releasing tapes under the name "Girlysound." She had settled in the Wicker Park area of Chicago known as "Guyville" (hence the title) and made connections in the local indie music scene, pairing up with local drummer Brad Wood to flesh out her material and continue making her tapes. A friend of hers from Oberlin, Chris Brokaw, was playing guitar for the Matador Records band Come, and sent the label head a Girlysound demo, earning Phair a contract. Phair culled her catalog for her best cuts and organized them into a loose (though she claimed song-by-song) response to the Rolling Stones' 1972 classic *Exile on Main St.*

Exile in Guyville was a refined form of feminism with the politics filtered out, cutting to the heart of male–female relationships and a woman's self-awareness with absolutely brutal honesty and matter-of-fact directness and using blush-worthy profanities with an almost clinical coldness. To put it as directly as possible, she was a woman who had something to say, and she came right out and said it. She hardly expected so many people would be listening, and admitted that if she had, the album would have turned out very differently. "I hope I don't forget where my head was when I was making it," she stated about her debut release. "I make this joke—If you took a mile radious around that studio, that was as far as I needed that album to go. My neighbourhood. I don't have to be loved by the whole world. I just have to have reached the people that I wanted to reach."[13]

Phair's reach, however, was exceeded by her grasp, and her clear stature as an unspoiled, independent artist gained her an even more devoted following as her audiences identified with the honesty and quick wit masked by a veneer of amateurism. Her regular bouts with stage fright were almost endearing, and the low fidelity four-track sound on *Exile in Guyville* smacked of converted-bedroom studio work (as sophisticated as it was for a low-budget recording), fueling the anyone-can-do-it element of the budding indie-rock movement. Suddenly "lo-fi" recording was all the rage, and dozens of Phair-ish imitators crowded the ever-growing roster of female singer-songwriters.

Within a year, *Exile in Guyville* had sold 200,000 copies—an extraordinary number for an indie LP—and high expectations for a sophomore release put Phair in danger of losing her indie cache. Matador Records signed a distribution deal with the mammoth Atlantic Records, and plans were made to heavily market Phair's follow-up album. Though Phair hadn't quite broken into the mainstream, she had become a very large fish in the small indie pond, and had to invent ways of dealing with her success, using what she called "My theory of the puppet," as she related it to one interviewer. "There's Liz Phair now, and when I'm holding her and I'm doing it, then I'm saying whatever I'm saying, and I get to hold her most of the time—I'm the one who's the main puppeteer. You use the puppet to say what you want to say, so you're in collaboration with yourself, as a performer and as an artist."[14] To stretch the metaphor, the timing of *Exile in Guyville* coincided with the puppet-master politics of major-label money versus independent artistic integrity, as indie artists were falling over themselves to not be corrupted and major labels were falling over indie artists to cash in on the street cache of their anti-corporate stance. With Phair's sharp, poignant debut album, she became a model for countless other indie artists who wanted to have their music heard while still pulling their own strings.

Album Title: *Enter The Wu-Tang (36 Chambers)*
Artist: The Wu-Tang Clan
Recorded: 1993, at Firehouse Studio in New York City
U.S. release: November 9, 1993 (Loud)
Producer: The RZA

The path to world domination usually starts with a good plan, and the Wu-Tang plan was as good as any (and using their critical, commercial, and cultural accomplishments as a measuring stick, it was better than most). Hip-hop acts often consisted of collaborations between MCs, writers, producers, and sometimes traditional musicians pooling their resources for an album, with each member contributing their particular talent. After a collaboration was finished, members might stick together for another release or go solo or move on to collaborations with other artists. Often, however, the artists were trapped within the confines of label contracts and commercial expectations that limited their career options, not to mention their artistic freedom.

Enter the Wu-Tang, to quote the title of the outfit's stunning 1993 debut. A collaboration between nine talented MCs—RZA, GZA, Ghostface Killah, Ol' Dirty Bastard, Raekwon, Method Man, U-God, Inspectah Deck, and Masta Killa—*Enter the Wu-Tang (36 Chambers)* was not only a seminal hip-hop album, but the cornerstone of one of the largest hip-hop empires ever. Led by RZA, the oldest of the group and one of the genre's top producers, the Wu-Tang Clan were more like a support group or an artists' collective than a band, planning from the beginning to arrive on the scene intact with an entire canned mythology, explode onto the charts with a monumental debut, then use the momentum to launch their members' solo careers while maintaining a professional solidarity and continuing to release albums as a group. Amazingly, this is exactly what happened, as the individual and collective efforts of the act swept over hip-hop in the 1990s like one giant wu-wave.

Before and during the late 1980s, despite the rap-rock fusion that the Beastie Boys and Run-D.M.C. had slathered all over the radio and MTV, hip-hop was still very much a cultural phenomenon of New York City street-corner DJs. In neighborhoods spanning all five boroughs, from Bushwick to Brownsville, MCs would battle for lyrical supremacy and DJs would improve on the scratching and mixing techniques of their predecessors. Occasionally a single would surface that made its way into dance clubs or, very rarely, onto the radio or the charts. Future Wu-Tang members RZA, GZA (who went by "Genius" at the time), and Ol' Dirty Bastard would work out routines as the All In Together Crew, battling other MCs, releasing the occasional single, and doing their best to make names for themselves in the hip-hop scene.

By 1992, all three artists had released either singles or albums, but none of them had found much success beyond the respect of their peers. GZA and Ol' Dirty Bastard decided to team up and form a crew, with RZA and the remaining six members quickly jumping on board. The collective formed a business as much as an artistic collaboration, agreeing to work together to ensure their mutual success. As part of their new endeavor, they created a pop-culture and martial-arts-themed mythology wherein their home base of Staten Island was known as Shaolin, after the ancient Buddhist temple in China. The name "Wu-Tang" is derivative of China's Wudang mountains, a center of Chinese martial arts for more than 1,000 years (as well as the name of a magical kung-fu sword thought to be wielded by invincible warriors). All of the group's members adopted names from martial arts films, and soon an entire backstory was developed for the group based on eastern mythology and popular culture references, with themes that included comic books, warrior codes, organized crime, chess, and principles of capitalism.

After scoring an underground hit with their debut single "Protect Ya Neck," the group spurned a number of offers from major labels until they could find one that would agree to allow all Wu-Tang members to operate as independent agents (i.e., not contractually obligated to the label) for their solo efforts to follow. RCA agreed to these conditions and released *Enter the Wu-Tang (36 Chambers)* under their Loud subsidiary in November of 1993 to critical acclaim. With RZA's sparse, coarse production style that retained hip-hop's gritty street origins, the album slowly climbed the charts over the next year. Rap fans gradually bought into the mysticism related through lyrics as dense as Don McLean's famous crossword puzzle "American Pie," with references ranging from Lucky Charms to Barbra Streisand. The Wu-Tang Clan ensured all members contributed lyrics to the songs, and after the album's single "C.R.E.A.M." hit big in 1994, five of the band's members were offered label contracts.

Within two years, solo efforts from Raekwon (*Only Built 4 Cuban Linx*), GZA (*Liquid Swords*), and Ghostface Killah (*Ironman*)—all produced by RZA—were among the best hip-hop albums available. RZA's defining production technique had grown to include more ominous, cinematic elements, including speeding up sampled soul music, largely replacing Dr. Dre's gangsta rap as the dominant sound in hip-hop. The Wu-Tang Clan graduated from a cultural curiosity to a cottage industry to a full-blown empire, eventually saturating the market (much like KISS in the 1970s) with an endless stream of commercial products, from clothing ("Wu Wear") to video games (*Wu-Tang: Shaolin Style*) to books unlocking the mysteries of the Wu-Tang code. With the success of Wu-Tang's group and solo efforts, as well as the extended Wu family the outfit supported through the decade, the Wu-Tang Clan became the country's most influential hip-hop act by the turn of the century, spinning their remarkable debut *Enter the Wu-Tang* into a cultural dynasty.

Album Title: *Dookie*
Artist: Green Day
Recorded: September–October 1993, at Fantasy Studios in Berkeley, California
U.S. release: February 1, 1994 (Reprise)
Producer: Rob Cavallo, Green Day

The story of punk rock is an endless cycle of worship and accusation from the genre's fan base—a band is either an unknown pioneer or a successful sellout, and there is very little room for negotiating an identity in the liminal space between. Perhaps the only punk band ever to find enduring popularity without being accused of selling out were British antidarlings the Sex Pistols, who, ironically, were one big publicity gimmick from the very beginning.

But Green Day—despite what their fans and the press called them—did not consider themselves a punk band. They believed their music to be good old fashioned rock and roll, all labels as the "saviors of punk" to the contrary. "So what kind of band are they? In a nutshell: supersonic hardcore bubblegum brats. A bright, crazy, brilliant cartoon with fast, tight, good-time songs. Songs about the important things in life: beer, birds, boredom, dope, wanking, television.... They're exactly what they intended to be— punk put through a dayglo California blender that's more skateboards than Sex Pistols, more sex than social conscience, more Beavis & Butt-head than Sid & Nancy, more Dickies and Ramones than Black Flag and The Germs."[15]

Putting all labels aside for a moment, Green Day were simply the most important thing to happen to rock music in the 1990s after Nirvana revitalized the genre in 1991 with *Nevermind* (see p. 214). Capturing the charm and three-chord wit that punk godfathers the Ramones used to launch punk rock in the mid-1970s, Green Day churned out bored sermons reinforced by short, catchy riffs on crunchy, treble-heavy guitars that provided a lighter counterbalance to the moody angst of Seattle grunge.

A notable difference between Californians Green Day and their petulant neighbors to the north concerned the young age of Green Day's members, who were still teenagers when they burst, fully formed, onto the national stage before they had had a chance to become jaded. The bay-area band was born as Sweet Children in 1988 when founding members Billy Joe Armstrong and Mike Dirnt were only fourteen years of age. After releasing a debut under indie label Lookout Records, the duo traded drummers to make Tre Cool (Frank Wright) the third leg of their defining trio, and slowly began to build a following in California's punk underground.

The release of their second effort, 1992's *Kerplunk*, brought them minor national attention with sales in the hundreds of thousands, a remarkable achievement for an indie-label act. Critics scrambled to affix a title to their bubblegum punk, many settling on the unappetizing sticker "popcore"—an attempt to capture the energy of west-coast hardcore and the radio-friendly appeal of their likable delivery. Singer Billy Joe Armstrong was impossible to take seriously with his high-pitched nasal whine, and the upbeat rhythm section of bassist Dirnt and drummer Cool was simple and tight, all three musicians reflecting Armstrong's captivating but uncomplicated lyrics. Taken as a whole, their sound was simple and stimulating, as if the Monkees were composing material for a very young version of the Who.

It was with their massive third album, *Dookie*—after the band signed with Reprise Records—that the rock and roll torch was passed to a new generation of budding adolescents. From the potty-humor title to the snotty juvenilia of the material, *Dookie* brought punk and rock and roll's lighter aesthetics to a mainstream audience, while still managing to convey their seemingly dichotomous brand of teenage boredom and garage-rock energy. "See, 80 percent of *Dookie* is in the trademark Green Day raging pop-punk," wrote Metal Mike Saunders, one of the country's top punk critics. "It's this deviant 20 percent that makes one suspect they can pull off almost anything they want out of the trash-dump of earlier under appreciated rock styles. A mainstream audience could forge a very, very interesting alliance with this group. . . . *Dookie* is one of the rawest melodically oriented rock records to show up on a major label in the last zillion years."[16]

With *Dookie*, Green Day twisted the Seattle grunge formula on its head, turning the weighty themes of Nirvana and Pearl Jam into fodder for tightly controlled wisecracking, as if Billy Joe Armstrong were Kurt Cobain's annoying little brother to whom everything was still just a game. This is not to discount Armstrong's significant strength and impact as a lyricist—his masterfully simple and direct approach put his words on the lips of millions of teens and young adults throughout 1994 and beyond. *Dookie* was a smash out of the box, selling ten million albums within five years, and quickly establishing a new template for alternative rock on mainstream radio. Naturally punk purists screamed "sellout," because that is their job. But Green Day, who had once railed against major labels, were pleased with the complete control that Reprise had given them in creating their music, and quickly moved past the criticism and continued playing their impish rock and roll. "I couldn't go back to the punk scene, whether we were the biggest success in the world or the biggest failure," Armstrong later told *Spin* magazine. "The only thing I could do was get on my bike and go forward."[17] The success of *Dookie* highlighted a new sound (or reminded everyone of an old sound) coming out of California, as the commercial popularity of Offspring's *Smash*, released two months later, and the underground sensation of Rancid's *Let's Go* two months after that reinforced the simplistic garage-pop of Green Day, influencing future mainstream acts like Blink-182, Fall Out Boy, and Good Charlotte, further propelling *Dookie* into the spotlight as one of the seminal releases of the decade.

Album Title: *Not a Pretty Girl*
Artist: Ani Difranco
Recorded: 1995, at the Recording Complex in Buffalo, New York
and 1:2:1 in Toronto
U.S. release: July 18, 1995 (Righteous Babe)
Producer: Ani Difranco

If ever an artist displayed such a mind-numbing gap between her stature as a seminal musical figure and her near invisibility in the mainstream music consciousness, Ani Difranco is that artist. Those aware of her name but unfamiliar with her history and music have often ignorantly lumped her together with one or another of her peer acts—the angry riot-grrl chick-rock of L7 and Bikini Kill, the haunted singer-songwriter efforts of Tori Amos and Suzanne Vega, the atmospheric Lilith-pop of Sarah McLachlan and Lisa Loeb—but those who have dipped more than their toe into her impressive canon or have seen the effect she's had on independent music know she is among the truly unique personalities in any genre, and may be seen by future generations as one of the most important artists of the 20th century.

More accurately compared to early, pre-*Highway 61* Bob Dylan than any of her contemporaneous peers, Difranco set a new standard for independence and musicianship that predated and outlasted most of the woman-oriented musical scenes that came and went in the 1990s. Where past chart-topping artists like Linda Ronstadt and Madonna used their sexuality as a weapon to gain equal footing in the male-dominated rock world, Difranco more closely emulated punk goddess Patti Smith, who simply powered through the male hierarchy with a sharp mind, fiery bravado, and groundbreaking music.

As a child, Difranco befriended a small-time promoter in her hometown of Buffalo, New York, and by the time she was ten years old, she was a fixture in the local (albeit small) folk scene. The promoter staged minor folk gatherings in Buffalo and would invite Greenwich Village artists to participate, some of them crashing at Difranco's house (Suzanne Vega once shared Difranco's room). "I had a strange childhood that way in that I didn't have set dreams about rockstars: my experience with music was very immediate. I had a lot of music in my childhood, but it was all done by the people I knew in the room and we'd all play and sing together. So I think I was always well acquainted with the idea of non-commercial music. Music wasn't a product or a fantasy, it was a social act—something you did after you couldn't eat any more."[18]

By the time she was fifteen she was writing songs, by sixteen she was on her own, and by eighteen she took up the touring lifestyle, driving hundreds of miles to play a gig for five people, sleeping at truckstops in the back of her hand-painted Volkswagen, and selling tapes out of her car and from the stage. These tapes became part of the Ani mythology and an early version of her word-of-mouth distribution—fans would buy the tapes, copy them, and send them to friends, who would copy them for other friends until they built a big enough fan base to invite her to come play their town. Thousands of artists would practice a similar touring and recording style more than a decade later after college radio exploded in popularity and a rash of small, local venues flowered around the country, but Difranco was one of the pioneers of the folk boom, a genre with which she proudly claims affiliation. "I think of folk music not in terms of tambourines or long pretty dresses or even acoustic guitars," she claimed, "to me folk music is just sub-corporate music, community-based music, song music."[19]

Before long Difranco had attracted the interest of record labels, but decided to brave the unknown when she went to City Hall and paid $50 to incorporate Righteous Babe Records, whose world headquarters occupied a corner of her friend Scot Fisher's living room. With Fisher's managing assistance, Difranco set out on a furious pace, releasing an average of an album per year, as well as constantly touring to the tune of 200+ shows annually. Larger and larger offers came and went from major labels, but Difranco stayed the independent course and over the next decade grew to be—with the possible exception of Frank Zappa—the defining presence in the world of independent music.

Fifteen years after her first release, Difranco came to be considered, by some measurements, the most successful artist in American music. Though her entire catalog has sold less than a single album by big-label competitors such as Jewel or Alanis Morissette, Difranco retained complete artistic freedom throughout her career, and allied herself with similarly independent companies in the music industry to loosen the stranglehold of corporate control and inspire thousands of other artists to assert their independence. Even framed in financial terms—something Difranco always criticized as a measure of success—her small empire was enormously successful, including several million albums sold and three times the return that she would have gotten as an artist on a major label. But such money talk made Difranco queasy. When several major newspapers and financial magazines drew attention to her business savvy in 1997, she responded in an open letter to *Ms.* magazine, "I'm just a folksinger, not an entrepreneur. My hope is that my music and poetry will be enjoyable and/or meaningful to someone, somewhere, not that I maximize my profit margins. . . . That's just the way I see it. Statistical plateau or no. I'll bust ass for 60 people, or 6,000, watch me."[20]

Though it was the enormity of her influence on independent artists that makes Difranco stand out as a public figure, it was the strength of her music that gathered thousands to her side in the first place. Her fan base was as rabidly devoted as any musician has ever had, and nowhere were the reasons for this more evident than on Difranco's exceptional 1995 album *Not a Pretty Girl*. After two individual albums and several more with a backing band, Difranco returned to her mostly solo origins (aided by the percussion work of Andy Stochansky) with a powerful release considered by many to be the best in her catalog. Tackling sensitive subjects that she had never shied away from, from abortion to politics to homosexuality, *Not a Pretty Girl* sent her standard alternative press and word-of-mouth publicity network into buzzing overdrive, exponentially increasing her fan base and turning her from a struggling artist into a role model for other independents. She soon began receiving wide acclaim for both her music and her autonomy, accolades she largely ignored, because, as one interviewer noted, "her definition of success is based solely on her art, and her ability to communicate that art. The rest is the reward that came from years of hard work, treating people with kindness and respect, surrounding herself with people who share her vision, and staying true to her beliefs. If Ani is to be made an example of anything, it should be that all things are possible to those who honor these basic truths. And that's something that nobody can mess with, argue over, pick apart, or turn into a chart."[21]

Album Title: *Odelay*
Artist: Beck
Recorded: 1994–1995
U.S. release: June 18, 1996 (DGC)
Producer: Beck Hansen, the Dust Brothers, Mario Caldato Jr., Brian Paulson, Tom Rothrock, Rob Schnopf

Beck's 1996 masterpiece *Odelay*, perhaps the most original and indefinable pop release of the decade. *Courtesy of Universal Music Enterprises.*

Bon Jovi of the '60s. Kip Winger with a protein shake. Glen Campbell with his clothes on inside out. Just some guy running around with his shoes on backwards, playing footsie with Richard Simmons.

These are not phrases that journalists used to describe Beck Hansen; these are phrases Beck Hansen used to describe himself (though journalists did jump on the bandwagon with descriptions ranging from the obvious "Woody Guthrie on LSD" to the simple but accurate "Slacker Dylan"). And why not? From the moment he slacked onto the scene with his bizarrely anthemic single "Loser" in 1993 (a cultural follow-up to Nirvana's "Smells Like Teen Spirit") he was a walking theater of the absurd, reeling out streams of nonsensical expressions in both his music and in interviews, showing a complete lack of interest in his own celebrity. "Have you seen the new *BAM* magazine cover that just came out with you on it and the coverline: "Who is Beck?" asked one of his earliest interviewers. "Yeah, I saw it yesterday," Beck responded, "and my first reaction was: "Who cares?""[22]

Maybe no one actually "cared," but many were interested. "Loser" was a 12" single released on the indie Bong Load label, and made such a splash on the Los Angeles underground when it was released that Bong Load couldn't keep production up to match the demand. The labels swarmed, and Beck landed a contract with Geffen that contained an unusual stipulation allowing Beck to continue recording radio-unfriendly material for indie labels. Not that it was easy to tell the difference—this was a man whose live shows included donning a *Star Wars* storm trooper mask and dancing solo to a beatbox. But his oddball antics and incredibly original music were an attempt to break American music out of a rut, where everything was "too neutral, stale and static," he told a later critic. "The nihilism of the whole grunge thing in America was just a purge. A purging of the materialism and elitism that was the '80s. But ultimately there's a place to go after that. Trouble is, people have got stuck in that. A lot of people are still there, y'know? It's very easy for people to uprise and rebel against something, but it's harder once you've done that to come up with something better. To get a functioning state of things back."[23]

If it were possible to move American music forward, Beck was as good a hope as anybody. His eccentric sound collages were the byproduct of an unusual upbringing that would rival Michael Jackson's childhood on the weirdness scale. His grandfather, Al Hansen, was a regular in Andy Warhol's circus of extreme art (reportedly he was present immediately after Warhol was shot in 1968). Al's daughter (Beck's mother) inherited her father's connections, acting in a Warhol film and marrying musician David Campbell, who wrote string arrangements for some of rock's top artists. The family's Los Angeles household saw a parade of artists, from Yoko Ono to Darby Crash, and Beck alternated back and forth between the L. A. spectacle, Europe (where his grandfather Al lived), and Kansas City, where his other grandfather was a Presbyterian minister. It was from these disparate influences that Beck learned an appreciation for a wide range of musical sounds (he claims to have started as a musician by playing with the buttons on a musical calculator). After dropping out of high school following tenth grade, he busked on street corners and paid his dues in the folk circuit as an acoustic artist before earning recognition for his unusual tapes made at home with an eight-track recorder.

After achieving local success in Los Angeles with the "Loser" single and his Geffen deal, Beck continued writing and releasing unusual lo-fi recordings through indie labels while recording his debut LP *Mellow Gold* for Geffen. Powered by a national re-release of "Loser," *Mellow Gold* was an instant hit, met with both praise and question marks from critics and the public. "Though clearly steeped in the acoustic folk and blues traditions of artists such as Woody Guthrie and Blind Willie McTell, Beck utilises a freeform stream of baffling surrealist imagery to encapsulate his impressions of modern American life, mangling together pop-culture references, droll *apercus* and bizarre *non sequiturs* in a manner reminiscent at times of the electric Dylan, while exhibiting an openness to modern pop styles that would stretch even His Bobness at his '60s best."[24]

"Loser" outshined its parent album, and though everyone agreed Beck was a refreshingly original voice, many wrote him off as a one-hit wonder. But concerns were put to rest with his stunning sophomore LP, 1996's *Odelay*, a mind-altering pastiche of genres and pop culture references that managed to be simultaneously undecipherable and prophetic. The singles "Where It's At," "Devil's Haircut," and "The New Pollution" were minor hits, with "Where It's At" receiving extensive play on the radio and MTV. The full weight of Beck's prolific compositional talents were brought to bear by the production team the Dust Brothers, who had saved the Beastie Boys from novelty status when they produced the Beasties' landmark sophomore release *Paul's Boutique* in 1989. On *Odelay*, the Dust Brothers managed to shape Beck's endless originality into a more cohesive, flowing work than *Mellow Gold*, creating an album that synthesized an impossible range of ideas. *Odelay* topped many critics' polls and received the highest honors from *Spin*, *Rolling Stone*, and the *Village Voice*, opening the door for studio experimentation in a way that hadn't been achieved since

Sgt. Pepper's in 1967, dissolving any notion of Beck as a one-hit wonder or novelty act. "I don't ever want to release a record that's seen as a novelty," Beck claimed, "but at the same time I want to avoid sounding contemporary because then it's already dated, if you see what I mean. So I'm trying to get to this place where you can stand outside the parameters of what's possible. If you can get outside there, out of the designated standards, then you'll preserve yourself."[25]

Album Title: *Spice*
Artist: The Spice Girls
Recorded: 1996
U.S. release: February 4, 1997 (Virgin)
Producer: Richard Stannard, Matt Rowe, Absolute, Andy Bradfield

Described by *Rolling Stone* as creators of "well-made music to Stairmaster to," the Spice Girls were an anomaly in the arena of 1990s femipop. Trapped between the energetic dance grooves of Madonna and Janet Jackson and the painfully self-aware manifestos from the Lilith Fair ranks, England's chief cultural export of the 1990s wowed American audiences with a blend of unapologetically vapid ear candy and lightweight feminism that put their catch-phrase "girl power" on the lips and lunchboxes of every tween in the country. "The Spice Girls take us deep into pop's heart of lightness, a happy place filled not with music of good taste but with music that tastes good—at least to a substantial portion of the planet," claimed the *Rolling Stone* article. "To get to the toppermost of the poppermost, the Spice Girls have traded shamelessly—which is not to say shamefully—on their much-vaunted Girl Power, selling themselves as feminist cheesecake...In the great pop tradition, their message is this: Have a good time, believe in yourself, and while you're at it, don't forget to buy a lot of Spice Girls merchandise."[26]

In 1994, the story goes, a manager placed an ad in a British paper seeking women who could sing and dance to form a new pop group. Hundreds of women attended the auditions, and five—Melanie Chisholm, Geri Halliwell, Melanie Brown, Victoria Adams, and Michelle Stephenson—were chosen for the lineup (with Stephenson soon replaced by Emma Bunton). The quintet found not only that they gelled well as a group, but that they were interested in controlling their own destiny and message, and soon fired the overbearing manager that had assembled them and struck out on their own. For the next year they lived together in a small house, recording demos and practicing dance routines, until finally landing a recording contract with Virgin and a new management deal with Annie Lennox's manager Simon Fuller, who would later find great fortune as creator of the television show *American Idol*.

With the release of their first single "Wannabe" in July 1996, the Spice Girls exploded onto the British music scene. The song's video was released weeks earlier and saw heavy airplay, causing "Wannabe" to debut at No. 3

on the charts and climb to No. 1 the following week. Before long the tune was a worldwide smash, reaching No. 1 in approximately two dozen other countries and debuting at No. 11 in the United States in early 1997—beating the Beatles for the highest charting debut by a foreign act. The western press, perhaps weary of the slacker rock, rap wars, and mixed-genre experiments that had dominated the decade, latched onto the group like they were pop music's life preserver, categorizing their music and their membership into neat boxes that made for easy digesting. "Chisholm is a keep-fit fanatic rarely seen without her Adidas sportswear, Addams is a fan of expensive labels, Halliwell has '70s style with a '90s edge, Brown likes rap, hip hop and jungle and dresses accordingly, while Emma Bunton favours chart pop and garage and hot-pink High Street fashion."[27] Easy to remember nicknames for the girls followed—Posh Spice, Scary Spice, Sexy Spice, Sporty Spice, and Baby Spice—creating a pre-packaged juggernaut for music fans who had tired of trying to "figure out" bands on their own.

The release of the equally lively-but-insipid singles "Say You'll Be There" and "2 Become 1" helped *Spice* continue its domination of the American charts and airwaves. By the end of the year, the follow-up album *Spiceworld* was released to similar sales figures, reportedly pushing six million copies worldwide in the first two weeks. The following summer a film version of the album hit the big screen, and with more than twenty endorsement deals signed by the band in that period, the group began to see a backlash from their oversaturation of the market. As often ridiculed for their lacking musical skills as applauded for their bravado, the group nonetheless reigned at the top of the musical food chain in 1997 and 1998. "We want to bring some of the glamour back to pop, like Madonna had when we were growing up," claimed Halliwell in one article. "Pop is about fantasy and escapism, but there's so much bullshit around at the moment. We want to be relevant to girls our age."[28]

It is *Spice*'s relevance (certainly not its intentionally derivative music) that makes the album such a significant document in the 1990s' musical canon. More than their musical talents, the Spice Girls coasted through the airwaves on the greased wheels of *Spice*'s "girl power" philosophy. The outspoken fivesome were well known for their extensive involvement in their career, from management decisions to musical and dance arrangements to songwriting. To what extent the group were actually a creative force rather then a commodification of independence itself (most of their work is co-credited to industry professionals) is buried under mounds of conflicting data and opinion, but it was their *image* as owners of their image and purveyors of that image to other women (particularly impressionable young girls) that made them a significant social force.

"Girl power" did not originate with the Spice Girls, but with the third-wave feminism of American riot grrls and the underground Welsh disco-punk band Helen Love, who used the phrase as a hook in their riot-grrl homage "Formula One Racing Girls" in 1993. "Girl Power" was a gateway cultural term that, when brought into the wider American consciousness by the Spice Girls, fueled an emerging interest in the study of empowered women in popular culture, ranging from Wonder Woman to *The Terminator*'s Sarah Connor to *Alien's* Ellen Ripley to the character of Buffy the Vampire Slayer, who earned her own academic discipline of "Buffy Studies." Where second-wave feminism of the 1960s and 1970s fostered a collective female identity with a somewhat strict and universal interpretation of what "feminism" meant, third-wave feminism expanded the term beyond the political collective and into shades of individual interpretation. In terms of musical idols, the overtly sexual identity emitted by Madonna to further her career would have been regarded as degrading by second-wave feminists and empowering by third-wave feminists. The release and overwhelming popularity of *Spice*, and the explosion of interest in female empowerment at the micro level that was towed along on the trailer hitch of its "girl power" posturing, was a watershed moment in a suddenly epidemic interest in gender identity and its related disciplines, making *Spice* an unlikely but worthy candidate as one of the most important releases of the 1990s.

Album Title: *Wide Open Spaces*
Artist: The Dixie Chicks
Recorded: March–August 1997
U.S. release: January 23, 1998 (Monument)
Producer: Paul Worley, Blake Chancey

Though earning a respectable following and some acclaim as an indie act throughout the 1990s, no one expected the tremendous success of the Dixie Chicks' major label debut *Wide Open Spaces*. Building on the rural sounds of formidable predecessors like Bonnie Raitt and Emmylou Harris, as well as the recent surge in alternative music that found women like Liz Phair, Tori Amos, and Alanis Morissette asserting a strong female viewpoint, the Dixie Chicks brought an unapologetic straightforwardness to both country and pop, annoying traditional listeners but garnering massive audiences that made *Wide Open Spaces* one of the all-time bestselling country albums.

"Looking at the cover of the Dixie Chicks' smash major label debut, *Wide Open Spaces*, it's hard not to huff, "How cute, Country Spice Girls,""" teased *Rolling Stone* as the trio's album was riding a wave of commercial success. "Three attractive, stylin' young blondes strolling confidently along a sidewalk, two with sleeveless tops and big smiles and the third wearing a black suit and a Posh-worthy little smirk...Ah, but witness the Chicks in action, and you'll eat those words. If country ain't your bag, by the time sisters Emily Erwin and Martie Seidel storm their way through their first banjo and fiddle leads and new-Chick-on-the-block Natalie Maines belts out her first chorus of rockin' honky tonk, it may well be."[31]

With the new popularization of country music brought about by artists like Garth Brooks and Clint Black—making Nashville an unexpected hotbed of popular music in the 1990s—came the inevitable intersections with other genres to garner massive crossover audiences (best exemplified by Brooks, who considered himself a rock star as much as a country act and employed all manner of arena-rock flash to illustrate this idea). But these were suburban cowboys, with more in common with slick country pop than with country and western's deep roots.

The Dixie Chicks, on the other hand, balanced traditional sounds with modern women's bold assertiveness, fostering a group persona that was as much 21st-century Susan Sontag as it was 20th-century Maybelle Carter. Formed in Dallas, Texas in 1989 by sisters Martie Seidel and Emily Erwin with Laura Lynch on bass and Robin Lynn Macy on guitar, the group courted a country bluegrass sound with fiddler Seidel and banjo player Erwin. They built up a small Texas following and released *Thank Heavens for Dale Evans* in 1990 and *Little Ol' Cowgirl in 1992* on the independent Crystal Clear label, and following the departure of Macy, *Shouldn't a Told You That* in 1993. After signing a deal with Sony's Monument label two years later, the group ousted Lynch and picked up twenty-one-year-old Natalie Maines as lead singer, whose father Lloyd Maines was the most respected pedal-steel player in Texas, and often sat in with the group.

The group's move to Nashville worried some of their Texas fans that their sound would be changed by the notoriously stiff Nashville "system," but the Dixies went in with their eyes wide open. "We stuck to our guns about a lot of stuff," said Maines. "We were ready to put up our dukes with Sony, and it turned out we didn't have to at all. They were sort of laughing at us because we thought they'd say we couldn't play on the album, and they were saying 'Well of course you can play on the album, that's why we're signing you—because you *can* play on your album.'"[32] Rather than use session musicians as was the Nashville way, the studio took a chance on three extraordinarily talented performers belting out their own material like seasoned pros. Accompanying their dynamic sound was a carefully cultivated image as being smart, sassy, and young in a genre whose women were expected to possess no more than one of those qualities at a time.

On the strength of the singles "Wide Open Spaces," "I Can Love You Better," and "There's Your Trouble"—all of which broke the Top Ten singles charts—the album blew past the gold and platinum rankings and became one of the fifty bestselling albums of all time, reaching No. 1 on the country chart and No. 4 on the pop chart. The boldness of the trio, from their lyrics to their personalities, rattled the country music world that was unaccustomed to seeing female musicians wearing business suits and evening wear instead of cowboy hats and cotton scarves. Telling modern stories of breakups and breakdowns with a distinctly Bill Monroe and Lloyd Maines touch was an unusual combination that created a crossover monster. Not since Garth Brooks' 1990 breakthrough *No Fences* had a country album had such an impact on both the country and rock worlds.

"To stay true to the music, and to stay true to Texas," is what Natalie Maines said her father told her as the Dixie star was on the ascent. "The Texas music industry is very honest. You don't compromise things when it has to do with your soul or your belief. I think that's why we have the album that we have."[33] Their follow-up release one year later, *Fly*, was equally successful, reaching No. 1 on both the country and pop charts, and proving that the Dixie Chicks were no fluke. True to the album's title, the Dixie Chicks opened wide country's musical space, bringing to a close a decade of significant advancement for women as artists and owners of their music and image.

Album Title: *The Slim Shady LP*
Artist: Eminem
Recorded: 1998
U.S. release: February 23, 1999 (Aftermath/Interscope)
Producer: Dr. Dre, M. Mathers, Marky Bass, Jeff Bass, Mel Man

Eminem's 1999 *The Slim Shady LP*, his first album with Dr. Dre producing and a milestone in the genre of hip-hop. *Courtesy of Universal Music Enterprises.*

Among Dr. Dre's more significant contributions to music in the 1990s—second only to his pioneering work as producer of N.W.A's 1989 *Straight Outta Compton* (see p. 198) and his own 1992 *The Chronic* (see p. 220)—was his discovery of rappers Snoop Doggy Dogg and Eminem, the former among the most popular gangsta rappers of the decade, and the latter one the most gifted lyricists and MCs the genre has ever known, as well as the most famous white rapper in what is generally regarded as a black genre. For two decades, give or take, rap music was the sound of the black urban experience in the dense and forgotten ghettos of cities like New York, Los Angeles, and Philadelphia—first as celebratory street-corner party music, then a much darker commentary on gang life and societal ostracism that many of these artists endured. In all that time, white rappers came and went, but Eminem was the first significant MC to pay an honest visit to the white ghetto in his rhymes, not by pretending to be black, but by telling his own story—in uncomfortably powerful and sophisticated verse—as white trailer-park trash trying to make it in a black genre.

Marshall Mathers (his nom de guerre was a variant spelling of his initials, M&M) was born near Kansas City, but grew up in the wasteland of

Detroit's ghettos. Dropping out of high school after reportedly failing ninth grade three times, he worked low-paying jobs and took on black rappers in MC battles to earn his street credibility. As he spelled out in painful detail in his autobiographical songs, he never knew his father, believed his mother to be an abusive drug addict, and seemed doomed to a life of obscurity, poverty, and powerlessness. His only escape was through his music, and he would spend hours sitting in places like Burger King composing lyrics. Through the early 1990s he alternated between dead-end jobs and attempts to jump-start a music career, interrupted by his girlfriend's pregnancy, his best friend's suicide, and his own attempt to overdose on Tylenol.

His music was as much wide-screen drama as his life, unsurprising since they were one in the same. After some directionless group work with other MCs and a forgettable solo debut in 1996 with *Infinite*, one of Eminem's demo tapes fell into the hands of Dr. Dre, who was sufficiently impressed to bring him into the studio. In one interview Eminem claimed that they hit it off so well they recorded three songs the first day they met. Like some gritty urban fairy tale, Eminem translated his personal demons into a stunning work of art—both bitingly witty and deeply disturbing—releasing *The Slim Shady LP* in 1999 to a round of gasps from both the hip-hop and pop-music worlds. "[T]he Eminem story does more than just restore the faith of those who feared that pop had lost its power to divide the generations. It is at once an unlikely romance, a strange new twist on the American dream, and—last, but not least—an aesthetic triumph, since in swapping the self-aggrandisement which is rap's traditional stock in trade for a self-loathing whose eloquence and wit are utterly compulsive, he has not only taken an upbringing of grinding poverty and violence and made it painfully funny, but also effected the most successful translation of alienation into art since Dostoevsky imagined the murder of his landlady."[29]

The Slim Shady LP's cinematic sweep was musically sparse, lyrically dense, and deeply personal, conveying the soul of a top-rank rap battle on a sweat-soaked stage. Initially met with some skepticism (rap's last great white hope, Vanilla Ice, was less than truthful about his comfortable background), Eminem's rhymes were even more devastating when the public learned how close they were to the truth. "My album is so autobiographical that there shouldn't really be any more questions to answer," he told an early interviewer. "It's just the story of a white kid who grew up in a black neighbourhood who had a pretty shitty life—not the worst life in the world, but still a fairly shitty life."[30]

At a time when the most popular hip-hop was fueled by ego-manic braggadocio and general themes of violence and misogyny, Eminem took it to a personal level, sparking outrage for his vicious attack on his wife in the song "'97' Bonnie and Clyde," in which he imagines murdering her and disposing the body in a lake as his young daughter tags along. Gangsta rap was at least as equally violent, but Eminem's lyrical mastery and passionate delivery sent shivers down the spines of listeners, especially when it was revealed that he had used his toddler daughter, Hailie, on background vocals (he had reportedly told his wife, Kim, that he was taking her to a kids restaurant, but carted her off to the studio instead—Eminem and Kim's contentious relationship would be the subject of much news fodder and many of his songs in the future).

Often compared to Elvis Presley for his ability to synthesize a predominantly black genre with his own experiences as a poor, white artist, Eminem burst into the hip-hop world with almost as much force as Elvis burst into the blues. Propelled by the hit single "My Name Is"—which was not only the first rap song to reach the top spot on MTV's request show "Total Request Live," but was retired after thirty days straight at No. 1—*The Slim Shady LP* won accolades from every corner of the industry, ultimately becoming one of the bestselling rap albums of all time and vastly expanding the artistic possibilities of rap music as a mainstream genre.

NOTES

1. David Szatmary, *A Time to Rock: A Social History of Rock And Roll.* New York: Schirmer, 1996 (1987), 332.

2. Szatmary, 1996, 337.

3. Steve Huey, www.allmusic.com.

4. Mark Coleman, "Ice-T: *O.G. Original Gangster*," *Rolling Stone*, June 13, 1991.

5. Simon Reynolds, "Nirvana: *Nevermind*," *The New York Times*, November 1991.

6. Ben Thompson, "Here They Are Now: Nirvana," *Independent on Sunday*, November 1991.

7. Glenn O'Brien, "What's Red Hot and Chili? Red Hot Chili Peppers," *Spin*, 1984.

8. Danny (Shredder) Weizmann, "The Red Hot Chili Peppers Will Pose Nude in Public," *L.A. Weekly*, 1984.

9. Simon Reynolds, "Red Hot Chili Peppers: Magicians followed but not chaste," *The Observer*, September 29, 1991.

10. Ben Edmonds, "I Believe in Peace, Bitch. Tori Amos Talks Back," *Creem*, March 1994.

11. "Dr. Dre: *The Chronic*," *Rolling Stone*, March 18, 1993.

12. Barney Hoskyns, "Liz Phair," *Vogue*, 1994.

13. Gerrie Lim, "Phair Enough: The Girl from Guyville," *The Big O*, February 1994.

14. Ibid.

15. Sylvie Simmons, "Green Day: Brixton Academy, London," *Raw*, 1995.

16. Metal Mike Saunders, "Green Day Rising," *Barn*, January 28, 1994.

17. RJ Smith, "Top 90 Albums of the 90s," *Spin*, August 1999.

18. Sylvie Simmons, "Ani Difranco," *Mojo*, April 1998.

19. Ibid.

20. Ani Difranco, November 5, 1997.

21. Lydia Hutchinson, "Ani Difranco: The Little Folk Singer Who Could," *Performing Songwriter*, June 1999, 61.

22. Gerrie Lim, "Kip Winger with a Protein Shake," *The Big O*, April 1994.

23. Paul Moody, "Beck," *Dazed + Confused*, 1996.

24. Andy Gill, "Beck," *Mojo*, February 1995.

25. Moody, 1996.

26. David Wild, "Spice Girls: *Spiceworld*," November 20, 1997.

27. Paul Gorman, "Taking on the Britboys: Spice Girls," *Music Week*, April 1996.

28. Ibid.

29. Ben Thompson, "His Name Is: Eminem," *Daily Telegraph*, October 1999.

30. Ibid.

31. Richard Skanse, "There's Your Trouble," *Rolling Stone*, September 2, 1998.

32. Ibid.

33. Ibid.

Appendix 1

TEN ALBUMS THAT ALMOST MADE IT

It would be ridiculous to claim that these 100 albums encapsulate every important development in American music. An entire second list could be constructed of other essential LPs that would rival those featured here. Following are ten "for further listening" albums that did not quite make the final list, but have proven to be significant in the evolution of American music.

***The Shape of Jazz to Come*, Ornette Coleman, 1959.** One of the more ridiculed members of the jazz avant-garde, Ornette Coleman's penchant for following his instincts and playing his alto saxophone in a free-flowing, emotional style frightened jazz purists in the late 1950s, costing him many opportunities for club gigs and record deals. *The Shape of Jazz to Come* was Coleman's major-label debut, on which he omits the grounding chords of a piano in favor of complete freedom for the saxophone, cornet, double bass, and drums to wander where they like. Though a startling advancement in the progression of jazz and a cornerstone of the free-jazz movement, the album is overshadowed by Miles Davis' *Kind of Blue* (see p. 12), recorded one month earlier, which had freed jazz from the confines of chords and defined modal jazz, similar to the directionless meanderings of free jazz but based on modal underpinnings.

***Live at the Apollo*, James Brown, 1963.** Often hailed as the greatest live album ever recorded, James Brown's *Live at the Apollo* set the benchmark for performances captured on vinyl. By 1963 Brown had released several hit R&B singles, but had not placed any albums on the pop charts. Though he had earned a reputation as an energetic performer, his recordings failed to capture the vigor and force of his wildly animated shows. Over his label's objections, Brown had his October 24, 1962 performance at the Apollo Theater in Harlem recorded, and when it was released the following year, it catapulted Brown from rumor to legend. Jumping all the way to No. 2 on the pop charts, *Live at the Apollo* became the most popular release of his career, demonstrating the skill with which Brown could whip a crowd into a frenzy and proving that he lived up to his reputation as the hardest working man in show business.

***Aftermath*, The Rolling Stones, 1966.**   Though the Rolling Stones' catalog is stock full of important releases, there are a half dozen or so that are often mentioned as their greatest works, including 1968's *Beggar's Banquet*, 1969's *Let it Bleed*, 1971's *Sticky Fingers*, 1972's *Exile on Main St.*, and 1978's *Some Girls*. But it was their 1966 album *Aftermath* that elevated the band to new heights as an immortal rock group. Whereas their previous LPs had been at least half cover songs, *Aftermath* was their first album of all original material from the young, fertile minds of Keith Richards and Mick Jagger. The transition from blues and soul cover band to innovative rockers is highlighted on this album by works of impressive variety that outlined their themes for world domination in their future releases, including the jazzy and misogynistic "Under My Thumb," the near-punkish venom of "Stupid Girl," the use of dulcimer on the fragile "Lady Jane," and the inclusion of the sitar on the darkly psychedelic "Paint It Black."

***Revolver*, The Beatles, 1966.**   Widely considered one of the most revolutionary albums in all of rock music, the Beatles' *Revolver* was omitted from the main list only because of the strength of its neighbors—1965's *Rubber Soul* and 1967's *Sgt. Pepper's Lonely Hearts Club Band*. It was on *Rubber Soul* that the Beatles elevated themselves from pop phenoms to truly gifted artists, exploring new philosophical lyrics and undiscovered sonic territory. On *Sgt. Pepper's* the band would achieve the pinnacle of these experiments with one of the most groundbreaking works in the musical canon. But it was *Revolver* that connected the two, delving even deeper into experiments with orchestral instruments (strings and French horn), ambient noise (coughing), studio trickery (tape looping and syncopation), and far-reaching lyrics (including an interpretation of the Tibetan *Book of the Dead*). Even compared to *Sgt. Pepper's* (widely held as their magnum opus), *Revolver* holds its own among the most daring releases of the century.

***Talking Book*, Stevie Wonder, 1972.**   Stevie Wonder had been one of Motown's bankable artists since his 1963 album *The 12 Year Old Genius* and its single "Fingertips" both went to No. 1 on the pop charts. A string of modestly successful albums followed through the decade before Wonder turned 21 and gained artistic control over his music. Though Wonder's first two albums with himself at the helm were as good as anything he had done before, he really hit his stride as a songwriter and performer with 1972's *Talking Book*, a masterpiece of poppy soul that ranged from the child-like "You Are the Sunshine of My Life" to the funktacular "Superstition." Reaching No. 3 on the charts, *Talking Book* was the first album since *The*

12 Year Old Genius to reach the Top 20, beginning Wonder's most celebrated period over the next four years with *Innervisions*, *Fulfillingness' First Finale*, and *Songs in the Key of Life*, all three of which were named Album of the Year, and the last resting at the top of the charts for fourteen weeks.

***Hotel California*, The Eagles, 1976.**   No matter how overplayed on classic-rock radio, *Hotel California* never lost its sheen as one of the most popular and engaging examples of 1970s West Coast rock and one of the smoothest blends of rock and country ever to emerge from the sunshine state. California is the home, title, and theme of this monumental work, a simultaneously romantic and nihilistic painting of American life in broad, depressing strokes that are somehow balanced by the upbeat twang of new guitarist Joe Walsh. A soundtrack for those 1960s refugees desperately trying to avoid punk and disco, *Hotel California* was almost as successful as the band's *Greatest Hits 1971–1975* that preceded it, both albums ranking in America's Top 20 all-time bestsellers.

***The Wall*, Pink Floyd, 1979.**   As much as the Who's "My Generation" did a decade before and Nirvana's *Nevermind* would do a decade later, Pink Floyd's album *The Wall* captured the angst and bewilderment of its teenage fans and defined a generation gap between those fans and their parents. A grand, sweeping concept album, *The Wall* tells the story of a neurotic rock star who goes mad trying to find separation between himself and the rest of the world. The film version starring Bob Geldof, released two years later, became a cult classic, and the song "Another Brick in the Wall" featuring the immortal line "We don't need no education" was a favorite among rebellious high schoolers across the country. *The Wall* ultimately became Pink Floyd's bestselling album, and at over twenty million copies sold domestically, the fourth bestselling album of all time.

***Synchronicity*, The Police, 1983.**   The Police's final album and the one that launched them to superstardom in the United States, *Synchronicity* was a landmark in sophisticated pop, featuring enduring hits like "Wrapped Around Your Finger," "King of Pain," and "Every Breath You Take," a deceptively simple stalker ditty that rose to No. 1 in both the United States and the United Kingdom and became the biggest hit of the year in America. The album camped at the top of the charts for seventeen weeks, ending Michael Jackson's *Thriller* reign with an easy-listening treat. Though undemanding on the ear, *Synchronicity* was grounded in the cerebral literature consumed by lead singer Sting, and with beats too slow to boogie to, provided American pop audiences with a refreshingly mature hero in a decade of dance-pop and hair-metal.

***The Joshua Tree*, U2, 1987.**   Though U2's unique brand of upbeat, anthemic rock is represented in these pages by their landmark 1983 album *War*, there is no avoiding the enormous popularity of their 1987 album *The Joshua Tree* that elevated them from popular rock group to worldwide phenomenon. Their first album to crack the Top 10, *The Joshua Tree* spent nine weeks at No. 1 and immortalized the band with a string of powerful anthems including "Where the Streets Have No Name," "I Still Haven't Found What I'm Looking For," "With or Without You," and "Bullet the Blue Sky." When stacked against the other high-charting albums of 1987— the Beastie Boys' *Licensed to Ill*, Whitney Houston's *Whitney*, Michael Jackson's *Bad*, and the *Dirty Dancing* soundtrack—*The Joshua Tree* reminded audiences of the passion and meaning that had gone missing in rock.

***Jagged Little Pill*, Alanis Morissette, 1995.**   Following on the heels of Tori Amos' confessional *Little Earthquakes* and Liz Phair's emotionally distant *Exile in Guyville*, Alanis Morissette became an out-of-nowhere superstar with her third album *Jagged Little Pill* in 1995, a release as personal as *Earthquakes* and as shocking as *Guyville* but with a chilling degree of undirected rage not usually heard from the singer-songwriter crowd. Among the twenty bestselling albums of the century, *Jagged Little Pill* brought energy and tension to the growing catalog of 1990s chick-rock. Though performed with an excellent backing band, the LP is thematically a solo album chronicling a woman's troubled relationships with brute force and intensity through hit songs such as "You Oughta Know," "Ironic," "You Learn," and "Head Over Feet," helping to quicken the rise of the solo female artist to the forefront of 1990s independent music.

Appendix 2

TEN IMPORTANT PRODUCERS

It is the artist's name on the cover, but it is the producer that determines how that artist sounds. There are as many styles of producing out there as there are producers, ranging from those who have their nose in every tiny detail to those who take the hands-off approach. Following are ten producers who have significantly shaped the sound of recorded popular music in the 20th century.

JOHN HAMMOND SR. John Henry Hammond, a wealthy descendent of the Vanderbilt family and father to musician John Hammond Jr., poured plenty of his personal fortune into the music industry. With a career spanning nearly fifty years, Hammond was one of the most respected men in the field, first working as a music journalist and then funding up-and-coming talents he believed in. Though most of his fame lies with his work as a talent scout—he discovered or helped Bessie Smith, Billie Holiday, Benny Goodman, Count Basie, Bob Dylan, and Bruce Springsteen—he also produced many of their albums. A fan of traditional jazz, his credits include Bob Dylan's self-titled debut album, his later *The Freewheelin' Bob Dylan* (see p. 25), Aretha Franklin's *Amazing Grace*, and Stevie Ray Vaughan and Double Trouble's *Texas Flood* (see p. 166).

PHIL SPECTOR. Known primarily for his "Wall of Sound" production technique—in which he recorded acts in an echo chamber with extra musicians to give the music a layered effect—Phil Spector was one of the top producers of the 1960s, using innovative instrument combinations and his studio prowess to make stars of the Chiffons, the Ronettes, the Crystals, and the Righteous Brothers. Spector's imaginative arrangements influenced some of the most important figures of the decade, including Beach Boy Brian Wilson, the Beatles, and the Rolling Stones. Among his credits are

George Harrison's post-Beatle triple album *All Things Must Pass*, the Beatles' *Let It Be*, John Lennon's *Imagine*, Leonard Cohen's *Death of a Ladies Man*, the Ramones' *End of the Century*, and Eric Clapton's *Crossroads*.

GEORGE MARTIN.   For his work behind the soundboard, George Martin was known as "the fifth Beatle," having signed them onto his Parlophone label and produced most of their albums between their 1963 debut *Please Please Me* and their 1969 *Abbey Road*. He is often given significant credit as one of the primary authors of the band's studio adventures, particularly on the groundbreaking mid-1960s trio *Rubber Soul*, *Revolver*, and *Sgt. Pepper's Lonely Hearts Club Band* (see pp. 34 and 46). His post-Beatles work included America's *Holiday*, Jeff Beck's *Wired*, and much of Paul McCartney's later catalog.

TOM WILSON.   Paul Simon and Art Garfunkel owed Tom Wilson their career when, inspired by the Byrds' folk-rock version of "Mr. Tambourine Man," he laid electric instrument tracks over Simon and Garfunkel's song "The Sounds of Silence" (without permission) and turned it into a hit, forcing a hasty reunification of the duo and a brilliant future. His work through the 1960s spanned many genres and spawned several of the decade's most important releases, from early folk-rock with Bob Dylan's *Bringing It All Back Home* (see p. 30), early freak-rock with Frank Zappa's *Freak Out!* (see p. 38), and the New York proto-punk debut of the Velvet Underground's *The Velvet Underground and Nico* (see p. 44).

BERRY GORDY JR.   As the founder and heart of Motown, Berry Gordy Jr. was the chief architect of 1960s soul music, producing three times the average percentage of hit records from his Detroit label. Gordy carefully crafted black soul music for a white American audience, creating a hit machine with artists like Smokey Robinson, Stevie Wonder, Diana Ross, Michael Jackson, the Four Tops, and Marvin Gaye. Though challenged in the 1970s by the Philadelphia soul coming out of Gamble and Huff's studio, Gordy left an indelible signature on American rhythm and blues in the 1960s and 1970s.

GAMBLE AND HUFF.   Considered the originators of the Philadelphia sound while they worked at the record label Philadelphia International, Kenneth Gamble and Leon Huff were to 1970s soul what Berry Gordy Jr. had been to Detroit soul in the 1960s. Before joining Philadelphia International in 1971, the duo had worked with several Atlantic Records artists like Wilson Pickett and Aretha Franklin before making a name for themselves producing some of the 1970s top soul acts, including the O'Jays, Harold Melvin and the Blue Notes, and Billy Paul, most notably his hit "Me and Mrs. Jones."

BRIAN ENO. Since he did not play any musical instruments, Brian Eno was a very unusual artist, but his mastery of studio techniques made him one of the most sought after producers of the 1970s and 1980s. He began his career as a nonkeyboardist for the band Roxy Music before turning his talents to creating electronic music with studio experiments, resulting in the landmark *Discreet Music* in 1975 (see p. 121) as well as pioneering work with Robert Fripp and several albums of ambient noise. From the 1970s through the 1990s, Eno helped shape the sounds of some of music's most groundbreaking acts, producing landmarks like Talking Heads' *More Songs about Buildings and Food*, Devo's *Are We Not Men?*, U2's *Joshua Tree*, and Jane Siberry's *When I Was a Boy*.

QUINCY JONES. As early as the 1950s Quincy Jones was conducting, arranging, and producing a who's who of musical acts, including Count Basie, Dizzy Gillespie, Sarah Vaughan, Duke Ellington, Gene Krupa, Miles Davis, Frank Sinatra, and Ray Charles, later penning theme songs for TV programs like *Sanford and Son* and *The Cosby Show* and a host of movie scores. By the 1980s he was a legend, best known to the public for helping make Michael Jackson the king of pop by applying his talents to *Off the Wall*, *Thriller* (see p. 157), and *Bad*, as well as orchestrating one of the largest collaborative efforts in popular music, U.S.A. for Africa's "We Are the World."

ROBERT JOHN "MUTT" LANGE. One of the architects behind the heavy-metal sound that permeated the 1980s, Robert Lange found his first major success with the Australian band AC/DC, producing their breakout albums *Highway to Hell* and *Back in Black* (see p. 155). The furious but well-paced sound set a template for the decade's metal as *Back in Black* became one of the world's most successful albums. Lange repeated this feat with the English band Def Leppard in the mid-1980s, producing their megasellers *Pyromania* (see p. 160) and *Hysteria*, as well as calmer albums like Foreigner's *4*, Bryan Adams' *Waking up the Neighbors*, and Shania Twain's *Come on Over*, Lange's fifth album to sell more than ten million copies.

RICK RUBIN. As co-founder of New York's Def Jam Records in the 1980s, Rick Rubin was at the forefront of hip-hop's saturation into the mainstream. His pioneering work in rap/metal fusion and bare-bones production technique launched the careers of three of the 1980s' biggest rap acts, producing LL Cool J's *Radio*, Run-D.M.C.'s *Raising Hell* (see p. 185), and the Beastie Boys' *Licensed to Ill* (see p. 188). His talents became much in demand in the 1990s as he earned a reputation for creating breakthroughs for up-and-coming bands [the Red Hot Chili Peppers' *Blood Sugar Sex Magik* (see p. 216) and Danzig's *Danzig*], as well as new hits for older acts such as Johnny Cash's *American Recordings*, Tom Petty's *Wildflowers*, and AC/DC's *Ballbreaker*.

Appendix 3

ALBUMS LISTED CHRONOLOGICALLY

Anthology of American Folk Music (1952)
Various

Elvis Presley (1956)
Elvis Presley

Birth of the Cool (1957)
Miles Davis

The Weavers at Carnegie Hall (1957)
The Weavers

Kind of Blue (1959)
Miles Davis

Time Out (1959)
The Dave Brubeck Quartet

Muddy Waters at Newport (1960)
Muddy Waters

King of the Delta Blues Singers (1961)
Robert Johnson

Modern Sounds in Country and Western Music (1962)
Ray Charles

The Freewheelin' Bob Dylan (1963)
Bob Dylan

Please Please Me (1963)
The Beatles

Bringing It All Back Home (1965)
Bob Dylan

Mr. Tambourine Man (1965)
The Byrds

Rubber Soul (1965)
The Beatles

Freak Out! (1966)
Frank Zappa and the Mothers of Invention

Pet Sounds (1966)
The Beach Boys

The Doors (1967)
The Doors

Surrealistic Pillow (1967)
Jefferson Airplane

The Velvet Underground and Nico (1967)
The Velvet Underground

Sgt. Pepper's Lonely Hearts Club Band (1967)
The Beatles

Are You Experienced (1967)
The Jimi Hendrix Experience

Days of Future Passed (1968)
The Moody Blues

Music from Big Pink (1968)
The Band

Sweetheart of the Rodeo (1968)
The Byrds

Led Zeppelin (1969)
Led Zeppelin

Kick Out the Jams (1969)
MC5

Tommy (1969)
The Who

In the Court of the Crimson King (1969)
King Crimson

Trout Mask Replica (1969)
Captain Beefheart and His Magic Band

Sweet Baby James (1970)
James Taylor

Bitches Brew (1970)
Miles Davis

Paranoid (1971)
Black Sabbath

Tapestry (1971)
Carole King

What's Going On (1971)
Marvin Gaye

There's a Riot Goin' On (1971)
Sly and the Family Stone

The Inner Mounting Flame (1971)
The Mahavishnu Orchestra

*Nuggets: Original Artyfacts from the First Psychedelic Era,
    1965–1968* (1972)
Various

*The Rise and Fall of Ziggy Stardust and the Spiders from
    Mars* (1972)
David Bowie

Raw Power (1973)
Iggy and the Stooges

The Dark Side of the Moon (1973)
Pink Floyd

New York Dolls (1973)
The New York Dolls

Head Hunters (1973)
Herbie Hancock

Autobahn (1974)
Kraftwerk

Heart Like a Wheel (1974)
Linda Ronstadt

Toys in the Attic (1975)
Aerosmith

Born to Run (1975)
Bruce Springsteen

Alive! (1975)
KISS

Horses (1975)
Patti Smith

Discreet Music (1975)
Brian Eno

A Night at the Opera (1975)
Queen

Wanted! The Outlaws (1976)
Waylon Jennings, Willie Nelson, Jessi Colter, Tompall Glaser

Mothership Connection (1976)
Parliament

Ramones (1976)
The Ramones

Boston (1976)
Boston

Exodus (1977)
Bob Marley and the Wailers

Saturday Night Fever (1977)
Various

Never Mind the Bollocks, Here's the Sex Pistols (1977)
The Sex Pistols

Marquee Moon (1977)
Television

The Modern Dance (1978)
Pere Ubu

Van Halen (1978)
Van Halen

One Nation Under a Groove (1978)
Funkadelic

Rust Never Sleeps (1979)
Neil Young

London Calling (1980)
The Clash

Back in Black (1980)
AC/DC

Thriller (1982)
Michael Jackson

Future Shock (1983)
Herbie Hancock

Pyromania (1983)
Def Leppard

War (1983)
U2

Murmur (1983)
R.E.M.

Texas Flood (1983)
Stevie Ray Vaughan and Double Trouble

Kill 'em All (1983)
Metallica

Born in the U.S.A. (1984)
Bruce Springsteen

Purple Rain (1984)
Prince

Zen Arcade (1984)
Hüsker Dü

Like a Virgin (1984)
Madonna

Raising Hell (1986)
Run-D.M.C.

Graceland (1986)
Paul Simon

Licensed to Ill (1986)
The Beastie Boys

Solitude Standing (1987)
Suzanne Vega

Appetite for Destruction (1987)
Guns N' Roses

It Takes a Nation of Millions to Hold Us Back (1988)
Public Enemy

Daydream Nation (1988)
Sonic Youth

3 Feet High and Rising (1989)
De La Soul

Straight Outta Compton (1989)
N.W.A

Pretty Hate Machine (1989)
Nine Inch Nails

No Depression (1990)
Uncle Tupelo

No Fences (1990)
Garth Brooks

O. G. Original Gangster (1991)
Ice-T

Nevermind (1991)
Nirvana

Blood Sugar Sex Magik (1991)
The Red Hot Chili Peppers

Little Earthquakes (1992)
Tori Amos

The Chronic (1992)
Dr. Dre

Exile in Guyville (1993)
Liz Phair

Enter the Wu-Tang (36 Chambers) (1993)
The Wu-Tang Clan

Dookie (1994)
Green Day

Not a Pretty Girl (1995)
Ani Difranco

Odelay (1996)
Beck

Spice (1997)
The Spice Girls

Wide Open Spaces (1998)
The Dixie Chicks

The Slim Shady LP (1999)
Eminem

Appendix 4
ALBUMS LISTED ALPHABETICALLY

Alive! (1975)
KISS

A Night at the Opera (1975)
Queen

Anthology of American Folk Music (1952)
Various

Appetite for Destruction (1987)
Guns N' Roses

Are You Experienced (1967)
The Jimi Hendrix Experience

Autobahn (1974)
Kraftwerk

Back in Black (1980)
AC/DC

Birth of the Cool (1957)
Miles Davis

Bitches Brew (1970)
Miles Davis

Blood Sugar Sex Magik (1991)
The Red Hot Chili Peppers

Born in the U.S.A. (1984)
Bruce Springsteen

Born to Run (1975)
Bruce Springsteen

Boston (1976)
Boston

Bringing It All Back Home (1965)
Bob Dylan

The Chronic (1992)
Dr. Dre

The Dark Side of the Moon (1973)
Pink Floyd

Daydream Nation (1988)
Sonic Youth

Days of Future Passed (1968)
The Moody Blues

Discreet Music (1975)
Brian Eno

Dookie (1994)
Green Day

The Doors (1967)
The Doors

Elvis Presley (1956)
Elvis Presley

Enter the Wu-Tang (36 Chambers) (1993)
The Wu-Tang Clan

Exile in Guyville (1993)
Liz Phair

Exodus (1977)
Bob Marley and the Wailers

Freak Out! (1966)
Frank Zappa and the Mothers of Invention

The Freewheelin' Bob Dylan (1963)
Bob Dylan

Future Shock (1983)
Herbie Hancock

Graceland (1986)
Paul Simon

Head Hunters (1973)
Herbie Hancock

Heart Like a Wheel (1974)
Linda Ronstadt

Horses (1975)
Patti Smith

The Inner Mounting Flame (1971)
The Mahavishnu Orchestra

In the Court of the Crimson King (1969)
King Crimson

It Takes a Nation of Millions to Hold Us Back (1988)
Public Enemy

Kick Out the Jams (1969)
MC5

Kill 'em All (1983)
Metallica

Kind of Blue (1959)
Miles Davis

King of the Delta Blues Singers (1961)
Robert Johnson

Led Zeppelin (1969)
Led Zeppelin

Licensed to Ill (1986)
The Beastie Boys

Like a Virgin (1984)
Madonna

Little Earthquakes (1992)
Tori Amos

London Calling (1980)
The Clash

Marquee Moon (1977)
Television

The Modern Dance (1978)
Pere Ubu

Modern Sounds in Country and Western Music (1962)
Ray Charles

Mothership Connection (1976)
Parliament

Mr. Tambourine Man (1965)
The Byrds

Muddy Waters at Newport (1960)
Muddy Waters

Murmur (1983)
R.E.M.

Music from Big Pink (1968)
The Band

Nevermind (1991)
Nirvana

Never Mind the Bollocks, Here's the Sex Pistols (1977)
The Sex Pistols

New York Dolls (1973)
The New York Dolls

No Depression (1990)
Uncle Tupelo

No Fences (1990)
Garth Brooks

Not a Pretty Girl (1995)
Ani Difranco

Nuggets: Original Artyfacts from the First Psychedelic Era, 1965–1968 (1972)
Various

Odelay (1996)
Beck

O. G. Original Gangster (1991)
Ice-T

One Nation Under a Groove (1978)
Funkadelic

Paranoid (1971)
Black Sabbath

Pet Sounds (1966)
The Beach Boys

Please Please Me (1963)
The Beatles

Pretty Hate Machine (1989)
Nine Inch Nails

Purple Rain (1984)
Prince

Pyromania (1983)
Def Leppard

Raising Hell (1986)
Run-D.M.C.

Ramones (1976)
The Ramones

Raw Power (1973)
Iggy and the Stooges

*The Rise and Fall of Ziggy Stardust and the Spiders from
     Mars* (1972)
David Bowie

Rubber Soul (1965)
The Beatles

Rust Never Sleeps (1979)
Neil Young

Saturday Night Fever (1977)
Various

Sgt. Pepper's Lonely Hearts Club Band (1967)
The Beatles

The Slim Shady LP (1999)
Eminem

Solitude Standing (1987)
Suzanne Vega

Spice (1997)
The Spice Girls

Straight Outta Compton (1989)
N.W.A

Surrealistic Pillow (1967)
Jefferson Airplane

Sweet Baby James (1970)
James Taylor

Sweetheart of the Rodeo (1968)
The Byrds

Tapestry (1971)
Carole King

Texas Flood (1983)
Stevie Ray Vaughan and Double Trouble

There's a Riot Goin' On (1971)
Sly and the Family Stone

3 Feet High and Rising (1989)
De La Soul

Thriller (1982)
Michael Jackson

Time Out (1959)
The Dave Brubeck Quartet

Tommy (1969)
The Who

Toys in the Attic (1975)
Aerosmith

Trout Mask Replica (1969)
Captain Beefheart and His Magic Band

Van Halen (1978)
Van Halen

The Velvet Underground and Nico (1967)
The Velvet Underground

Wanted! The Outlaws (1976)
Waylon Jennings, Willie Nelson, Jessi Colter, Tompall Glaser

War (1983)
U2

The Weavers at Carnegie Hall (1957)
The Weavers

What's Going On (1971)
Marvin Gaye

Wide Open Spaces (1998)
The Dixie Chicks

Zen Arcade (1984)
Hüsker Dü

BIBLIOGRAPHY

PRINT

Altschuler, Glenn C., *All Shook Up: How Rock 'n' Roll Changed America*. New York: Oxford, 2003.

Azerrad, Michael, *Our Band Could Be Your Life*. New York: Little Brown, 2001.

Bangs, Lester, *Psychotic Reactions and Carburetor Dung*. New York: Anchor Books, 2003.

Bordowitz, Hank, *The U2 Reader: A Quarter Century of Commentary, Criticism, and Reviews*. Milwaukee, WI: Hal Leonard, 2003.

Bronson, Fred, *The Billboard Book of Number One Hits*. New York: Billboard, 1985.

Buckley, Peter, *Rough Guide to Rock*. New York: Rough Guides, 1999.

Campbell, Michael and James Brody, *Rock and Roll: An Introduction*. New York: Schirmer, 1999.

Christgau, Robert, *Grown Up All Wrong: 75 Great Rock and Pop Artists from Vaudeville to Techno*. Cambridge: Harvard, 1998.

Dalton, David and Lenny Kaye, *Rock 100*. New York: Putnam, 1977.

Eno, Brian, *A Year with Swollen Appendices: Brian Eno's Diary*. London: Faber & Faber, 1996.

Ewen, David, *All the Years of American Popular Music*. London: Prentice-Hall, 1977.

Fong-Torres, Ben, *Not Fade Away: A Backstage Pass to 20 Years of Rock & Roll*. San Francisco: Miller Freeman Books, 1999.

Friedlander, Paul, *Rock And Roll: A Social History*. Boulder, CO: Westview, 1996.

Frith, Simon, *The Sociology of Rock*. London: Constable and Company, 1978.

Halfin, Ross and Pete Makowski, *Heavy Metal: The Power Age*. New York: Putnam, 1982.

Hopkins, Jerry, *Hit and Run: The Jimi Hendrix Story*. New York: Perigee, 1983.

Huxley, Aldous, *The Doors of Perception*. New York: Harper and Row, 1963.

Janosik, Maryann, *The Greenwood Encyclopedia of Rock History: The Video Generation, 1981–1990*. Westport, CT: Greenwood, 2005.

Kahn, Ashley, *Kind of Blue: The Making of the Miles Davis Masterpiece*. New York: De Capo.

Laing, Dave et al. *The Electric Muse: The Story of Folk into Rock*. London: Methuen, 1975.

Larkin, Colin, ed., *The Virgin Encyclopedia of Popular Music*. London: Muse UK, 1997.

Macan, Edward, *Rocking the Classics: English Progressive Rock and the Counterculture*. New York: Oxford University Press, 1997.

Malone, Bill C., *Country Music, U.S.A.* Austin: University of Texas, 2002.

Marsh, Dave and John Swenson, *The New Rolling Stone Record Guide*. New York: Random House, 1983 (1979).

Martin, Linda and Kerry Segrave, *Anti-Rock: The Opposition to Rock 'n' Roll*. Hamden, CT: Archon, 1988.

Miller, Jim, *Rolling Stone Illustrated History of Rock and Roll*. New York: Random House, 1980.

Morley, Paul, *Words and Music: A History of Pop in the Shape of a City*. Athens: University of Georgia Press, 2005.

Sarig, Ron, *The Secret History of Rock: The Most Influential Bands You've Never Heard*. New York: Billboard Books, 1998.

Smith, Chris, *The Greenwood Encyclopedia of Rock History: The Rise of Album Rock, 1967–1973*. Westport, CT: Greenwood, 2005a.

Smith, Chris, *The Greenwood Encyclopedia of Rock History: From Arenas to the Underground, 1974–1980*. Westport, CT: Greenwood, 2005b.

Strausbaugh, John, *Rock 'Til You Drop: The Decline from Rebellion to Nostalgia*. New York: Verso, 2001.

Szatmary, David, *A Time to Rock: A Social History of Rock And Roll*. New York: Schirmer, 1996 (1987).

Tingen, Paul, *Miles Beyond: The Electric Explorations of Miles Davis*. New York: Watson Guptill, 2001.

Tobler, John, *100 Greatest Albums of the Sixties*. New York: The Overlook Press, 1994.

Waksman, Steve, *Instruments of Desire: The Electric Guitar and the Shaping of Musical Experience*. Cambridge: Harvard University, 1999.

Warner, Jay, ed., *Billboard's American Rock 'N' Roll in Review*. New York: Schirmer, 1997.

Whitburn, Joel, ed., *The Billboard Book of Top 40 Albums*. New York: Billboard, 1987.

Whitburn, Joel, ed., *The Billboard Book of Top 40 Albums, 1955–1992*. New York: Billboard, 1993.

Whitburn, Joel ed., *The Billboard Book of Top 40 Hits*. New York: Billboard, 1996.

Whitburn, Joel ed., *Joel Whitburn Presents a Century of Pop Music*. New York: Billboard, 1999.

ELECTRONIC

Allmusic
A comprehensive musical reference source covering albums and artists of all genres. www.allmusic.com

Beach Boys Fan Club
The official website of the Beach Boys Fan Club tracking the history of the Beach
   Boys and the current status of the bands' members.
www.beachboysfanclub.com

Bob Dylan
The official Bob Dylan website featuring news, tour information, album archives,
   and other information on all things Bob.
www.bobdylan.com

Make My Day
An archive of interviews and articles about the Detroit band MC5.
makemyday.free.fr/library.htm

National Public Radio
The website of the not-for-profit radio network that includes interviews with a
   large number of notable musical figures.
www.npr.org

The Recording Industry Association of America
A trade group representing the music industry that keeps track of album sales in
   the United States.
www.riaa.com

Robert Christgau
The official website of music critic Robert Christgau, featuring thousands of his
   album reviews and articles published since 1967.
www.robertchristgau.com

Rock's Back Pages
An online archive of rock journalism from the 1960s to the present.
www.rocksbackpages.com

Rolling Stone
The official website of the music publication *Rolling Stone*.
www.rollingstone.com

Salon.com
An online magazine of arts and culture.
www.salon.com

Smithsonian Folkways
The official website of Smithsonian Folkways Recordings.
www.folkways.si.edu

Trouser Press
An online reference source for alternative music.
www.trouserpress.com

INDEX

About the Author

CHRIS SMITH is a Vancouver-based writer and photographer whose credits range from *Rolling Stone, Billboard*, and MTV to the *University of Chicago Magazine* and the *Journal of Visual Anthropology*. In addition to music and film journalism, he has worked as a combat correspondent, a festival producer, a travel writer, an anthropologist, a wildlife photographer, and a musician. He is the author of two volumes of the *Greenwood Encyclopedia of Rock History* (Greenwood, 2005) and currently teaches cultural criticism at the University of British Columbia.